Public Sector Activity in Capital Accumulation and Synthesis of Capital Fractions

Bilal Kargi
Ankara Yıldırım Beyazıt University, Turkey

A volume in the Advances in Public Policy and Administration (APPA) Book Series

Published in the United States of America by
IGI Global
Information Science Reference (an imprint of IGI Global)
701 E. Chocolate Avenue
Hershey PA, USA 17033
Tel: 717-533-8845
Fax: 717-533-8661
E-mail: cust@igi-global.com
Web site: http://www.igi-global.com

Library of Congress Cataloging-in-Publication Data

CIP Pending
ISBN: 979-8-3693-5996-9
EISBN: 979-8-3693-5998-3

British Cataloguing in Publication Data
A Cataloguing in Publication record for this book is available from the British Library.

All work contributed to this book is new, previously-unpublished material.
The views expressed in this book are those of the authors, but not necessarily of the publisher.

For electronic access to this publication, please contact: eresources@igi-global.com.

Advances in Public Policy and Administration (APPA) Book Series

ISSN:2475-6644
EISSN:2475-6652

MISSION

Proper management of the public sphere is necessary in order to maintain order in modern society. Research developments in the field of public policy and administration can assist in uncovering the latest tools, practices, and methodologies for governing societies around the world.

The **Advances in Public Policy and Administration (APPA) Book Series** aims to publish scholarly publications focused on topics pertaining to the governance of the public domain. APPA's focus on timely topics relating to government, public funding, politics, public safety, policy, and law enforcement is particularly relevant to academicians, government officials, and upper-level students seeking the most up-to-date research in their field.

Coverage

- Government
- Law Enforcement
- Political Economy
- Politics
- Public Administration
- Public Funding
- Public Policy
- Resource allocation
- Urban Planning

IGI Global is currently accepting manuscripts for publication within this series. To submit a proposal for a volume in this series, please contact our Acquisition Editors at Acquisitions@igi-global.com or visit: http://www.igi-global.com/publish/.

The (ISSN) is published by IGI Global, 701 E. Chocolate Avenue, Hershey, PA 17033-1240, USA, www.igi-global.com. This series is composed of titles available for purchase individually; each title is edited to be contextually exclusive from any other title within the series. For pricing and ordering information please visit http://www.igi-global.com/book-series/advances-public-policy-administration/97862. Postmaster: Send all address changes to above address.

Titles in this Series

For a list of additional titles in this series, please visit: www.igi-global.com/book-series

Holistic Public Agency in Complex Environments
Mirko Pečarič (Faculty of Public Administration, University of Ljubljana, Slovenia)
Information Science Reference • copyright 2024 • 322pp • H/C (ISBN: 9798369305072) • US $265.00 (our price)

Infrastructure Development Strategies for Empowerment and Inclusion
Neeta Baporikar (Namibia University of Science and Technology, Namibia & SP Pune, University, India)
Information Science Reference • copyright 2024 • 510pp • H/C (ISBN: 9798369329177) • US $315.00 (our price)

Global Geopolitical Impacts and Dynamics of the Indo-Pacific
K. Vinay Kumar (Maharashtra National Law University, India) Nina Slama (Reichman University, Israel) and Monojit Das (Indian Aerospace Defence News, India)
Information Science Reference • copyright 2024 • 307pp • H/C (ISBN: 9798369316900) • US $255.00 (our price)

Enhancing Democracy With Coalition Governments and Politics
Ndwakhulu Stephen Tshishonga (University of KwaZulu-Natal, South Africa)
Information Science Reference • copyright 2024 • 392pp • H/C (ISBN: 9798369316542) • US $255.00 (our price)

Global Trends in Governance and Policy Paradigms
Mahani Hamdan (Universiti Brunei Darussalam, Brunei) Muhammad Anshari (Universiti Brunei Darussalam, Brunei) Norainie Ahmad (Universiti Brunei Darussalam, Brunei) and Emil Ali (Universiti Brunei Darussalam, Brunei)
Information Science Publishing • copyright 2024 • 453pp • H/C (ISBN: 9798369317426) • US $240.00 (our price)

IGI Global
PUBLISHER of TIMELY KNOWLEDGE

701 East Chocolate Avenue, Hershey, PA 17033, USA
Tel: 717-533-8845 x100 • Fax: 717-533-8661
E-Mail: cust@igi-global.com • www.igi-global.com

Table of Contents

Detailed Table of Contents

This chapter highlights the crucial role of the introduction in scientific studies, which outlines the study's paradigm, current status, and new insights from observations. It covers epistemology, semantics, and historical philosophy, aiming to clarify the observer's perspective and methodological approach. Core elements include information theory, semantics, and historical philosophy, providing a framework to question concepts and recognize the dynamic nature of phenomena. It critiques mainstream economic views that see privatization as a natural shift from public to private ownership, challenging the notion that public ownership is unnatural. The study questions the pragmatic/utilitarian perspective of mainstream economics, assumptions about market efficiency, and the role of the state. It discusses expected outcomes of privatization, such as consumer benefit and resource optimization, highlighting contradictions and varied economic contexts.

This chapter contrasts feudalism and capitalism, highlighting capitalism's key features: high commodity production, labor commodification, and the social relations between owners and non-owners of production means. Capitalism is characterized by "generalized commodity production," where even labor power is traded. The chapter explores the production relations, focusing on how owners and non-owners interact to generate surplus value and concentrate property among capitalists. It examines the state's role in regulating these relations, discussing the "form of value" as a core social relation in capitalist development and the state's role in capital accumulation. The chapter addresses simple and extended reproduction mechanisms, production element mutations, and their historical evolution. It contrasts Marxist and Keynesian wage theories, emphasizing value as key to accumulation. It also covers Marx's value categorizations, the "transformation problem," and macro-level value-form, highlighting regulation's role in factor mobilities and international profit transfers.

This chapter explores the dynamics and implications of inward-looking versus outward-looking accumulation strategies in economic development. It finds that prioritizing one strategy inherently downplays the variables of the other, revealing a fundamental trade-off. The state's role in choosing and implementing these strategies is crucial, shaped by internal political actors and external economic conditions, raising questions about the interplay between state policy and economic actors. The concept of strategy is examined at both micro and macro levels: micro-level adjustments among economic actors create a dynamic, complex environment, while macro-level strategies may overlook certain variables to achieve broader goals. The chapter aligns with capitalist development and dependency theories, highlighting the state's role in sustaining capitalist economies. It covers stages of capitalist development and their global interplay, focusing on inward-looking strategies like import substitution and state intervention.

This chapter explores capital accumulation, total output, and economic growth in various economic models, highlighting their roles and interactions. It distinguishes "total output" as the monetary value of goods and services produced at a given time from "growth," defined as the increase in investable surplus value over periods. "Capital accumulation" is the addition to capital stock from surplus value, crucial for expanding productive capacity. The chapter examines how public sector activities, especially privatization, influence these models under different economic conditions. It delves into productivity and capital stock's roles in economic growth, factors transforming accumulated capital into productive assets, and the impact of international capital flows and market dynamics on surplus value utilization and economic development trajectories. Critiquing classical, neo-classical, and Marxist growth models, it discusses technological advancements, population dynamics, and income distribution within capitalist economies.

The state is a central topic of debate in social sciences, defined by its institutional framework and legal authority as the embodiment of collective societal will. Its role and legitimacy are continually contested. The state wields a monopoly on legitimate violence and governs through laws and institutions, reflecting social consensus but often leading to divergent perspectives. Some view the state as a necessary evil, curbing individual freedoms for communal order and security, while others see it as a vehicle for social justice and welfare. Historically, the state's role has evolved, expanding during the rise of Keynesian economics to mitigate market failures and contracting under neoliberalism, which advocates for market efficiency, privatization, and deregulation. Ideological differences shape perceptions of the state: socialists see it as a tool for wealth redistribution and equality, while liberals favor a minimal state prioritizing individual liberty and market mechanisms.

The relationship between individuals in society, driven by economic interests, defines societal character and poses challenges. Economicization views individuals as utilitarian agents within economic frameworks, a duality sparking debate. Proponents say it aligns with human nature and enhances freedom, while critics argue it erodes human essence. Political economy examines the dynamics among economic actors, focusing on the state's role. Historically, state involvement has shifted between central intervention and laissez-faire policies. Recent trends toward market efficiency and privatization highlight a reduced state role, fueling debate over its optimal function. Liberal economics, favoring minimal state interference, emphasizes market mechanisms for efficient resource allocation. Hayek's idea of organic societal structures opposes central planning, arguing that imposed orders disrupt economic balances. The principal-agent relationship reveals tensions in economic governance, especially in public enterprises.

This chapter explores economic theories within the context of capitalism, public sector activities, and privatization. The first part establishes a philosophical and historical foundation, identifying key concepts and their definitions within different levels of capitalism. The second part examines terms like strategy, development, policy, accumulation, and growth, differentiating their roles in economic theories and practices. It distinguishes between economic growth (total output increase) and accumulation (capacity to produce output increase), highlighting their implications for development and policy. The chapter critically analyzes capitalism's tendencies to generate crises and cyclical fluctuations, exploring their impact on social structures and public sector activities. It also examines capitalism's historical continuity, recognizing its renewal and adaptation. A significant portion contrasts economic theories regarding public ownership and privatization, highlighting ideological and practical differences in addressing economic challenges within capitalist frameworks.

This chapter distinguishes between analytical and synthetic propositions in social sciences, focusing on their roles in knowledge production and empirical validation. Analytical propositions, such as "Privatization is an economic policy," are true by definition and need no empirical verification. In contrast, synthetic propositions, like "Privatization fosters capital accumulation," require empirical evidence to validate. The chapter also discusses the holistic integration of phenomena within broader frameworks, emphasizing their interconnected, context-dependent nature. Concepts evolve over time and across different contexts due to subjective interpretations, challenging uniform application. Theoretical foundations in surplus-value formation and economic crises are explored, showing how capital accumulation fluctuations influence public sector strategies. Shifts from public ownership to privatization reflect changing alignments with dominant capital factions, illustrating cyclical transformations in public policy under varying economic conditions.

Preface

This book delves into the complexities surrounding privatization, offering a critical and historically informed perspective that challenges the limited view presented by mainstream economics. The following pages advocate for a more nuanced understanding, one grounded in the principles of political economy.

Privatization, as we will explore, transcends the narrow definition of an economic tool focused solely on efficiency. Rather, it represents a significant historical transformation with deep roots. Its story is intricately linked to the evolution of the state, the concentration of capital, and the ever-present power dynamics within the global capitalist system. Simple cause-and-effect relationships will be cast aside as we delve into the interconnectedness of historical events, highlighting the crucial role of context in understanding privatization's multifaceted nature.

The book takes aim at mainstream economics, critiquing its singular focus on efficiency and its portrayal of researchers as passive observers. In contrast, a political economy approach acknowledges the influence of power dynamics and the active role researchers play in shaping their interpretations. This broader perspective recognizes that privatization extends beyond economic impacts, potentially impacting social and political spheres in profound ways. It can exacerbate inequalities and weaken democratic principles. To fully grasp these broader ramifications, a comprehensive approach is necessary, one that examines historical context, political dynamics, and the complex web of social relations affected by privatization.

The concepts used in social science are not static entities, the book argues. They evolve alongside the phenomena they represent, reflecting the dynamic nature of society. This necessitates a critical approach that meticulously defines key concepts, considering their historical context, potential biases, and any existing counter-definitions. Further enriching this critical lens, the book delves into the philosophical underpinnings of studying privatization. Emphasis is placed on the importance of both observation and analysis, as outlined by Kant. Without observation, concepts lack meaning, and without analysis, observations remain uninterpreted. Hegel's proposition is also explored, which suggests that reason can be used to understand the underlying logic behind social events. Human freedom is a central theme that will be woven throughout the book. We will explore the tension between individual freedom and the state's role in regulating power imbalances. While some advocate for a minimal state to maximize freedom, others see it as a necessary check on concentrated power. The global context plays a crucial role as well. The book acknowledges the influence of the global capitalist system on national economies and cautions against applying past privatization experiences as a one-size-fits-all solution. Instead, it suggests examining how privatization practices relate to a country's sovereignty and the dominant power structures within it.

Finally, the book views privatization as a policy tool used by neo-liberal ideology, which emphasizes deregulation and reducing the state's role in the economy. This book, in essence, argues for a critical and multifaceted approach grounded in political economy and "fuzzy logic" to understand the complex social and political ramifications of privatization. This approach acknowledges the limitations of a purely economic view and emphasizes the importance of power dynamics, historical context, and the global system in shaping privatization's impact on human freedom. Prepare to embark on a journey that challenges assumptions and delves into the complexities surrounding privatization.

Introduction

ABSTRACT

This book challenges traditional views on privatization by advocating for a critical, historically informed approach rooted in political economy. It contends that privatization transcends mere economic efficiency, embodying a profound transformation of property relations shaped by historical context and power dynamics. Critiquing mainstream economics' portrayal of privatization as a natural progression, the text highlights its ideological underpinnings and implications for social justice. Emphasizing the dynamic nature of social science concepts and the evolving interplay between state, capital, and society, the book underscores the necessity of understanding privatization through a multidimensional lens. It argues for scrutinizing concepts beyond their surface definitions, acknowledging their historical biases and contextual nuances. Ultimately, the book advocates for a nuanced understanding that considers historical contingencies and power relations, challenging simplistic economic narratives to better grasp privatization's impact on human freedom and societal well-being.

INTRODUCTION

It argues that a good introduction to a scientific research book should lay the groundwork for the entire study, outlining the topic, its complexities, and the researcher's perspective. The core of the research hinges on the concept of a paradigm, which essentially represents the set of values and assumptions that guide the investigation. This paradigm is shaped by the researcher's approach to knowledge acquisition, how concepts are formed, and the historical context surrounding the topic. The book emphasizes that social science concepts are not fixed. They evolve alongside the phenomena they represent, reflecting the ever-changing nature of society. Studying social phenomena requires acknowledging this dynamism and considering the historical context that shapes them. Focusing solely on a single snapshot of a phenomenon can be misleading, as it fails to capture the ongoing transformations that occur over time. A well-structured introduction should establish what is being studied, why it's important, and how the researcher plans to analyze it. The book then critiques the way mainstream economics views privatization, which is as a natural progression towards efficiency. This perspective, the text argues, overlooks the historical background and the power dynamics at play when considering privatization. The concept of a "natural" market mechanism is also challenged. The book argues that the free market often requires specific conditions to function perfectly, conditions that might not exist in reality. Furthermore, liberal economics prioritizes individual goods over the common good. The text suggests that for the market to function smoothly under this focus, actors might need to possess certain similar characteristics. In essence, the book advocates for a critical approach to studying privatization, one that is informed by history. It argues that mainstream economics presents a limited view and that power dynamics and social structures significantly influence the outcomes of privatization practices.

This book delves into the philosophical underpinnings of studying privatization through a critical lens. It argues that privatization goes beyond a simple economic tool and instead represents a significant transformation of property ownership. This transformation is intricately linked to the accumulation of capital, the dynamics of political economy, and the dominance of specific capital groups. The book critiques mainstream economics, which often portrays decision-making as purely rational. In contrast, a political economy approach acknowledges the potential influence of political agendas on these decisions. It also recognizes the role of power dynamics in shaping economic policies. To establish a solid foundation for the study, the text emphasizes the importance of philosophical grounding. It highlights two key propositions:

Kant's proposition: This principle stresses the need for both observation and analysis. Without observation, concepts lack meaning, and without analysis, observations remain uninterpreted.

Hegel's proposition: This suggests that phenomena can be understood through reason. There's an underlying logic behind social events that can be unraveled through critical analysis.

History is another crucial factor. Social phenomena are not isolated occurrences. They have a rich past and are interconnected across time. The text challenges the idea of a linear cause-and-effect relationship in history. Human behavior is a dynamic variable that actively shapes historical processes. This book goes on to argue that the observer's position significantly influences their interpretation. Just like observing a falling stone from different vantage points, the observer's perspective can alter their understanding of the phenomenon.

Furthermore, the text emphasizes the role of the researcher. Unlike mainstream economics, which positions the researcher as a passive observer, political economy views the researcher as an active participant. Researchers acknowledge their own role and the impact of human actions on social phenomena. This book acknowledges

Karl Marx's significant contributions to political economy, particularly his work on identifying the internal relations of capitalism. Finally, the text argues that neutrality is impossible when studying social phenomena. Researchers must acknowledge the influence of human agency and their own position within the historical context. In essence, this book advocates for a critical and historically informed approach to studying privatization. It emphasizes the limitations of a purely economic view and the importance of considering power dynamics and social structures within a historical framework.

This book delves into the philosophical and methodological underpinnings of critically studying privatization. It argues for a social theory approach that examines how privatization shapes human freedom over the long term, rather than a purely economic focus on efficiency. Central to this approach is understanding history and its role in shaping social phenomena. Privatization isn't simply an economic policy, but rather a transformation with deep historical roots. It's intricately linked to the evolution of the state, the concentration of capital, and the ongoing power dynamics within the global capitalist system. Simple cause-and-effect relationships are challenged; the text emphasizes the interconnectedness of events across time. This book critiques mainstream economics for portraying researchers as passive observers. In contrast, a critical approach acknowledges the researcher's role and the impact of human agency on social phenomena. This includes recognizing how the researcher's own position can influence their interpretation. Human freedom is a central theme. The text explores the tension between individual freedom and the role of the state in regulating power imbalances. While some advocate for a minimal state to maximize freedom, others see the state as a necessary check on concentrated power. The global context is crucial. The text acknowledges the influence of the global capitalist system on national economies. Privatization is seen as one way national economies respond to and integrate with this larger system. The text cautions against simply applying past experiences with privatization to new situations. Different historical conditions and power dynamics can lead to vastly different outcomes. Instead, the text suggests examining how privatization practices relate to a country's sovereignty and the dominant power structures within it. While various social theories may disagree on the best path to achieving greater freedom, the text argues that all ultimately aim for a form of humanism. The debate centers on the role of the state in balancing individual freedom and social order. The text acknowledges the state's role in regulating relationships within society, even if this might limit absolute freedom. Finally, this book views privatization as a policy tool used by neo-liberal ideology, which emphasizes deregulation and reducing the role of the state in the economy. In essence, the text advocates for a critical and historically informed approach to studying privatization. It argues that a purely economic view is insufficient and that power dynamics, historical context, and the global system all play a significant role in understanding privatization's impact on human freedom.

This book emphasizes the importance of clear definitions, especially for concepts used in social science research. It argues that the meaning of concepts can shift over time, shaped by history and context. Simply accepting prevailing definitions is risky. Researchers should consider a concept's origins and how it's been used throughout history to avoid hidden biases. Proposes a method for scrutinizing concepts. First, explore the concept alongside its opposite or a critical counter-definition. This contrasting view helps expose limitations and underlying assumptions within the original concept. Second, examine how the concept's meaning might be influenced by its historical roots. For example, the seemingly neutral concept of "development" might imply progress without acknowledging potential downsides. This book acknowledges that the meaning of a phrase can be more than the sum of its parts. How individual concepts are combined can create a new implication that goes beyond the meaning of each concept alone. The text uses the example of "good" and "bad" to illustrate how these concepts are historically and socially constructed, not absolute. Overall, the text advocates for a critical approach to studying social phenomena. The first part of the research will focus on meticulously defining key concepts. This definition process will involve considering the concept's historical context, potential biases, and any critical counter-definitions that exist. The text delves into the philosophical and methodological underpinnings of studying privatization through a political economy lens. It argues against a purely economic focus on efficiency and instead advocates for a social theory approach that examines the long-term impact of privatization on human freedom.

Central to this approach is understanding history's role in shaping social phenomena. Privatization isn't simply an economic policy, but a transformation with deep historical roots. It's intricately linked to the evolution of the state, the concentration of capital, and the ongoing power dynamics within the global capitalist system. Challenges simplistic cause-and-effect relationships, emphasizing the interconnectedness of events across time. Critiques mainstream economics for portraying researchers as passive observers. In contrast, a critical approach acknowledges the researcher's role and the impact of human agency on social phenomena. This includes recognizing how the researcher's own position can influence their interpretation. Human freedom is a central theme. Explores the tension between individual freedom and the role of the state in regulating power imbalances. While some advocate for a minimal state to maximize freedom, others see the state as a necessary check on concentrated power. The global context is crucial. The text acknowledges the influence of the global capitalist system on national economies. Cautions against simply applying past experiences with privatization to new situations. Different historical conditions and power dynamics can lead to vastly different outcomes. Instead, the text suggests examining how privatization practices relate to a country's sovereignty and the dominant power structures within it. While various social theories may disagree on the best path to achieving greater freedom, the text argues that all ultimately aim for a form of humanism. The debate centers on the role of the state in balancing individual freedom and social order. The text acknowledges the state's role in regulating relationships within society, even if this might limit absolute freedom. Finally, the text views privatization as a policy tool used by neo-liberal ideology, which emphasizes deregulation and reducing the role of the state in the economy. In essence, the book advocates for a critical and historically informed approach to studying privatization. It argues that a purely economic view is insufficient and that power dynamics, historical context, and the global system all play a significant role in understanding privatization's impact on human freedom.

This book dives into the philosophy of studying privatization, particularly through a critical political economy lens. It rejects the rigid, cause-and-effect logic of traditional approaches and instead proposes a more flexible, nuanced understanding based on "fuzzy logic." This allows for the examination of complex social dynamics and historical transformations. Central to this approach is the concept of the state as a fluid entity, shaped by historical power struggles and property ownership. The state's role in regulating economic activity is constantly evolving alongside economic development. Privatization isn't simply a policy decision; it's a reflection of this ongoing transformation, a shift in the state's relationship with property power. Highlights the tension between the state's responsibility for the well-being of its citizens and the profit-driven nature of capitalism. It questions how individuals can define themselves meaningfully within a system focused on maximizing profit, where social alienation can be a consequence of privatization. The analysis goes beyond pure economics. It argues that privatization can have significant social and political ramifications, potentially exacerbating social inequalities and weakening democratic principles. The text acknowledges the limitations of studying privatization solely through an economic lens. A comprehensive understanding requires examining historical context, political dynamics, and the complex web of social relations that privatization affects. In essence, the text argues for a critical and multifaceted approach to studying privatization. It emphasizes the state's role in shaping economic development, but recognizes the interconnectedness of social relations, power struggles, and historical forces that all play a part in the complex phenomenon of privatization.

Chapter 1
Scientific and Philosophical Perspective

ABSTRACT

This chapter highlights the crucial role of the introduction in scientific studies, which outlines the study's paradigm, current status, and new insights from observations. It covers epistemology, semantics, and historical philosophy, aiming to clarify the observer's perspective and methodological approach. Core elements include information theory, semantics, and historical philosophy, providing a framework to question concepts and recognize the dynamic nature of phenomena. It critiques mainstream economic views that see privatization as a natural shift from public to private ownership, challenging the notion that public ownership is unnatural. The study questions the pragmatic/utilitarian perspective of mainstream economics, assumptions about market efficiency, and the role of the state. It discusses expected outcomes of privatization, such as consumer benefit and resource optimization, highlighting contradictions and varied economic contexts.

PARADIGM, METHODOLOGICAL SCOPE AND PROPOSITIONS

In scientific studies, the "Introduction" is the heart of that study and should present the characteristics of the study within a holistic framework. There are three main elements that make up this integrity; the paradigm of the work as a set and whole of values; The current static situation regarding t he observed phenomenon; Imagination that emerges from new observation of the phenomenon with the defined paradigm.

Paradigm, as a whole and series of values, must first of all include epistemology as a philosophy and theory of knowledge. Secondly, it can be formed from semantics with the structure of propositions that produce concepts, and finally, thirdly, from the philosophy of history. A paradigm created from these elements aims to clearly determine from which direction the observer observes the phenomenon and in what

DOI: 10.4018/979-8-3693-5996-9.ch001

position the observer himself is. In this way, the logical system that will provide the connections between the propositions will be explained from the beginning. In this way, it will be determined and specified how the phenomenon is defined as a phenomenon and how the observer will observe the phenomenon through which mechanisms.

As the first element of the paradigm, information theory recommends creating a critical language to question the information contained in any concept.

The second element, semantics, presupposes that the concepts formed by the observation of any phenomenon have a dynamic character. As a matter of fact, in social sciences, the nature of the phenomena is in motion in endless variations, and both the social phenomenon and the concept are in internal integrity with this movement. A social phenomenon that occurs at any point in history; When the same phenomenon that tries to be explained with a concept reappears at a later stage of history, it will contain differences. For this reason, the concept developed for the first observed phenomenon constantly changes its content in parallel with the movement in the phenomenon. For example, while a concept related to a phenomenon that emerged at any point in history may be considered as a positive concept in the same time period, it may take on a negative meaning in later periods of time in connection with the change in the phenomenon. They may even contain completely different meanings compared to each other.

The philosophy of history is; It implies the character of the causal relations observed under certain historical conditions of the phenomenon under investigation. And this character is dynamic. Therefore, any scientific study will not be able to produce transcendental data. For this reason, in addition to emphasizing the set of dynamic relationships, one should focus on a static analysis isolated from other conditions by taking only a section of the movement of the phenomenon in the space of facts. In this way, preliminary information about dynamic processes can be produced and data can be provided for further studies. Moreover, a study that claims to address the entire dynamic process may be stuck among the endless variations of social sciences. Scientific studies that contain propositions regarding historical sections will also emphasize the continuity and holism of the term science.

Therefore, the "Introduction" should include a scaled body of information about "what" is being done and "why" it is being done. The "how" of analysis and synthesis should be included in the next section of the study text. In short, the "Introduction" carries the character of a pre-discourse regarding the method and philosophical/ intellectual assumptions of the observer.

Within the framework of the above passages, this "introduction" article covers three main topics. The first of these draws the current framework of the concept and problematic of privatization as a "general view". In doing so, the general definitions of pragmatic assumptions and the points open to criticism in these definitions are outlined. Secondly, it determines the framework of the epistemological infrastructure that this book study will try to establish with its analysis methods and philosophical assumptions. Thirdly and finally, the claims to be made and the analysis methods of these claims are explained, indicating the connections that will be tried to be shown throughout the study. In addition, propositions regarding the general topics included in the chapters in the study are mentioned. This content attempts to indicate the general integrity of the content and method of the study as a whole.

Accordingly, the transfer of public sector economic enterprises to private capital envisages a growth/development process oriented to the market mechanism. Thus, growth and development can be achieved by combining the accumulation in the public sector with the productivity of the private sector (AlHussaini & Molz, 2009).

In the field of Mainstream Economics, privatization is not perceived as a "ownership change" or "ownership transformation" (Beesley & Littlechild, 1989). For this reason, analyzes on privatization adopt a pragmatic/utilitarian perspective. Because the prerequisite for increasing the efficiency of markets is to reduce state effectiveness, and the shift of state ownership to the private sector is seen as a natural necessity of this assumption. In this context, certain justifications have been put forward for privatization. These reasons are broadly evaluated under the headings of ideological, pragmatic, commercial and populist (Savas, 2008, p.2). Privatization of public property, which is external to the market mechanism, is perceived as a transition to the natural state.

However, before these reasons put forward for privatization, the reasons for the "dogma" of the organizations that are the basis for privatization are more striking. Because, in its first sense, privatization means "transferring an existing public/state institution to the private sector/market actors", but it neglects the "birth" of those institutions, that is, how they were formed in the hands of the public sector, and the reason for the existence of the "existing". Because, according to mainstream economics, public ownership is an unnatural situation and privatization is the naturalization of this "unnatural situation". As a matter of fact, the state is an unnatural structure that is external to the market mechanism, the functioning of which it disrupts and limits by intervening. Especially in neo-classical economics, "equilibrium is theoretically automatic […] crisis is logically impossible [... and] markets do not function well and most state interventions do not yield good results" (Rosier, 1994, p.29), and state activities are at least theoretically completely excludes it. However, as Sweezy points out, "Few people would deny that the state plays a very important role in the economic process. However, there are many who say that the state can and should be kept away from economic theory" (Sweezy, 2007, p.239). This actually reveals the disconnection between phenomenon and theory.

While there is an intense debate about what is "natural" and how it works, utilitarian logic should generally be placed at the origin of the analysis. However, the "essentialist" tradition, which has been going on since Aristotle, assumes that objects have a common essence and that this is natural.

Neo-classical economics, due to its emulation of physical sciences and the influence of the paradigms of the 18th and 19th centuries, predicted that human and more generally social behavior could be explained by mechanical-deterministic progression models, acting on the stable behavior of objects, that is, stable units. However, if Simmel and Marx's understandings of history are combined - and this combination shapes the basic perception of history in the study - economic decisions may not always yield the same results. Therefore, a privatization practice may yield different results in each economy and may not result in the envisaged "removal of obstacles to the functioning of markets". In fact, diametrically opposite results may arise for different economies.

The main result expected from privatization is to 'maximize consumer benefit' (Beesley & Littlechild, 2009) and ensure optimal resource use. With the realization of privatization, market actors will become more effective, they will be able to find new profit and investment opportunities, and these already rational actors will be able to maximize their benefits. However, the fact that the market is controlled or intervened by factors that restrict the free movements of the actors is an obstacle to this maximization attempt. The ultimate goal is to increase the effectiveness of market forces, which is necessary to increase the effectiveness of the market mechanism: As a result, maximum benefit will be achieved. In other words, it is approaching the assumptions of neo-classical economics; It will ensure the most effective use of resources under the freedom of action of rational actors in the market where there is no intervention under competition conditions (Guerrien, 1989, p.7-12). However, the following point is noteworthy here: The market is a natural mechanism, and its functionality is disrupted and disrupted only due to an unnatural intervention in that naturalness. In that case, it can be considered as an attempt to realize some special conditions for a market mechanism that was only "designed" to be possible in reality, and which was "assumed" that that mechanism would function perfectly, but which did not find its counterpart in reality. As a result, an attempt is made to achieve a market mechanism that has not been experienced but has been designed.

Essentially, liberal doctrine, which carefully avoids the concept of "common good", bases the flawless functioning of the market mechanism on the above-mentioned assumptions, but in society, which is the arithmetic sum of individuals, there are "different goods" for each individual. The market is a neutral mechanism against these "different goods" so that authoritarian and totalitarian results do not arise (O'Neil, 2001, p.35) and the mechanism automatically reaches an optimal result of "different goods". The idea that this representation and its assumptions are "natural" is the basic method of mainstream economics. Approaching the assumptions of neo-classical economics actually shows that the "natural order" as a design does not exist naturally, on the contrary, it is based on designing the field of reality according to the elements that will establish that order. As a matter of fact, in a society where the idea of "common good" is not recommended, the market, which will impartially regulate the conflicts of individual "goods", only implicitly requires that the actors be at least similar to each other in terms of their essential qualities. This common feature, which seems at first glance, is individual freedom.

Neo-classical economics predicts the narrowing of the field of public activities in order to expand individual freedoms. This will mean increased individual freedoms. Therefore, privatization is only an economic tool, and only an economic policy. However, it should also be said that, like other economic policies, it has a greater impact on the political risks undertaken by governments than others. As a matter of fact, freedom is negative freedom and it is the elimination of restrictions in the field of action that limit individuals without interfering with the freedom of other individuals. In fact, a main debate that emerges at this point is the nature of the concept of freedom, which reveals the necessity of considering freedom as different definitions as "negative freedom" and "positive freedom". Because the state, as an institution that emerges unnaturally and is formed (and maintains its continuity) by extracting value from economic relations unnaturally, is like an actor that simultaneously restricts the economic movements, that is, the freedom, of individuals.

Recent privatization studies emerge pragmatically within the framework of this general paradigm. As a linear equation, it is based on a data definition of privatization, which is defined as the shrinking of the state that restricts freedoms and the withdrawal of the state from the field of production in this shrinking process. In my opinion, a scientific study should never be pragmatic, and although the liberal doctrine is based on pragmatism on the basis of individual benefit, the development of thought by individuals according to their own positions is directly based on their own interests, and in fact, this is inherently true for a liberal thought. Because, when "individual interest" is the basis, an individual's view is absolutely focused on maximizing his own interest.

The "Introduction" passages so far generally provide a framework answer to three basic questions: 1- How the ownership in the hands of the public sector is formed; 2- The requirements of transferring this property to the private sector and; 3- What are the expected results when the ownership changes hands? However, the emergence of questions as "questions/problems" is related to the formation and results of an economic policy under the mainstream neo-classical economic paradigm of a given state mechanism. In other words, it includes concepts belonging to the basic paradigm of studies on privatization. However, this study aims to address privatization from a critical perspective, especially by touching on the implications of these concepts. As the most basic assumption to be used in doing this: The main axis around which the study will be shaped is: privatization, which will be defined as a "transformation in the form of property", the continuity of capital accumulation, especially international political economy relations, capital fractions and the dominance of these fractions in accumulation strategies, or hegemony in general. It is based on its relationship with the form of public activity in the accumulation regime. It tries to handle privatization as a concrete indicator that will try to observe the transformation of the state's form of activity. Naturally, this study is a study of political economy, and a study of political economy differs from the given neo-classical analysis. While neo-classical economics deals with decision-making units as rational, political economy is critical in that it prefers to understand and explain the phenomena based on the acceptance that decision-making units can be political as well as being rational. In addition to being critical of political economy (avoiding pragmatism), another point that differs from economism is that, as one of the basic assumptions of this study, position taking between actors creates certain foundations not only in economic but also in the context of political and social relations. In this case, the term political economy is adopted in the sense used by Anikin (1975) in the sense that "production relations [...] have a general and social character".

This meaning attributed to the concept of political economy necessitates touching on its philosophical roots while evaluating the concrete elements of a scientific study to be conducted under its paradigm. Based on this main foundation, the framework of the study's philosophical assumptions and economic assumptions are discussed in the following passages.

The first condition for analyzing social phenomena must be starting from a certain philosophical proposition or set of propositions. This book will proceed under the umbrella of two philosophical propositions. These are the famous propositions of both philosophers; Kant's "concept without intuition is empty, intuition without concept is blind" (2007, p.13) and Hegel's proposition, "The rational is real and the real is rational". An observer must first observe a situation that occurs in the social field (the space of phenomena that includes human behavior). However, this observation, under the assumption that the observer's world view is neutral, first and foremost requires that the phenomenon have occurred and become observable. The observable state assumes that this state is in the realm of "reality" and therefore finished/completed. Subsequently, the realized phenomenon can be analyzed using rational arguments. On the other hand, phenomena that have occurred and can be analyzed by rational arguments, separated from mysticism, must be conceptualized or at least conceptualizable. Finally, at this point, Kant's proposition is used.

Another field with which the actually observed phenomenon is in relationship is the "historical-field". The historical field is the clarification of the phenomenon to be analyzed, where it emerged in history, its conceptualization and the content of the concept. Because, as one of the general principles in the universe, no physical or social phenomenon is outside the relationship of causality, and each phenomenon is a "result" of the phenomena before it and a "cause" and antecedent of the phenomena after it. This will reveal the transformation of both the concept and the phenomenon within cause-effect relationships. But again, no social phenomenon forms a linear system. Therefore, history is not linear. Even if the shot is made with an automatic mechanism by determining the angle of the cue that affects the billiard ball at a stationary point with the finest adjustments, it is very unlikely to repeat a shot exactly, depending on the temperature of the table, the newness or oldness of the broadcloth, and the hardness of the tapes. Moreover, if the shooter is a "human", it can be said that it is almost impossible to make the same shot. This situation, which Weber calls "sensitive dependence on the initial condition" (Ringer, 2000, p.104-105), also means that the historical process that includes human behavior will not be linear. Moreover, physics in general adopts the same principle (Hawking, 1998, p.113). A phenomenon and the factors that reveal that phenomenon cannot be created once again and the same results cannot be expected to be obtained again. On the other hand, while the analysis of social phenomena can be done for "here and now", it cannot be pragmatic (detached from history) and requires an analysis that cannot be considered separately from its historical background. Because man and his thought are active and this activity is a non-neutral variable in the causality equation. For this reason, the "active person" directly affects/can influence the phenomenon, causality ties and, in short, its outcome.

The conditions of the phenomenon occurring "Here and Now" belong to the here and now, and its consequences will be independent even of what happens "here and now". Because it will not be possible to expect history to produce the same results "every time and everywhere". Indeterminate human behavior in circumstances will separate circumstances from what is "here and now", which is completely different from what is "here and now", so that humans, as agents between "there" and "here", are completely different and completely different agents, and this alteration is historical. It is a separation that inevitably took place.

In addition to the differences of people as agents, it is also in direct relationship with the worldview of the observer who analyzes the "realized-now-here" phenomenon, which is perhaps the most important factor that removes historicity from linearity. It is like the difference between Einstein's (2002, p.18) example of a stone being thrown from a train, between the window of a moving train and the observer standing still on the ground outside, observing the trajectory of the stone as it falls. In this example, the observer on the moving train sees the path of the stone dropped from the window as a "line", while for the observer standing still outside, the path followed by the falling stone is in the form of an "ellipse". Moreover, considering that the planet rotates on its axis at a certain speed and that the planet is in constant motion in space, the path followed by the stone may be much different for other observers. This means that the importance of the position of the observer, even when observing a physical situation, in relation to the phenomenon taking place, contains a decisive difference for the entire observation.

Every observer who analyzes social facts is actually making a historical analysis. By comparing a phenomenon that occurred "today" with how it occurred "yesterday", an attempt is made to understand and explain how the phenomenon has undergone formal or essential changes in the historical process. However, the most powerful researchers of social phenomena are successful in obtaining the most consistent results in determining whether the change or development between "yesterday" and "today" carries an essential and inherent set of relationships in its occurrence.

When the phenomenon to be analyzed is capitalism, that is, an economic, social or political phenomenon within an economic-social system, one of the achievements of determining the set of internal relations of capitalism in the most consistent and detailed way belongs to Marx. Marx defines himself as a "political economist". If a definition of "political economy" or, in other words, "political economy" is made in this study, a study about "today" can be made.

Mainstream economics starts from neo-classical assumptions and mostly accepts the observer as a "passive spectator". That is, the observer is essentially passive and the result is neutral. However, a political economy researcher, above all, scrupulously keeps himself/herself away from seeing or being seen as passive, and thus is an obvious factor in social phenomena. Because it is impossible for the researcher to keep himself neutral in a space where active and effective human behavior cannot be denied within social phenomena. So much so that he accepts the effectiveness of all people, as well as himself, in the realization of the phenomenon. In this case, the linearity of history is naturally eliminated. Because "movement", which would require a linear history, is not a "movement" for the political economist, but an active "action". Action is conscious movement. In pure movement, there is no consciousness. While the apple falling to the ground is a pure action, the apple being thrown to the ground by a child is a clear "action" and the child is a clear agent. Because the child carries out a conscious action by moving an apple that will fall to the ground after a long time, with a conscious action, long before this process. Therefore, how the apple falls to the ground is clearly "sensitively dependent" on the child's attitudes as an "initial condition".

The explanations made so far are an attempt to establish the field of study and philosophical/intellectual axis of this book study. In addition to this axis framework, it would be useful to make the distinction between "economics" and "political economy" (or other terms such as political economy, political economy, political economy) more clearly than made above. When economics is mentioned, a scientific field is meant/implied. However, in this scientific field, when "pure economics" is mentioned, neo-classical economics is understood, and this movement is generally called “mainstream economics”. Because, to put it bluntly, the most effective and accepted paradigm in explaining today's economic world is the assumptions and paradigm of neo-classical economics. In economics, moreover in mainstream economics, the behavior of actors -that is, neo-classical economics- is based on predetermined assumptions. However, in sociology and in the political field, all actors are active, dynamic, changing, transforming and always in a process of evolution. They constantly change position and even shape. Therefore, sociologically, roles and statuses always change places in the historical process, and decisions are made within the conditions of a historical section. Therefore, the behavior of a social actor is not universal as accepted by neo-classical mainstream economics, but changes according to historical conditions. It would be appropriate to call this situation “historical continuity”, which means the continuity of change in thoughts and behaviors, not certain conditions. Accordingly, under historical continuity, phenomena in any section of history are linked to before and after within cause-effect relationships as a universal general principle. Today's “state”, “capitalist state” or “modern state” or whatever it is called, is causally linked to the previous processes of history. This means that any social phenomenon cannot be detached from historicity.

This shows that social research can be approached in at least two ways. Pragmatic (here, now and linear deterministic) perception and historical (holistic and specific) perception. My view is parallel to Hegel (2004, p.31) at this point and is based on the principle of “reality integrity”. Therefore, a social phenomenon should be considered within a whole network of relationships surrounding that phenomenon, which may/may necessitate taking into account the whole set of philosophical, political, sociological, anthropological and even more deeply psychological factors.

In this form, the work deals with the phenomenon through a process of abstraction; Although it tries to examine it with the “suspension” method (Husserl, 1975, p.33), it should not be seen as simple reductionism. Therefore, it is already useful to make some determinations regarding the analysis of a social phenomenon in general, and it can be said that these determinations form the characteristics of the study.

In general, social theory (holding social theory as a whole above the concept of political economy as a sub-field, but not focusing on sociology as used by sociologists, on the contrary, attaching a predominant meaning to economic relations) is all of them, regardless of which scientific discipline and philosophical approach within these disciplines are considered. focuses on human freedom and investigates how human freedom is shaped in the long term and, along with this formation process, the variables, character, characteristics and similar structural qualities of the process. So much so that, at the height of the Enlightenment, Prince II of Prussia. In Frederich's (1740-1786) view, which appears as “think whatever you want, but obey the orders”, although it paves the way for free thought, it requires “obedience” (Kojéve, 1980).

This obedience effect is a natural consequence of modernism, and this uniformity was effective in the formation of neo-classical economics, so that a homogeneous human definition was attempted as an economic method. In general, the only point that all social scientists, from Hegel to Marx, from Hume to Schumpeter, agree on, even though their methods and perceptions are completely different, is "How can a person be freer/(and happier)?" They are looking for an answer to the question. However, how a person "accepts" to be under the will of another person also causes the answers to this question to vary greatly and is at the basis of the aforementioned differences in method and perception.

For this reason, in the concrete economic field, when the change of hands of state property is put on a pragmatic intellectual basis with a simple economic approach, it can be concluded that it expands the mentioned freedoms. However, when viewed from a social theoretical perspective in general and a political economy perspective in particular, it produces results that can also be viewed as "transforming the state" as a naturally acceptable result of the centralization and concentration of capital that capitalism has come from. This is a difference in perception that varies depending on the "passive-spectator" position and the "active-doer" position of the observer, which was emphasized from the beginning. Because the transformation of the state is a conscious human action.

In the first part of the passages, the general acceptance of the phenomenon of "privatization" as the object of the study is emphasized, and in the following passages, an attempt is made to draw a philosophical/methodological framework for the way of handling the object, which will be used to reach the aspects of the research object that will be criticized. Within the limits of this framework, the propositions that will be put forward and tried to be demonstrated throughout the study and the a priori basis of these propositions will be presented. In this way, this "introduction" text will be completed, and the integrity of the study content will be completed at this level. However, some philosophical/intellectual propositions continue to be presented along with propositions related to the specific field of the study. Although philosophical/intellectual/methodological principles refer to the "general field" and the specific subject refers to the "private field" for a scientific study, there is no need to exhibit/explain the holistic "general field" of the observer, but to approach the private field and in this approach, the private field is related to the general field. It is necessary to determine the connections.

The first condition for examining an object, or more clearly a social phenomenon, is the definition of the phenomenon. The main concepts of this study are: state, ownership, privatization, globalization, capital cycle, business cycle movements. Accordingly, the following basic passage is largely sufficient to explain how to establish the structure of these concepts.

The global capitalist conjuncture as a whole system (under the assumption that capital refers to a mode of production and a set of social relations) is a system of relatively independent and relatively dependent economies (even though they are relatively independent of each other in terms of regulations and other policies of the country's economies), asymmetrically or symmetrically according to this conjuncture is directly effective and decisive on their behavior. With a simple description; The whole has an effect on the parts, but these parts constitute the whole. In response to the global main conjuncture, national economies; 1- National conjunctures, 2- Capital fraction conjunctures and finally 3- General public sector activity conjunctures, specifically the ownership transfer and/or public activity conjunctures. Therefore, the relationship between four separate conjuncture functions is discussed.

In order to deal with the business cycles of different economic variables, a preliminary assumption must be made regarding the historical flow as a series of events. The flow of history can be considered as the history of mood events, as Simmel (2019, p.9) suggests, or as the history of mode of production and class conflicts from a materialist perspective, or as the history of the liberation of the individual from a liberal perspective. Each of these historical review assumptions is a research topic in itself, which is outside the boundaries of this study. However, I will argue that human freedom is a whole and that it includes the actions of the physical world and the state of mind. This can be considered an attempt at reconciliation between Simmel and Marx.

The results of the experiences of the countries where privatization was first carried out should not constitute data for this study. This data set contains uncertainty. Because, just as the initial conditions of a "finished-completed" action "there" and "in the past" are different, the variables in the completion process of the action and the activities, degree of influence and forms of these variables are also different; Since the initial conditions, process variables and dynamics of an action that starts "now" and "here" will be different, there will not be a necessary deterministic relationship between the results of both actions. Therefore, "there" and "in the past" means a "finished-completed" action; It should not be expected that "here" and "now" will coincide with the results of the same action expressed with the same term, which means that the data and observation set of the first action may not be a source of the second action to a large extent due to non-deterministic results. In short, the starting point, conditions, processes, dynamics and results that require a "finished" action arise from the differences in the starting conditions of different societies and societies in adopting the same practice. Therefore, the sovereignty and hegemony relations in "developed" countries should be examined in terms of privatization periods and it should be determined which areas were privatized. The connection between these three variables (sovereignty, hegemony and privatization areas - in this study, the phrase privatization areas is used as "privatization period" or "privatization conjuncture" and this is discussed on a sectoral basis) can be used both to demonstrate state activity and to determine the connections between conjunctures.

Any scientific or political approach that claims to have a humanism that it explains and/or justifies with its own reasons does not consider itself anti-humanist. The claim of anti-humanism for any thought necessarily comes from another thought. For this reason, all thoughts ultimately contain a humanism that expands human freedom. The debate arises from the formation process and conditions of this freedom. While some ideas see the state as necessary for absolute freedom, some consider the absence of the state or argue that it should be minimal. This actually shows that social scientific analyzes do not create an absolute set of relationships.

In the field of freedom, the "state" is, in any case, a mechanism that hinders freedoms to a greater or lesser extent. Because, under the assumption that absolute freedom can be valid, even a minimal state can mean that there is minimal distance from absolute freedom. On the other hand, the state may emerge as an inevitable necessity in terms of regulating relations between people.

The principles of neo-liberalism as the most current ideological basis of mainstream economics and its view on ownership and privatization; It inevitably recommends policy practices that include regulation (liberalization), and privatization is one of the most prominent areas of these practices. Because there are many actors involved in the impact of a privatization application.

At this point, the division of the study and the processes and topics to be discussed in these sections can be shown. Accordingly, in the first part of the study, which consists of three main parts, first of all, the concepts that will be used throughout the study will be defined, and while doing this, the concepts, along with their current acceptances and controversial aspects, will be evaluated dynamically within the phenomenon-concept-history formulation (epistemology) within the study. Character definitions are also attempted. In this way, a concept can be removed from the way it is used for current privatization studies. The purpose of doing this is that a concept will emerge depending on how it is defined and/or accepted, and the results may differ accordingly. If mainstream concepts are used, a different result should not be expected. As Myrdal (cited in Türkay, 2006, p.5) states, semantics as conceptual knowledge and transformation is important in terms of the quality of a study; It is important for the social scientist to "not purify concepts from values, but to clarify the attributed values" and, as suggested by Poulantzas, "the prerequisite of any scientific approach to the 'concrete' is to clearly reveal the epistemological principles of its mode of operation" (Poulantzas, 2008, p.16) is also of great importance. As a matter of fact, considering that the most important feature of social sciences is to develop and expand concepts, concepts for propositions that will be tried to be proven and/or put forward can be handled with the acceptances of certain authors, or it will be possible to make a synthesis between the acceptances of different authors.

Moreover, the meaning of the concept may differ with a certain epistemology. The process can be briefly summarized as follows; concept, counter-concept, essential parallels, essential distinctions and the accepted (adopted) concept. For example, if the concept of development can be defined as "policies and/or strategies aimed at ensuring capital accumulation for an underdeveloped economy to enter the growth process", there should also be an opposite of this version of the concept. For this reason, another definition of development is "economic growth in social areas, increasing the living standards of people and societies" or "a curtain covering capitalist inequalities" or "a set of proposed or adopted policies and/or strategies that will provide the expansion area needed by capital in capitalism". We encounter counter-definitions such as ". By trying to reveal the explicit or implicit essential unity and contradictions/distinctions between this concept and its counter-concepts, the connection of the concept with the phenomenon can be opened to criticism. And finally, as the last stage of this process, it will be possible to adopt an optimum or radical concept that will support the propositions of the study, and this acceptance can start from the criticisms made in the previous stage.

The key concepts of the study are development, strategy, policy, state, ownership and privatization. It should be noted right away that the study does not claim to cover every aspect and all depth of these concepts on which there is no consensus, and it is only tried to be of interest to the aspects that will support the main proposition. Along with the definitions of these concepts, the used phrases and their implications, and the differences between them are mentioned. For example, while the concept of strategy was originally a military concept, today it is frequently used, especially in business and economic fields, and is still used in the military field. The popular version of this concept has become completely independent of its origin, and the negativity in its content is almost completely ignored in the current version of the concept. Therefore, it can be seen that the concepts differ in usage and/or completely lose their meaning over time. The origins of concepts, differences in usage over time, and changes in meaning when passing from one field of origin to another field can make concepts flexible. Therefore, the above key concepts of the study have to be handled through this filter. The reason why so much emphasis is placed on the meanings and implications of concepts is that "the assumption that there is a world of phenomena independent of the theories that reveal the meanings of the phenomena is completely unscientific, and science is based on the deceptive obviousness [as expressed in this study, pragmatism] of daily observations and common sense." This is due to the fact that the view that it can progress with challenges" (Blackburn, 1972, p.10 from Claessen & Skalnik 1993, p.4) was adopted in the study. In other words, scientific creativity and extraordinaryness constitute the driving source of scientific studies, as looking at a phenomenon with everyday simplicity can lead to deceptive observations. Therefore, a given concept will not be accepted for this study, but the concepts will be filtered through the mentioned filter and made adoptable.

Another issue that will be discussed in the first part, which is known as the literature review, is phrases. Phrases such as "development policy", "development strategy" or "accumulation strategy" will be discussed through the meanings and implications that complementary concepts attach to each other. As a matter of fact, a phrase formed by two different concepts will affect the implications and contents of both concepts. Since optimistic meanings are attributed to the concept of development and strategy, the concept of "development strategy" will generally be optimistic, that is, "good". If any of these (the concepts that make up the phrase) are given a pessimistic, pessimistic or non-optimistic meaning other than its optimistic meaning - for example, by updating the relationship of the concept of strategy with its military roots - the phrase is different; It may shift to a "bad" insinuation. It is possible to show the concepts of "good" and "bad" as the basis of this view. For the meaning of the term "good", "When Agamemnon tries to take the slave girl Briseis from Achilles by force, Nestor says to him; An area of action can be created through the expression "You, Agamemnon, even if you are "good", do not take the girl away from him" (MacIntyre, 2002, p.12). In the continuation of this example, MacIntyre explains that Agamemnon is "good" because he is "Agamemnon" and that taking the slave by force does not make him "good". This example is important in that, as a concept, "good" in ancient times was the behavior, wish, desire and thought of the emperor as the absolute authority, and this covers and represents the entire society. In other words, "good" and "bad" are perceptions that transform historically and socially. For example, today the concept of market speaks of an infinite space of "goods". Therefore, any concept to be discussed in the study may still be connected to the roots of the period in which the concept was developed. Because Goethe (2008) is implicitly talking about this when he says, "What you call the spirit of the era is nothing but the spirit of the rulers of the era." In other words, a concept may have taken the form defined by the rulers of the time in the period in which it was used, and it is possible to extract the concept from this, and this will be possible by revealing the relationship of the concept with its roots.

In short, the first part will be the concept definition and phrase formation part. For example, if it is possible to define the concepts of "accumulation" and "strategy" by: 1- departing from the dominant views and acceptances of the time and 2- establishing the relationship of the concept with its origins, the phrase "accumulation strategy" will be able to reveal new meanings and implications accordingly.

In the second part, the propositions that form the main axis of the study will be revealed. For this reason, it is tried to be built on the temporal progressions to be used and the logic system formed by four main processes and one phenomenon. 1- Capitalist (system) conjuncture, 2- Country economies conjunctures (more generally, economic cyclical fluctuations), 3- Capital fractions conjuncture, 4- privatization conjunctures (taking into account sectoral distinctions) and finally these conjunctures/waves have the strongest relationship with each other. An attempt is made to develop propositions about state transformations (as phenomena) in the periods in which they are related. A simple set of propositions can be presented here as premises. Capitalism as a system (by distinguishing between system crises in capitalism and economic crises. 1929 and 1974 can be shown as system crises. On the other hand, periodic fluctuations are defined outside the definition of "crisis". As a matter of fact, it is a theoretical arrangement that requires state intervention towards the basic form of capitalism (Levi-Faur, 2005). As is the case, these crises have also changed the modes of production. Capitalist economic fluctuations other than this will be evaluated as capitalist economic fluctuations as economic processes that create shocks in macroeconomic variables but do not have an impact on the mode of production and do not provide basic theoretical system explanations. In short, economic fluctuations are regulations in the capitalist economy. System crises are defined by the transformations experienced within the theoretical framework of the system.

As such, in my opinion, Capitalism should be considered as a social formation, and the term crisis implies a term that encompasses it and shakes its essence. However, this impact includes not only macroeconomic consequences but also permanent effects on production and consumption styles, habits and forms. However, I will not deny that economic fluctuations have an impact that transforms the essence of the system, the human spirit at its core, and affects its position. However, this effect is not a shocking effect; as an effect spread over time, it can remain as residues that can be considered as much milder effects than the "crisis" phenomenon. Therefore, the conjunctures to be discussed will not include capitalism's current spiritual plan and future views. They will only be used as indicators to address the position of the state apparatus in the field of economic production as one of the effects of accumulation strategies in the current periods through the relationship of economic conjunctures.

To summarize, the book proposition of the study can be shown by gathering the opinions tried to be discussed in the entire study into five propositions.

Proposition 1: First of all, there is "Action/movement". Action/movement is discovered and conceptualized a priori by the observer. This conceptualization can be made without the historical consequences of the action/movement occurring. Even if the consequences emerge, the concept begins to change with new actions/movements due to the invalidity of historical determinism. Its content varies greatly and its implications differ. Therefore, the concept that comes after the action always changes/transforms in response to new actions. So much so that the adequacy of a concept that emerged anywhere in history to explain today's action is questionable.

To be able to abstract from these debates, it is clearly critical how the concept is accepted.

Proposition 2: The concepts of strategy, policy, accumulation and growth are discussed as follows, depending on proposition 1. Although strategy seems to imply a positive meaning, from a broad perspective strategy involves a choice among different action/movement alternatives. Moreover, no matter which alternative is preferred, the chosen strategy has a cost, variables that are given up, neglected or sacrificed for the sake of a certain goal, and as such, the term strategy does not always have a positive connotation. While politics has taken on a very general meaning as the set of practices of the state sector, political actors are not only politicians, all parties in an economic policy are political actors who constantly regulate their positions against any public policy and the attitude/policy of any actor. Therefore, the term policy does not include a set of public sector administrations and practices, but rather the positions determined by all segments of society that are subject to these policies. However, public sector policies are not independent from other actors, but also include the effects of the dynamic characters of the actors. As a result, economic actors are political entities that are constantly mobile in an infinite universe of positions. While the term growth has a general meaning such as increases in the monetary size of final goods and services produced in a certain period, the term accumulation includes the stock of means of production in the economy used in the production of these goods and services and the increases in this stock.

Proposition 3: History and society, and therefore capital accumulation, do not contain linear models. While public ownership supports the accumulation process in a certain phase, privatization supports accumulation in another period. That is, teleological opposites are at different stages of the same process. Therefore, when talking about an accumulation strategy and/or growth strategy, the set of alternative paths made in the accumulation/growth process necessarily neglects another variable or variables, and these variable transformations may contain constant differences throughout history in a way that ensures the accumulation/growth process in general. In this case, while market forces are neglected at a certain stage, the public sector may be neglected in the following stage. In short, while public economic enterprises are necessary in an accumulation process, in another period of the process, on the contrary, privatization of public economic enterprises may be seen as the optimum strategy.

Proposition 4: Disposal of public property is not the withdrawal of the state from "intervention" in the economic field, but on the contrary, it is another form of intervention and, as per Proposition 3, it is an intervention in a "changed form" form. The state continues its intervention by increasing its size in the field of expenditures with the income it provides.

Proposition 5: The form of state intervention in the economic field is in harmony with the basic economic conjuncture. The relationship between capital forms, the general economic conjuncture and international trend conjunctures determines the form of state activity, that is, intervention.

Thesis proposition: These five basic sub-propositions give the main thesis proposition: In the capital accumulation process, capital fractions follow a harmonious course to ensure capital accumulation. Within this path, public sector ownership also changes from time to time and is in transformation with simultaneous interaction with the accumulation process. However, the process is dynamic and each economic actor is a political economy character within this dynamism and they constantly determine political positions in the endless space of actions as a result of their mutual interactions, and privatization is a normal form of this process.

SUBJECT, PURPOSE AND IMPORTANCE OF THE BOOK

Although it is stated that a scientific view of a phenomenon must be based on an intellectual, or more generally philosophical, infrastructure, this character of the study has been tried to be determined. As will be mentioned under the heading of "Method", this acceptance appears to be the main assumption of the book study. In general, starting from the set of relations between the state, that is, the "political sphere" and the "economic field", we will try to address the transformation of the property relationship in the dynamic process (to analyze the dynamic mobility of this set of relations) under the assumption of "moving continuity", which can be said based on the historical background of this set of relations. .

The study deals with the attempt to explain the activity of the state in the economic field, or in other words, the relationship between the political sphere and the economic field, through the change/transformation in the perspective of both of them on the "phenomenon of property" or in the "perception of property". As an indicator of this, it tries to concretize the transformation in the perception of ownership of the two areas (along with their own internal relations) by grasping it as "privatization" and using it.

For example, it is accepted that "change" is linear and that the transfer of ownership from the state to the private sector will increase competition, which will increase the general welfare of the society, based on the basic assumptions of classical economics. However, it is seen that the institutions that moved from the public sector to the private sector have become monopolized, and the study will also focus on such transformation dynamics and results.

On the other hand, from the perspective of rationalism, the private sector is always thought to be rational, and the most severe criticism of public sector activities comes from the point that the public sector cannot be rational. However, it is often seen that resources are used ineffectively and inefficiently in the private sector. However, this is said only for public institutions. Here is the study: Are the failures of the private sector or the failures of public institutions generally similar in terms of economic domination and economic hegemony processes changing hands or transformations, and do public and private sector failures overlap in these periods of change of ownership? It is about analyzing a main question such as.

The main purpose of the study, while dealing with a social science phenomenon, is to make the phenomenon of privatization explainable in accordance with this procedure, by taking into account the position of the phenomenon within its integrity and trying to understand the cause-effect-form relations between the phenomenon and the whole, and adopting the phenomenon to be explained. Attempts are made to bring it in. In short, it takes the whole and tries to make sense of the change in that whole based on the change in a part of that whole. Because there is an internal relationship between the part and the whole.

In the mainstream economics literature, it is possible to understand from the concept of "development" initially "industrialization" and then "capital accumulation" and/or "growth". However, political economists have focused on how capital goes through certain stages in different capital segments in the implementation of capital accumulation and related strategies. While the mainstream view thinks of the state in terms of a road map that becomes increasingly smaller and ineffective in this accumulation/growth process, political economists are interested in the form, method, continuity, causalities and method in the growth or shrinkage of this sphere of influence, but ultimately "a shrunken state". If a "state" emerges, it also focuses on the interest and power relations in this process by asking the question "who" to this situation.

While trying to understand privatization as an economic policy practice, the concept of "policy" is defined as "taking a position". In addition, the term economic policy also includes the meaning of "assigning a role" to other actors based on public authority. Thus, the term "political economy" can be defined as the position of economic actors, and "economic policy" will imply "how economic trends change or transform according to the positions of the actors." Grounding this conceptualization constitutes the terminological aim of the study.

The importance of the study can be criticized for the fact that studies on privatization generally do not mention the perception of the state and the transformation of this perception, or the superficiality of the references. In other words, a "data state" is being put forward. And for example, a concept such as "privatization" is discussed based on the "data state". However, when the state is not taken as a "given" and the “state” phenomenon is considered based on its existence or reasons for existence, the phenomenon of “privatization” reveals that it is a phenomenon that makes it a “given”, not its “behavior while it is a given”. Thus, the state is a dynamic element of a holistic system. Therefore, this point can be shown as a fundamental difference adopted by this study in terms of method.

The study analyzes the phenomenon of privatization by considering the state organization within a dynamic structure. As a matter of fact, as a criticism of the privatization efforts, it focuses on why and how privatization “should” or “should not be done”. However, here it is considered as its place within a process.

Therefore, the study tries to criticize pragmatic and popular arguments based on mainstream economics. In addition, it is aimed to make an analysis from the perspective of political economy. However, anti-privatization views within political economy are also subject to criticism. The most obvious importance here is that it treats privatization not as a “movement” but as an action with a “reason” or “specific purpose”, in which case privatization is defined as an “action” rather than a “movement”. While movement is not a state of certainty, action is a conscious movement. But it is driven by too many variables.

Finally, an important indicator is that it is known how much of the total R&D expenditures in the country - a very significant share - are made by public institutions (even more so by privatized institutions). In this case, it can be said that the role of being effective in technology development and technology transfers, which is attributed to public institutions as an important “duty”, has also disappeared. However, it will also be tried to determine to what extent privatized organizations focus on R&D expenditures.

METHOD, CONCEPTUAL FRAMEWORK AND ASSUMPTIONS

The method determines the main character of a book study. For this reason, it is necessary to briefly summarize the references and acceptances regarding the method here. First of all, it should be noted that the Enlightenment movement, which started in the 18th century, built a paradigm for scientific thought that is still heavily influential today. It has been strongly suggested that scientific thought should become secularized in a way that covers the entire universe of thought and adopt rationalism based on the mind and perception of this worldliness. In fact, the main reason for this is an attempt to purify the act of thinking from dogmas outside of thought itself.

The most fundamental similarity between positivism and realism is that they are both deterministic, and that is why they produce propositions with the principles of classical logic. However, in this study, we will try to produce propositions with the principles of "fuzzy logic". Because fuzzy logic is not deterministic, and this is the point where social sciences become natural sciences.

In this state, the basic method of the research will be based on Kant's proposition that "vision without a concept is blind, a concept without vision is empty", and the conceptual and theoretical basis of the subject to be discussed will be touched upon, and in doing so, the intellectual infrastructure that forms this basis will be touched upon. As a matter of fact, while deriving Hegel's proposition "The real is rational, the rational is real" as the most impressive attempt to bring together/reconcile 19th Century Romanticism and Rationalism, he stated that the rational way of understanding and explaining the transformation, change or metamorphosis in a phenomenon is related to the reality in this process (i.e. It suggests that there must be a connection with the actual concreteness. (The emergence of realism after Hegel and the separation of materialism - materialism, realist rational - and idealism - idealism, realistic rational as the phenomenon of ideas) This is considered as the second basic proposition regarding the method of the study.

Although rational and moreover a priori analyzes are an active form in human thought, modernism, which emerged with the rational paradigm brought by rationalism declaring itself "the end" just as every thought declares itself "the end", is actually dialectical. As such, rationalism also embeds its own opposite within itself. This is Empiricism. Because capitalism, as a narrative and explanation within modernism (in fact, as a historical phase), has created/built a one-dimensional homoeconumicus to explain its own internal and complex relationships. The most appropriate analysis tool for this created/constructed "man in capitalist society" also legitimizes Empiricism for non-critical thought. For this reason, empiricism has managed to hold a large place in economic research today. He was able to do this thanks to pragmatism, which was the strongest support he received in the early 20th century.

Natural science is a deterministic analysis. It develops propositions based on the beginning, occurrence, end and results of an action that is taking place (unless, of course, the position of the observer is considered first). However, in a social science, as in natural sciences, the observer's indifference to the processes of the event is unthinkable. Therefore, the observer is not only an observer, but also inherent in the processes of the event. Moreover, the observer's immanence in the event and its processes develops propositions based on the continuity of the movement, not on the completedness of the world that the observer observes. Therefore, the fact that the processes of the phenomenon are not completed inevitably keeps the observer in a state of mobility. For this reason, Empirism can only put forward static propositions about the state of mobility at a certain time, not propositions containing "results" for social sciences, and more importantly, it can testify to the internal connections within mobility. Therefore, empiricism is not a basic research method, but can only be used as a criterion, an indicator, for rationalism and sometimes realism. Thus, it can only be a concrete indicator for mental reality. For example, a thermometer has no effect on increasing or decreasing the temperature in the human body. This is just a measuring process. Conceptual, semantic and epistemological propositions are created by reasoning theoretical facts.

Although the study asks the questions "what" and "how" as it is an economic study in the usual sense, it also asks the questions "why" and "who" since it aims to be a stronger political economy study. This is the most effective aspect where it differs from positivism. However, while doing this, it differs from realism in that it does not confine itself to abstract propositions obtained on the plane of purely phenomenological relations, but rather asks the "who" and "why" questions between these propositions. In particular, it strictly stays away from pragmatism, which is one of the practical consequences of the "observer being a pure observer in the rationalist sense", which can be called "situation analysis", which is frequently seen in privatization studies. In this form, the study, which can also refer to mainstream economic arguments in general, essentially has the character of a critical political economy study oriented towards the mainstream.

Privatization studies generally (and mostly) focus on the reasons, methods and results, processes and success-failures of privatization practices. And very few studies deal with privatization in relation to economic development processes. Moreover, in this study, there are a very limited number of studies on privatization within the framework of economic development through the transformation of the state.

Not the empirical side of privatization in general or specifically, but privatization itself will be used as an empirical indicator. In other words, in a realistic sense, "privatization" will be examined as a phenomenon of the relationship between economic development and the structure and/or transformation of the state. In short, the main point is not direct privatization as an economic policy, but rather to reveal how the public sector that implements economic policies in the economic development process adapts to the general character of the economic development process.

The power of a concept within a knowledge-producing proposition depends on the definition of the concept in terms of meaning and/or origin. When we define the state as a relationship and form of power and property, we see the power in this (analytical) proposition as a form of the will to power (the field of struggle of those who want power) and the power in which "good" is seen as legitimate in itself as a thing-in-itself against "bad". (or the ability to create and react and set rules). In this case, what remains is the "good-bad" distinction (an ethical issue) and its implications, which is precisely a conceptually integrated (intertwined) situation: "The strong is good". This explains all forms of the state. So much so that one can look at all the historical phases that the state has gone through as a form of property and power. (every form of state is a form of property relations).

Privatization, on the other hand, involves a transformation in the form of property power of the nation-state form, a "transfer" phase, in the form of "privatization" and "publicization" at different stages in line with economic development. So much so that the change, development and transfer of ownership of the state's economic entities can be interpreted with this conceptual acceptance. In this case, it is tried to follow whether the capital takes shape according to its fractions and, if so, the traces of its conceptual transformation. The conceptual main questions that will be focused on and addressed to the state in this process can be summarized as follows; Is the state a phenomenon that should be taken as a given in the first place? Does the state take on changing roles and forms in the process of economic development?

Is the state transforming through the process of the emancipation of the individual and the parallel unrestricted economic activity, according to the factions of capital, on the basis of class relations, or through a set of relations that this book aims to explore?

Realism; the state is transforming. The state is transforming/changing based on the phenomenon of economic growth/development or a certain perception of accumulation. This change or transformation can be shown by the transformation in the perception of property (and the power and authority of power) as the main phenomenon that makes the state a state. Privatization is the most obvious example of this. The general aim of the state is to regulate and, moreover, to improve the economic living conditions of the governed, that is, the people.

But for this it must support production. Once the process of increasing production has begun, in order to increase production the state can a) itself use the channels of production or b) support and develop the sectors (class) that will produce. However, the internal attitude of the capitalist class drives it with profit fetishism and the capitalist class, which wants to maximize surplus-value and confiscate it at the highest possible level, is born/strengthened. A fundamental problem, a contradiction arises. How is it that governments are able to seize power in spite of a very large electorate, the lower classes, while the capitalist class is very small and the lower classes are very large? Of course, the answer to this question is beyond the scope of this study, but it is presented as an effective example to illustrate the thinking of the study.

The fact that the consciousness of "profit" can be kept alive in capitalist society and that "man" can still define himself within this structure, that is, still make sense of his own life, somehow reproduces the continuity of the system. Moreover, any prediction about the future of any social formation must be built on this basis. In this social formation, is the human being able to define/make sense of himself/herself as a "human being"?

This (and other assumptions that could be derived) isolates privatization from social pressure and society becomes alienated from the privatization of its own public goods. This is because capitalism can create an ever-differentiating human form and relation of production.

The analysis will be based on "shifts" in the cause-and-effect relationships of social mobility in interactions between societies. Therefore, by showing that determinism does not work, tests are made by adopting the principles of fuzzy logic.

Accordingly, the assumptions that can be made in addition to the assumptions in the above methodological framework can be listed as follows:

- The state is an abstract phenomenon and this abstract phenomenon changes/ transforms historically within the framework of a set of social relations
- The most prominent characteristic of the state in the economic sphere is its dominance over the phenomenon of property.
- But this dominance always affects the policies of the state as a field of struggle.
- The general character of capital and the processes of development of capital fractions define the main character of economic development.
- This main character is linked to the form of international "sovereignty" and "hegemony".
- In connection with the processes of international "sovereignty" and "hegemony", public activity supports/feeds the processes of accumulation and capital fractionalization.
- A transformation in the phenomenon of property implies the transformation of the state.
- The political and economic spheres are intertwined. Because both share the common denominator of property relations. And the form of property directly affects the economic sphere.
- Since the state is the centralization of authority, capitalism is the centralization of capital. On the other hand, the state taking the form of a nation-state is based on the principle that communities can govern themselves (democracy, republic). In economic relations, on the other hand, it is assumed that rational individuals can manage their own decisions in the right way (i.e. the political sphere and the economic sphere imply that the individual is capable of self-governance. However, centralization occurs both in the state and in the economic sphere)

Scope and Limitations: It can be argued that the transformation of the state should be addressed simultaneously on historical, political, power relations and economic fronts. However, this study on economic development deals with the transformation or development of the state from the economic front. In this framework, privatization as an area of state action in the economic sphere, which can be called "economic modes of the state", will be tried to be explained. In addition to this, although public policies that can be multiplied such as 1) on the production front, 2) on the demand, i.e. consumption front, 3) income redistribution, 4) state financing and its exclusion effect.

REFERENCES

AlHussaini, W., & Molz, R. (2009). A Post-Keynesian regulatory model of privatization. *Journal of Socio-Economics*, 38(2), 391–398. 10.1016/j.socec.2008.10.011

Anikin, A. (1975). *A Science in its Youth: Pre-Marxian Political Economy*. Morkow: Progress Publishers.

Beesley, M., & Littlechild, S. (1989). The regulation of privatized monopolies in the United Kingdom. *The RAND Journal of Economics*, 20(3), 454–472. 10.2307/2555582

Claessen, H., & Skalnik, P. (1978). *The Early State*. DeGruyter Books., 10.1515/9783110813326

Einstein, A. (2002). *Relativity: The Special And The General Theory*. Fingerprint Publishing.

Goethe, J. W. (2008). *Faust*. Oxford University Press.

Guerrien, B. (1989). *L'economie Neo-Classique*. La Découverte.

Hawking, S. (1998). *A Brief History of Time: From the Big Bang to Black Holes*. Bantam Press.

Hegel, G. W. F. (2004). *The Philosophy of History*. Dover Publications.

Husserl, E. (1975). *Introduction to the Logical Investigations: A Draft of a Preface to the Logical Investigations*. Springer. 10.1007/978-94-010-1655-1

Kant, I. (2007). *Critique of Pure Reason* (2nd ed.). Palgrave Macmillan. 10.1007/978-1-137-10016-0

Kojéve, A. (1980). *Introduction to the Reading of Hegel: Lectures on the "Phenomenology of Spirit"*. Cornell University Press.

Levi-Faur, D. (2005). The global diffusion of regulatory capitalism. *The Annals of the American Academy of Political and Social Science*, 598(1), 12–32. 10.1177/0002716204272371

MacIntyre, A. (2002). *A Short History of Ethics*. Routledge.

O'Neill, J. (1998). *The Market: Ethics, Knowledge and Politics*. Routledge. 10.4324/9780203358467

Poulantzas, N. (2008). *Marxism, Law and the State*. Verso.

Ringer, F. (2000). *Max Weber's Methodology*. Harvard University Press.

Savas, E.S. (1994). *Özelleştirme*. MPM Yayınları, No.517.

Simmel, G. (2019). *Superiority and Subordination as Subject-Matter of Sociology*. LM Publishers.

Sweezy, P. (2018). *Theory of Capital Development*. Monthly Review Press.

Türkay, M. (1994). *Gelişme iktisadı: Ekonomik büyüme merkezli yaklaşımın yükseliş ve gerilemesi, Yayınlanmamış Doktora Tezi*. Marmara Üniversitesi SBE.

Chapter 2
Strategy and Political Concepts in Accumulation Theories

ABSTRACT

This chapter contrasts feudalism and capitalism, highlighting capitalism's key features: high commodity production, labor commodification, and the social relations between owners and non-owners of production means. Capitalism is characterized by "generalized commodity production," where even labor power is traded. The chapter explores the production relations, focusing on how owners and non-owners interact to generate surplus value and concentrate property among capitalists. It examines the state's role in regulating these relations, discussing the "form of value" as a core social relation in capitalist development and the state's role in capital accumulation. The chapter addresses simple and extended reproduction mechanisms, production element mutations, and their historical evolution. It contrasts Marxist and Keynesian wage theories, emphasizing value as key to accumulation. It also covers Marx's value categorizations, the "transformation problem," and macro-level value-form, highlighting regulation's role in factor mobilities and international profit transfers.

VALUE FORM AND CAPITAL ACCUMALATION

The sharpest and most defining differences between the feudal social form and the capitalist mode of production are that capitalist production is characterized by a very high level of commodity production, the transformation of labor into a commodity that is (also) bought and sold, and a set of social relations between those who own the means of production and those who do not (Sweezy, 2007, pp.65-68). The simplest answer to the question of what capitalism is is "generalized commodity production".

DOI: 10.4018/979-8-3693-5996-9.ch002

The elements of the term are "first, a commodity is a good or service that is brought to the market to sell or rent. It can either be exchanged for another commodity or exchanged for money. [...] Secondly, the word "generalized" is included in the term for two reasons. It points to the fact that under capitalism most goods and services are commodities [... secondly] it points to the special characteristic of capitalism that labor-power is also a commodity" (Hodgson, 2006, p.101).

Consequently, in capitalism as a form of relations of production, "relations of production" are its most fundamental characteristic. Production, in turn, is a relation of production that emerges between the "owners" and the "non-owners", how the ownership of the means of production is concentrated in the hands of some while depriving others of this ownership. And it is this relationship, the mechanism that produces "surplus-value", which is the deep core of the mode of production, that ensures the concentration of property in one party.

In this passage, property is meant to be concentrated in the hands of a social class, which in capitalist production is characterized as "capitalists" or "owners of capital", and the relationship between capitalists and owners of labor power is implied. However, capitalism is a more complex system than a mere relationship between the owner of capital and the owner of labor power, and this study will try to focus on the "state" and its ability/power to regulate relations as an actor and/or party in this complex set of relations, on which the debates of all economic thought have not yet ended and on which even consensus has not yet been reached.

The term "form of value" is defined as "the basic social relation that defines the matrix of capitalist development" (Jessop, 2008, p.264). That is to say, it implies the combinations of a set of arguments that can be formed within the general limits of a certain matrix in order to ensure the self-sustainability of capitalist capital accumulation as a system. Although in general the means/arguments do not change, in the process of reproduction, the relations between these arguments change their positions and priorities in order not to break away from the deep core. For example, in the continuity of accumulation, the state as an actor can be quite active in some cases, while in others it can be completely passive. In more detail, in some cases it demonstrates its effectiveness through monetary policies, while in other cases it defines its actions within the matrix of effectiveness through fiscal policies.

"The form of value is the most general form of the commodity economy" (Rubin, 1975, p.114 cited in Saad-Filho, 2006, p.59). This "most general form" applies to this study - though not to the authors who defined it - from the micro scale for an economic level of perception to the macro scale up to the international level. Indeed, the "simple" and "extended" reproduction functions, which describe the relations between commodity production and consumption, do not seem to be concerned with where the elements of production "come from" and where production takes place. That is, the commodity produced is produced and consumed in the same place as the labor power that produces it. More precisely, the producer and the consumer, the means of production and the market are in the same spatial dimension.

However, the wheat for the dough for the pizza consumed by an American is produced in Brazil, the meat is produced in Canada, and the order taker is in India. An American worker in the production of Sector 1 goods (production goods) pays the pizza company in the United States for the Sector 2 goods (consumption goods) ordered with his wage income. The pizza company, however, has brought its production inputs from these countries and pays each of them out of its gross income. And most critically, all this mobility is taxed by the public sector whenever political boundaries are crossed.

In order to discuss these relations in more detail, two key concepts need to be mentioned: "simple" and "extended" mechanisms of reproduction. Before turning to these mechanisms, it is important to note the following: In a capitalist society, the appropriation of surplus-value from labor by the capitalist is, in general, capitalist production. And the surplus-value derived from labor is its essence, the deepest core that gives it its form. But the general validity of the appropriation of value and its concentration in certain hands can take different forms and forms. Elements within the system, such as the mode of production, the form of value, the formation of sales and distribution and price, mutate in such a way as to maintain the system, that is, to reproduce it. Understanding this mutation requires historical observation. For example, the Marxist analysis suggests that wages always tend to fall, but only to a level that allows reproduction, while the Keynesian analysis speaks of the stickiness of wages due to the existence of trade unions. Today, by shifting production to places where labor is considerably cheaper, the share of labor in production costs can be unexpectedly reduced.

What is important here is to understand the value mechanism at the core of accumulation. Without understanding this, accumulation cannot be understood. Therefore, the most fundamental of the parts that make up the accumulation mechanism is value. And then the emergence and accumulation of this value. Here, we first take the term "value-form" as Marx's "value-form" and call it "micro-form of value". Then, as "macro-form of value", we make a distinction between "value-form" and "macro-form of value", meaning the "value-production-form" that finds expression in macroeconomic functions. At the same time, Marginal Theory should also be analyzed as a micro-form of value.

Marx makes four categorizations of "value" in his analysis: 1- the intrinsic forms of value; use-exchange; 2- the simple form of value (the relative-value-form) 3- the extended relative-value-form and 4- the money-form.

First, the intrinsic form of value is subject to the distinction between the use-value and exchange-value of a commodity. Whereas use-value is a value determined by the utility to be derived from a commodity, exchange-value "appears as a relation of quantity, as the proportion of different kinds of use-values exchanged with each other, a relation which varies constantly according to time and place. As such, exchange-value appears as a value that is contingent, purely relative and consequently inherent in the commodity" (Marx, 2003, p.46). In short, while the value of a commodity in satisfying one person's needs is "use-value", the thing or things that one can ask for in return for that commodity, for example, when giving the same commodity to another person, is "exchange-value".

Secondly, the simple form of value is also called "relative-value-form" and "co-value-form". In this distinction, the expression of the value of the first of two different commodities in terms of the second is called the relative-value-form of the first commodity. The second commodity, which is the basis for determining the relative-value-form of the first commodity, is the value-value-form, and these two forms are interdependent. Which of the two commodities will appear as a relative-value-form and which as an equivalent-value-form, i.e. which commodity will be used to determine the value of the other commodity, is purely arbitrary. For the equivalent-value-form, the commodities whose relative-value-form is to be expressed must be interchangeable, and finally, by placing both commodities in a reciprocal relation of value with each other, the amount of embodied labor in both is equalized. In short, in the equation of value in which commodity A is equivalent to commodity B, commodity A serves as the value-form (Marx, 2003, pp.58-59). Putting commodities into this value-form relationship with each other and equating them means putting them both into the same equation as concrete accumulations of labor, and this is the essence and starting point of the labor theory of value since they express the abstract human labor between them.

Thirdly, there is the extended relative-value-form. In the simple relative-value-form the determination of the value of two different commodities, which are compared and equalized, is purely arbitrary. In the extended relative-value-form, however, the commodity on which the relative-value-form is based is compared with all other commodities in the commodity universe and equalizing equations are established. "Every commodity, such as a jacket, tea, wheat, iron, etc., is included in the value-expression of linen as an equivalent, and therefore as something that has value. The material form of each of these commodities is now one special equivalent form among many commodities. In the same way, the many-sided concrete useful forms of labor embodied in these different commodities now manifest themselves as these many different forms of realization or forms of emergence of undifferentiated human labor" (Marx, 2003, pp.69-70).

Finally, *fourthly*, the money-form. Instead of another commodity being necessary for the equivalent-value-form used to express the relative-value-form of a commodity, money is now used to express the extended relative-value-form of all commodities. The value of each commodity is thus indicated not by the quantity of another commodity but by a quantity of money. The commodity used for the equivalent-value-form used to determine the expanded relative-value-form is replaced by money, and "that particular commodity, which has thus acquired a social character through the equivalent form, its material form, now becomes a money-commodity, or functions as money. This is the special social function of that commodity, and it is therefore its social monopoly to play the role of universal equivalent in the world of commodities" (Marx, 2003, pp.73-74). In all this categorization of forms of value, Marx attributes value to abstract human labor. However, the answer to the other question "on the other hand, what is the value of a commodity/how is it determined?" is not limited to this. Especially in the early twentieth century, when pragmatism dominated the intellectual field, neo-classical economics came up with the concept of "marginal value".

With the concept of "marginal utility" as a substitute for the classical economists' and Marx's answer to the question "What is the value of a commodity or how is it determined?", the labor theory of value was tried to be removed from the basis of general economic theory.

Against the prediction that "naturally" capitalism will transform society into a class structure with the contradictions that will arise with the concentration and centralization of capital and that it will disappear as a result of conflicts between these classes, neo-classicists come up with the prediction that "naturally" capitalism will gradually increase human welfare in the natural functioning of the market mechanism.

However, the main theoretical debate arose in the transformation of exchange value into price, which is called "transformation" or the "problem of transformation". The above-mentioned "value-form" issue is not a price formation, but an attempt to develop/find a universal "value-measure". Consequently, the solution of the "transformation problem" provides one of the most important arguments for this study. Namely, the fact that prices may differ from the values of commodities, and finally that prices fluctuate around values, the severity of the fluctuations can be relatively controlled by differentiations in the "value-form" as we use the term. In this way, the capitalist's ability to control the rate of profit reaches a much more advanced level. And this ability to control is directly and obviously possible through changes in the "value-form". It is for this reason that the term "value-form" is used in a different sense from that of Marx.

s+v+a, namely constant capital (s), variable capital (d) and surplus value (a), shows the integrity of capitalist production. "The value of every commodity consists of two parts. "One part shows the value transferred directly to production, the other part shows the newly produced value" (Mandel, 1998, p.45). In the long run, the basic tendency of the economic system is that while the value of inputs such as machinery, buildings and tools that constitute the constant capital increases, the tendency for labor to work more efficiently will increase the (s) in the s/s+d equation called the "organic composition of capital" and (It will reduce d). As a result, the organic composition of capital grows continuously in the long run. As long as the producer sells the goods he produces, (s) will increase. Finally, "the realization of surplus value [by selling the commodity] is the condition for capital accumulation, which means nothing other than the transformation of surplus value into capital" (Mandel, 1998, p.46).

While total capital (S), constant capital (s), variable capital (d) and surplus-value (a), the rate of surplus-value is (a')=a/d and a = a'*d. If total capital is substituted for variable capital in the surplus value, profit (k) occurs and the rate of profit (k') is obtained. That is, k'=a/S; (k'=a/S=a/a+s) (Marx, 2004c, p.50).

Although the discussion of the transformation problem means that it moves away from the purpose of this study, it should be noted that Böhm-Bawerk, who argues that there are different organic compositions in different sectors, states that "in different branches of production, there is a different difference between the fixed capital invested in the means of production and the variable capital spent on the purchase of labor." They create ratio. As a result, each branch of economic production requires a special, unique "organic composition" for the capital invested in it. Hence, according to the previous argument, given an equal rate of surplus-value, each branch of production has a different value (subject, of course, to the condition that Marx had hitherto always assumed, that commodities are exchanged with each other "according to their value" or in proportion to the labor embodied in them). must show a special rate of profit" (Böhm-Bawerk, 2011, p.15).

Based on this basis, the neo-classical theory, which takes into account different profit rates in different production areas, also recommends that the commodities produced in different production areas have different levels of utility. In his work, Böhm-Bawerk talks about "different forms of use" of capital. This actually implies different forms of value. Marx defines the term "value form" rather as a micro-scale variable and categorization. However, here, the term "value form" is tried to indicate the macro-scale categorization of the value-producing mechanism. However, while doing this, micro-scale value forms should not be separated from their roots. For this reason, concepts such as Taylorism, Fordism and Post-Fordism, which have recently been presented as "mode of production", are "forms of value", that is, value creation mechanisms developed to create value. These mechanisms are discussed at a macro level, including the micro-scale reproduction mechanisms of value determined by the triad of producer, producer and commodity, as well as production spaces and spatial differences between producers and consumers, as well as the supply processes of production factors. Because any value-creating mode of production consists of different components, and these components are now beyond the same space dimension, and even the components of the value-producing mechanism are both prone to and need to constantly change shape according to their value-creating power. For example, union activities and effectiveness, wage policies and taxation policies, raw material supply potentials, and company management culture are some elements of these mechanisms.

The reason why the term value-form has been expanded so much is to focus on the distribution effect created by profit transfers as one of the most important items of the international balance of payments balance sheet. Moreover, regulation practices lie at the basis of factor mobilities, and thanks to regulation, capital can become more liquid-permeable.

Periodization of Economic Development

We define "mobility" as the movement of any object or phenomenon from one particular position/situation to another in a certain period of time. Movement only occurs over time. Even in theoretical physics, no explanation has been given that motion and therefore the movement of phenomena and/or objects from one state A to another B state will occur in a space where there is no time.

In space where time exists, every object or phenomenon is in motion and constantly moves from one state to another. This mobility may cause the object or phenomenon to change, transform, or even become metamorphosed during the movement. However, in object sciences, objects exhibit stable behavior under certain conditions. Therefore, the mobility of an object from state A to state B can be repeated in experimental environments, and thus mobility can be explained based on certain principles under certain assumptions. Many phenomena, especially on the planet Earth, where the change of natural conditions takes place over long periods of time, can be explained to a large extent due to the fundamentally valid principles of nature.

However, in social and human sciences, the situation is not as clear and convenient to be understood and explained. There may even be major problems in perceiving the observer according to his observation skills. Moreover, in natural sciences, the position of the observer can affect the results of the observation. Perception plays a key role in the human and social sciences. Because perceiving the social phenomenon is deeply connected with being or not being in the society where the mobility takes place, and also the class of the social structure one belongs to has important effects. For example, far from understanding and explaining inflation, the perceptions of an observer under the pressure of this problem and another observer who does not experience the phenomenon differ greatly.

Likewise, there are great differences in perception of the phenomenon of privatization between an employee in the privatized institution and another observer who studies the phenomenon. Although it is thought that the observer should be outside the phenomenon in scientific observations, in social systems each individual is in a relationship with the phenomenon indirectly, if not directly. In fact, this relationship is not only in the emotional and emotional spheres, they are also connected and even dependent on each other with material ties. Although the financing to be obtained through privatization will contribute to the financial discipline of governments for a temporary period, it will also affect all observers in the medium and long term, as it will result in the government increasing borrowing or tax rates in order to maintain the same width due to the fiscal habits that have expanded due to high financing.

In summary, with the realization of a phenomenon, a three-stage intellectual process will occur on the phenomenon: Perception (observation ability and position), understanding (conceptualization), explanation (Declaration).

The phenomenon is primarily perceived by observers at different levels and degrees. Perception shows depth to the extent of the dependence/attachment of the phenomenon and the observer to the phenomenon. The observer brings an explanation to the phenomenon with a certain terminology, epistemology and paradigm, depending on his distance. This takes place in the light of a paradigm that the observer will adopt depending on his distance from the phenomenon (for example, Poulantzas says that liberal concepts should not be used, while Hahnel sees no harm in this). Thirdly, it is based on the explanation brought by the observer and all the other elements that are directly or indirectly involved in the actual phenomenon, gathered around his own explanation. Generally speaking, it is generally an attempt to persuade some of the actors in the phenomenon.

In the light of this theoretical/abstract pre-discourse, what emerges is that dividing capitalism into periods is a very difficult task. Although such a periodization attempt is not made in this study, it should be mentioned in order to determine the basic movement patterns of economic processes.

While the concept of "development" in general is the "transition" of any being with the ability to move from one state to another, economic development specifically refers to the transition from any economic level to another economic level.

In this passage, the verb "transition" is especially used, but care is taken to avoid the verb "proceed". The act of transition, which means "the movement takes a willing, desired, conscious direction", is also meant to keep the possibility of uncertainty on the agenda. This is basically a visible result of this study's perception of history, which is too complex and contains uncertainties to show a linear progression.

Just like the "law of gravity" in physics, every mass has a gravitational force. However, the gravitational force of the mass changes over time. While the gravitational powers of celestial bodies are directly determined by their core temperatures, the gravitational powers of bodies that have lost their heat decrease accordingly. However, it still maintains a gravitational force based on the fundamental power of matter. Therefore, while we can talk about a "law of gravity", the gravitational force is not a constant, but a variable. In the social sciences in general and in economics in particular, although the economic developments of societies follow a constantly growing course in quantity, they fluctuate in different characters, as will be seen later. A study that aims to remain within economics should dare to explain the economic world in terms of its characteristics in a certain period, instead of searching for universal constants that fully comprehend the economic world; just like the effort of this study. On the other hand, economists' "prediction forms" that deal with economic data and mathematical models within econometrics, and the writers' surrender of their responsibilities to the undisputed power of mathematics, have become an effective shield to defend themselves: "That's what the numbers said"!

In particular, the emergence of econometrics by adorning economic theory with mathematical models has progressed to the explanation of economic history with statistics and mathematics in recent times. The view called climetry and defined as "the application of economic theory and quantitative techniques to historical research" (Uzun, 2002, p.82) tries to bring new approaches to cause-effect relationships, based on past economic data. However, in the light of the above trilogy, it is possible to make a very fundamental criticism of Klimetri and remove it from the agenda of this study. Namely; Perpetrators who "act" an event that has already been completed in the past never have full knowledge of all the variables of the event. Therefore, when implementing any economic policy, there are only "expected results" about the results of that policy. These consequences may or may not have occurred. Its realization does not depend on the full knowledge of the variables of the policy, but only on the fact that one of the fifty percent possibilities such as success or failure has occurred. On the other hand, although there is no "complete information" regarding the policy, the existence of sufficient information and strong authorities to control other elements related to the implementation of the policy can strengthen the possibility of this success. That is, even if the variables are unknown, the control power and effectiveness regarding the variables is sufficient. The failure occurred due to insufficient information about the variables and subsequently insufficient control power regarding the variables. As a result, the perpetrators completed a policy with the knowledge and control ability of that day. Although the "cause-effect" relationships that will be created by reconsidering the completed events of the past with their antecedent and consequent data and re-writing the variables that no longer need to be controlled into the equations "today" may produce striking results, they should not be seen as sufficient to grasp a general understanding of history.

Although there are studies on economic development or on the mode of production called capitalism and more generally on how the social system functions and determines its internal dynamics, it is no longer a common field of research to study the periodization of capitalism today. However, in the early periods of capitalism and economics, the most popular field of study, in addition to micro topics such as value and accumulation, was the periodization of economic development, in other words, the phases or stages of capitalism.

Therefore, by adopting Hobsbawm's dilemma, it is possible to explain the periodization of the relationship between economy and history in general and the capitalist mode of production in particular: According to him; “There are two economic histories that we can call the economic history of historians and the economic history of economists” (Hobsbawm, 1996, p.144). It is useful to add the following to this view here: While historians' economic history actually deals with economic causes, results and processes between already completed events, economists' perception of history generally involves being busy looking for propositions for the present and the future. In understanding today, it is to use the relative recurrence power of causalities in the chain of events that have happened, are over, and have been completed in the past. For example, Luxenburg's (2004) proposition that “every major economic crisis brings about a war” may justify predicting that “now” and “future” wars will result in a regulatory war (See also Smith, 2000, pp.76-86). However, this is of course not a universal proposition under changing world conditions.

However, on the other hand, studies on the past of capitalism - economic history studies - are constantly decreasing (Hobsbawm, 1998, p.147), studies on the future of capitalism are almost disappearing and even the effort to develop a holistic theory cannot be observed. According to Gréau, “it is now very rare to find a person who would take the risk of predicting the future holistically.” Because, “all writers who have previously attempted such a prediction have been astonished by the world history that has passed since 1945” (Gréau, 2005).

This much is necessary when used as a means of proof to demonstrate the propositions of a scientific book: measuring concretely observed large fluctuations in the chain of completed events in the past can prove propositions developed for certain conditions. For example, the fact that all or the overwhelming majority of depositors in a country want to withdraw their deposits from banks on a Thursday morning for a certain reason is more than enough to instantly destroy that country's economy with a fission effect.

Here, we will not attempt an original periodization of the past, nor will we make theoretical or empirical propositions for the future. However, the suggestions of some authors regarding the periodization of capitalism also provide a great source of information for the post-1980 period we are considering.

Maillet collects the dual distinction made by Hobsbawm into three main approaches and work plans for economists to make economic history: Chronological Approach, Geographically Based Approach and Conceptual Based Approach. Chronological Approach is based on the chronological order of historical periods. Age classifications such as early, middle, new and recent are the most obvious application. “When we talk about antiquity or the Middle Ages, we should think of events that have common characteristics and can be gathered under the same concept, rather than a heterogeneous set of events that are not connected to each other. That is why one age ends and another begins instead; It shows that the basic features that give the characteristics of the events in that age have also changed and new features have emerged." However, in an "era" definition that indicates the same time period, there may not be homogeneous developments all over the world. For example, in terms of the consequences of world wars, it had different results in almost every region. However, the strongest aspects of the chronological approach are; It presents the events with a certain clarity, gives the causality and continuity relations between the events in the form of a certain chain, and finally provides the opportunity to compare societies in the same period and observe the developments comparatively. Its weaknesses are that it is difficult to find equally suitable periods for all societies and that the criteria to be taken as criteria in determining historical periods are difficult to be valid for every place. As the second approach, the Geographically Based Approach, based on the assumption that different forms of evolution have emerged in different parts of the world, "[different geographical regions] each has its own history, so instead of trying to divide history into chronological slices, it is divided into geographical parts or regions and examined." It is an approach that focuses on [k]". For this reason, first of all, homogeneous regions with their own characteristics should be determined. "This solves the problem of heterogeneity." In the Chronological Approach, first historical phases are determined and then regional historical differences are examined by taking into account the differences of regions or countries. However, in the Geographical Approach, regional differences are first identified and then chronological periods appropriate to each are determined. In this way, geographical slicing takes precedence over dividing history into time periods." The criticisms directed at this approach are that "it is difficult for each geographical region to maintain and maintain the homogeneity it has in certain periods in the flow of history; "This homogeneity may have disappeared in other periods." Another criticism of this approach is that "general homogeneity is sacrificed for the sake of providing partial homogeneity in the examined periods." As the last approach, the basis of the Conceptual Based Approach is defined as "investigating the common factors that direct the evolution of various economies or allow to describe this evolution and thus determine the criteria that are or tend to be the same for all economies." In simpler terms, it is a field of research on essences based on conceptual qualities. With these essences, an attempt is made to reach "a level of generalization that would be meaningful for all societies". Naturally this tends towards abstract qualities and will ignore differences. For example, for each society, concepts such as agricultural economies, market economies or industrial economies are determined and historical-economic distinctions are made based on these concepts. By definition, these concepts must be applicable to all economies and therefore require a level of homogeneity. "From here it is said that every economy goes through these same successive stages in history." "Then, in order to write a history based on a consistent perspective that does not change within itself, it is necessary to determine in which periods of history (chronological segmentation) the various economies went through each of these stages, and where the regions that went through similar stages in the same historical period and formed a consistent, homogeneous whole. (geographic slicing) it is enough to determine which ones they are. It seems that the chronological or geographical distinction that we encounter in all views of history is no longer at the forefront in the conceptual approach." There are four main groups of criticism towards this approach: First, the assumption that different economies follow the same line of evolution and development is rejected due to the very different ethnic, religious and geographical differences of societies. Secondly, even if a general scheme of development can be obtained, the differences of societies outweigh these general characteristics. Another is that believing in a certain scheme of development causes all societies to adapt to this scheme in some way, leading to the development of compelling factors. Finally, different societies may have gone through or are going through the same developmental stages in quite different time periods (Maillet, 1953, pp.11-26).

According to the Chronological Approach, capitalism is a phase of general history and the concepts that define capitalism are still ongoing, so the Conceptual Approach, which includes generalizations, offers us more information in understanding the facts. As Carr mentioned, generalization is the main element that nourishes history. In his words, "it is absurd to say that generalization is alien to history; "History thrives on generalizations." Again, the proposition that Carr quotes from Elton, "What distinguishes the historian from the collector of historical facts is generalization" (Carr, 1991, p.75) is also a very strong proposition. A historical angle, then, should focus on the concepts of how capitalism was able to sustain itself and, more deeply, how these concepts harmonized with changes in other elements of history. In short, "capitalism as a stage" in history falls directly into the research field of economic history, or it is a partial or general history research that can be explained by general historians connecting the causality they create regarding the flow of history to economic developments and relations. However, a study on capitalism that remains within economics deals with "capitalism as a system", which means examining the transformation in theory from the basis of economic theory to action by establishing a relationship between the data of the past and the present. This is an effort to answer the question of how capitalism transforms and how it evolves and ensures the continuity of its existence. In short, the theoretical examination of how capitalism as a phenomenon transforms in ongoing history must be an economic examination, and the use of past data will only facilitate understanding the movement of a historical period whose continuity is in question. In essence, although capitalism is not a finished phenomenon, it is an ongoing and dynamic system that can constantly transform.

Based on this basis, it is necessary to distinguish between the concepts of economic history and the periodization of capitalism. While economic history can tell us about the process of economic growth with a harmonious trend in the long term and how capitalism emerged and progressed through historical stages in this long-term process, capitalism is a historical stage determined by economic history and, in general, a unique development within a certain framework with its qualities. As a structure, it will be able to show how it can take different forms in harmony with this long-term trend. In conclusion, capitalism is a historical stage in economic history; Periodization, on the other hand, deals with the forms that this historical phase has changed with its own unique qualities and the stages it has gone through during its existence.

Capitalism is dynamic and open to changes in its form in order to continue its existence throughout history, just as a living organism evolves in the long term to adapt to its environment. Therefore, the economic and political criticisms regarding the state, which were clearly visible in the political philosophy of Smith and his parallels when it first emerged, could be seen as the necessity of an optimum in Keynes and his followers. However, after 1974, as the second crisis of capitalism, Keynesian views began to withdraw their activities from the field of political and economic policy practices, although not from the theoretical field. However, as has been emphasized, regulatory activities related to the continuity of capitalism continue to create their existence and new forms within the mainstream economics, the most effective and specific example of which stands before us as "supreme boards".

However, to be brief, the first author to define economic development according to stages is F. List. List addresses economic development from a serious historical school perspective. Its basic paradigm can be grouped in three important aspects, and these aspects have significantly influenced the "German historical political economy school [...]: 1) "Historians", like List, do not see political economy as the science of general laws of economic development, they emphasize the decision-making role of the state; 2) They were critical of the attitude of the classical school and its followers, specifically attacking the cosmopolitan and abstract nature of the theory of the classics; 3) They were starting from the given economic development stage of the country" (Anikin, 1975). It is the third element of this paradigm that attracts our attention here. However, List divided economic development, not capitalism, into stages within a holistic history. Accordingly, he suggested that societies pass through the stages of hunting and fishing, animal husbandry, shepherding and farming, shepherding-farming and industry, and finally shepherding-farming-industria l-trade economies, and "thus, List has a unique and important role in each stage." has determined typical economic activities as the basic criterion in its approach"

(Maillet, 1953, p.20). Each stage is therefore defined by the economic activity that is active.

Another staging initiative, more widely known than List, came from Rostow in 1966. Rostow, with the five stages he identified, claimed that societies go through these economic stages. The first of these stages is the Traditional Society stage based on tradition. In this stage, where there is more or less efficiency, basic material production is in question, and the boundary of the stage is drawn by Newtonian science and scientific perception. The second stage is the Preparation for Action stage, where the conditions that will constitute the beginning of economic development are prepared. At this stage, the results of the beginning of modern sciences, that is, Newtonian science, began to be used. The most fundamental of these results is that, thanks to inventions, the world market has unilaterally created economic developments in favor of Western Europe. The Mobilization phase is defined as the "great phase in the history of modern society" and is a phase in which the obstacles and restrictions to economic development are completely eliminated. "The forces that make economic development develop at this stage and dominate society. [...] The idea that prosperity will increase geometrically if profits are reinvested has now entered the minds of individuals and the institutions themselves." In the fourth stage, Going to Maturity, a regular economic development is experienced in which mechanisms are formed where 10-20% of the national income is reinvested. Modern technology has spread to every field, and a long and strong phase of progress has occurred. The economy has also found its place internationally. "At this stage, an economy demonstrates the ability to go beyond the initial industrial activities that propelled it and to adopt the most advanced benefits of modern technology and apply them to a large part, if not all, of its resources." In the Mass Consumption phase, which is the last stage of the development of an economy, production shifts to the services sector. National income per capita has exceeded the ability to meet basic needs such as shelter, food and clothing, and the population now largely lives in cities. Another final character of the stage is that it considers technological development as a goal (Rostow, 1999, p.17-25).

Another phasing wing was made by Marx. Marx put "relations of production" and "modes of production" as the basis of his phasing. There is class conflict in some form at all stages. Thus, a five-stage general scheme emerged: Primitive Communism, Slavery, Feudalism, Capitalism and Socialism. Although Marx used the term "modern bourgeois society" instead of "capitalism", each of these stages emerged historically; Each stage is seeded in the previous stage, and each stage prepares the conditions for the next stage (Marx & Engels, 2003b). According to this view, which is based on historical materialism, humanity is in a great spiral and this spiral has the above order. However, there are small spirals within this big spiral. Each of these is the history of the class form of society. They create internal contradictions that arise from a starting point for progress, but which will become the shackles of human history" (Sutcliffe, 2002, p. 42-43), and therefore each link of the chain of human history originates from the previous link and shapes the next link, which is an understanding In short, it is called the understanding of historical materialism.

Apart from these three basic approaches, many more general schemes have been created. However, the interest of this study is not economic development in general, but the periodization of capitalism itself as a special phase of general economic development. In this context, capitalism can be periodized within the framework of different definitions. This periodization is made by subjecting it to the following categorization: 1- Periodization of capitalism as a system; 2- Periodization of capital fractions; 3- Periodization within the framework of development theories and 4- Periodization on economic fluctuations. However, this bet will be reopened in more detail later.

However, it should be noted that "this situation has resulted in the separation of the "world", "more concretely, the world market into three segments: monopoly capitalism, state socialism, the "third world" (the third world is all the underdeveloped countries. These countries Their economies are in the phase of "take-off" in non-Marxist terms, and "primitive accumulation" in Marxist terms" (Lefebvre, 1966; Itoh, 2001, p.113-114).

What we are trying to do here is to focus on determining the place of economic policy options, which form a wide range and depend on the origin of capitalism's continuity, in the internal progress of capitalism in question: to try to determine the cause-effect links of these policy options in the internal progress. Concretely and specifically, the formal cause-effect relationship of privatization of public economic enterprises, as one of the forms of state ownership in the internal progress of capitalism, is discussed. However, in order to move on to this process, the models developed regarding the process that capitalism has gone through must be addressed.

To put it briefly, while historians deal with the economic elements in the general course of history as a side field "economic history", economic historians deal with general history by categorizing it according to its economic characters. However, a political economy study is about how the capitalist system, defined by "capitalist production relations" as a common intersection period within general history and economic history, works, the phases, processes, changes and transformations in the economic division of labor in the history of the capitalist system, in short, the period of capitalism. examines its own internal dynamics. Therefore, capitalism, as a dynamic system, can be considered in "different periods within capitalist development" in order to constantly reproduce itself.

The most important criticism of Rostow's Model was made by Kuznets. According to this;

* A particular stage must have some common features that are found in others and can be measured.
* The features of a particular stage should not necessarily be distinctive individually, but as a whole, that is, they should not be specific to only one stage.
* The analytical relationship of a stage with the stages before and after it should be determined and shown.
* The age of departure and transition to maturity cannot be clearly distinguished. If the existence of a social and institutional structure is meant, it is also present in this take-off phase.
* A fast-growing economic activity branch does not necessarily have to be a leading segment (Kuznets, 1955).

Mentality, politics and social institutions are matters that cannot be measured. For this reason, Kuznets excluded these features of the phases from his studies and criticisms. According to Kuznets, when the current statistics of Western countries are examined and these observations are made, it is not possible to accept Rostow's take-off phase assumption and development should be seen as a process that lasts much longer and occurs gradually (Hiç, 1994, p.157-158).

Capitalist Development and Periodization of Capitalism

First of all, the answer to the question of how capital accumulation takes place in a world where the capitalist social formation is a given can be given by saying "capitalism is periodized in accordance with accumulation". Secondly, how the continuity of the mode of production and, directly related to it, accumulation are ensured in a world where the capitalist mode of production is given, can be answered with the question of "how capitalism is periodized through classes and the state". However, as the third term, the answer to the question of "initial conditions of capital accumulation", in other words, under what given conditions capital accumulation does not start or what conditions are necessary to ensure that it starts and/or how these conditions can be created, is development economics, with its different names. will be able to provide a field of study in development economics or underdevelopment economics. "The developments in the 1980s provided rich material for development economists and policy practitioners. The external financial saturation of the 1970s showed that increasing capital supply was not sufficient to drive development. This development is natural as long as the capital does not remain within the country and is not used in productive areas, and the bottleneck in the supply of complementary inputs (infrastructure, management skills, etc.) is not eliminated" (Pio, 1994).

Therefore, it can be said that the term capital accumulation has a different content from the term "development" and even the term "growth".

Although the third of the terms given in the passage above will be discussed in this chapter and only in later topics, it is necessary to examine the other first two terms in the passage. The term "periodization of capitalism in line with accumulation" includes the differentiations in the mode of production within the general framework of production relations envisaged by the capitalist social formation. This means that they are regulations in the mode of production that enable the mechanism that produces surplus value to control the rate of surplus value and profit by those who appropriate the surplus value, and naturally to attract the surplus value more effectively.

As is known and will be discussed clearly and in detail later, in the micro sense, "the [capitalist] wants to produce more commodities than the total value of the commodities used in production; That is, the value of what he produces must be more than the means of production and labor power he buys from the free market" (Marx, 2003, p.172), and this excess is surplus value. To put it more clearly, it is "nothing other than the money form of the social surplus product, that is, the money form of the part of the production of the wage worker that is left unrequited to the owners of the means of production" (Mandel, 1998, p.26). The term "social" in this second definition allowed us to expand the term micro surplus value to the term macro surplus value. Surplus value in the macro sense is the difference between total production and total consumption in a certain period, and this difference is appropriated by a segment of the economy. P. Baran defines the concept we call "surplus value in the macro sense" as "economic surplus" and divides it into three main categories. Namely, the first one is the concept of actual economic surplus and "the difference between the total production of the society in a certain period and the total consumption in the same period is called actual economic surplus. The actual economic surplus is then equal to the actual saving or accumulation; It is defined as the "sum of various contributions made to the wealth of society in a certain period" (Baran, 1957, p.39). The second is the concept of Potential economic surplus. This concept refers to "potential economic surplus, the difference between the total production that can be achieved with the help of available productive resources in a certain natural and technological environment and the total production segment that can be defined as basic consumption" (Emphasis belongs to the author), (Baran, 2007, p.40).) is defined as . Finally, thirdly, planned economic surplus "only makes sense in terms of undertaking comprehensive planning in a socialist order. [...] will be obtained by subtracting the planned and "optimal" consumption level from the planned and "optimal" production level that can be achieved under historically given natural and technological conditions at an "optimal utilization level" selected for all productive resources. It is defined as "value" (Baran, 2007, p.61).

Surplus value in both micro and macro senses has the character of the need to be increased due to the productive/capitalist social formation in the micro sense and the capitalist social formation in the macro sense. However, here the whole economic theory is divided into two main branches. To briefly mention, Mainstream Economic Theory and Marxist Economic Theory. The first of these main views calls this increase in value "added value", while the second calls it "surplus-value".

First of all, it is necessary to touch upon the production function, which is at the origin of both concepts. Production function refers to the factors of production used in the production process of a commodity. The production function in the Marxist sense is "the object of labor, nature, in different forms (including "natural energy", which must always be "captured" or used in all its forms – gravity), whether simple wind or stream, but primarily, passive (raw materials in (mineral) or active (animals, soil): - instruments of production [and] -actants of production (or labour-power)". The term means of production refers to the sum of the working object and working tools and is defined as "Productive Forces = (Unit) Means of Production + Labor-Power" (Emphasis by the author), (Althusser, 1967, and 2011). The issue that draws attention for now on this subject, which will be discussed in detail later, is to touch upon the continuity of production factor components and accumulation under certain material conditions and the material conditions necessary for the realization of production.

To further enable the comparison between both approaches, the term "technology" is encountered as the most key concept and variable. This term/variable was introduced into the equations to increase the marginal efficiency of capital in the production functions in the first stage, while increasing the marginal efficiency of labor in the second stage (in endogenous growth models). In the Marxist view, it appears as a result of the organic composition of capital, deepening the rate of exploitation of labor and class differences.

In general, the course of production corresponds to following the organic composition of capital. Accordingly, the sum of "constant capital" (s), "variable capital" (d) (wage for labor) and "surplus-value" (a) formed by the means of production (machine, raw materials, buildings, etc.), that is, s +d+a is a general function that creates production. Within this function, in the ratio of (s) used in production to total capital (s+d), (s) always tends to increase within the capitalist system. What triggers this increasing tendency of constant capital (s) and keeps it dynamic is the constant increase of competition and mechanization. In short, the ratio of constant capital to total capital is called the "organic composition of capital" and is written with the equation s/s+d, which shows the ratio of constant capital to total capital and this ratio always grows in the process (Mandel, 1998, p.45-46). For example, in period A, s=10, and d=15; In period B, s=12 and d=13; While s=14 and d=11 in period C: SOB= 10/10+15= 0.4 in period A; It tends to increase as SOB= 12/12+13=

0.48 in period B and SOB=14/14+11= 0.56 in period C. This increase indicates the mechanization of at least a part of the surplus value obtained by purchasing the machinery and equipment used in production, and, in turn, the continuous decrease in the amount of labor used in production. This "continuous decrease" forces the marginal productivity of labor to increase.

Ricardo puts forward his familiar "pessimism" due to this constant decrease in the amount of labor. On the other hand, while mainstream economics focuses on the final increase of total output, the Marxist current argues that the "exploitation" that the final increase in total output will create, inevitably, through the use of labor in the production function, will lead to both the structural crises of the system - overproduction - and the class structure of the system. It focuses on its unsustainability with a pro-labor attitude. As the key to observing this difference, it is necessary to touch upon the production functions used to explain the production process. For example, Koutsoyiannis regarding a production function; It compares the situations of using 2 units of labor and 3 units of capital (scenario A) and using 3 units of labor and 3 units of capital as different uses of factors in the same production function (scenario B) and presents the result that "production method A is more technically efficient than B." On the other hand, "basic production theory considers only efficient production processes. It puts forward the proposition "Inefficient production methods are not used by rational entrepreneurs" (Koutsoyiannis, 1979, p.77-78). Therefore, there is no choice between labor and capital at the same output level, and the main thing is to use the most efficient, that is, the lowest factor that enables the same output level. In fact, "if one of the production methods [scenarios] such as A and B requires less of some inputs than the other, while using more of the other inputs, it is impossible to compare these two production methods in terms of efficiency" (Koutsoyiannis, 1979, p.78) . That is, while the factor composition in scenario A is 2 units of labor and 3 units of capital, and scenario B is 1 unit of labor and 4 units of capital, it is impossible to compare these two scenarios in terms of efficiency.

In short, the main argument of mainstream economics, which is dominated by positive thinking and pragmatism, is profit maximization. Profit-maximizing production conditions, as mentioned above, do not include a choice between labor and capital within the production function consisting of production factors in which capital and labor substitute each other. The relationship established between the profit rate and the capital-labor ratio shows that, "When the profit rates decrease, the increase in the capital-labor ratio accelerates, and when the profit rates increase, it slows down" and "the same periodicity occurs, the increase or decrease in the profit rates moves in line with the change in capital productivity." ". As a result, "the process of technological development has brought about a rapid technical change with a large increase in profit rates while increasing the capital-labor ratio". "In addition to the increase in capital productivity in the period from 1900 to 1953, there was also an average annual growth rate of 2.4% in labor productivity. This rate is slightly higher than the average growth of 2.1% in the general period of 1869-2000" (Duménil & Lévy, 2009, p.31-33).

The basis of this relationality is the character of the production function. The most frequently used production function is the Cobb-Douglas Production Function. According to the relationship presented by the function, "Growth in output occurs as a result of increases in inputs, increases in productivity due to technological advances and more skilled labor force" [(from Barro, 1999)], "the production function establishes a quantitative connection between inputs and outputs" (Dornbusch et al., 2010, p.58). In this production function where two production factors are used, the assumption of constant productivity to scale is valid and;

$$Y = kC^{a}L^{1-a} \tag{1}$$

It is formulated as, in Equation (1), "Y" indicates the total output, "L" indicates the amount of labor and "C" indicates the amount of capital; "k" and "a" are coefficients. The sum of the coefficients "a" and "1-a" is always equal to 1, and these are the coefficients that will show the shares of labor and capital in the total output. Therefore, the effect of 1 unit of labor or capital to be used in production on the total output is obtained, which gives the marginal product of capital and labor. The "k" coefficient is a coefficient that represents the technology level that affects both production inputs.

Growth from one particular period to another is determined by the increases in the inputs in equation (2). Accordingly, the increase in L is ΔL, the increase in C is ΔC, and the increase in Y is ΔY;

$$\Delta Y = EMU * \Delta L + SMU * \Delta C + f(C, L) * \Delta k \tag{2}$$

It is written that equation (2) forms the basis of accumulation. Because ultimately it shows an increase in Y. EMU in the equation gives the "marginal product of labor" and SMU gives the "marginal product of capital. To simplify equation (2), divide both sides by $Y = kC^{a} L^{1-a}$ and obtain equation (3).

$$\frac{\Delta Y}{Y} = \frac{EMU}{Y}\Delta L + \frac{SMU}{Y}\Delta C + \frac{\Delta k}{k} \tag{3}$$

When the first term of equation (3) is multiplied and divided by "L" and the second term by "C";

$$\frac{\Delta Y}{Y} = \left[\frac{EMU * L}{Y}\right]\frac{\Delta L}{L}\left[\frac{SMU * C}{Y}\right]\frac{\Delta C}{C} + \frac{\Delta A}{A} \tag{4}$$

the equation is obtained. The basic drive to increase profits makes competition a leading assumption in the capitalist economy. "In a competitive economy, factors are paid their marginal products. Thus EMU=w. Here w is the real wage. The total payment to labor is wage times labor quantity w*L; The total payments to labor as a fraction of all payments – that is, the "labor share" – is EMU*L/Y. (The reasoning regarding capital is similar.) Now, by substituting 1-a = share of labor force into EMU*L/Y and a= share of capital into SMU*C/Y in equation (4), equation (5) is reached.

$$\frac{\Delta Y}{Y} = \left[(1-a)*\frac{\Delta L}{L}\right] + \left(a*\frac{\Delta C}{C}\right) + \frac{\Delta k}{k} \tag{5}$$

the left side of Equation (5) represents output growth and the right side respectively; "labour share * labor force growth rate"; It shows "capital share * capital growth rate" and finally "technical development" (Dornbusch et al., 2007, p.79-80).

The term "marginal product" refers to the increase in output that a unit of any production factor entering the production function will create. But the main issue that concerns one is the term "returns to scale". The Cobb-Douglas production function mentioned above basically assumes constant returns to scale. That is, if the inputs on the right side of the production function increase at an equal rate, output will also increase at an equal rate. However, increasing the marginal product of labor is not always achieved by increasing the amount of labor. Therefore, the capitalist mode of production can be periodized by different methods of increasing the marginal product of labor. In this context, we divide the periodization into four periods.

Taylorism, which we will define as the First Period, basically has two pillars: "separation of work into its smallest components and top-down management" (Amsden, 1990). The essence of Taylor's approach is to develop a working efficiency based on improving managerial measures to reduce production efficiency and eliminate waste in the use of labor, raw materials and time. Accordingly, it is necessary to increase the production efficiency of employees by specializing them and dividing production into very small units. To put it more clearly and strikingly, Taylorism is the first effective thought attempt to create a functional and harmonious corporate identity within capitalism. In parallel, "the effort towards scientific management of the workplace is precisely an effort to destroy practical knowledge. "it involves the development of many rules, laws, or formulas which replace thc individual worker's day of judgment [...] The worker is told at every moment what to do and how to do it; Any improvement he makes in addition to the orders given to him is fatal to success" (Power, 1994). The task of scientific management is to "bring together all the traditional knowledge that the worker had in the past, then classify, tabulate and reduce this knowledge to rules, laws and formulas" (Taylor, 1966, narrated by O'Neil, 2001, p. 232). With a reductionism that can be considered among the results of modernism, Taylor turned to establishing the ideology of the ruling elite, "reducing employees to individuals who are dependent on their ordinary daily habits, even lazy, but who can be activated by some material rewards." Taylor provided a classic description of this view of employees and the methods used to employ them in ways that will maximize profit for employers" (Touraine, 2007, p.73).

Fordism, considered as the Second Period, is a more complicated approach than Taylorism. "Fordism creates an accumulation regime that ensures the balance between the production of means of production and the production of means of consumption. Lipietz refers to this as "a regulatory mode of internalized rules and institutionalized social procedures" and regards it as a condition for long-term stability (Callinicos, 2001, p.233; and 2007). Although Fordism, like Taylorism, had a middle denominator on the basis of ensuring efficiency through the internal structuring of the business, what was unique to Ford (and ultimately distinguished Fordism from Taylorism) was his vision: mass consumption of mass production, a new system in the reproduction of labor power, control of labor. and that he clearly saw that his management meant a new politics, a new aesthetics and psychology, in short, a new kind of democratic society, rationalized, modernist, populist" (Harvey, 1991, p.148). In short, Fordism, in addition to the workplace formatting that regulates the conditions of mass production, also proposes a society model suitable for this mode of production. Namely, "The goal of eight-hour, five-dollar labor was not simply to ensure that the worker adhered to the discipline required by the highly productive assembly line system. This practice was also aimed at ensuring that workers had sufficient income and free time to consume the mass-produced products that large corporations were preparing to release in ever larger quantities... Ford believed so deeply in the power of big business to organize society that as soon as the great depression began, increased wages. He believed that wage increases would stimulate the market by increasing effective demand and strengthen the confidence of the business world" (Harvey, 1991, p.148-149). Therefore, apart from the common denominator of Fordism and Taylorism, which focuses on mass production by increasing the productivity and efficiency of the enterprise, Fordism also proposes a society model. This social structure was "above all an extreme form of class domination through the transformation of work into efficiency" (Touraine, 2007, p.40).

In the Third Period, the production volume, which reached high levels by increasing its "rapidity" and "efficiency", created a demand crisis, as it was in the 1929 Crisis. The response of the mode of production to the 1929 Crisis was manifested in the form of public initiatives to stimulate effective demand. However, in the second crisis of capitalism in 1974, the response to the crisis was reversed and the attempt to revive the public-motivated effective demand, which was the first solution to the continuity of capitalism, this time focused on reducing the effectiveness of the public in the markets and eliminating the effective demand gap that would arise with the Post-Fordist mode of production. As a response to the markets saturated with the "monotype" products of Fordism, he proposed a constantly diversifying product and therefore the restructuring of the mode of production towards a constantly differentiable product. "The key to flexible production is the ability to change production lines quickly and manufacture small assemblies for suitable markets. To do this, manufacturers use more versatile workers, information technology, and computerized production systems that can adapt to fewer new conditions. It also plans advertising and other strategies to create constant changes in demand for new and fashionable products. By constantly changing production lines and encouraging fads and fashions, the wheels of consumerism and capitalism are kept turning" (Smith, 2007, p.302). The basic thesis of Fordism was that for standardized and cheaply produced products, a standard audience was ready to demand these products. However, the problem remained unanswered as to what would happen when the standard-mass consumers waiting their turn for these standard products ran out. Flexible specialization and flexible production are "dependent on new information technologies (and thus already explain the intertwining and overlapping of theories of social change"). Numerically controlled machines allow the economical production of goods for specific segments of the market – both capital goods and consumer goods – in small sets [...] numerically controlled machines are universal machines without any specialisation. New designs and new products can be achieved with relatively simple changes made in the computer-controlled programs that direct the tools (Kumar, 2004, p.60-61). In short, Flexible Accumulation or Post-Fordism: 1- Flexibility of labor use/flexibility of the producer; 2- Product differentiation / flexibility of what is produced; 3- It is a style of production that focuses on the scattering of production/flexibility of space. While Taylorism and Fordism focus on the level of production through management, Post-Fordism focuses directly on the duration of production itself, not on the form of production, that is, the time, place and efficiency of production. "Indeed, production is becoming increasingly decentralized as managers seek to increase their flexibility in the face of rising market entry barriers and chronic uncertainty about political and consumer demands in distant locations" (Harrison, 1996, p. 77).

The Fourth Period is the most current approach to expanding labor productivity, called Endogenous Growth Models. However, the most obvious difference of this approach from other periods is that, although the first three periods were company-oriented approaches, these modelings were incorporated into this periodization in terms of their macroeconomic content and results. At its core is the assumption that capital accumulation is not the focus of economic growth.

As the First Term, the importance of periodization through the production processes of capitalism and the activities of production factors in the production function is that this periodization also sheds light on the globalization process, as will be discussed later. Because the capital-intensive mode of production in developed capitalist countries makes it easier to provide an enlightening explanation for the low marginal productivity of labor and the shifting of production to "peripheral" countries where the marginal productivity of capital will be high.

In sociological terms, this First Term periodization attempt includes definitions such as "industrial society", "post-industrial society", "information society", "consumer society", which are based not on the accumulation principles of capitalism, but on the principles of accumulation and the mode of production, and which correspond to transformations in the mode of production. It has a wide place in the literature. "Standardized" and "uniform" production and social formations, which basically correspond to Modernism, had to transform with the second crisis of capitalism in 1974, as mentioned above, and all sociological views took on critical identities with the prefix "post". Although these attempts actually contain strong criticisms of the "uniform" structure of modernism, what they want to do is formulated in Derrida's aphorism. Although Derrida builds all critical initiatives on the "deconstruction" model, he also stays away from proposing anything new; "I'm taking the risk of not saying anything," he says. For all these discussions, sociology-based and sociological transformation-origin studies such as Giddens (1995; 1999; 2013), Megill (1998), Murphy (1989), Hollinger (1994) can be consulted.

As the First Term, a new phase has begun to emerge in this periodization, focusing on the transformation in the modes of production, that is, the production function. This new era reveals a flawed side of the previous periods. In the mentioned periodization, the period of "economical" and "cost-free" products begins during the operation of the products, in order to eliminate wastefulness in the maintenance, parts and especially energy usage that the product needs, in the post-production, that is, consumer use phase. In the 2008-2009 world financial period, General Motor did not enter this production process and lost its competitiveness and came to the point of bankruptcy due to its insistence on luxury products that required intensive expenditure during the usage process. For this reason, the company's managers apologized to their consumers and had to decide to focus especially on hybrid engine technologies and research.

The Second Term is a periodization made more generally and in the literature. However, as will be shown in due course, in addition to this periodization conceptualization, efforts are being made to harmonize the terms/stages of "globalization" and subsequently "regionalization". According to the known periodization; The First is called and defined as "Classical or Competitive Capitalism" and the Second is "Imperialism or Monopoly Capitalism".

Simple and Extended Reproduction

Before describing the simple reproduction process, Marx begins with the following sentence, which will cause us to see the passages above: “Whatever the form of the production process in a society, this process must be continuous, going through the same phases as cycles” (Marx, 2003, p.487). There are or may emerge more than one form/”shape” that will ensure this “continuation”, that is, continuity. The term “reproduction” then refers to the basic self-sustaining mechanism of a social order. Thus, society continues its social existence.

Since societies cannot give up consuming, they cannot give up producing, and when the social production process is seen as “an interrelated whole, an event that flows with continuous renewals, every social production process is also a process of reproduction [and] the conditions of production are also a process of reproduction.” -they are also the conditions of production” (Marx, 2016, p.487).

In one sentence, simple reproduction is the increase of a capital owner with this capital in a certain period and in a certain amount (surplus value), and if the new income obtained at the end of that period from the initial amount of capital is used as a “pure consumption fund” and is consumed within the period in which it was earned. Ceteris paribus simple reproduction takes place [by the capitalist]” (Marx, 2016, p.488). Sweezy defines these conditions, where there is no accumulation but production only maintains itself and its own dynamism, as “a capitalist system that maintains the volume and proportions between its different parts without changing at all” (Sweezy, 2018, p.82). Then, this changeless and non-accumulated process can be simply formulated as follows: After deducting the shares of raw materials and other means of production (fixed capital shares), wage fund and depreciations from the monetary value of the total product obtained at the end of the period, the remaining surplus value is transferred to the capitalist economy. It must be consumed by. In this case, there is no saving level by those who use the wage fund or by the capitalist to reinvest through a certain mechanism, that is, to create an increase in production at the end of another period compared to previous periods. In short, there is a static economic model in which there is no economic growth in the usual sense and net investments are zero.

However, since the capitalist or entrepreneur produces not use value but exchange value and to increase this value, he will want to increase his constant capital and, as a result, the amount of production. Therefore, a part of the surplus value is consumed by the capitalist as income, the other part is used and accumulated as capital. If the mass of surplus-value is of a certain size, the larger one of them becomes, the smaller the other becomes. The proportion between these parts determines the size of the accumulation” (Marx, 2016, p.510). In short, surplus value is a quantity in mass form. Part of this will be converted into the capitalist's own consumption fund - which includes basic consumption as well as luxury consumption - and the other part will be converted into new fixed capital investment, creating an increase in total output. Here, the difference between simple reproduction and expanded forms of reproduction is the savings segment that remains outside the capitalist's consumption fund and is converted into fixed capital to create an increase in total output. However, the degree/ratio of this saving relative to consumption, again in Marx's terms; It also points out a difference between "classical capitalist" and "modern capitalist". While the classical capitalist makes a choice between "savings" and his own "personal consumption pleasure", he chooses the passion for "savings" at the expense of giving up "consumption for personal pleasure"; The modern capitalist uses his choice to forego "savings" for "individual consumption pleasure". Therefore, the process formulated as "accumulation for accumulation's sake", that is, the process of taking a larger share of the surplus value and transforming this share into new investments, is defined as "expanded-reproduction". Therefore, the general character of capitalists, that is, the producing class, in an economy in the process of development is to save as much as possible and transform these savings into new investments, instead of satisfying the desire for consumption.

Here, a language created on the basis of "saving-consumption" for the concept of accumulation arises and is nourished from quite different roots in political and political economy thought. Mandeville deals with the increase in consumption of the capitalist class (if you pay attention, the process followed by Marx, in which the capitalist first saves and then tends to consume) in a discontinuous manner, and focuses on the direct consumption/consumption increase of the capitalists. However, in the process, the capitalist, which is the pioneer stage in Marx that fuels accumulation, It misses the tendency to save) and argues that it organizes accumulation in an indirect way that increases the total welfare of the society. In the debate arising from the "moral dimension of accumulation", which we have not addressed here; On the one hand, the consuming capitalist ensures the general welfare of the society, on the other hand, he gathers ideas that the same consumption (indirectly increasing the surplus value and the confiscated labor of the employees) reduces the total welfare of the society. Mandeville also argues that "commerce and virtue are opposites of each other and that a society that seeks economic wealth must encourage avarice [...]" (Barry, 1974, p.286). Thus, what is essential is the continuity of production and consumption, that is, the maintenance of the system through expanded reproduction, which is the main mechanism of social development.

On the other hand, Ricardo, partly contrary to Mandeville, recommends that capitalists significantly avoid luxury consumption. According to him, what is essential is the idea of social progress, so that the share of consumption - especially luxury consumption - in the net surplus value that capitalists obtain should be restrained and the share of net investments should be increased.

The problem that expanded reproduction poses here can be formulated as follows: does expanded reproduction focus on the existence and continuity of the capitalist class on which the continuity of social order is built, or is it a mechanism that fuels class conflicts that are predicted to destroy regularity? While, on the one hand, social progress keeps alive the trend of social development undertaken by capitalist-entrepreneurs, the same situation also forms the basis for the deepening of class tensions. In short, does expanded reproduction perpetuate the capitalist system or fuel its deep contradiction? For this reason, the dialectic that determines the long-term ultimate existence of one of the two segments within the extended reproduction mechanism over the other represents the unity of opposites. While thinkers such as Mandeville, Ricardo and Schumpeter identify continuity and expanded reproduction with the existence of the capitalist class as the production mechanism of the social system, thinkers such as Marx, Mandel, Swezzy and Baran argue that this contradictory unity is a historical phase and that what will be withdrawn from history in the contradictory unity is the capitalist class. They recommend that it is a class.

As Schumpeter expresses most clearly, "the relations between social consciousness and capitalism are so tense that thinkers immediately condemn capitalism and blame the system and its products without any discussion [...] When criticizing capitalist practices, they are rushed and the capitalists are scolded." . He even goes further, describing capitalism as a new "social religion" and stating that such reactions may be normal in periods when social religions have just emerged (Schumpeter, 2007, p.80). He goes on to say that "the one who keeps the capitalist mechanism working; Stating that "new consumer goods, new production methods, new transportation routes, new markets, new types of industrial organizations" are constantly created by the "capitalist initiative", the author explains that the dynamics of change and development are caused by "these elements are constantly destroying the old factors." He argues that "creating new ones" and explains this process, that is, the dynamic character of capitalism, with the concept of "creative destruction". (Schumpeter, 2007, p.103-104). In short, the development of capitalism is fundamentally characterized by the capitalist, the mechanism that transforms the surplus value drawn from the reproduction process into new fixed investment and increases total output as new production.

Sombart, who tries to give character to capitalism parallel to Schumpeter and Mandeville but from a different dimension, albeit implicitly and indirectly, identifies the development of capitalism with luxury consumption and states that the industries he calls "luxury industries" - as it will be noted, the consumption of the workforce and capitalist segments in the extended reproduction mechanism are the same. While Sombart is talking about a completely different sectoral dimension - he defines personal use goods of a quality and value that only capitalist wealth can consume. "What essentially Marx the concept of luxury industry is the generic [quality] of the good produced: Whether this good is a high-value good or not determines whether the business in which it is produced is a luxury business. The spinning mill is therefore a luxury industry, although it produces a luxury good of the third order; On the other hand, the timber cutter, which provides a secondary luxury good, is not included in the luxury industry. If capitalism comes into being thanks to luxury in industries that produce valueless goods, that is, specifically low-value goods, then what is it but a mass release that makes this possible? Of course: a mass release for the sake of luxury demand" (Sombart, 1967, p.191-194). Therefore, the dynamics, immersion and dynamism in capitalism are clearly based on capitalist luxury consumption.

In short, the extended reproduction mechanism is the fundamental mechanism that defines the continuity of capitalism as a "system" and is said to always hold together the opposites within it. In other words, it hides and contains a duality within itself. The functionality of this duality can be expressed with the description of a lever, a seesaw. On the one hand, the labor that embodies the essence of value, and on the other hand, the entrepreneurial segment that accumulates the surplus value obtained from production. For the continuity of the system, the seesaw must be balanced. Balance requires preserving formality and essentiality.

A Simple Law of Physics

Physics is the science that uses the term "law" the most. The main reason for this is the strength of the mathematical expressions of the propositions. The attraction of using mathematics, especially in economics, drives the effort to give the same power to the propositions of economics. In physics, there are such complex equation requirements and propositions derived from complex and in-depth models that, after a point, "laws" emerge and these propositions also have mathematical representations. Feynman defines the term "conservation law" as follows; "At any given time there is a number being calculated. Later, after nature has changed in masses, when this quantity is calculated again, the previous number is found again: the number does not change. An example of this is conservation of energy. There is a number calculated according to a certain rule, and no matter what, the number is always the same" (Feynman, 2017, p.62). Feynman expresses what is meant here more clearly with a simple chessboard example. In a giant chess game with an infinite number of elements and constant moves, the location of the pieces is constantly changing. However, if the character of the bishop piece in this game and the style of play can be known, no matter how many moves are made, the bishop in the white square at the beginning will be in a different but white square after all the moves.

The second law of physics is the "lever law", which is related to the law of conservation of energy. Accordingly, a rod is turned into a lever/seesaw with 1 unit on one side and 4 units on the other side. Of course, there is no balance here. To ensure balance, the lever will balance when a 2-unit weight is placed on the long end and an 8-unit weight is placed on the short end. More interestingly, when the short end (which has a weight of 4 units, but is 1 unit long) is moved down, the 1 unit down movement of the short end will move the long end (with a 2 unit weight, but 4 units long) up 4 units. Conversely, when the long end 4 is moved down one unit, the short end will move up 1 unit. In other words, the change at one end of the lever, that is, the difference in energy, passes to the other end of the lever to a certain extent and causes a reaction. The size of the reaction can be determined by the distance between the arms of the lever and the ratio of the weights at both ends of the lever.

There are three basic inferences from this simple law of physics that concern us: The first of these is that economic actors are constantly making moves that are not calculable in advance, as in physics, from which the term "market anarchism" is derived. Although propositions can be derived about the functioning of markets in general at a certain moment, when the time dimension enters the equation, the behavior of all actors is irregular and anarchic. Moreover, the behavior of these actors is far from the determined behavior of the elephant, which always remains in the white square. A capital directed to financial markets under certain conditions can be directed to the real sector as a fixed investment when conditions change; He can move from the white square to the black square and even stay away from making a move. Moreover, no economic actor has a moral or intellectual obligation to ensure the functioning of the economic system in general and/or to assume responsibility for its functioning.

The second is based on the principle of conservation of energy. In the simple reproduction mechanism, there is an unchanging energy, a protected energy. As in the proposition "There is a certain electrical charge on the planet Earth and this charge never changes", in the simple model, there is an unchanging productive power. In a stagnant economy where there is no growth - while the population is stable - this productive power will always be preserved. In the dynamic model, a transition is made from the closed model, which is also the assumption of the principle of conservation of energy, to the open model, and the energy/productivity in the system increases. However, in physics, while there is external energy input to the closed model, the energy/productivity increase in the extended reproduction model is produced within the system itself. In addition, opening to the outside world and external financing issues, which are at the foundations of development economics and considered "strategies", also assume that energy/productivity will enter the system from outside at the macro level.

Third, in the extended reproduction model, the energy/productivity increase that makes the system dynamic has a leverage effect. While the labor and capital components within the system aim to grow by always increasing the rate of surplus value obtained from labor, due to the expected behavior of capital, this will have a decreasing effect on the reproduction of labor on the other side of the lever.

The subject that interests our study is the state that emerged in the accumulation process to regulate the relations between social classes. In order to maintain the formula of saving for the sake of saving, the state undertakes the aim of "primarily extending wage contracts, legally restricting the possibility of dominant strikes, prohibiting unauthorized strikes and regulating the income policy against the danger of inflation" (Mandel, 1998, p.80). In the process of development, the state authority not only supports capital expansion, but also undertakes initiatives to revive the idea of savings in other segments of society. With this dual function, the state is focused on the continuity of expanded reproduction.

However, beforehand, it is necessary to touch upon the concepts of concentration and centralization of capital. As a matter of fact, these key concepts contain the basic logic of regulating the relations between state authority and the parties of economic development. On the other hand, active firms in the expanded reproduction process are, in neo-classical theory, present and compete with each other. Therefore, the birth of the company is not mentioned. However, neo-classical theory explains the emergence of state enterprises with the "optimum firm size" model for the emergence of publicly owned production facilities. The emergence of state enterprise, that is, state ownership, is at its core a form of centralization-concentration. However, this is an exceptional or external formality to the functioning of the market itself - in its default form.

Concentration and Centralization of Capital

These two key concepts need to be addressed for several reasons. The first of these is important as it can be used to explain the capital fraction circuits on which we are trying to focus our attention. Secondly, because state-owned production facilities as concentrated capital – because these facilities are largely monopolies, at least initially – are a form of very large concentration. Thirdly, during the privatization process of these facilities, the capital amounts that were sold to the institutions were centralized private capitals. Therefore, it would not be wrong to describe it as the privatization of publicly owned production facilities as a concentrated capital enterprise and its transfer to centralized private capital. In this way, we will get closer to our main research topic.

After accumulation, that is, the production of surplus value in the micro sense, begins, the centralization of capital; It is the expansion of the amount of capital and the scale of production controlled by only one capitalist producer. As a result, accumulation will not occur unless there is surplus value, and concentration will not occur unless accumulation occurs (Sweezy, 2018, p.253). More clearly, centralization is the unity of multiple capitals. While small entrepreneurs are in competition with each other at the initial level, some of them disappear under competitive conditions and begin to gather with other entrepreneurs. Essentially, this points to the emergence of very large centralized capitals, that is, the transition to monopoly capitalism, as small firms withdraw from the market under competitive capitalism conditions.

However, it is necessary to make a clear distinction between "concentrated publicly owned production capital" and "centralized private sector capital". While centralized private capital is realized in the form of adding the capital of small companies that cannot withstand this competition and withdraw from the market to other private capitals under certain conditions of competition, "concentrated public-owned production capital" is a capital formed from the shares - taxes - taken from the surplus value in the state of monopoly and in the public sector from the very beginning. created with; It is an inherently centralized form of capital. In fact, it is the growth models themselves that support this process, and subsequently, with the importance given to public investments and conscious planning in development economics; emerged away from competitive conditions.

EPISTEMOLOGICAL DETERMINATION

A scientific study realizes the concrete reality it will try to explain by relying on concepts related to that reality. For this reason, all key concepts to be used should be handled as a whole and acceptable definitions should be made according to the character of the study. As a matter of fact, concepts will contain subjective judgments, subject to development and/or modification by the person who introduced the concept and/or users after the period in which it was conceptualized. For this reason, no concept emerges without containing a certain personal value judgment, and the concept cannot be protected from personal value judgments throughout the process. Therefore, concepts continue with the burden of subjective value judgments at the beginning and afterwards. This will be called the "Subjectivity Problem". Due to the time that has passed between the introduction of the concept and/or subsequent users and the present, its power to explain the phenomenon may weaken or become much stronger. And even as the phenomenon implied by the concept will also undergo transformation and change, over time the ties between the phenomenon and the concept may reach the point of breaking. We call this situation the "Time Problem". On the other hand, concepts are introduced by the observer who observes and conceptualizes the phenomenon. However, especially in social sciences, when concepts are translated from one language to another, they may not have an exact equivalent in the new language, and the concept may be transferred to a language with a meaning more or less than the language of origin. Therefore, a fact-meaning inequality may arise, which we call the "Language Problem". Finally, the phenomenon that caused the emergence of the concept may not occur in the same way and with the same qualities and causalities all over the world, which is unique to social sciences. Therefore, although the meaning of the concept in the place where it emerged and the way the phenomenon occurs in another place cannot be expressed with the same concept, phenomena that are derivatives of each other can be tried to be expressed with the same concept, which we consider as the "Problem of Place".

Due to Concept-Meaning inequalities, the key concepts in the study need to be redefined by taking these problems into consideration. This "redefinition" does not necessarily imply that it will include "new" meanings with ultimate differences. By comparing different conceptualizations of different views, it is actually recreated, mostly in parallel with the essence of the work and the perception it creates today. Key concepts are reviewed respectively under this heading. Because the necessity of these definitions is to bring a critical perspective to some concepts, especially concepts such as "development" and "strategy", which are affirmed today, that is, concepts that can be handled positively, and to show that these concepts actually contain negations in their essence.

Semantics focuses on the evolution of concepts and the transformation principles of the concept-fact relationship and defines itself as concept-history. Semantics, which considers concepts as storing factual experiences, focuses not on the ability of a concept to explain the same phenomenon at the same level at every point in time, but on the dynamics that drive change behind the changes in the phenomenon and/or concept, and focuses on "[these] changes, but only in the background, these repeated "If it happens, it can be detected and recorded." In fact, by focusing on the fact that the changes in each concept-fact relationship may differ according to temporality, it seeks an answer to the question of "how the temporal relationship between the concept and the factual content is shaped." This problematic logically envisages four different forms. "First: The meaning of a word and the content it comprehends are the same as synchronous and diachronous. Second: The meaning of a word remains the same, but the content it grasps changes. It moves away from the previous meaning. Therefore, the changing reality must be linguistically reconstructed and re-conceived. Third: The meaning of a word changes, but the reality it grasped before the change remains the same. Therefore, in order for the changing semantics to be compatible with reality, it must find new linguistic expression forms. Fourth: Situations and the meanings of words develop completely independently of each other, so that old correspondences can no longer be established. "Which reality corresponds to which concept can only be understood through the concept-history method" (Koselleck, 2004, p.58-62).

This logical framework is valid for almost every concept, and especially for social-science concepts. Apart from the examples given by Koselleck, two more basic examples can be given here for the concepts of "morality" and "development". Since Homeric times the "family of concepts presupposes a certain kind of social order, characterized by a recognized hierarchy of functions. It is worth noting that value predicates can be applied to people who fall under the definitions that, taken together, constitute the social acceptances of the system. "Those who fall outside the system also fall outside the moral order." In this context, Aristocratic behavior is virtuous and moral behavior for the feudal society (MacIntyre, 2002, p.12-13). In the same vein, its transformation can be observed in the 18th century with the term "spirit of the age", and Goethe advises that "the so-called spirit of the time is the spirit of the rulers of the time".

Strategy Concept

The word meaning of the concept of strategy in the dictionary of the Turkish Language Association is given as "impression, the science and art of using political, economic, psychological and military forces together in order to support the policies adopted by a nation or a group of nations in peace and war". However, the concept is basically a military concept and Clausewitz (1989, p.148) defines the concept as "the use of battles to serve the purpose of war". In addition, Hart (1991, p.247) adds the necessity of "designing the flow" in order to win the war and contributes by stating that strategy is not only about taking advantage of the battle, which is a criticism and deficiency in Clausewitz. The main goal is to win the war and use battles as a tool for this. In fact, the concept is almost a purely military concept, as it means "to lead an army" in Ancient Greek.

However, strategy, as a frequently used concept in recent times, especially in the business field, is defined as strategic management, with a phrase formed by the suffix "management"; "A management technique that reveals what an organization does, its reason for existence, and the goals it wants to achieve in the future" (Bryson, 1988, p.5) or "the It is defined as "the analysis of the goals and the process showing how to achieve these goals" (Barry, 1974, p.10, as cited in Can, 2008, p. 1). In its latest and most popular form, the concept aims to use market and production arguments "effectively" to achieve a future goal (such as maximum profit, growth and market expansion and dominance), especially for companies.

In the economic field, the concept of strategy is used as a suffix to many concepts such as industrialization, growth and development. However, there is a need to make a difference between "development strategy" or "accumulation strategy" by specifically touching on the implications of the concept. However, first of all, it is necessary to give a meaning to the content of the concept of "strategy".

It is possible to combine the definitions of the concept of strategy under the following categories and derive a composite definition from this categorization. These categories are military, populist, political and economic. At first glance, the most superficial and analogous categorization emerged in the economic field. In fact, the main purpose of this study and what it tries to do in its conceptual analysis is to draw attention to this situation.

This means that strategy is a concept that can be defined as "positioning the available arguments for a certain purpose together with each other in accordance with that purpose and being able to sacrifice some arguments while doing this." In broader terms, it is to determine the combinations of actions to be followed to achieve the overall goal. While there is a variation of 1, 2, 3 and 4 stage actions to achieve the general goal A, the action determined in the 1st stage is to determine the preference for the 2nd stage, assuming the results in the 2nd stage. For example, while there is an alternative space with 4 stages and a total of 20 actions to reach the "Result" level from the "Start" level, we define the chain of actions carried out after the start, designed for action "a2" and beyond, until the result is reached, as "strategy". However, the action taken at each stage will change the characteristics of the actions in the next stage. Therefore, the action in each stage always carries the assumption that the actions in the next stage will deviate from the course determined at the beginning. In other words, for example, even though the action in stage 2 was determined "in advance" as b1; In the process of performing action a2 in stage 1, all actions in stage 2 may undergo unexpected quality changes and the implementers of the strategy may choose another action in stage 2 instead of action b1 determined at the beginning. Additionally, a new phase may emerge and the action space may expand.

Figure 1. Strategy map

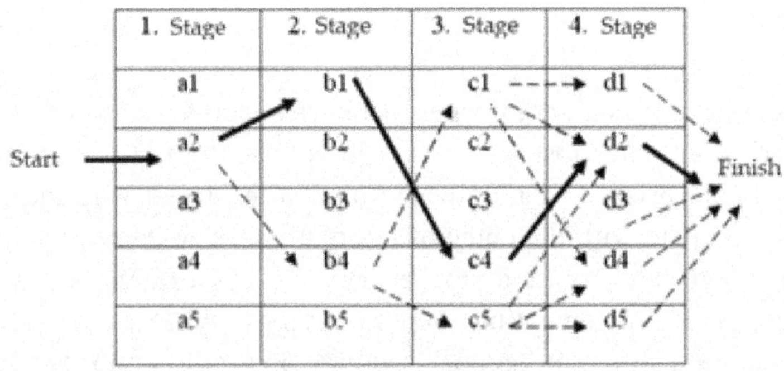

Therefore, strategy is a very dynamic process in itself, in the space of actions, and action variations can constantly change. Strategy, as a military concept, when examined from the language of military war experts, envisages using battles spread across a large front as a tool to win a holistic war, as seen in the passage above. This implicitly implies that it is possible to risk losing some battles in order to win the overall war. On the other hand, when the TDK definition is taken, a broader definition such as "using the union of forces consisting of "political, economic, psychological and military" forces for a national purpose" is obtained. In this case, strategy also includes the meaning that, in order to achieve a certain national goal, some of the factors such as political, economic, military and psychological can be neglected or even sacrificed by using them as "pawns", just like in the game of chess, to achieve the general goal. Moreover, many economic policy tools such as support purchases, subsidies, tax reductions or increases are implemented at the expense of creating a budget deficit. Moreover, many economic policies also distort income distribution.

It is possible to transfer the perceptions of both definitions to the economic field, and if the general meaning of "being able to sacrifice some sub-objectives for a basic purpose" in the concept is taken away from the definition, the meaning of being able to sacrifice or neglect some sub-elements for an economic basis and general purpose is obtained. Then, a strategy in the economic field means adopting to use (lose/neglect) some sub-goals (battles) for a certain general goal (Development/ Winning the War). But for which sub-objectives would the risk of losing economic battles be taken?

Answering this question does not seem possible under the assumptions of neo-classical economics. Because neo-classical economics, in terms of its assumptions, looks after "everyone's interest". However, capitalism, as a system that creates monopolies, operates in a way that is contrary to the interests of a segment or class, in accordance with the theory of surplus value. For example, when it comes to import substitution growth strategy; While companies in the domestic market are restricted from acquiring more qualified raw materials, they are also protected against stronger foreign companies with which they will compete in the domestic market. Or, when an outward-open growth strategy is adopted, while outward expansion provides new market opportunities for companies that have become sufficiently strong in the domestic market and have lost the sufficiency of the domestic market, small and medium-sized enterprises in the domestic market are faced with the risks of not being able to compete with the entry of international companies into the market. Therefore, a “good” strategy for almost every actor has different implications.

On the other hand, implementing a general strategy within the market as a neutral mechanism between different “goods” requires a certain authority. Because this “authority” has to assume the role of guaranteeing reconciliation and coexistence between different “good” people. At this point, another critical concept should be considered: Politics.

Policy Term

Again, in the TDK dictionary, policy is defined as “the whole of the principles of regulating and developing the activities of the state in terms of purpose, method and content: Behavior style, mentality: flattering the feelings of others in order to achieve a goal, taking advantage of their weak points or disagreements between them, etc. Three different definitions are given, such as “conducting one's business by means of means”, the third of which is metaphorical. In general, these definitions are used for many studies and ideas.

However, it is necessary to expand the content of the term policy and not be a term related only to state activities, with a dictionary definition such as “the whole of the principles of regulating and carrying out the activities of the state in terms of purpose, method and content, politics”. As a matter of fact, the concept of policy is used in the form of a phrase in many fields. For example, just as it is used in economic fields such as “business policy”, “economic policy”, “privatization policy”, a term used in almost every field such as “agricultural policy” and “tourism policy” should be defined more broadly.

Schmitt's view of the concept of “political”, that is, “politics”, is original and speculative. Because the concept of “politics” is often mentioned after the concept of “state”. When the above dictionary meanings are examined, it is obvious that it is considered as a term that comes from a predecessor state. However, Schmitt argues the opposite and puts forward the idea that “the concept of the political comes before the concept of the state.” “In its current usage, the state is the political status of a people organized on a certain piece of land. In this definition, the state is only described, there is no conceptualization of the state" and in this case, it is necessary to clarify not the nature of the state but the nature of the concept of politics. As Schmitt also mentioned, the concept of "the political" is somehow considered equivalent to "relating to the state", or at least associated with the state. Thus, the state appears as something political, and the political as something related to the state - a clearly unsatisfactory cycle" (Schmitt, 2006, pp.39-40). Based on this, it will be possible to define the concept in a speculative field and remove it from the narrow-state field.

Policy is a reaction: An action (primary action) carried out by an actor in any field to achieve certain results, depending on a certain reason, and other actors, directly and/or indirectly, accept this action as a "cause" and act accordingly. They are actions that are compatible with the action from their own perspective and that they develop to achieve their own results (second actions). However, secondary actions are a variable in the equations created for the expected results of the primary action, and secondary actions directly and/or indirectly change/affect the equation of the primary action as they react to the effects of the primary action. It is possible to conceptualize this situation as an "internal reaction".

On the other hand, when the internal reaction that occurs in an independent area tries to be repeated in another independent area in an expansion area it will create; A state of repetition emerges in which the active actors who emerge as a result of the completed action in the repeated field can also intervene in an equation created to include primary and secondary actions in the repeating field. Therefore, since there will be intervention from the field that has completed its internal reaction to the field that tries to repeat the internal reaction, the results obtained in the first field that has completed its internal reaction will not be deterministic for the repeating field, and it is possible to conceptualize this situation as "external reaction".

In this case, it can be concluded that politics is an anarchic component of internal and external actors. For example, privatization in England, as an economic policy, is an action (internal reaction) in which many actors in the country are dynamically active, and the resulting action produces certain results. On the other hand, if the privatization policy in England gave "positive" results and is attempted to be repeated in Turkey; It is possible that the private sector actors and/or actors who purchased the privatized institution in the UK and aim to grow in this field are involved in the process in Turkey.

The concept of politics is a dual activity. As a policy, it is a dynamic mechanism that operates together with the action taken by another actor in response to an action taken by one actor. Then, politics that includes these dual activism; Given a certain policy field of action, it is the position taken by other actors and actors against the action taken by any actor within this field of action. Therefore, the action of any actor is perceived by all other actors and they act accordingly. However, the process is not limited to this. As a matter of fact, in response to the action of the actor exhibiting the first policy (primary action), together with the actions of other actors (secondary actions), all actors in the action field will exhibit actions aimed at re-producing policies, that is, taking a position (tertiary action), over a period of time. In short, actors in the field of politics will constantly change positions and therefore constantly make policies. Therefore, politics is the action that creates the "infinite universe of positions" of the actors within the policy field.

The phrase "economic policy" is the economic practices that have emerged historically and/or determined by the public authority as the decision-making and implementation authority of decisions that concern the economy of a whole country on a macro scale. In economic policy practices, although there are generally no actors as deep as the term policy, many actors may not be effective enough in the equation to be effective. For example, in the privatization practices in Turkey, working classes have not been able to create and/or create sufficient areas of activity on their own. However, the reason for this should be sought in the network of political relations rather than the economic field, and this problem is outside the boundaries of the study.

Development and Accumulation

The first clear meaning of the term development appears as "industrialization". However, the reason for using the term "accumulation" in this study is due to the acceptance of Jessop's definition of "accumulation strategy". According to Jessop, an "accumulation strategy" defines a specific economic "growth model" complete with its various extra-economic prerequisites and draws a general strategy line suitable for its realization. A definition is made as follows: "For such a model to be successful, it must unite different moments of capital circulation under the hegemony of a fraction" (Jessop, 2003, p.266).

While accumulation implies a continuity and does not involve a certain initial level but strategies in later stages, "the adoption of a particular strategy offers, at least, a stable framework within which competition and conflicting interests can be managed without endangering the overall integrity of the capital circulation" (Jessop, 1982, p. 268). The concept of development implies the initial conditions of accumulation.

The basis of the linear perception of history is the regularity of the natural situation in nature. One of the first to express this view was Aristotle in "Physics", who stated that "natural objects [are] objects that move ceaselessly towards a certain goal, in accordance with a principle inherent in them, and… if there is no intervention in the process, it always leads to a similar result." "There is a trend," he says. Again, according to Aristotle, every object in nature changes by exhibiting a certain purposeful movement, but this change also includes differences between species (Bock, 2004). It is possible to see the same view in the Enlightenment thought, which emerged from Christian influence, and Kant calls this situation "the plan of nature". He suggests that nature changes, transforms and progresses in order to achieve a certain goal. However, the problem is about what the "subject or object" that is subject to change is. Because if objects have certain essences, change and therefore progress can be observed under certain conditions. However, when the subject of change is the individual or the society, different views emerge from the perspective of social sciences. Because, if individuals and therefore societies have certain and infallible essential qualities (just like objects), change and observation can be measured and observed with linear equations. However, under the assumption that individuals and/or societies are completely independent of each other and have no essential ties, it becomes impossible to observe change. In fact, this situation draws us into the wide-ranging debate about whether the models or theories of economics are general or not. However, this study does not foresee a volume that could enter into this discussion.

By agreeing with the view that mono-economy is not possible in the light of mainstream economics and Hirschman's conceptualization of "mono-economics", in addition to the view that this is not possible in terms of social dynamics, in my opinion, it may be possible to put forward another difference in terms of causality relations.

The behavior of stable objects can yield deterministic results under equivalent conditions. In Einstein's "stone thrown from a train" example, also mentioned in the "Introduction", let the stone be thrown at time t and fall to the ground at time t+10. While the observer on the train and dropping the stone observes the route the stone follows as it falls to the ground as a "line"; The observer standing stationary on the ground outside the train will observe the path of the stone as an "ellipse". In other words, the route followed by a stable object can be observed on a different route by two different observers in different locations. This situation can be repeated at different times and for different observers, and while the stone always falls to the ground and exhibits a stable behavior, observers will always observe "ellipse" and "correct" routes. However, after the experiences gained by the observers through their observations, they will come to know that the observation made as an "ellipse" is not actually an ellipse and that this is due only to the observer. However, when the observed phenomenon is not a stable object but dynamic subjects, observations will never reach universal, general-valid conclusions. Because when each observation is acquired as information by dynamic subjects, it is internalized and each information brings the subjects' behaviors to infinite possible variations. The acting subject is then independent of object determination and is directly active in the action. Therefore, objective events can be repeated even after time t. For example, no pitcher can make an attempt to avoid falling off the table, inspired by the experience that the pitchers before him will break as a result of falling off the table. However, for example, as the results of a social phenomenon in society A, these results are reflected in another social process, and since society B, which wants to repeat the action of society A, will also include these result-effects reflected from society A, it will not be possible to repeat the same action under the same conditions. There will be differences in terms of the variables involved in the actions of the two societies and the results to be achieved. But still, although universal social principles cannot be demonstrated; A social phenomenon may have a tendency to spread among societies and/or people, and may unite human or social essences on certain common denominators.

In short, the validity of economic theories is also considered under this basic assumption. As a matter of fact, this element is responsible for the emergence of development economics; It has been extremely influential that economic theories developed for developed countries are not/cannot be valid for developing or underdeveloped countries. Therefore, almost every country may have very different economic policies.

Development, Accumulation and Strategy

Based on the concept of development mentioned above, the concept of development was emphasized with a certain idea of linear progress. However, although accumulation is not linear, it ultimately implies a certain capital stock, albeit through different methods. The process called development is the process of changing the conditions of space A in order to obtain the desired results for space B at the earliest time t+n or at time t+n+x in space B, in terms of the results of a phenomenon that occurred at time t in place A, at time t+n. It does not seem possible to create the and process and obtain the results of space A.

"The totality of policies created according to the requirements of capital accumulation processes" (Gülalp, 1987, p.58) can be defined as accumulation strategy. However, when talking about strategy, Gülalp talks about "strategy choice" (Gülalp, 1987, p.58), and although he says that alternative strategies are determined by the global division of labor and the country's management style, this is treated as a simple choice. However, this is not a simple choice (in fact, although his own criticism of liberals is that they ignore historicity, he also talks about a choice among options, not in historical continuity). He also defines choices or transitions with different class structures and changes in the international division of labor.

The accumulation strategy is to position the arguments that can be used to achieve a certain economic size in a certain way. "Capital is a form-determined social relation. Capital accumulation is the complex component of the changing balance of class forces in the struggle that takes place within a framework determined by the value form" (Jessop, 2013, p.154).

Economics tries to perceive and explain economic relations through economic variables. While doing this, it tries to connect the static determinations of the variables to the results as historical series. However, political economy also tries to see the effects of political ideologies on the formation of economic data and treats the formation of data not as natural processes, but as a presupposition that they are created. In other words, while according to economics, the trade-off between inflation and unemployment is a situation to be determined by data, political economy tries to see this as a result of the choices of certain political effects.

The spread of capitalism occurs in two stages. The first is the theoretical and the second is the practical stage. The theoretical stage is the intellectual theoretical current coming from the countries that contain early capitalist and systematized large capitalist capital, and the second is the actual expansion of capitalism, that is, the tendency of advanced capitalist countries to spread capital / seek new profit areas due to the internal structure of capitalism, and the international division of labor that is formed in accordance with the international division of labor. As a result of the structure, developing and underdeveloped economies need foreign capital.

REFERENCES

Althusser, L. (1967). *Philosophie et philosophie spontanée des savants*. Fronçois Maspero.

Althusser, L. (2011). *Sur la reproduction: Préface d'Étienne Balibar* (2nd ed.). Fronçois Maspero. 10.3917/puf.althu.2011.01

Amsden, A. (1990). The world industrialization: 'Global Fordism' or a new model. *New Left Review*, 182, 5–31.

Anikin, A. (1975). *A Science in its Youth: Pre-Marxian Political Economy*. Morkow: Progress Publishers.

Baran, P. A. (1957). *The Political Economy of Growth*. Monthly Review Press.

Barro, R. (1999). Human capital and growth in cross country regressions. *Swedish Economic Policy Review*, 6, 237–277.

Barry, N. (1974). *Scientific Knowledge and Sociological Theory*. Routledge.

Bock, K. (2004). Theories of progress, development, evolution. In Bottomore, T., & Bisbet, R. (Eds.), *A History of Sociological Analysis*. Heinemann.

Böhm-Bawerk, E. (2011). *Karl Marx and the Close of His System*. Ludwig von Mises Institute.

Bryson, J. M., & Einsweiler, R. C. (1988). *Strategic Planning: Threat and Opportunities for Planners*. Planner Press.

Callinicos, A. (2001). Periodising capitalism and analysing imperialism: Classical Marxism and capitalist evolution. In Albritton, R., Itoh, M., Westra, R., & Zuege, A. (Eds.), *Phases of Capitalist Development: Booms, Crises and Globalisations* (pp. 230–245). Palgrave. 10.1057/9781403900081_14

Callinicos, A. (2007). *Social Theory: A Historical Introduction* (2nd ed.). Polity.

Carr, E. (1991). *What Is History*. Penguin.

Clausewitz, C. (1989). *On War*. Princeton University Press.

Dornbush, R., Fisher, S., & Startz, R. (2010). *Macroeconomics* (11th ed.). McGraw-Hill.

Duménil, G., & Lévy, D. (2009). *La grande bifurcation En finir avec le néolibéralisme*. Ouvrières.

Feynman, R. (2017). *The Character of Physical Law*. Piper Books. 10.7551/mit-press/11068.001.0001

Giddens, A. (1995). *A Contemporary Critique of Historical Materialism*. Palgrave. 10.1007/978-1-349-24187-3

Giddens, A. (1999). The Constitution of Society: Outline of the Theory of Structuration. *Polity*.

Giddens, A. (2013). The Nation-State and Violence. *Polity*.

Gréau, J. L. (2005). *L'Avenir du Capitalisme*. Gallimard.

Gülalp, H. (1987). *Gelişme Stratejileri ve Gelişme İdeolojileri*. Yurt Yayınları.

Harrison, B. (1996). Küçük firmalar miti, K. Tanyılmaz (çev.). *Ekonomik Yaklaşım*, 7(20), 77–94.

Hart, B. H. L. (1991). *Strategy*. Plume.

Harvey, D. (1991). *The Condition of Postmodernity: An Enquiry into the Origins of Cultural Change*. Wiley-Blackwell.

Hiç, M. (1994). *Büyüme ve Gelişme Ekonomisi*. Filiz Kitabevi.

Hobsbawm, E. (1996). *The Age of Revolution: 1789-1848*. Vintage.

Hobsbawm, E. (1998). *On History*. The New Press.

Hodgson, G. (2006). Demokratik ekonomi: Planlama, piyasa ve iktidara yeni bir bakış, S. Çaklı (çev.). *Ekonomik Yaklaşım*, 17(59), 99–113. 10.5455/ey.10612

Hollinger, R. (1994). *Postmodernism and the Social Sciences: A Thematic Approach*. Sage Publications.

Itoh, M. (2001). Spiral revelsal of capitalist development: What does it imply for the Twenty-First Centry? In Albritton, R., Itoh, M., Westra, R., & Zuege, A. (Eds.), *Phases of Capitalist Development: Booms, Crises and Globalisations* (pp. 110–124). Palgrave. 10.1057/9781403900081_7

Jessop, B. (1982). *The Capitalist State*. New York University Press.

Jessop, B. (2003). The Future of the Capitalist State. *Polity*.

Koselleck, R. (2004). *Futures Past: On the Semantics of Historical Time*. Columbia University Press.

Koutsoyiannis, A. (1979). *Modern Microeconomics*, 2Rev Ed Edition, Palgrave. 10.1007/9781349160778

Kumar, K. (2004). *Sanayi Sonrası Toplumdan Postmodern Topluma Çağdaş Dünyanın Yeni Kuramları*. Dost Kitabevi.

Kuznets, S. (1955). Economic growth and income inequality. *The American Economic Review*, 45(1), 1–28.

Lefebvre, H. (1966). Sociologie de Marx. *Revue Philosophique de Louvain*, 86, 173–241.

Luxemburg, R. (2003). *The Accumulation of Capital*. Routledge.

MacIntyre, A. (2002). *A Short History of Ethics*. Routledge.

Maillet, J. (1953). *Histoire des faits économiques*. Payot.

Mandel, E. (1973). *An Introduction to Marxist Economic Theory*. Pathfinder.

Marx, K. (1988). The Economic and Philosophic Manuscripts of 1844 and the Communist Manifesto. *Prometheus*.

Marx, K. (2016). *Capital, Vol.1, 2, 3.*, Fingerprint Publishing.

Marx, K., & Engels, F. (2003). The German Ideology. *Prometheus*.

Marx, K., & Engels, F. (2003b). *The Communist Manifesto*. Penguin Classics. 10.1522/cla.mak.man

Murphy, J. (1989). *Postmodern Social Analysis and Criticism*. Praeger.

O'Neill, J. (1998). *The Market: Ethics, Knowledge and Politics*. Routledge. 10.4324/9780203358467

Pio, A. (1994). New growth theory and old development problems: How recent developments in endogenous growth theory apply to developing countries. *Development Policy Review*, 12(3), 277–300. 10.1111/j.1467-7679.1994.tb00068.x

Power, M. (1994). *The Audit Explosion*. Demos.

Rostow, W. W. (1966). *The Stages of Economic Growth: A Non-Communist Manifesto*. Barakaldo Books.

Saad-Filho, A. (2006). *Marx's 'Capital*. Pluto Press.

Schmitt, C. (2006). *The Concept of the Political*. The University of Chicago Press.

Schumpeter, J. A. (2007). *Capitalism, Socialism and Democracy*. Lebooks Editora.

Smith, A. (1994). *The Wealth of Nations*. Modern Library.

Smith, R. (2000). Military expenditure and globalization. In Toporowski, J. (Ed.), *Political Economy and the New Capitalism: Essays in Honour of Sam Aaronovitch* (pp. 76–86). Routledge.

Sombart, W. (1967). *Luxury and Capitalism*. University of Michigan Press.

Sutcliffe, B. (2002). How many capitalism? Historical materyalism in the debates about imperialism and globalization, *in* M. Rupert, & H. Smith (edt.), *Historical Materialism and Globalization*. (pp.40-58), Routledge

Sweezy, P. (2018). *Theory of Capital Development*. Monthly Review Press.

Touraine, A. (2007). *New Paradigm for Understanding Today s World*. Polity Press.

Uzun, A. (2002). Yeni iktisat tarihi akımı ve iktisat tarihi yazımına katkıları. *CÜ İİBF Dergisi*, 2(1), 80–93.

Chapter 3
Capitalism and Development

ABSTRACT

This chapter explores the dynamics and implications of inward-looking versus outward-looking accumulation strategies in economic development. It finds that prioritizing one strategy inherently downplays the variables of the other, revealing a fundamental trade-off. The state's role in choosing and implementing these strategies is crucial, shaped by internal political actors and external economic conditions, raising questions about the interplay between state policy and economic actors. The concept of strategy is examined at both micro and macro levels: micro-level adjustments among economic actors create a dynamic, complex environment, while macro-level strategies may overlook certain variables to achieve broader goals. The chapter aligns with capitalist development and dependency theories, highlighting the state's role in sustaining capitalist economies. It covers stages of capitalist development and their global interplay, focusing on inward-looking strategies like import substitution and state intervention.

CAPITAL ACCUMULATION STRATEGIES

The main result we obtained from the term strategy is that when one of the strategy options within a whole is preferred, the variables of the function that make up the other strategy can be neglected, ignored, or even if not ignored, in the most optimistic case, they can be put on hold. With this adoption, talking about any accumulation strategy also requires pre-assuming that at least some of the elements contained in the alternative strategy or strategies can be neglected in their overall integrity. In short, the "inward-looking accumulation strategy" to be adopted in order to create, develop and maintain the functionality of the accumulation mechanism shows that

DOI: 10.4018/979-8-3693-5996-9.ch003

some elements of the "outward-looking accumulation strategy" have been ignored since the choice was made. Or the same negligence applies to the opposite situation.

However, the findings observed from capitalist development theories, whether through the Keynesian influence in mainstream economics or in the periodization of state capitalism from the perspective of political economy, show that the state plays a functional role in the establishment and continued functioning of capitalism.

First of all, the political power that will make the strategy choice is the state itself. However, this policy determination is not completely independent. The main result obtained from the term policy is that if any political actor determines a policy in the policy space, other political actors also harmonize their positions, including causal links. The basic question here is; What is the direction of the causality relationship between the state's implementation of its choice of accumulation strategy as a policy and the compatibility of other actors within the framework of the same strategy? In other words, is the premise that "the state politicizes its choice of accumulation strategy as a result of the political positions of other actors in the basic integrity of accumulation?" or, "in a political determination compatible with the accumulation strategy adopted politically by the state, other actors also take political positions in accordance with this political determination" is to answer the validity of the proposition "Is it adapting to the preferred strategy by determining the

Of the dual meanings we attribute to the concept of strategy, the micro one is; Actors in the economy determine their own positions by observing or at least predicting the behavior of other actors, even though they do not have the chance to know them exactly. Since it is clear that one of the "n" number of actors in the economy cannot reach the optimum of observing all the other actors and determining the most appropriate position, and the fact that the "n" number of actors mutually switch to constantly dynamic positions shows that the actors in the market have "infinite position alternatives". This is why the term "market anarchism" is brought to the agenda.

In the macro sense, it means that in a universe where perfect competition conditions are not possible, among the "n" number of actors, the actors who have the scope to direct the overall economy can "neglect" some other elements in the economy in order to achieve a segment of the economy or an anchor target. In short, while strategy in the micro sense refers to an unobservable field of action, the concept of strategy in the macro sense indicates that some sub-variables can be ignored or neglected for a general goal.

By assigning these meanings, we should refer to the forms of strategy that are often referred to as "development strategy" but defined as "growth strategy" or "accumulation strategy", which include how the economy can grow with its relations with the outside world. In short, if an "inward-looking" or "outward-looking" development strategy is talked about, this means that some variables in the equation can be neglected in order to achieve some anchors. Therefore, in this study, "introvert" or "extrovert" strategies are considered only as strategies before using them as phrases with the terms "growth", "development" and "accumulation". Because it is necessary to determine the dividing lines between these terms.

The Problem of Choice-Periodality

No matter how the phrase is made, the term strategy as a part of the phrase arises on the basis that, in order to achieve a certain general goal, in a system of equations with more than one variable, some variables of the system can be prioritized while other variables can be ostensibly neglected for a certain period of time. Therefore, there are alternative options to achieve the said overall goal, that is, alternatives on which variable can be neglected. However, which variable can be taken as basis in the equation system and which variables can be neglected is not in the form of alternatives that can be linearly "determined" or "chosen". In short, there are some apparent options, but the option that emerges from them may not or may not be fully based on a will. More generally, a system of social equations is not always voluntary and controllable. There are many actors and therefore political attitudes that affect the system from inside and outside. Therefore, in order to observe the conditions under which a certain strategy emerged, it will be possible to explain the historical position of internal and external actors and dynamics and to define the situation in which the strategy emerged in these contexts.

While the basic and final expectation is that the economic growth process will "begin" and be grounded and "continued", all actors in the economy will take their political positions according to these conditions. As stated by Bina and Yaghmanian, the preliminary knowledge/assumptions of economic actors about the characteristics of such a process are the stages in the historical continuity of capitalist development. While the principles of historicity and capitalist periodization discussed previously have been determined, the periodization about the accumulation strategy; [considering] that it "represents three historically specific stages in global development: (I) the early stage of primitive accumulation, (II) the advanced stage of primitive accumulation and import substitution industrialization (IIS), and (III) export-oriented accumulation and global articulation". What is meant by the early stage of primitive accumulation includes the peasants breaking away from the land, starting to turn to the labor market, and the beginning of the formation of commodity capital. The second stage, the "advanced stage of primitive accumulation and the import substitution period", includes a preparation process for the demolition of pre-capitalist obstacles to production and integration into the world economy. After the process, it is "preparation for import substitution industrialization, export-oriented accumulation process and production directly for the world market". In addition to this view of

Bina and Yaghmanian, it is also a preliminary preparation and creation of conditions for consuming from the world market. Finally, "export-oriented accumulation is the internationalization of productive capital at a higher stage. "This is a phase in which various parts of the global capitalist market are interconnected around large networks of production and exchange." (Bina & Yaghmanian, 1988, p.234-248).

The fact that three different economic forms can appear simultaneously in the global capitalist process also shows that each form is effective on the other and that the existence of other forms is needed, at least in some form. These three forms; They appear as Advanced (Early) Capitalist Economies, Late Capitalist Economies and Primitive Economies. While the first two of these are generally accepted as developed and developing countries, respectively, in this study, they refer to desert Asia and desert Africa as "primitive economies", which have not developed production mechanisms, operate mostly on natural resources. As is known, these countries still contain social dynamics that can be called "feudal". The natural resources obtained from these countries are resources that contradict the labor theory of value and carry a very high value with less labor than the amount of labor used for the product obtained and even less than the average social labor amount. In these economies, where feudal relations are also strong, differences between classes also include large gaps. Although it is not the aim of this study, these economies, the values they produce and labor-value still need a theoretical explanation. According to Frank, the industrialized capitalist West draws the socialist East into a new international division of labor, and the failure of the third world countries in their development puts these southern countries "under the burden of cheap labor and political oppression" (Frank, 2014, p.131). The relationship between these triple forms, which at first glance is partially similar to the view that it is) and takes part in the system; It is a "partial-relative interest relationship" and requires mutual dependence. However, while this "dependence" provides cheap labor, new markets and the necessary raw material opportunities for advanced capitalist countries, it also provides relative benefits for late-capitalist economies. "Dependency theory emerged after industrialization processes began in the South. Accordingly, the environment depends on the market, technology, financial resources, etc. He was dependent on the center to reach him. Against this self-producing state of extroversion, self-centered development models" (Assidon, 1996, p.13) began to be put forward. On the other hand, economies called primitive economies provide the opportunity to preserve their feudal relations within themselves. Moreover, feudal governments in primitive economies generally do not have a social purpose other than the continuation of their power. In this way, economies at all levels get what they want from the process.

According to the approach of the dependency school, "the structure of the global political economy has made the underdeveloped economies of the south dependent on the developed economies of the north [...] there are three different phases of dependency in modern history: colonial dependency (18th, 19th centuries); financial and industrial dependence (19th, 20th centuries), dependence on the basis of multinational corporations in the post-war period. G. Frank, on the other hand, rejects Marx's thesis that societies pass through stages of different modes of production and adheres to the thesis of imperialism. According to him, developing countries have never been underdeveloped countries, they are countries that have been left behind. The question that needs to be asked to this thesis is how can developing countries that are exploited by developed countries develop? (Balaam & Veseth, 2001, p.81).

For example, no economy in Africa, except Egypt and South Africa, can even receive the title of "developing". The same situation is valid for almost all Arab countries. Countries at each level will not be compared to each other, but it appears that their scale has improved compared to previous periods. Therefore, this approach contains a synthesis with the "unequal development" approach.

What mainly interests us here is in which of these seemingly alternative strategy periods public enterprises in particular and public ownership in general emerged. Of course, however, inward- or outward-looking growth paradigms/strategies defined through international trade, in terms of mechanism; It brings about the development of public enterprises in the inward-looking strategy period, and privatization in the outward-looking strategy periods.

Therefore, I wonder whether the capitalist historical developments in the world economy are generally categorized as import or export substitution, and that there are different divisions of labor in these stages, or whether these strategies start from the initial level and move on to other stages one by one, as if a country's economy is isolated, and finally become integrated into the world economy. Should we think? This is a process that goes together. The world economy, which is articulated with each other in some way and/or historically at different levels, creates a hegemony within itself and maintains its hegemony on the basis of mutual interest and partial interest. As will be discussed later, we should be talking about absolute sovereignty, in Jessop's term, not a sovereignty aimed at destroying other elements, but a hegemony that shapes other elements in line with their own interests.

Two basic strategies are generally accepted to realize capital accumulation: Inward accumulation strategy and outward accumulation strategy. "Growth strategies based on the expansion of the domestic market are the strategies that correspond to the "expansion period" of capitalism, and the outward-looking model corresponds to the "structural crisis" period of capitalism" (Başkaya, 2000, p.99). Based on this determination, it can be seen that accumulation strategies are not strategies implemented by making a clear choice between these two strategies, but they emerge in accordance with the phase process of capitalist development. However, the transition from one phase to another requires that the conditions are mature enough and the economic agents, especially the large capital segments and the public authority, decide to start implementing it, that is, to move from one phase to the other, as seen in the experience of Turkey in 1980. In short, the conditions must mature and the economic agents must want and decide to transition to the next phase, in which case there is no "choice between alternatives" and this transition cannot be possible without the practices and decisions of the economic agents, and both situations (preference-stage/period) occur together.

Inward-Looking Accumulation Strategy

Mainstream economics, starting from Smith, has focused on the basic assumption that foreign trade will have positive consequences for the economies of both parties involved in trade, and this focus is an important element of the basic paradigm. However, in the process of development economics, although it was emphasized that foreign trade would have negative effects on economic development under "some" conditions, a strategic acceptance emerged that was inward-looking, that is, aimed at regulating domestic markets and ensuring capital accumulation.

This strategy is basically an answer to the question of how a country's economy can use its own resources to initiate and advance the accumulation process. Therefore, the inward-looking accumulation strategy reveals two basic assumptions (in terms of development economics): First, economies defined as "underdeveloped" do not have the structural qualities that will directly respond to the explanations of mainstream neo-classical economic theory and sustain accumulation. For this reason, there was a need for approaches that could explain these economies and accumulation processes that neo-classical economics could not explain. The second was that the economic differences that emerged and deepened between the "developed" and "under-developed" economies required the creation of new areas that would adapt to the expansion/expansion process of capitalism due to the capitalist logic of the "developed" countries. The first of these can be cited as Lewis's "unlimited labor supply" approach. Lewis states that all the classics, from Smith to Marx, analyzed on the assumption that "they could only find an unlimited supply of labor in return for a living wage that would ensure survival", but over time, especially in Europe, the limitlessness of labor disappeared. On the other hand, he argued that there is still an unlimited supply of labor in underdeveloped economies and that this unlimited supply of labor provides an opportunity for development. Lewis, who clearly states that the assumption of unlimited labor supply is only valid for underdeveloped economies and aims to "clarify a different framework" without following neo-classical economics, states that in a closed economy, "in countries where the population is high compared to capital and natural resources, there is unlimited labor force in many sectors of the economy." It is considered as an assumption that "the marginal productivity of the workforce is negligible, zero or negative" (Lewis, 1954).

The second acceptance has more political characteristics. New states that emerged with the dissolution of great empires, as a result of their political independence, resulted in the necessity of saving their economic development from dependency. Accordingly, "once we moved away from the environment of political dependence, the problem was perceived as a pure capital accumulation problem. Development was perceived as the increase (growth) of production factors" (Başkaya, 2000, 103-104). For this reason, political freedom also triggered economic freedom and made it necessary. However, this had to be developed with the country's own resources. On the other hand, the fact that development theories are of Western origin has also affected the economic thoughts in developing countries that have the idea of "independence". As a matter of fact, development theories originating from the West and "Asia's problems attracted the attention of very few economists" in the early periods. (Even Asian economists accepted the assumptions and views of European economists)" (Lewis, 1954). However, the reactions to this situation, especially from South America, began to emphasize that economic dependency is the main cause of underdevelopment. For this reason, the necessity of development with internal resources and economic independence, in other words, with an inward-looking strategy, has been put forward. In fact, "developmental thought within the framework of social sciences belongs entirely to the West. This idea that we are as foreign as those who came and colonized us (from Goonahlake, & Hettne, 1990, p.74, 2006, Ercan, 2006, p.125) has become decisive. Due to these two basic reasons, restrictions and obstructions in foreign trade and therefore an import substitution accumulation strategy with internal resources began to be adopted.

The inward-looking accumulation strategy envisaged for the accumulation process to take place in an underdeveloped economy is based on "import substitution", that is, restricting foreign trade to different degrees and facilitating state interventions in the economy and even central planning, and furthermore, deeming it necessary.

The first of these, in a terminology where economic development and/or development is considered identical with industrialization, is to support local industries, to ensure their strengthening, to create an industry and capital accumulation that can produce at least the consumer goods and, in a broader sense, industrial goods that the economy needs, domestic sectors. It is based on the idea of protection. This process can be considered as an attempt to gain time for local sectors that do not have the power to compete in international markets to strengthen themselves within customs walls until they have competitive power. In the import substitution period, it is thought that first consumer goods and then capital goods will be produced domestically.

The main disadvantages of the import substitution strategy, that is, within the framework of the terminology of this study, the elements that the strategy neglects/ignores are as follows. The production capacity required for the production of consumer goods can develop rapidly, but the production of elements such as technology and information required for the development of industrial goods production in the domestic markets may become a big problem (Prebish, 1973, p. 27, narrated by Egeli, 2001, p.152).). On the other hand, the success of the strategy emerges at the point where the economy that produces basic goods generates foreign exchange income from the import of these goods. "[It requires] high levels of imported inputs at every stage of the production process. Since there is not sufficient articulation between the sectors of the economy in general, and the sub-sectors of the industry in particular, and since "machines that produce machines" cannot be produced, establishing a new production unit each time can only be achieved through imported input (Başkaya, 2000, p.114). may be possible. However, the strategy also limits meeting these requirements.

Secondly, public ownership and especially public economic enterprises emerge intensively in this phase of economic development. Considering that the private sector does not have sufficient capital power, many large production facilities are established and put into production in this period. In short, in this period, which is considered as the "industrialization strategy", the Neo-Liberal Approach states that the market system and therefore competition will achieve complete success, and in this case, the "only legitimate duty of the state is to create a completely open economy with a stable macroeconomic environment in which the rules of the game are clearly determined." While the Structural Approach places "less reliance on the free market as a driver of competitiveness and more emphasis on the state's ability to intervene effectively [...] While acknowledging the mistakes of past strategies, it places greater emphasis on markets." He argues that the way to get better is through the state taking more priority" (Lall, 2005, p.145). These views form the core of development economics, and it will become inevitable that the state will be much more effective in a strategy based on import substitution.

The economic policies followed by especially developed countries in the twentieth century are mostly attributed to the gradual separation of ownership from control and the continuous centralization of technological power. "The private and public sectors of national economic systems are interconnected in a network of both complementary and competing relationships" (Ballance, Ansari & Singer, 1985, p.237). If you pay attention, since there was no international market that could compete with the developed countries' own industries during the stages of creating a capitalist system, an intense set of relationships was formed between the public sector and the private sector in this period and mutual dependency/dependence was formed. On the other hand, in the import substitution period, at the point of creating/strengthening the domestic bourgeoisie, "the state may be an indispensable element [...] to ensure the balance between classes" (Keyder, 1987, p.14).

On the other hand, the import substitution inward-looking strategy also creates a demand for special political relations between the private sector and the public sector. In other words, it can also lead to a developing private sector by establishing organic or inorganic ties with public resources and public policies, which is one of the most important points of criticism of the inward-looking strategy. In addition, weak competitive conditions may cause the private sector to operate with very high profit margins.

Outward-Looking Accumulation Strategy

With the import substitution period; domestic capital accumulation has been achieved, the creation of the domestic bourgeoisie, a sectoral activity that can compete in international markets has been achieved, the necessity of new technologies has emerged at the point reached in the domestic markets and the resources required for the production of new industrial goods have become unable to be procured internally, an inward-looking industrial strategy These are the main reasons for the end of the period and the transition to an outward-looking strategy. Globalization is generally defined as "the volumetric growth of cross-border economic connections and resource flows that produce a qualitative change in the relations between national economies and nation states" (Kotz, 2001, p.98-99). In particular, goods trade flows are characterized as foreign direct investments and cross-border portfolio investments. In other words, this period includes the adoption of policies that are defined as the free movement of production factors and that will ensure "liberalization" in international factor circulation.

Liberalization implies that, along with the liberalization of factor circulations, public effects in economies, that is, in the functioning of market mechanisms, will also decrease and be minimized, and privatization exactly corresponds to this stage of the economic development process.

On the other hand, there was an increase in production resulting from the high growth rates that emerged in Europe and the United States after World War II. In the same period, "policies based on the concepts of "welfare state", "social state" and "clientelistic state" were implemented in industrialized capitalist countries, and generally an import substitution growth model was implemented in underdeveloped countries (Başkaya, 2000, p.131). However, due to the internal tendencies of the capitalist system, it began to cause a decrease in profit rates in developed countries in the 1970s. For this reason, capital that has reached a certain volume in developed countries tends to shift towards underdeveloped or developed countries where profit margins are higher or the "marginal efficiency of capital" is high and production costs are low. Therefore, the outward-looking strategy emerges as a result of being exposed to this pressure from the outside world.

In the 1980s, policies in line with foreign trade liberalization through structural adjustment and stabilization programs began to be advocated. These policies continued to be implemented in the early 1990s under the name of "Washington Consensus" (Shafaeddin, 2005). However, in the 2000s, the term and understanding of the Post-Washington Consensus emerged. This "new approach, at least at the principle level, was shaped by pro-stability macroeconomic and pro-price incentives microeconomic prejudices, and attempted to move away from the reductionist development approach that defines physical capital as the main obstacle to growth" (Wayenberge, 2006). Thus, an attempt was made to redefine the relations between the state and society.

The continuity of recent liberalization policies often brings new restrictions and regulations to governments through supranational organizations. "These regulations are not about limiting companies' options, as the concept of regulation normally implies. These regulations are more about limiting the ability of developing country governments to restrict the options of companies operating or wishing to operate within their borders. The new regulations are, in effect, designed to expand the options for developed country companies to enter and exit markets more easily, with fewer restrictions and obligations, and to ensure that these companies can appropriate the technology rents" (Wade, 2003).

The most obvious negative result of the outward-looking strategy is that, due to the integration of the world economy through trade and especially financial interconnectedness, it has increased the spread and permeability of real or financial crises, especially in large economies, throughout the world. "The process of financial liberalization eliminates the effectiveness of this previous system of surveillance and control. Moreover, even the surveillance and control system or institutions do not fully know the changing rules of the game and thus remain inadequate. Therefore, financial liberalization, which motivates and enables risk-taking, combined with incomplete supervision and control, will be effective in the emergence of banking crises. "If an effective surveillance and audit system is established, excessive risk taking will not occur and the adverse effects of financial liberalization on the banking sector will probably not be seen" (Noy, 2004, p.343).

One of the most important channels of the permeability of crises/fluctuations is that the accounts called "toxic assets", which grow especially in the balance sheets of banks and play an important role in the financial fluctuation that emerged in 2009, constitute the accounts of funds coming from international and almost all countries of the world. The fact that the banking system's balance sheets contain so many of these assets poses certain risks regarding a potential fluctuation. Husson divides these risks into two categories. The first of these risks is that "the assets of banks [continue to contain] a toxic backlog of assets and bad debts, which could increase the severity of fluctuations through future financial ruin of households and business bankruptcies." On the other hand, the second risk is "banks returning to speculative behavior and creating new bubbles" (Husson, 2010, p.57-58).

As a result, international money and commodity circulation has gained such an intricate and intense character that "liberalization" is accepted or accepted by almost every country. So much so that "today, no territory is closed neither to the circulation of goods nor to international means of payment. Even when states try to prevent this movement, the dizzying progress in transportation and communication systems makes it difficult to control the borders. The most diverse products and payment instruments reach the most remote corners of the world" (Corm, 2013, p.23-24). Therefore, the "choice-seasonality" problem has almost disappeared from the agenda, and almost all countries in the world have removed the option of not being included in this trade and financial network from the agenda. There are two main reasons for this, as discussed at the end of this section. The first of these is the dominance, directing power and influence of transnational companies on the world economy. The second is that international economic organizations direct the world economy to articulation with their liberal policy practices and recommendations on a world scale.

ON THE CONCEPT OF UNDERDEVELOPMENT

As with every concept, the concept of "underdevelopment" has an opposite: "development". Since economic development expresses that the measure of economic welfare of a society is at high levels, first and foremost, "underdevelopment" expresses economic underdevelopment, underdevelopment, poverty, and that some social and economic mechanisms either do not exist at all or the mechanisms do not affect the economic development process. It also states that it is insufficient to put it into dynamic motion. In short, underdevelopment refers not only to an economic level but also to a structural situation. That is why the concept is about being agreed upon; It carries contradictions due to its content and different definitions can be put forward from many different angles.

Albertini (1983) tried to determine the "underdevelopment of a country" by using two different approaches. The first of these is the "statistical approach" and states that the level of development of a guinea pig country can be decided by macroeconomic variables such as demographic characteristics, health, education, nutritional level, education, labor force, income per capita, sectoral distribution, and investment rates. Secondly, it refers to the "structural approach". Accordingly, he states that "the economy is divided into sectors more or less independent from each other [and] remains under a number of dominations that hinder development" (Albertini, 1983, p.19-39). This distinction essentially shows that, as mentioned above, it is a concept that presents both numerical and structural problems in unity. However, the problem does not end there.

As an economic historian, Maillet (1953, p.191-192) regarding the difficulties of research on the historical roots of the concept of underdevelopment; Due to the lack of usable documents and data, the uncertainties in the definition of the concept, the fact that it cannot be said exactly in which phase of history underdevelopment emerged, and the radical effects of ideological and moral approaches on the concept, and finally, the fact that underdevelopment in the past and underdevelopment in the present are not the same although they are different from each other. It points out the difficulty of analyzing underdevelopment due to the way it is handled.

It is possible to define the social form called capitalism, taking into account its multi-dimensionality, as "the creation of a material value production mechanism and the integration of people into this mechanism in order to provide the necessary and sufficient material conditions to meet people's material needs." In summary, capitalism is a social form in which the main goal is to provide wealth to ensure the material conditions of people's happiness. Then, the term "developed economies" can be used for the economies where this mechanism has been established. And this term implies economies in which people can become "rich" - so that they can increase their material consumption - within those economic conditions, or where mechanisms have been created to make them. Like every term, the term "underdevelopment" and "underdeveloped economies" were developed and used as the opposite of the term "development" - where capitalist mechanisms are formed. So, the term "development" examines a dual movement from one point of underdevelopment to another point of development. The first of these is to provide an explanation for the static situation of underdevelopment and to determine the preconditions for how this static situation can become dynamic. Secondly, it is to investigate the dynamic observations and conditions on the course of the state of dynamism, that is, the course of an underdeveloped economy that is "on the move". Although an attempt has been made to clarify the previous issues, it is necessary to first make a static analysis of an underdeveloped economy as a stagnant state, that is, to determine the conditions for it to be mentioned with this term.

Although Bernstein and Patel stated in their studies that the definition of underdevelopment should not be made in terms of industrialization and that it is possible to obtain high income from agricultural production even though the incomes of some countries are low from industrial production (Bernstein & Patel, 1952, p.41), underdeveloped economies are generally Although it is shown that their characteristics are based on agriculture, the industrial sector is underdeveloped and even agriculture does not have industries to process agricultural products and modern industrial tools and tools are not used in obtaining the product. Therefore, when an underdeveloped economy is mentioned, the first thing that is meant is that the industry is underdeveloped or underdeveloped. Therefore, what is recommended for these economies is the development of industry. For this reason, by applying import substitution, "rapid industrialization, at least under temporary protectionist conditions, is shown as a way out [of underdevelopment]" (Schmitz, & Musyck, 1994). However, industrialization strategy based on protectionism, that is, import substitution; The industrialization results expected from protectionist import substitution could not be achieved due to the formation of excessive bureaucracy and the restriction of private enterprise, the increase in exchange rates and the decrease in the attractive earnings from imports, the increase in exchange rates, the decrease in the earnings of agricultural imports, the inefficiencies in capacity utilization and the decrease in labor use (Schmitz, & Musyck, 1994).

Over time, these differentiations have led the world economy to a significant differentiation into "industrialized core" countries and "periphery" countries. Thus, "even though international conditions do not determine the pace or nature of industrialization in underdeveloped countries, they have created a series of limiting parameters." It appears that in some periods international conditions are particularly favorable to industrial development in Third World countries, while in others they are less favorable" (Jenkins, 2003, p.212). The industrialization indicators that differed between these periods also affected the world economy's view of the underdeveloped economies and caused the disappearance of the ideas described as the "third world". Three main reasons for the emergence of third world thought; It was "decolonization, separation of the world into two blocks, and the belief that the economic sphere needed a political regulation" (Bessis, 1998, p.45). However, this idea disappeared with the disappearance of the stated reasons.

Finally, countries described as underdeveloped have now begun to be depicted as "developing" or "developing" countries. Despite these differences in definition, as of the Nineties, these countries continue to experience major problems, albeit with differences. Some of these problems can be listed as increasing poverty based on income distribution injustices, continental hunger problems, excessive population growth, constant increase in environmental problems, the disappearance of natural resources, and external financing deficits that have reached unfinable levels (Nunnenkamp, 1991). In addition to these socio-economic problems, the most important economic problem is seen as the debt problem. As a direct result of the steep increase in debt, "the drive for industrialization and economic restructuring for long-term development has stalled in many countries." Instead, efforts are being made to develop programs aimed at a short-term goal: finding resources to pay off debt (Gibson & Tsakalatos, 1992).

ON FAILURE: DEVELOPMENT ECONOMICS

Development economics includes, on the one hand, "market failure" as the failure of the functioning of markets due to public sector interventions, and then "public sector failure" as the failure of public sector interventions and guidance with the liberalization policies reached today. In short, development economics lies between two failures. Public sector interventions, which found a partial legitimacy especially with Keynes, are the most important characteristic of development economics. Especially in the post-war period, "economists who followed Kalecki on the necessity of additional controls [began] to be called "Gosplanners", inspired by the Soviet planning organization." The inspiration for development economics was not the post-Keynesian economists, who were only interested in aggregate demand, but also the Gosplanists' approach, which directly addressed supply-side problems (Toye, 2005). Sweezy argues that Keynes was also a neo-classical, stating that "his education was neo-classical and he was not open to other ideas than neo-classical [economics]. In fact, Keynes [can be said] to be the most important and brilliant person created by the neo-classical school. This is the basis of Keynes' success. Keynes' task was to reform neo-classical economics, to bring it back to the real world, from which it had become increasingly distant after its departure from the classical tradition in the nineteenth century" (Sweezy, 2018, pp.56-57). During this period, "analyses regarding developed countries were deepened and a large degree of precision and certainty were given to these analyses. However, [... this] has been done at the expense of limiting and stereotyping the problems with specific and specific assumptions. Studies in this field are a more dynamic expression of Keynes' savings-investment analysis. An opposite approach has been used regarding the development of underdeveloped countries. The problems were often drawn in broad outlines, no limitations were made, and the analyzes were kept away from precision (Bruton, 1966, p. 129), and development economics rose under these conditions and on this basic research logic.

As a result of the Second War, a very extensive literature has emerged on the value and duty attributed to the state at the level of the emergence of development economics. In particular, the end of development economics in 1974 also coincides with the end of Keynesian economics. The 1974 crisis discredited both Keynes and development economics. In the same period, the Fordism mode of production began to lose its popularity. Competition for political takeover over the underdeveloped has also increased. The capitalist golden age between 1950-70 also corresponds to the same period. So, the end of a golden age changed the entire economic thought. After this period, the state entered a period of ineffectiveness again, and neo-classical economics increased its power. Particular emphasis should be placed on the Washington consensus. In the 1980s, the neo-liberal wave started and the privatization of state-owned production mechanisms spread all over the world.

The terms "Underdevelopment Economics", "Development Economics", "Development Economics" are terms with the same content, referring to the same study subjects that have emerged as a sub-discipline of economics. The general problem of these terms is the question "Why are we richer and others poorer?", which is the problem of the entire science of economics and has been asked since Smith. (Landes, 1990, cited in James, 2007, p.1) brought up the question again and expanded it a little further: "Why are some countries rich, while other countries are not and cannot be rich?" Easterlin, who initiated the beginning of the modern technology era with Watts' invention of the steam engine, says that in the time since then, "the world has developed first in Northern and Western Europe and North America, then in Japan, in Southern and Eastern Europe, and in Latin America and Oceania." [Economic growth] increased in some parts of the country (Easterlin, 1981). The contrast in earlier periods was so great that Simon Kuznets called this period a new era in world history, the age of modern economic growth (Kuznets, 1955). However, two centuries later, most of the world's population continues to live in a situation not very different from their situation at the beginning of this period" (Easterlin, 1981). And he goes on to ask these extended questions: "Why isn't the whole world developed? Beyond this, there is also a question that concerns the future: Will the whole world develop? If it will develop, when? What does the future of the "modern era of economic growth" look like?" (Easterlin, 1981). These questions have essentially become the fundamental questions and problematics of the development economics discipline and include attempts to find answers to these questions.

The basic criticisms of development economists towards orthodox economics and the points where they differ from orthodoxy based on this can be summarized as follows. "Firstly, they emphasize the realism of trying to adapt standard models of theoretical analysis designed for advanced countries to the different economic and institutional environment of underdeveloped countries [... Secondly], they focus on the realism of static neo-classical economics, which deals with the problem of the distribution of certain resources within the existing economic framework; underdeveloped countries are concerned with the degree of relevance to the problem of accelerating development that will break this framework, such as increasing their existing resources, improving technique and generally initiating a self-reinforcing dynamic process of economic change [...Thirdly], Orthodox economic theory, laissez-faire in Orthodox economic policy, argues that it is inextricably linked with preconceptions and tendencies in favor of free trade and conservative fiscal and monetary policy" (Myint, 1973, pp. 314-315).

In terms of conceptual knowledge, the terms development, development, progress and evolution contain differences between each other. Most of the time, there is no accepted distinction between these concepts, and they are confused with each other. For example, Bock describes the distinction between these terms as "interesting efforts" and tries to keep the terms in general under the common denominator of "the idea of progress", but he adds: "However, in the majority of studies focusing on human phenomena, this distinction has not yet been made and there is a lot of confusion", comes from assuming that this distinction has not been realized [...] It emerges when contemporary concepts of social development, as well as today's efforts to explain the changes seen in "underdeveloped" countries, are confused with the "development assumption" of the 19th century biological science" (Bock, 2004).

Whatever the term is, the basic hypothesis of economics is that people's quality of life increases. The increase in the quality of life is considered as a function of greater consumption. However, in periods of crisis, especially cyclical movements, and in theoretical studies, it is a matter of debate what kind of limitations there are in human needs and therefore consumption behavior. However, the term "welfare economics", conceptualized especially by Pigou in the literature, reveals this impulse underlying the phenomenon of development. In Pigou's definition, "the part of social welfare that can be directly or indirectly measured by money" is called social welfare, and Kuznets' definition is actually expanded as "some positive elements in the satisfaction of the desires of people we consider as members of a society". Because while Pigou's definition is based on "values that can be measured in money" and the term "measurable", Kuznets criticizes this issue and expands the definition and uses the term "desire". According to Kuznets, "close attention must be paid to the changes in the measurement possibilities of money over time and place," and he points out that the self-sufficient agricultural competence of the industrialized market economy in the United States a century ago is different from the monetary evaluations of the highly industrialized economy at the time the article was written. vary (Kuznets, 1955).

The term development, on the other hand, has more complex internal differences. So much so that, while the concept can sometimes be used as a positive concept, sometimes it can have completely negative meanings within the framework of the determined "development strategy". Since the question "who" is asked, especially in political economy studies, the question "for whom development is" may arise, and here there is an implicit reference to the problem of distribution, that is, income distribution.

Pieterse defines the concept of development as "essentially a field of multi-level struggles and negotiations between different interest groups" and that "different interest groups in the field of development have different views on development and how to achieve it. As a result, generalizations about development are meaningless and there is always the question "development but for whom?" "The question needs to be asked," he adds (Pieterse, 2013).

Table 1. Evolution of development thought

Development Thought	Historical Context	Hegemony	Explanation
Progress, Evolutionism	19th century	British Empire	Social Darwinism, Colonial Anthropology
Classic Development	1890-1930	Coming After / Colonialism	Classical Political Economy
modernism	Postwar	United States Hegemony	Growth Theory, Structural Functionalism
Dependence	Decolonization	3. World Nationalism	Neo-Marxism
Neo-Liberalism	1980s and After	Finance Capital and Company Capital	Neo-Classical Economics, Monetarism
Human Development	1980s and After	The Rise of Asia and the Pacific, Major Emerging Markets	Capacity, Powers Developmental State

Note: (Pieterse, 2013).

The defining characteristics of the economies defined as "underdeveloped countries", which are subject to the concept of development and development theories and which will be the research object of capital accumulation strategy within the terminology of this study, have been subject to three types of definitions by Kuznets. These are as far as Freyssinet explains; "underdevelopment can be defined as a comparative concept, according to possibility, necessity and other considerations" (Freyssinet, 1980, p.7-8).

First of all, in the most general sense of the term, it implies that natural resources, other internal forces and labor are not utilized sufficiently or are used inefficiently. More specifically, underdevelopment is the difference between a country's current level of underdevelopment and the level of development it may have in the future. Secondly, in order to define a situation of "underdevelopment", a "developed" country is needed to make a comparison. At the third level of definition, it is a definition that can be made by referring to the ability to meet basic needs and human living standards (Freyssinet, 1980, pp.8-9). As a result, and in short, a country being "underdeveloped" means that the economy cannot use all its economic resources or uses them inefficiently. Compared to a country that has achieved significant improvements in general living standards, countries that have not reached sufficient levels in providing the same standards are "underdeveloped" countries. theories have emerged as a sub-discipline that analyzes the conditions, reasons and consequences of how these countries' economies can reach the mentioned level of economic efficiency and development.

However, due to the activities dependent on mutual effects discussed under the previous heading and defined as the "universe of positions", "underdevelopment" cannot be clearly attributed to a specific cause. As a matter of fact, the underdevelopment of a country may occur due to the positions, that is, policies, exhibited by interest groups within the country, as well as by actors in the field of international politics, that bring that country to this level of development or keep it at this level.

The models and ideas developed on how capital accumulation can be initiated and continued, called development economics, are a phenomenon of modernism. On the one hand, development economics aims to provide enlightening information to eliminate the destruction caused by the Second War, and on the other hand, it tries to determine the mechanisms that will create the accumulation process in countries where the accumulation mechanism has not been formed and which are called "underdeveloped".

The picture drawn by Tinbergen regarding the period in which development economics emerged and the general view of the basic political and economic characteristics of the world of the period are summarized as follows. Along with the existence of a socialist 'bloc', there are countries other than these that are not socialist. On the other hand, there are countries that are sectorally developed and developing, although they are not socialist. Developing countries consist of some countries in Asia, Africa, Latin America and Southern Europe, with relative differences among them. In addition to this picture, Tinbergen suggests that colonialism has also disappeared. However, the Dependency School, which emerged as a reflex to the development literature and will be discussed later, treats the period and development literature discussed by Tinbergen as another form of colonialism. Finally, Tinbergen argues that some country groups have a "tendency to give up some of the elements that constitute their national sovereignty" through integration. He places two basic reasons for underdevelopment at the basis of his analysis: 1- Direct Causes and 2- Indirect Causes. The last link in the chain of indirect causes is direct causes, and the chain contains a one-way causality relationship. Indirect causes extending to the last link of the chain; people in the relevant country; They include human behavior and other issues, geographical and political, including their concern for material well-being, desire to look ahead, readiness to bear risks, interest in technology, readiness to cooperate, ability to persevere, and readiness to accept the "rules of the game." Direct reasons are "the low level of technical and organizational ability in the human factor of production, [and] the scarcity of the complementary factors of production, namely land and capital" (Tinbergen, 1965).

It is possible to think of the initial question of development economics through Nurkse's proposition that "a country is poor because it is poor" (Nurkse, 1953, p.61). Development literature focuses on the causes and consequences of this vicious circle and how to get out of it. In economics, "the desire to invest is limited by the size of the market. [The size of the market] is determined by the general level of productivity. Productivity depends – largely, if not entirely, on its level – on the capital used in production. However, the use of capital was first limited by the small size of the market" (Nurkse, 1953, p.61). In short, in some countries, since there is not enough capital accumulation, sufficient investment will not be made, since there is not enough investment, there will not be sufficient employment and therefore sufficient consumption, and finally, when there is not sufficient consumption, we will go back to the beginning and not be able to obtain sufficient investment and capital accumulation.

There have been intense discussions on how to get out of this vicious circle arising from economic underdevelopment resulting from insufficient capital accumulation. The most common categorization emerged as "balanced" and "unbalanced" development models. In the most general sense, these approaches are based on the sectoral distribution of available resources in the country that can be used for capital accumulation. For example, according to Nurkse, "in cases where more or less harmony is achieved by investing in different industries, this difficulty [producing in a sector where there will be no demand] does not arise. Because in such a situation, the deadlock [vicious circle] is broken as the market expands completely. Many of the industries that respond to mass consumption are considered "complementary" because they provide markets for each other. The state of "balanced growth" is ultimately based on the need for "balanced nutrition" (Nurkse, 1953, p.52).

Another classification regarding the development economics literature belongs to Hirschman. Accordingly, it makes a classification between Orthodox economics, development economics, Marx and finally Neo-Marxist theories, based on their mutual views on development. Accordingly, development theories are grouped into two basic approaches: "rejection of the single-economic understanding" and "acceptance of the assertive understanding of mutual interest". Rejection of the single-economic approach; "The understanding that underdeveloped countries should be kept separate from advanced industrial countries due to a number of specific economic characteristics they share as a group, and therefore traditional economic analysis focusing on industrialized countries must be changed in many respects when it comes to underdeveloped countries. The claim of mutual interest is based on the determination that the economic relations between these two groups of countries can be shaped in a way that will benefit both parties (Hirschman, 1958, p.25-26).

"The orthodox approach starts from two propositions; a) economics consists of a set of simple but "powerful" theorems with universal validity; There is only one economy; b) According to one of these theorems, the market economy provides profit to all participants, whether individuals or countries, in all voluntary economic relations they enter into [...] thus, it adopts the claims of mono-economy and mutual benefit. The opposite approach is that of the main Neo-Marxist theories. Accordingly:

a) Exploitation or "uneven development" is the fundamental, permanent component of relations between the capitalist "center" and the underdeveloped "periphery" countries; b) this long process of exploitation has caused the political-economic structure of the peripheral countries to be very different from those seen in the center. For this reason, it is impossible for development to follow the same path." Marx accepts mono-economy but completely rejects the claim of mutual benefit. Orthodox economics and Marxism unite in a common bracket in development economics. And for this reason, Development economics is described as a "hybrid approach". As a result, this hybrid approach is based on two basic arguments: "a) Some features of the economic structure of underdeveloped countries [make] a significant part of the orthodox analysis inapplicable and misleading; b) It consists of the combination of the proposition that "the relations between developed and underdeveloped countries are based on mutual benefit and that it is possible for developed countries to contribute to the development of the underdeveloped" (Hirschman, 1958, pp.26-28). In this context, although development economics has developed especially in the USA and England, it has brought to the agenda the modeling that the economists who form the discipline will develop for the development of underdeveloped countries.

On the other hand, developmental economists of developed countries make suggestions to underdeveloped countries, in line with the second proposition mentioned by Hirschman. However, Chang argues that the prescriptions that developmentists propose to underdeveloped countries are not actually the same processes, directly proportional to the experiences their own countries have gone through. According to him, the arguments put forward by developmentalists as the method and process of their own development are as follows: "The industrial success of laissez faire Britain since the eighteenth century proves the superiority of free-market and free-trade policies. These policies unleashed the entrepreneurial energy of the nation, gave it an advantage over interventionist France, Britain's greatest rival at the time, and enabled Britain to establish itself as the world's greatest economic power [...] This led other countries to limit mercantilist policies. It caused them to realize that and to adopt the principles of free trade in the 1860s [...] On the basis of the liberal world order, which reached perfection in the 1870s, laissez faire industrial policies within the country and low barriers to international goods, capital and labor movements; There is macroeconomic stability guaranteed by the balanced budget principle and the Gold Standard" (Chang, 2007, p.33-35). According to development economists, the protectionist policies implemented after this stable period, which was disrupted by the First World War, were shown as the main cause of the 1929 Crisis. According to the author, development economists drew these conclusions from the early structures of developed countries and suggested these policies by analyzing underdeveloped countries through theoretical studies. However, developed countries have not even implemented these policies suggested at the beginning of their development processes. Finally, although Chang accepts that the nineteenth century was a laissez faire period, he later argues that developed countries did not actually implement the policies and processes that development economists presented above and said were implemented in the development processes of developed countries (Chang, 2007, p.37-38).

However, it is necessary to examine the theories of the major developmentalists. Because no thought can ever be completely right, nor will it ever be completely wrong. Economic development implicitly implies planning. In fact, Mason clearly suggests that this planning should be based on central planning (Mason, 1964, p. 39). It combines a similar approach, that is, "all modern forms, some measures of public planning, with the necessary amount of freedom for individual decision-making", regardless of the economic system. Even in the freest market economies, the state's own budget is planned according to annual and long-term needs. At the same time, many large private organizations plan their investment and market development programs five or ten years ahead" (Colm & Geiger, 1962, p.11). In short, in addition to seeing central planning as a prerequisite, the long-term nature of planning and leaving a certain area of action for the private sector, but sharing the knowledge created by their movements within this area of action with the central authority and providing the necessary infrastructure for this, make development processes easier. It is considered as the starting level. Claiming that there can be no question of decentralized planning, Mason states that for the success of planning, it is necessary to establish an effective relationship between the central government and decentralized governments by providing "an effective information and communication system" and "a strong management and incentive measures". It is also necessary to ensure "a good distribution of resources, a mass of information about macroeconomic quantities taken together, as well as a significant flow of information about price and income elasticity, production and deformation functions and inter-industry relations" (Mason, 1964, p. 39-40).

However, in the same period, there were also severe criticisms against planning for development. Hayek, a member of the Austrian School, comes first among these criticisms. Hayek considers the centrality of planning as arbitrariness and "this opinion has spread continuously and finally has become such that it has become the desire and enthusiasm to direct and manage the majority of human work for any purpose." Hayek's intended purpose is implicitly the term "planned development" and individuals and private enterprises should not be governed for this purpose. However, in the same period, Hayek's will for a market economy and his opposition to state intervention received serious criticism. For example, Aren and Gorvine put forward the view that "thinking that there is no means of control and management in a democratic system only indicates the absence of the ability to analyze events" (Aren & Gorvine, 1956, p.392).

The basis of an economic plan to be prepared for economic development is "generally, a budget prepared for the state investment sector (at all levels of state organization), in addition to recommendations on money, finance, exchange rates, worker training programs and similar activities to encourage and manage investments in the private sector." With, preferences about what is expected from private sector investments [should be specified]. The target is often investment, income, output, employment, etc. It is expressed as the shape and levels of elements such as: but the plan also requires that there be a certain place of establishment of the industry, a certain distribution of the population and a certain way of utilizing the land. All the efforts of the economic development plan are concentrated on utilizing capital; As a rule, it does not contain a plan for land utilization" (Haar, Higgins & Rodwin, 1961, p.232-233).

Millikan states that one of the decision methods in economic development can be made within economic planning, and the second is "a more or less centrally autonomous price-market system, responded to by the decisions of consumers and those who have certain resources and efficient techniques." However, Millikan's remarkable observation is that "two sets of criteria [are involved] in both decision-making." Efficacy criterion and value criterion. Efficiency criteria are methods that help society reach the desired point and determine which are the most technically and economically effective ways. Value criteria, on the other hand, are ways that cover the problem of how to choose between many different technically and economically possible objectives. Since it depends on how possible it is to reach the desired place, they are evaluated on the strength of the effectiveness criterion and the value criterion or the distinction between these two criteria (Millikan, 1965, p.63).

In their study, Chenery and Kretschmer found that underdeveloped economies "deviate primarily from the competitive system that ensures optimal resource use." "First, these economies normally operate from a structural imbalance. The reasons for this are various; Ignorance about technological possibilities or consumer demand, widespread monopoly situations, inflation expectations, inadequacy of infrastructure facilities, etc. The inadequacy of investment funds and foreign exchange amounts at current prices, the widespread underemployment and unemployment are indicators that reflect the fact that these countries are far from optimum use of resources. Under all these conditions, current prices are inadequate to resolve the resource allocation outcome for both government agencies and private investors. [Second] is that foreign savings, which may exist even if other flaws in the competition system are not observed, have little place in these economies. This situation arises from the fact that, by definition, most of the economic activities in underdeveloped countries either do not exist or are carried out at a primitive level (Chenery & Kretschmer, 1969, p.138-139).

Kuznets expresses hesitation, but still recommends using National Income as a measure of welfare. Kuznets: "The realization of the desires of final consumers by using scarce material resources, taking advantage of the measure of money, constitutes economic prosperity. Therefore, looking at national income as a measure of economic well-being is not only justifiable but also necessary" (Kuznets, 1955). However, it should still be said that this approach adopts the paradigm of orthodox mainstream economics, which neglects income distribution analysis.

Cohn makes a general criticism of the developmental approaches, points out the inadequacy of these models, and puts forward the concept of "innovative entrepreneur", whose key role for development is defined as people who "apply new methods to conventional activities". This approach attributes a transformative role to the innovative entrepreneur. (Cohn, 1966, pp.18-19). Like Tinbergen, Cohn argues that society should be ready and willing to accept new products created by innovators. In this case, it refers to the activity power of minority innovators and the need for the majority of the population to be ready for these innovations or to be made ready. Harbison, too, "includes new discoveries and inventions achieved through creativity; But [it is something] bigger than invention, and it attaches great importance to the concept of "innovation", which goes far beyond the discovery of a new method, a machine, an organizational system[,] and includes the adaptation of known technologies to specific problems and the acceptance of new ideas and new facts. In addition to the fact that Schumpeter-type entrepreneurs play a key role in the critical concept of innovation, he recommends that there should be a social character that can adapt to innovations, just like Cohn, and suggests educational programs and systems to ensure this (Harbison, 1966, pp.36-41).

As a result, there has been much debate on ensuring capital accumulation in an economy. As a result, the sub-branch of economics generally called development economics failed. However, the problem that still exists today has not disappeared: what are the dynamics of capital accumulation in an economy?

The term industrialization lies behind the initial perception of the term development. In other words, "economic development", which is referred to as development, is equated with industrialization and the making of necessary and sufficient industrial investments. And being developed is identical to being industrialized. As Dobb also mentioned, these countries that have "achieved" industrialization are a small portion of the world's population and are generally concentrated in North America and Europe. And again, Dobb states that, apart from these industrialized countries that he mentions as "developed", "almost all of the countries that are described as "underdeveloped" have a significant difference, whether in terms of the sheer size of industrial production, productivity (per capita for working people), or production per capita for the general population and He states that they are at a "much lower level of economic development, measured by the standard of living" and points out that the primary reason for the underdevelopment of these countries is that these countries are the raw material hinterlands of developed capitalist states, since they are colonies or semi-colonies of today's developed countries (Dobb, 2012, p.193-194).

In short, economic development does not seem possible in all cases where the economic surplus produced in an economy is not invested in that country as employment-creating investment. The term economic-surplus, as will be discussed in detail later, is "between the total production that can be obtained with the help of usable, efficient resources in a certain natural and technological environment, and the total production segment that can be defined as basic consumption" (Baran, 1957, p.40). It is defined as the difference. Well, development, as an indicator of social economic development, can only be achieved by turning this economic surplus into investment that will create employment.

An important dimension of the discussions focuses on whether or not to approve this foreign capital inflow, if there is no capital accumulation in a country at a level that will sustain the movement and it comes to the fore that capital may come from another country's economy to initiate and continue this movement. At this point, the second important classification style regarding development economics emerges: the first is the orthodox theories, that is, the theories that define development in terms of the specific characteristics of any country and try to explain capital accumulation (i.e. the theories mentioned above), and the second is the theories that also include international economic relations into the equation. and international division of labor theories. It should be noted right away that the general criticisms and explanations directed towards these approaches are directed towards the state of being in a hinterland situation mentioned above by Dobb.

Classical theory adopted the principle of excluding public interventions in the functioning of the economic system. The no-classical theory, which emerged as a result of Marx's criticisms of the classical theory and developed by externalizing the labor theory of value and internalizing the marginal-value theory, focused on the complete exclusion of public interventions, especially on growth and foreign trade, and on economic functioning in general. However, public expenditure policies were actively included in the theory by Keynes to keep the effective demand alive, especially as a solution to the crisis that would arise with overproduction due to the increase in the organic composition of capital caused by supply-demand imbalances, in other words, the increase in the organic composition of capital created by the surplus-value producing mechanism. However, with the collapse of the international monetary system in the 1970s and the spread of a new balance approach in foreign payments, new restrictions on public sector activities became the focus of theoretical studies. Fixed exchange rates provided by the Bretton Woods agreement, which was valid between 1944 and 1973, were left to fluctuate with the adoption of developed countries. However, especially those who continue the Austrian school and who continue to work on neo-classical economics to explain the practical world, despite the developments in the practical world, have maintained their continuity by excluding the public sector activity.

When viewed from the perspective of developmental approaches, the BW System "could not fully meet the development needs of underdeveloped countries." Free trade and unlimited convertibility, which were the basic philosophy of the system, contradicted the economic reality of most developing countries at that time... In the face of frequent monetary crises, various projects were put forward by both governments and academic circles regarding the reform of the international monetary system in the 1960s. was thrown away. The common feature of these proposals is that they aim to eliminate one or more of the [problems] of the BW System [...] equalization, liquidity, insecurity, emission gains and development" (Seyidoğlu, 1998, p.561-562).

If we look at a wider period of time, as a result of World War I and the subsequent 1929 Crisis, we are entering a period of general protectionism and public sector activity. "Countries faced with external payment and external balance problems have resorted to protectionist policies in public sector activities and foreign trade by resorting to tools such as exchange control and direct trade controls in this environment of irregularity in the field of international money and payments" (Güran & Aktürk, 1999, p.18). In this general picture, an "anti-neo-classical line", in Tubiana's term, has begun to be advocated. "This interventionism finds itself in import substitution industrialization policies, and these policies were discussed and adopted in the Economic Commission for Latin America (ECLA) based on Prebisch's views" (Tubiana, 1998, p.22). During this period, protectionism and import substitution policies were intensively implemented in the developed countries of the post-war period. After World War II and especially in the 1960s, it came to the fore as the main starting point and solution to crises for other underdeveloped economies. In addition to these policies, an extensive planned development literature, the content of which was previously discussed, was created and much broader "duties" were assigned to the public sector. The most effective place of the public sector in the effective demand has changed from the form of expenditures to the form of investment, that is, production with fixed capital investments, and suggestions have been developed regarding this.

Behind the great importance of the 60s, "these years brought with them a change of equal value to the radical changes that occurred with the industrial revolution in the second half of the 19th century. On the one hand, a new economic understanding caused by the second technological and scientific revolution and the resulting consumption society structure emerged (Guichaoua, 1981, p.53), and the phenomenon of "globalization" began to gain its current character after this period.

Although development literature developed in the 1960s, its effects began to shake in the 1970s with the "neo-liberalization" period brought about by the 1974 crisis. In addition, the opposition literature that developed the development literature in the 1970s has continued until today. However, of course, it has changed form considerably since the 1960s. Today, when viewed from the perspective of positive developments within the general form of development literature, it can be seen that some important conceptual contributions have developed. The first of these can be classified under the broad theme of the political economy of development and the role of institutions. One of its key tenets is that more equal distributions of initial income and wealth are consistent with and conducive to growth. New political economy theories link rising income inequality to falling growth through the following channels: 1) Inefficient rent-seeking activities that reduce the security of property; 2) The spread of political and social instability, leading to greater uncertainty and lower investment; 3) Income redistribution policies triggered by income distribution inequalities and encouraging the rich to invest and accumulate resources; 4) Imperfect credit markets, resulting in underinvestment by the poor, especially in human capital; and 5) A relatively small share of income falling to the middle class has a strong positive effect on fertility, and increased fertility has a significant and negative effect on growth" (Thorbecke, 2009, p.164). As can be seen, development economics today focuses on income distribution rather than the initial years. As a matter of fact, while income generation was the main focus in the early years of the movement, today income distribution has become the focus.

EXPANSION OF CAPITALISM

As a result of the centralization and concentration of capital, capital acts to open up to new areas, to search for new spaces/areas in order to increase the total output by reducing the surplus-value production mechanism, the input values in the production function. Because, total savings, as the difference between total production and total consumption in a country, is at a level that can keep the rate of profit high, both because it increases the organic composition of capital in the expanded reproduction scheme and because of the mechanisms that produce relative and relative surplus value, under the assumption that it is transformed into reinvestment each time. It will need an expansion. The current name for this expansion is "globalization". The term globalization first suggests the freedom of movement of all production factors. On the other hand, in the Keynesian sense, due to the multiplier-accelerator mechanism, investments made in countries with high savings levels will create a higher income increase each time and, as a result, an ever-increasing level of savings. However, in the long run, the marginal return on capital in developed economies will begin to decline. Due to this decline, private sector capital will need to invest in international areas, that is, in low-cost production areas. However, there is a need to open the resulting high level of production to new markets and even create new markets. On the other hand, accumulated capital will need to be able to move easily internationally, especially in countries that do not have enough savings, in order to obtain interest income by financing the public sector. In short, "capitalism is expansionist by nature. "For capitalism to survive, access to cheap labor, land, natural resources and market resources is necessary" (Robinson, 2002).

This mobility of capital expands the capitalist mode of production and production relations, and a "global capitalism" emerges. However, this means that "globalization in its radical sense should be taken as the emergence of a new economic structure, not just as a cyclical change towards more international trade and investment within the framework of existing economic relations" and in this context, there are two different internationalization models. These are: "1) a fully globalized economy and 2) an open international economy characterized primarily by exchanges between still relatively separate national economies, with many outcomes, such as the competitive performance of firms and sectors, being determined by processes at the national level" (Hirst & Thompson, 2018) in other words, an "international economy" type of internationalization in which the vitality and interests of relatively national economies are pursued.

For the integration/articulation of the world economy, there are Multi-National/Supranational companies for both of these types of internationalization. As these corporatizations become more prevalent, the permeability/spreading speed of crises increases for both types of articulation. Discussions on the separation of these two types of integration gather at two points. The first is the effectiveness of the nation-state on international economic activities and the second is the degree of effectiveness of supranational economic organizations (Colas, 2002, p.197: Robinson, 2002, p.215). In addition, "the rise of multinational corporations, the movement, size and accessibility of international financial capital and the resulting interdependence of countries have fundamentally changed all expectations regarding the sovereignty, autonomy and future of nation states" (Arestis & Paliginis, 2000, p153).

First of all, the type of company called Transnational or Multinational (without distinguishing between them for now) implies, first of all, that production is spread on a world scale. Their emergence "can be traced back to the period of colonial empires and various early privately chartered trading companies" in the early 1800s and even earlier. (Jones & Sluyterman, 2011, p.163-164).

Although there is no agreed-upon definition, multinational company in general terms; These are listed as "functioning in more than one country, centralized control, following a uniform policy for all company divisions, and being enterprises that control the functions of subsidiary companies in various countries" (Tokol, 2001).

According to this definition, companies in this structure have spread their activities on a world scale, with their headquarters in a certain country, in terms of production and marketing, their policies and mostly their technologies are determined and developed in the centers in this 'source country', and finally they have acquired partners in the 'host' country of the investment, but their capital They are large companies with international stakeholders, as well as traded in securities markets.

These giant companies are defined as "Multinational companies" or "Supranational companies", but they are defined as the same and used interchangeably. However, by agreeing with Down's opinion, it is accepted that these two terms are different from each other. "The multinational corporation [...] is the ancestor of today's transnational corporations." "There are many similarities between a multinational company and a supranational company, but the differences are of greater importance." While multinational companies are the most powerful companies of their countries, transnational companies are the most powerful companies of the entire world economy (Dowd, 2006, p.202). A multinational company is a type of company that spreads its production and marketing on a global scale, but has its headquarters in a certain country. However, over time, and especially starting from the 1960s, these Multinational companies not only expanded their fields of activity, but also began to form transnational companies by merging with or acquiring other Multinational companies. Thus, "giant" companies operating in many fields and in many countries have emerged and have begun to clearly direct the world economy. In this case, "capital" emerged from a certain power field and was able to spread itself to the world scale (Wood, 2002, p.155-172). Despite the controversial aspects of the globalization phenomenon that emerged as a result of this expansion, many empirical studies have been conducted that "will indicate that joint-stock companies are effective in increasing the performance of industries and macroeconomies" (Kimura & Kiyota, 2004, p.2). However, these studies are mostly under the influence of economism.

Since transnational "companies can produce and sell their goods and services all over the world, they have initiated a strong movement towards worldwide standardization of technology and products" (Freeman & Soete, 2003, p.353-354). However, while there is indeed a strong trend in the standardization of products, it is difficult to say that the same level of standardization of technology has occurred. In particular, technology: A company that develops technology cannot be expected to share it because of the risk that its competitors or potential competitors will not be able to get their hands on it and the costs they incur in creating the relevant technology for themselves. On the other hand, with production being dispersed, it does not seem possible for a company that can somehow obtain the technology that has left the center in the country it goes to, to compete with the supranational company both in terms of technology, market share and price. For example, even if an innovative company that wants to produce a product that competes with the product of a transnational company succeeds in creating or acquiring technology, such a company "considering that they are social structures surrounded by institutional environments, the institution is subject to sectoral conditions [technology, market" in the process of historical transformation. and competition], organizational conditions [cognitive, behavioral and strategic] and institutional conditions [employment, financial and regulatory]" (Emphasis added by the author) (Lazonick, 2007, pp.48-49), which is quite difficult. .

On the other hand, recent transnational companies have been acquiring strong partners in host countries in order to reduce transaction costs and benefit from the facilities provided by the countries where the investment will be taken. In addition, since the shares of transnational companies are also traded in capital markets and these transactions are also acquired by international funds, it is now emphasized that transnational companies have become "deterritorialized". "The sovereignty of states has become extremely difficult to control by the power of transnational corporations and financial flows have become extremely difficult to control [... and] as the national identity of corporations has become increasingly blurred" (Nair, 2000, p.77-78), transnational corporations are now the mainstay of the world economy. It is suggested that they are actors and movers. However, critical studies also show that despite these powerful positions of transnational corporations, they have extra-economic effects by creating a pressure mechanism on host country governments in line with the interests of the states of the core countries in political critical periods. Moreover, the process subordinates "the interests of the global majority to the interests of multinational corporations and financial capital" (Hahnel, 2003, p.155 and 292).

Although transnational companies appear to display familiar firm behavior, they are closely associated with political authorities. Especially considering that they emerged as privileged trading companies of the imperial periods, their relations with political authorities date back to ancient times and are at a complex level. For example, American transnational companies differ from companies in countries such as Britain, the Netherlands, and Japan, whose history dates back to the colonial period: for example, "British companies have grown by internalizing the markets of assets they hold abroad, such as technology and brands [...] the role of protectionism in encouraging investments [in manufacturing companies] "emerges clearly". While American companies have a hierarchical management structure, British companies have small-scale headquarters. Americans have been able to survive longer in countries that do not have strong local governments. Small-government British were able to hold their own in the services and resource production sectors. However, Americans have mostly focused on high-tech fields. (Jones, 2011, p.394-397).

Although the world economy is in the process of integration/unification in the forms of "international economy" or "globalization", the first characteristic of this process is transnational companies, while the second is supranational economic organizations. The sum of these supranational institutional structures can be defined as the "supranational state", and accordingly, the "supranational capitalist class" and "supranational labor class" can also be conceptualized (Wood, 2002, p.164-168: Robinson, 2002, p.5).

As of this study, international economic relations are constantly expanding and deepening. The basis of this is that the global capital power that emerged, first of all, with international trade and then with international financial expansion and deepening, has become an effective actor on and within the national economic policies of the countries. The part of this effect that interests the study is that they are also effective in the change of public sector activities and privatization policies can be shown as an important indicator of this. Since privatization is considered as direct capital investments, it is more explanatory to exclude financial markets from the analysis and consider international trade theories.

International Trade Theories

As a result of the centralization and concentration of capital, capital will seek new spaces in order to expand into new areas, reduce the surplus value production mechanism, input values in the production function, and increase total output. Because capital accumulation, as the difference between total production and total consumption in a country, is at a level that can keep the rate of profit high, under the assumption that it turns into reinvestment each time, both because it increases the organic composition of capital in the expanded reproduction scheme and because of the mechanisms that produce relative and relative surplus value. It will need an expansion. The current name for this expansion is "globalization". The term globalization first suggests the freedom of movement of all production factors. However, here we are trying to emphasize the different forms of globalization of capital and especially the fact that the labor factor cannot be globalized.

"The volume and nature of international trade are determined by the amount of goods seeking buyers, the growth in the number of potential buyers and the removal of economic and political barriers between buyers and sellers. Changes in industrial and agricultural methods made it possible for some goods to be produced in quantities far beyond local or national requirements. "Long before the law of diminishing cost of production or "increasing returns" became obsolete, stocks of Lancashire cottons or German steel were far greater than could be sold to domestic customers, and the manufacturer had to seek foreign buyers" (Heaton, 1948, p.534).

The general assumption of foreign trade theories is that countries engaging in foreign trade obtain mutual benefits, albeit in different forms. Apart from this, other assumptions used to facilitate the analysis are summarized as follows: There is no use of money between countries, the exchange of goods for goods, the validity of full competition conditions in the markets, the absence of state intervention in the domestic and foreign economy, prices are real prices (i.e. the price of a good in terms of other goods or production). It is assumed that the labor theory of value is valid, especially in the classical ones, that the labor force is fully mobile domestically but fully immobile internationally, that full employment is valid and that transportation costs are zero. (Seyidoğlu, 1998, p.16).

International trade theories can be briefly summarized as follows. Smith's Theory of Absolute Superiority: If a country can produce any good at a lower cost than another country or countries, that country should specialize in that good and export the good in question, not producing goods that it can produce expensively, and importing them. Ricardo's Theory of Comparative Advantages: "In cases where comparative advantages occur, there is also absolute advantage, but the opposite is not true" (Seyidoğlu, 1998, p.18). While a country has an absolute advantage in any two goods, it should specialize in the good in which it has a proportionately stronger absolute advantage, and thus increase factor productivity. Other goods must be imported. (Bapat, 1981, p.89-106). Heckscher-Ohlin, Factor Productivity Theory: The main deficiency of the Ricardo model is the issue of why production costs and especially labor productivity are different. According to this theory, whichever production factor is abundant in a country, it should produce with that production factor. The two main assumptions on which the theory is based are: "a) Countries differ from each other in terms of factor endowments. In the two-country model, one country is rich in labor and the other is rich in capital. b) Goods also differ in terms of factor intensities" and other assumptions are "c) The production function of a good is the same in all countries. In other words, if a good is produced by capital or labor-intensive methods in one country, it is produced with the same method in other countries. This feature means that the production technology of a good is the same in all countries. d) Constant yield conditions according to scale are valid in production. e) The demand conditions of the countries are similar to each other. Therefore, it is not possible for the difference in demand to eliminate the difference in cost conditions. (Seyidoğlu, 1998, p.42). Other approaches are briefly as follows: Factor Price Equality Theorem; "free trade equalizes factor prices between countries and in this respect produces the same result as international free factor mobility" Stopler-Samuelson Income Distribution Theorem; "It is revealed that free trade will increase the real income of the factor that the country has in abundance and decrease the income of the scarce factor" Rybczynski Theorem; "It has been proven that under full employment conditions, when the supply of only one factor increases, the production of the good that uses this factor intensively will expand, while the production of the good that intensively uses the factor whose supply remains constant will absolutely shrink" (Seyidoğlu, 1998, p.67). Posner's Technology Gap Theory; "A large part of trade between industrialized countries is based on new goods and production processes. They are developed by innovative companies, most of which are based in advanced industrialized countries. Innovations are protected by patent and intellectual property laws. In other words, the company that finds an innovation first becomes its monopoly. According to the technology gap hypothesis, industrialized countries that find a new good or production process become the first exporters of these goods. However, over time, after the technology passes into the hands of other countries, either through imitation or by becoming a free good, those countries produce the good in question cheaper than the one that first invented it, due to the cheapness of labor or their superiority in natural resources. Thus, the mentioned goods begin to be exported by these less developed countries. "Those who first invented the product now import it from abroad because they cannot compete with these countries" (Seyidoğlu, 1998;79).

Vernon's Theory of Product Cycles: "some countries specialize in the production of existing goods and some in the production of new goods. However, the critical assumption is that as a good passes through life periods from the new good to the old good, the geographical location of production also changes. According to Vernon, technological innovations and the development of new goods occur in advanced industrialized countries, especially the United States. This situation is a result of a highly educated workforce and relatively high expenditures on R&D (Dunn & Mutti, 2004, p.89).

REFERENCES

Albertini, J. M. (1983). *Mécanisme du sous développement et développement.* Ouvrières.

Aren, S., & Gorvine, A. (1956). İktisadi Kalkınma ve Totaliter Liberaller. *Journal of SBF*, 11(3), 387–394. 10.1501/SBFder0000000254

Arestis, P., & Paliginis, E. (2000). Globalization, regionalism and national economic policies. In Toporowski, J. (Ed.), *Political Economy and the New Capitalism: Essays in Honour of Sam Aaronovitch* (pp. 153–166). Routledge.

Assidon, E. (1996). Les conceptions Nord-Sud: un oubli et le marché, *in* S. Cordellier (Edt.). *La fin du Tiers Monde?* La Decouverte.

Balaam, D. N., & Veseth, M. (2001). *Introduction to International Political Economy.* Prentice-Hall Inc.

Ballance, R. H., Ansari, J. A., & Singer, H. W. (1985). *The International Economy and Industrial Development.* Impetus.

Bapat, B. G. (1981). İthalat kısıtlamaları ya da karşılaştırmalı üstünlüklerin değişmesi, O. Esen (çev.). *Ekonomik Yaklaşım*, 2(5), 89–106. 10.5455/ey.10101

Baran, P. A. (1957). *The Political Economy of Growth.* Monthly Review Press.

Başkaya, F. (2000). *Kalkınma İktisadının Yükselişi ve Düşüşü* (3rd ed.). İmge Kitabevi.

Bernstein, E. M., & Patel, I. G. (1952). *Inflation in Relation to Economic Development.* IMF. 10.2307/3866200

Bessis, S. (1998). The current state of the third world, *in* S. Cordellier (Edt.). *La fin du Tiers Monde?* La Decouverte.

Bina, C., & Yaghmanian, B. (1988). Import substitution and export promotion within the context of the internationalization of capital. *The Review of Radical Political Economics*, 20(2-3), 234–240. 10.1177/048661348802000235

Bock, K. (2004). Theories of progress, development, evolution. In Bottomore, T., & Bisbet, R. (Eds.), *A History of Sociological Analysis.* Heinemann.

Bruton, H. J. (1966). Growth models and underdeveloped economies. *Journal of Political Economy*, 63(4), 322–336. 10.1086/257679

Chang, H.-C. (2007). *Kicking Away the Ladder: Development Strategy in Historical Perspective.* Anthem Press.

Chenery, H. B., & Kretschmer, K. S. (1969). Resource allocation for economic development. *Econometrica*, 24(4), 365–399. 10.2307/1905490

Cohn, E. J. (1966). *Yenilikçiler'in Rolü, Azgelişmiş Ülkeler*. Milliyet Kültür.

Colas, A. (2002). The class of globalisation, historical materialism and globalization. In *M. Rupert, & H. Smith (edt.), Historical Materialism and Globalization* (pp. 191–209). Routledge.

Colm, G., & Geiger, T. (1962). İktisadi ve toplumsal kalkınmada kamu planlaması ve ferdi karar alma, N. Serin (çev.). *SBF Dergisi*, 19(2), 11–29.

Corm, G. (2013). *Le Nouveau Gouvernement du Monde*. La Découverte.

Dobb, M. (2012). Papers on Capitalism, Development and Planning, Routledge.

Dowd, D. (2006). *Capitalism and Its Economics: A Critical History*. Pluto Press.

Dunn, R. M., & Mutti, J. (2004). *International Economics* (6th ed.). Routledge. 10.4324/9780203462041

Easterlin, R. A. (1981). Why isn't the whole World developed? *The Journal of Economic History*, 41(1), 1–17. 10.1017/S0022050700042674

Egeli, H. A. (2001). Dış ticaret açısından sanayileşme stratejileri ve Türkiye açısından değerlendirilmesi. *Sosyal Bilimler Dergisi*, 2, 149–161.

Ercan, F. (2006). *Modernizm, Kapitalizm ve Azgelişmişlik*. Bağlam Yayıncılık.

Frank, A. G. (2014). *The World System: Five Hundred Years or Five Thousand?* Routledge.

Freeman, C., & Soete, L. (2003). *The Economics of Industrial Innovation*. Psychology Press.

Freyssinet, J. (1980). *Le Concept de Sous-Développement*. Walter de Gruyter.

Gibson, H. D., & Tsakalatos, E. (1992). The international debt crisis: Causes, consequences and solutions. In Hewitt, T., Johnson, H., & Wield, D. (Eds.), *Industrialization and Development*. Oxford University Press.

Guichaoua, A. (1981). *Sciences Sociales et Développement*. CNRS Éditions.

Güran, N., & Aktürk, İ. (1999). *Uluslararası İktisadi Kuruluşlar*. Tuğra Ofset.

Haar, C., Higgins, B., & Rodwin, L. (1961). Metropolitan policy for developing areas. *Daedalus*, 90(1), 132–146.

Hahnel, R. (2003). *The ABC's of Political Economy: A Modern*. Pluto Press.

Harrison, B. (1996). Küçük firmalar miti, K. Tanyılmaz (çev.). *Ekonomik Yaklaşım*, 7(20), 77–94.

Heaton, H. (1948). *Economic History of Europe*, Harper & Brothers.

Hirschman, A. (1958). *The Strategy of Economic Development*. Yale University Press.

Hirst, P., & Thompson, G. (2018). *Globalization in Question*. Rawat.

Husson, M. (2010). *Marxist İktisat Teorisi, Çağdaş Kapitalizm ve Kriz*. S. Binaltı (çev.). İstanbul: Yazın Yayıncılık.

Jenkins, R. (2003). *Corporate Responsibility and Labour Rights: Codes of Conduct in the Global Economy*. Routledge.

Jones, G. (2011). Multinationals. In Amatori, F., & Jones, G. (Eds.), *Business History around the World*. Cambridge University Press.

Jones, G., & Sluyterman, K. (2007). British and Dutch business history. In Amatori, F., & Jones, G. (Eds.), *Business History around the World*. Cambridge University Press.

Keyder, Ç. (1987). İthal ikameci sanayileşme stratejisi ve çelişkileri, *in* Boratav, Ç. Keyder ve Ş. Pamuk (der.), *Kriz, Gelir Dağılımı ve Türkiye'nin Alternatif Sorunu*, (pp.13-36), Kaynak Yayınları.

Kimura, F., & Kiyota, K. (2004). Foreing-owned versus domestically-owned firms: Economic performance in Japan. *Review of Development Economics*, 11(1), 31–48. 10.1111/j.1467-9361.2006.00347.x

Kotz, D. M. (2001). The state, globalization and phases of capitalist development. In Albritton, R., Itoh, M., Westra, R., & Zuege, A. (Eds.), *Phases of Capitalist Development: Booms, Crises and Globalisations* (pp. 93–109). Palgrave. 10.1057/9781403900081_6

Kuznets, S. (1955). Economic growth and income inequality. *The American Economic Review*, 45(1), 1–28.

Lall, S. (2005). Reinventing industrial strategy: The role of government policy in building industrial competitiveness, *in* K.P. Gallanger (edt.), *Putting Development First: The Importance of Policy Space in the WTO and International Financial Institutions*, (pp.144-161), Zed Books.

Landes, D. S. (1990). Why are we so rich and they so poor? *The American Economic Review*, 80(2), 1–13.

Lazonick, W. (2007). The US stock market and the governance of innovative enterprise. *Industrial and Corporate Change*, 16(6), 983–1035. 10.1093/icc/dtm030

Lewis, W. A. (1954). Economic Development with Unlimited Supplies of Labour. *Manchester School*, 22(2), 139–191. 10.1111/j.1467-9957.1954.tb00021.x

Maillet, J. (1953). *Histoire des faits économiques*. Payot.

Mason, E. S. (1964). Kalkınma planlamasında metodoloji: Kalkınma planlamasında izlenen stratejinin yönleri", N. Serin (çev.). *SBF Dergisi*, 19(1), 39–57.

Millikan, M. F. (1965). İktisadi planlamada karar alma kriteri gelişen ülkelerde planlama hareketi ve planlama amaçları, N. Serin (çev.). *SBF Dergisi*, 20(1), 63–76.

Myint, H. (1973). Ekonomi teorisi ve kalkınma politikası", A.Y. Gökdere (çev.). *SBF Dergisi*, 29(3-4), 313–328.

Nair, S. (2000). İktisadi Liberalizmin Dünya Ölçeğinde Yayılması, S. Köm (çev.). Bir Uygarlık Siyaseti. İstanbul: Om Yayınevi.

Noy, I. (2004). Financial liberalization, prudential supervision, and the onset of banking crises. *Emerging Markets Review*, 5(3), 341–359. 10.1016/j.ememar.2004.05.001

Nunnenkamp, P. (1991). What are the future prospects for the Third World? Current problems and conclusions for development co-operation. *Economics*, 43, 7–27.

Nurkse, R. (1953). *Problems of Capital Formation in Underdeveloped Countries*. Oxford University Press.

Pieterse, J. N. (2013). Trends in development theory, *in* R. Palan (Edt.), *Global Political Economy: Contemporary Theories*. (pp.197-214), Routledge.

Robinson, W. (2002). Capitalist Globalization and the Transnationalization of the State, *in* M. Rupert, & H. Smith (edt.), *Historical Materialism and Globalization*. (pp.210-229), Routledge.

Robinson, W. I. (2004). *A Theory of Blobal Capitalism: Production, Class, And State in A Transnational World*. Johns Hopkins University Press. 10.56021/9780801878848

Schmitz, H., & Musyck, B. (1994). Industrial districts in Europe: Policy lessons for developing countries? *World Development*, 22(6), 889–910. 10.1016/0305-750X(94)90060-4

Seyidoğlu, H. (1998). *Uluslararası İktisat*. Güzem Yayınları.

Shafaeddin, S. M. (2005). Towards an alternative perspective on trade and industrial policies. *Development and Change*, 36(6), 1143–1162. 10.1111/j.0012-155X.2005.00453.x

Sweezy, P. (2018). *Theory of Capital Development.* Monthly Review Press.

Thorbecke, E. (2009). The evolution of the development doctrine, *in* G. Mavrotas, & A. Shorrocks, *Advancing Development: Core Themes in Global Economics*, (pp.3-36), Springer. https://doi.org/10.1057/9780230801462_1

Tinbergen, J. (1965). *A planning model for the educational requirements of economic development, Econometric Models of Education.* OECD.

Tokol, A. (2001). Çokuluslu şirketler ve endüstri ilişkilerine etkileri, *İş- Güç Dergisi*, 3(2), 35-52.

Toye, J. (2005). The significance of Keynes for development economies. In Jomo, K. S., & Fine, B. (Eds.), *The New Development Economics: Post Washington Consensus Neoliberal Thinking* (pp. 123–124). Zed Books.

Tubiana, L. (1998). The end of economic models, *in* S. Cordellier (Edt.). *La fin du Tiers Monde?* La Decouverte.

Wade, R. H. (2003). What strategies are viable for developing countries today? The World Trade Organization and the shrinking of 'development space'. *Review of International Political Economy*, 10(4), 621–644. 10.1080/09692290310001601902

Wayenberge, E. (2006). From Washington to post-Washington consensus illusions of development. In Jomo, K. S., & Fine, B. (Eds.), *The New Development Economics: Post Washington Consensus Neoliberal Thinking* (pp. 144–161). Zed Books.

Wood, E. M. (2002). Global capital, national state, *in* M. Rupert, & H. Smith (edt.), *Historical Materialism and Globalization.* (pp.17-39), Routledge.

Chapter 4
Growth, Accumulation, and Public Sector:
Conjuncture and Capital Fractions

ABSTRACT

This chapter explores capital accumulation, total output, and economic growth in various economic models, highlighting their roles and interactions. It distinguishes "total output" as the monetary value of goods and services produced at a given time from "growth," defined as the increase in investable surplus value over periods. "Capital accumulation" is the addition to capital stock from surplus value, crucial for expanding productive capacity. The chapter examines how public sector activities, especially privatization, influence these models under different economic conditions. It delves into productivity and capital stock's roles in economic growth, factors transforming accumulated capital into productive assets, and the impact of international capital flows and market dynamics on surplus value utilization and economic development trajectories. Critiquing classical, neo-classical, and Marxist growth models, it discusses technological advancements, population dynamics, and income distribution within capitalist economies.

GROWTH AND ACCUMULATION IN GENERAL

The purpose of this section is to distinguish terms such as capital accumulation, total output and economic growth, and to examine this triple terminology within a certain formal pattern, to examine different accumulation/growth models, to reveal the public sector activity within these models, and to The aim of this study is to determine how the privatization of public property is shaped in different conjunc-

DOI: 10.4018/979-8-3693-5996-9.ch004

ture periods within the framework of "public sector property acquisition" in the accumulation/growth models of the sector and subsequent conjunctural changes.

The increase in Gross Domestic Product (GDP) from one period to the next is classically defined with the term "growth", and the proportional value of this increase between two compared periods is called "growth rate". Growth is expressed as the total monetary value of final - finished, completed - goods and services produced in a certain period, which constitutes the definition of total output, that is, GDP.

However, in this study, it is necessary to distinguish between the term "total output" and "growth" and between "growth" and "accumulation". "Total output" is the monetary value of goods and services obtained at a time t. In other words, it is the total monetary value of final goods and services produced in an economy that can be converted into money. This total output that can be converted into money is converted into money and after the capitalist's consumption fund, wage fund and depreciations are separated from the resulting value (other costs related to production are subtracted from the total value before obtaining the total output term. Because the initial price of the goods is determined, at least before the market price, this costs have been calculated and deducted. The reduction of these costs is a function of technology and, accordingly, technology. However, wages are determined by many other variables. At least theoretically, the wage is determined by the marginal product of the labor itself. That is, the wage is inherent in itself compared to other cost items. is a variable.) a "surplus value" will remain. We define this increase of "surplus value" from one year to the next as growth. In short, or in other words, we define growth as the increase in investable after-tax surplus value from one year to the next.

Growth is the potential capacity to generate fixed capital that can be used to produce total output. The basic sources of growth are, first of all, the amount of "capital stock" as factors of production, labor and capital, which are the components of the basic production function, and fixed capital items used in production, such as machinery and buildings. The second is Productivity, that is, the effectiveness of the use of production factors and capital stock in the production process, and productivity increases are a function of specialization and knowledge accumulation from period to period. In short, growth is a component of capital stock and factors of production (other than capital). When we say Growth in the narrow sense, we mean the total increase in output in a certain period, while the term Capital Stock is the total of machinery, buildings and equipment required for the production of final goods and services. Finally, growth in its broad sense includes both an increase in final goods and services and an increase in the capital stock. Since the general character of capitalism is high-level commodity production, there is a need for a sufficient market to sell these products. "The increasing expansion of markets cannot be explained solely – nor especially – by the increase in purchasing power resulting from lowering production costs. Because the two factors that determine the demand volume of consumers cannot always be said to develop in a market-expanding direction. In other words, it does not follow that lower costs will necessarily lead to market expansion. There is nothing to prevent us from thinking that revenues may decrease along with costs, so that the income effect will reduce the cost effect to zero" (Denis, 1978).

The term capital accumulation (accumulation in short) is the additions to the capital stock from the potential surplus value that can be converted into investment. Therefore, accumulation is only one part of growth; It is an addition to the fixed capital stock. In other words, the concept of accumulation is a more specific concept and is investment, that is, capital increase added to the capital stock, at the end of a certain period. Although capital turned into investment increases the capital stock, accumulation may not add to the capital stock unless it turns into investment. The transformation of accumulation into capital stock through investment is a function of the productivity of the marginal product of capital. In other words, the transformation of capital accumulation into capital stock and consequently increasing total output is subject to certain conditions. The first of these conditions is the real interest rate. While a low real interest rate will encourage the capital stock to be converted into investment in parallel with the high profit rates, high interest rates are an obstacle to the transformation of potential surplus value into investment (accumulation).

The key point that is wanted to be emphasized by making this distinction is that capital accumulation is in the use of the person who obtains the potential surplus value that can be converted into accumulation, and in today's conditions where international capital movements are expanding, it should not always be seen as a net contribution to the capital stock, that is, to investment and therefore to total output. For example, the potential surplus value obtained in a country can be used to generate interest income instead of making a net addition to the capital stock in that country, instead of increasing profits by increasing investment by turning to high interest rates in international money and fund markets. Or, as is frequently seen in Turkey and constitutes the "non-core activity income and profits" item in company balance sheets, companies invest in public securities with increased returns, avoiding the risks and costs of investments, as the public sector borrowing requirement has increased, and they can finance their own finances. International financing at low interest rates can also be cited as an example. Therefore, potential surplus value is a monetary value and it cannot be said that it will always be converted into physical investment, that is, capital accumulation. Because, in line with the aim of profit maximization, the entrepreneur can maximize benefit/return by obtaining interest income by supplying funds (in international markets or to governments) instead of investing in physical capital. Therefore, under the assumption of a fully mobile international money market, in short, investment-saving inequality is mentioned.

Total output produced in a given period is expected to equal total demand. However, entrepreneurs want to increase the total output and therefore the total value of their enterprises by making new additions to the capital stock. For this reason, the potential surplus value they will have after payments such as total output, production factor shares in the production of output, depreciations and taxes should be at a level to finance the investments they plan in the future. When this level is not present, it can be said that sufficient capital accumulation cannot be achieved in the country's economy. As discussed in the previous section, the situation of "developing" or "underdeveloped" economies is explained by this inadequacy. If an economy cannot produce at a level that meets the social consumption of the society in that country, it means that the country's population cannot save enough to finance investments. Therefore, these countries cannot make new investments (accumulation) due to insufficient savings, and therefore total output (growth) cannot be increased to a level that can meet the consumption level of the society. On the other hand, it should be considered as a normal process that capital accumulation in "developed" countries shifts to "developing" and "underdeveloped" countries due to the marginal efficiency of capital.

Marginal productivity of capital expresses the increase in output if the amount of capital used in the production process is increased by one unit. In other words, an economy must be increasing its capital accumulation at a -relatively- stable level, and the marginal efficiency of the capital used for investments in that economy must be high.

The term we are trying to define as capital accumulation is a function of fixed capital investments and is related to the marginal efficiency of capital in the form of new fixed capital investments to be made, not to a marginal efficiency of capital investments to be made in existing investments, which is subject to the marginal efficiency of capital.

The marginal efficiency of capital is low in developed countries; It is higher in developing or underdeveloped countries. Because there are no new investment areas in developed economies, that is, sufficient investments have been made in almost every sector, the marginal efficiency of capital will be low. More clearly, since the supply in the markets of developed countries is sufficient, new investments to be made in these economies will increase the supply, thus reducing the market prices, which will keep the returns on investments low. Secondly, due to the law of diminishing returns, as production increases in any sector, the cost of the goods produced will also increase and the marginal efficiency of capital will be low. Finally, as production increases, the demand for investment goods will increase, so the prices of investment goods will also rise, which will reduce the marginal efficiency of capital in the area invested. For these three basic reasons, the marginal efficiency of capital is low in developed countries; It can be said that the marginal efficiency of capital is high in developing or underdeveloped economies.

Investment also represents the demand for capital by those willing to invest. But of course, investing at the desired level also creates the same level of capital demand. Of course, this capital demand cannot always be met. For this reason, foreign capital is needed to meet the capital demand that may remain unrequited due to insufficient savings within the country. This capital demand may be wanted to be met by funds in developed countries that do not have sufficient marginal efficiency in developed countries and therefore seek high marginal efficiency of capital. Thus, growth and accumulation are financed so that aggregate supply is a function of net investment, while aggregate demand is a function of gross investment.

For example, United States data reveal a clear divergence between capital accumulation and the capital stock, and finally total output. "In the United States, private capital is roughly equal to 2.5 years of GDP. Investment is around one-sixth of GDP. Therefore, the capital stock is worth approximately 15 years of investment. If capital demand were to fall by 1 percent, the investment-to-GDP ratio must fall from around 16 percent of GDP to around 13 percent to offset the decline within 1 year. To put it another way, a 1 percent decrease in the capital stock is achieved by a 15 percent decrease in annual investment transfer. [… so] at normal investment rates, approximately 15 years of flow are needed to [increase] the capital stock to its normal level. As a result, even a very small increase in the desired capital stock will open the investment tap wide, while a very small decrease in the desired capital stock will reduce investment to a trickle. This phenomenon, the ratio of large stocks to small flows, explains why investment is such a volatile part of total demand. This also explains why investment has little effect on aggregate supply in the short run: whether wide open or closed, the flow of investment is only a tiny ripple on the capital stock. Of course, in the long run, the height of the capital stock solely determines the flow of investment, and therefore investment is one of the most important determinants of total supply" (Dornbush, Fisher & Startz, 2010, p.399).

The investment activity of the public sector emerges to eliminate the investment deficiency that occurs in underdeveloped countries due to insufficient capital accumulation. However, before distinguishing between the investment activity of the public sector, that is, the acquisition of ownership of the means of production, it is necessary to touch upon the general explanations and contents of growth models.

FORMATION OF SURPLUS VALUE AND ACCUMULATION IN GENERAL

Economic growth appears as a general combination of positive movements in economic variables. However, it can generally be measured in a narrow area with GNP and/or GDP. Size in these two large mass definitions is frequently used as a measure of economic growth. It can also act as a cover over the problems of production, distribution and consumption in economics. It has become an indicator that has pushed the qualities of production, consumption and distribution into the background. In its most general sense, growth has become a frequently used definition as "the increase in the total monetary value of final goods and services produced in a one-year period compared to the previous period". The growth rate is the proportional size of this change. These definitions are taken as a reference for the quantitative increase in people's quality of life in the future, in order to cover a wide area of interest such as its quality, direction, impact and results on social relations. For this reason, under the previous heading, definitions have been tried to be developed by taking into account certain differences between concepts such as "accumulation", "growth" and "total output". Provided that these definitions and criteria can be adhered to, it is necessary to examine growth/accumulation theories that can be considered theoretically. As a matter of fact, the definitions reveal the critical character of this study in these models/approaches.

However, for now, by neglecting the theoretical foundations from this perspective and ignoring the characteristics of the phenomenon of "growth", in the words of Weisskopf, "a perfect dream [...] has happened and...] the growth of the GNP and, if possible, its growth at an increasing rate is almost It is necessary to consider the form and implications of the concepts until they become a form of worship and the rule of economic thought" (Weisskopf, 1971, p.127).

While growth is the total monetary value of goods and services produced in a certain period, what is expected is what is not consumed, that is, saved, and this savings turns into investment. Savings that do not turn into investments are a leak in the economy. This very simple explanation goes back to deep theoretical roots. Determining these extensions also determines the character of growth, that is, the nature of the phenomenon of capital accumulation.

Capital accumulation is a direct function of surplus value and the rate of profit. The difference between the costs of inputs and sales revenues in the production of goods or services is, in its simplest definition, surplus value, and it is the part of this surplus value that is added to fixed capital in a way that increases the total output. Addition to fixed capital is the second determinant of the equation, which is the rate of profit. High profit rates will trigger new investments and savings will be realized.

In short, theoretical approaches defined as growth models or growth theories consist of explanations that come together in the common bracket of investment, savings, total consumption and total output increases, but made from different aspects.

Many sources understand that growth theories emerged with Keynesian macroeconomics, and in fact, growth is a unique research field within economics. However, the phenomenon of growth has existed, explicitly or implicitly, since classical theory. Here, it is possible to categorize these modeling or explanations regarding growth/accumulation into two main categories, which are made with the formation of value. In this study, the distinction will be made primarily according to the definition of value and accordingly surplus value.

"Surplus-value is the "deep core" of the capitalist system [and…] is the source of profit" (Gouverneur, 2005, p.217). The concentration of capital at certain points means that profit increases gradually from the accumulation that started at one point. In other words, capital started to form at a starting point, and from this point onwards, capital "accumulates" by obtaining new profits each time as a return on capital. This starting point is, first of all, "value", and this value is the essential element that gives color to the system called capitalism. Therefore, surplus value, that is, profit, is the starting point of capital's self-reproduction as accumulation.

To define value as a starting point, "Marx generally starts from human labor". (Saad-Filho, 2002, p.74). Even Weber accepts, in Baechler's (1986, p.39) words, "without any difficulty" that the essence of capitalism is wage labor, suggesting that it is not solely dependent on value, and that this was first put forward by Marx.

In the simple commodity production cycle, it consists of selling the commodity that meets the needs of the buyers and converting it into money, and then converting this money back into a commodity that will meet the needs of the seller. However, in the capitalist period, the seller, that is, the capitalist, enters the market with money and buys labor and production tools, puts them into production, and sells the goods he produces in the market, transforming the starting point, that is, into money again. "If M [the amount of money] at the beginning and end of the process were the same, the whole process would become meaningless. Therefore, from the capitalist's point of view, the meaningful circuit must take place in the form C-C- C' [and] C'>M [is]" (Sweezy, 2018, p.66-67). Thus, this C'-producing circuit is the capitalist's "relentless, never-ending process of making profit [which is] its sole aim" (Marx, 2016, p.143). And this ambition and ambition is at the root of the economic crises called "bubbles" in today's capitalism.

C' is a value that carries profit. And profit is the driving force that triggers the production of ever more goods, by purchasing again and again more labor and means of production. However, profit attracts the attention of another actor, as much as the capitalist, on whom no consensus has been reached: the state. The state is a political structure that holds authority with the ideal of people's happiness, freedom and welfare. By providing the necessary conditions for profit, this structure will confiscate a portion of the profit and income from those who both make the profit and earn income by working hard in the process of obtaining the profit, in order to finance the happiness, prosperity and freedom it promises. However, as much as the state is a political entity, organization or structure, it is also an agent and actor in the economic field. However, the behavior of the state in the political and economic fields cannot be addressed within a generally accepted theory and involves deep debates on the subject. This issue is addressed later. The state, on whose political form and effectiveness, especially its economic effects in the economic development process, are endlessly debated, attracts as much attention as the value it extracts from the economy and fixed capital investments, which is only one of the ways of using this value.

However, it is still necessary to determine the different forms, effects and intentions of the state within the economic system. This contains the information necessary to analyze changes in the attitude of the economy over the cycles it goes through. Accumulation in the following process implicitly implies "economic growth". Thus, it was aimed to abstract the concept of "accumulation" from social and historical aspects. While discussing different accumulation or growth models, it is aimed to examine the model in general and define the role assigned to the state within the model. Because, in general, one can try to explain the relations between the state and growth in the light of Baechler's proposition, "economic development is only possible if all profit opportunities are perceived and used" (Baechler, 1986, p.91).

Here, first of all, the elements that constitute accumulation in pure economic terms and the discussions on these elements are mentioned; It is necessary to determine the deviations that may and have occurred in the accumulation process and the place of public sector activity in these deviations.

Classic Accumulation Description

The classical theory, which is accepted to have started with Smith's Wealth of Nations, does not actually offer a real theory of accumulation or growth. However, first of all, it should be noted that, as discussed in Chapter One, as the phenomena expand, the observer tries to discover the a priori or a posteriori principles in this phenomenon. For this reason, Smith's work should not be evaluated independently of what inspired him or, more precisely, the climate of the intellectual world of the period. The person who influenced Smith most deeply was his friend and thinker, Hume. So much so that Anikin describes this influence as an influence that both facilitates the understanding of Smith and the formation of Smith's ideas and says, "Hume's short and influential essays published in 1752 are a brief summary of the achievements of the pre-Smith classical school in its struggle with mercantilism." [...

and] plays an important role in preparing minds to perceive the Wealth of Nations" (Anikin, 1975, p.143).

However, Hume's world of thought contains the methodological influences of Newton, as he clearly mentions. The methodological influences passed from Newton to Smith through Hume will help us understand both Smith's and the general Classical theory's thoughts on accumulation. As a keyword, the concept of "natural" stands out. The natural laws of physics have been established in classical economics as a "natural mechanism" in explaining the economic world.

Therefore, economic growth has been far from being considered as a problem. The economy will continue to grow following a linear trend. Even the fluctuations that occur in the economy are not inherent in this linearity, but are merely the effects of uncontrollable external variables on the economy. However, the main point is what the "internal dynamics of capitalist forces" are and what is external to them, as well as what the "external conditions created by capitalist development" (Freeman, 2001, p.197) are and the consequences of these created externalities in both economic and political fields. What happens is that these are the most difficult boundaries to determine.

The basis of Smith's accumulation model is essentially "social welfare". What needs to be increased is the total social welfare. However, in order to achieve this, "sacrifice" is required from capitalists and especially workers. That is to say, "the gross income of a whole country includes the entire annual production of their land and labor; Their net income is the amount remaining to them after deducting the expenses necessary to sustain their lives, first their fixed capital and secondly their circulating capital" (Smith, 2009, p. 303). Barber offers the following explanation for this sacrifice: "the amount of the net income [...] lies in the shares received by the capitalists and landowners. Wage earners would probably not be allowed to earn more than their "maintenance" needs, and if they were, they would not be paid wages that would enable them to obtain much "surplus value". Landowners and capitalists need to save by keeping the "surplus value" (the remaining value after subtracting the production inputs of future periods and living according to their own living standards). Although landowners will mostly waste these savings (surplus value), the savings in the hands of capitalists will increase profits and therefore the speed of accumulation, and capitalists' savings and profits are a prerequisite for capital accumulation (Barber, 2007, p.61).

The second great architect of classical accumulation analysis is Ricardo. Regarding the deepest difference between Ricardo and Smith, Smith holds that the principle of diminishing returns is valid for capital but increasing returns for labor, while Ricardo accepts the principle of diminishing returns as valid for both factors of production. "But in both models, Malthus' population law was at the forefront, and in both models, the economy would sooner or later enter a period of stagnation"

(Hiç, 1994, p.14). Malthus predicts that even if capitalism is revised, it will maintain the continuity of a class structure in which wealthy property owners and poor laborers will always exist, and argues that the population will increase geometrically. Accordingly, he argued that an "uncontrolled" population would double every twenty-five years. Malthus' control mechanism for population growth was to turn a blind eye to the continuation of the misery of the poor classes and he also rejected income redistribution mechanisms (Hunt, 2005, p.110-113). This is essentially a part of classical economics' general rejection of the state. According to Ricardo, in the two-class structure consisting of capitalists (entrepreneurial landowners) and laborers, the distribution of the income obtained in the economy will decrease in the long run, profits will decrease and there will be no abnormal profit, and "the share of profit in the total output will increase over time." [If] the course of the wage over time, the wage per head will remain constant at the minimum physical level for a long time. However, as the population and the number of employees increase, and considering that the decreasing productivity is current, the share of total wages in total output will increase. Then, according to Ricardo, there is a conflict between the interests of the landowner and the entrepreneur-capitalist.

Classical theory is perhaps the approach that shows the clearest stance against the state until Mill's death. Smith's "invisible hand" phenomenon is a proposition that completely isolates the state from economic relations.

The amount of work in the market and the exchanges to return this amount of work will equalize supply and demand. Therefore, as the amount of work increases, that is, as the total supply increases, the supply will automatically create its own demand, as it will bring about a demand for the inputs used to realize this supply.

The classical theory is based on the fact that due to population growth and resource scarcity, the economy will stop growing in the long run, that is, it will not be able to exceed the stagnation level that will develop later. In particular, it was not brought to the agenda that technological developments could progress so rapidly and productivity would increase to this extent. That's why Solow's neo-classical model starts from this point.

Marxist Accumulation Statement

When it comes to Marxist crisis theory, it is not possible to clearly talk about a crisis theory belonging to Marx. Because Marx did not clearly develop a crisis theory. Marx's first explanation of the crisis appears in the Communist Manifesto as "trade crises" and about the effects of these crises, "[during these crises], not only the existing products but also a large part of the previously created productive forces are periodically destroyed." During these crises, a social epidemic occurs that would have seemed senseless in all previous ages; epidemic of overproduction"

(Marx & Engels, 1998; 2003b, pp.27-28). This is inadequate explanation; As a social system, in his words, "bourgeois society" is a crisis that produces contradiction in its structure. Because this "overproduction" will naturally lead to depression due to the lack of people who have the power to purchase that production.

Marx's most detailed explanations of the crisis are included in Theories of Surplus Value, mainly as a criticism of Say. The most important point that draws attention here is that among the supply-side economic explanations that become evident with the proposition that "every supply creates its own demand", which liberal classical economists state as the law of the Movements, and the opposite, demand-side economic explanations that become evident with Keynes' proposition that "every demand creates its own supply", Marx, this It states that "buying and selling", that is, supply and demand, are two phases of a unity, that is, they carry an integrity. In other words, instead of making an explanation based on neither one-way supply nor one-way demand, Marx states that these two are parts of the integrity within the system, even though they seem to be opposite to each other. That is, "the independence that these two complementary and binding phases [in their own terms, "buying and selling", that is, supply and demand] assume in relation to each other is forcibly eliminated. Therefore, crisis reveals the unity of two universes that have become independent from each other. There would be no crisis without the inherent unity of seemingly unrelated factors" (Marx, 2004a, p.186). With this view, Marx states that there is neither supply of demand nor demand of supply, but a mutual dependence and dependence. Making supply and demand independent from each other is the main reason for the crisis, and the capitalist production system is capable of disrupting this unity. Because as the capitalist tends to increase the rate of surplus-value, the wage fund will decrease and naturally overproduction will occur. However, in the capitalist mode of production, this unity is still a contradictory unity and is already the cause of the crisis. Because of these contradictions, capitalism always includes crisis-producing processes. Because the contradiction in this unity is the production for profit, not for the market, in the capitalist mode of production. That is why, in times of crisis, producers do not put the money they have converted by selling their goods back into production, and they interrupt the process, causing a crisis. The withdrawal of surplus value occurs in the organic composition of capital as wages decline and, finally, profits tend to decline.

"In a situation where people produce for themselves, which is simple reproduction, there is indeed no crisis, but neither is [this] capitalist production." Crisis is "the phase of disruption and interruption of the reproduction process" (Dobb, 2012, p.189-190).

In the Marxist school, accumulation or growth occurs directly as a result of the inherent imbalances in the expanded reproduction scheme. In other words, "capitalist growth means the reproduction of capital on an expanded scale, and this expanded production involves the accumulation of the surplus value created (Gouverneur, 2005, p.238).

In the Marxist approach, crisis means that before the Second War, since there was no market mechanism that expanded at the same rate despite the increase in production, and wage earners could not consume enough goods, the constant accumulation of surplus value in the capitalist forces the system to constantly grow, but it should also encourage consumption to the same extent. If it cannot do this, it enters into crisis due to overproduction. In the same period, the insufficiency of union activities created the assumption that wages are infinitely flexible, as seen in the classical theory, and the inability of wage earners to consume adequately despite excessive production emerges in an environment where union activities are insufficient. However, ironically, the crisis is a mechanism that brings the profit rates, which fell before the crisis, back to their previous levels.

Baran's Economic Surplus Categories

Baran (1957), on the other hand, groups the economic increases, which he describes as "economic surplus", into three main categories. The first of these is the "actual economic surplus" and is "the difference between the total production of the society in a certain period and the total consumption in the same period" (Baran, 1957, p.39). In the footnotes of his work, Baran distinguishes this concept from surplus value and considers the actual surplus value as a fraction of the surplus value and the fraction that goes to capital accumulation and says that "actual surplus value is equal to actual savings or accumulation; It is the sum of various contributions made to the wealth of society in a certain period" (Baran, 1957, p.63). Actual economic surplus is narrower than the scope of Marx's concept of surplus value. Because surplus value is obtained by subtracting the share of workers from the total net production. We can also define this as total national production minus the real income of workers. The actual economic surplus is only a part of the surplus value, the part that goes to capital accumulation. In other words, in the actual economy, there are no consumption expenses of capacities, the public is used for the administration, for the army, etc. Expenditures for organizations are not included in the current economic surplus.

The second category is "potential economic surplus". It is defined as the difference between "the total production that can be obtained with the help of usable, efficient resources in a certain natural and technological environment, and the total production segment that can be defined as basic consumption" (Baran, 1957, p.40).

Baran argues that this second category is the fundamental flaw in capitalism and that capitalism is irrational due to the explanations in this category. Because, the producer sector, which wants to constantly increase the total production, must always extract surplus value from the wage workers who will realize the total consumption in order to do this. In other words, capitalism is a system that simultaneously increases production and reduces total consumption.

The third and last economic surplus category is "planned economic surplus". This category is obtained by subtracting the "optimal" consumption level planned in the same way from the planned and "optimal" production level that can be achieved under historically given natural and technological conditions at an "optimal utilization level" selected for all productive resources. It is defined as "value" (Baran, 1957, p.61) and this surplus category is a category that can only be applied to socialist economies.

Neo-Classical Accumulation Explained

The primary growth theory of the neo-classical model was developed by Solow and starts from the "steady state" level, where the "pessimistic" views of the classics are blocked. And again, in this situation where there are no technology-based productivity increases that the classicists neglect, Solow starts with the assumption that technology is ineffective at the initial level. (Dornbush, Fisher & Startz, 2010, p.66).

Although its emergence dates back to the 1950s, intensive studies on it correspond to today and it is the last theoretical level that growth theory has reached. Solow, who developed a Neo-Classical based model, published his work in 1956 and received the Nobel Prize in 1987 for his other works based on this work. The assumptions of the Solow model are briefly as follows: it is simplified as follows: only one good is produced, there is no foreign trade, technology is external and random, and technology and R&D are not affected by firm behavior (Jones, 2007, p.18-19).

In the model, "although technological development does not cause an increase in the number of workers, each worker comes with more labor units over time. Thus, technological development leads to an increase in the number of effective workers." That is, although technological progress does not increase the number of workers in production, it can increase the working hours of workers in the production process due to the use of technology. On the other hand, "with the addition of technological development [...] observable increases in the standard of living will occur." New technological development [will be able to achieve] sustainable growth in output per worker. On the contrary, a high savings rate can only ensure growth until a steady state is reached. When the economy reaches a steady state, the growth rate of output per worker will depend solely on the rate of technological development (Mankiw, 2015, p.249-251). Therefore, the stagnation level in classical economics cannot be exceeded, but in the Solow model it can be overcome with technological development. In this way, growth will become sustainable and workers' living standards will increase. "According to the Solow model, the only source of sustainable growth is external technical change, as labor is kept constant as a result of the decreasing returns of capital accumulation" (Levine, 2000, p.105).

One of the most critical concepts of the model is the term "convergence". The measure of the proximity or distance of any economy to the steady-state level defines the concept of convergence. Accordingly, "the speed of convergence towards a steady state, the rate of growth of output per worker in an economy heading towards a steady state, or the rate of contraction of output per worker in an economy tending towards a steady state, varies depending on how far the economy is from the steady state. In this context, the further the economy is from a steady state, the higher the growth or contraction rate of output per capita will be (Ünsal, 2007, p.155). In short, for an economy that is positively or negatively distant from the stagnant state, the growth rate per worker will be higher, depending on the greater the distance, while there is a tendency towards the stagnant state.

Keynes[ian] Accumulation Explanation

In general, Keynes did not address the growth and accumulation phenomena in a static analysis; In other words, it did not reveal a growth or accumulation model. For example, "Keynes generally focused his arguments on a certain set of events at a certain time. He therefore temporarily takes the values of his variables as given, but will explain this as he puts all the arguments together in the final stage. [...] shows that liquidity preference theory can be used in the world of endogenous money, on the grounds that demand conditions as well as supply play a key role in determining the structure of interest rates" (Harcourt, 2000, p.16). Although Keynes did not introduce a long-term analysis, which was 'partially' separated from the short-term analyzes that neo-classicals and the marginalist school frequently and fundamentally used as a method of economic analysis, "with the mechanism activated by the multiplier coefficient, events occur at once and income reaches a new equilibrium." [a comparative static analysis]" (Ülgener, 1991, p.409). Although this new perspective is also a source for Keynesian growth, it can also be considered as an attempt to address the necessity of long-term analysis. Keynes, who made a distinction between Micro and Macro issues and therefore used the term "classical" for the economists before him who examined micro issues and whose analyzes were stated to be static, kept his macro analysis at the level of comparative static analysis on macro issues. However, many Keynesian economists have suggested that there are dynamic concepts in Keynes. One of them is Harrod, who also developed a Keynesian dynamic growth model. "According to Harrod, who argues that there is a dynamic concept in the Keynesian system, this concept is the concept of positive savings. Harrod argues that the concept of positive savings, which has a very important place in the General Theory, is a dynamic concept. The allocation of a certain amount of income to house rent each year is not a dynamic event. However, the allocation of a certain amount of income to savings each year is essentially dynamic. Because this implies constant changes in the amount of capital available, which is one of the main determinants of the system. [...But this] does not change the static character of Keynes' analysis. Because, as Schumpeter stated, these dynamic concepts are essentially attached to a static skeleton" (Karaosmanoğlu, 1958, p.1- 10). Another of the main reasons for considering the concept of "value" as the starting topic of this part of the study (while the first one is the beginning of accumulation) is that it lies in the meaning given to the concept of value as the basic and general cause of the crises. In other words, the arguments that emerge to explain the crisis differ from each other by showing similarities in terms of the meaning given to the concept of value (Ünsal, 2000, p.331).

The most important element that defines Keynesian economics is its fundamental opposition and rejection of the proposition that "every supply creates its own demand", known as the Law of Exchanges. Since classical economists took Say's Law as their theoretical basis, they created a supply-side economic idea. However, Keynes put forward and theorized the idea of a demand-side economy with the opposite proposition of the classics, that supply does not create demand, but demand creates supply. According to Keynes, the main weakness of the classics is that the "classical economists" before him, for whom he first used this name, included Say's Law, "that is, the logical impossibility of an economy with excessive production supply in every field of the economy, therefore the labor supply, and their inability to explain economy-based unemployment". (Laidler, 2016, p.4).

However, Keynes examined savings only in terms of their effects on aggregate demand, but did not address the effects of investments on capital accumulation. What drives investments is the marginal efficiency of capital. In essence, Keynes attributes the phenomenon of crisis to inadequacy in investments. Therefore, the characteristic of growth, on the contrary, depends on the consistent and regular increase in investments. Therefore, Keynes recommends that if a rhythmic investment trend occurs, the economy will reach the equilibrium level. However, he did not focus on its continuity. He carried out his analysis through the comparison of different equilibrium levels, independent of each other. In this case, explaining Keynes' process of reaching this equilibrium level can form the outline of the Keynesian growth model. There are two basic elements of the equilibrium state; It is the marginal efficiency of capital and the accelerator-multiplier mechanism. The marginal efficiency of capital is defined as "the discount rate that makes the present value of the investment project zero and therefore equals the present cost of the expected net returns of the investment projects - the present supply price of the capital good" (Ünsal, 2000, p.325). In other words, the entrepreneur who will make the investment decision, which is the source of growth and accumulation, is the result of the choice between the present value of the net investment, the interest income likely to be obtained in the future and the total profit, and the largeness of the expected profit is an effective factor in making the investment.

The Keynesian equilibrium condition is that planned total expenditures equal planned income. Consumption expenditures within total expenditures consist of autonomous and stimulated expenditures, and stimulated expenditures are a function of "disposable personal income", which is obtained by subtracting "net taxes", which consists of the difference between taxes and transfer payments, from "personal income". In this case, if other expenditures are defined as "autonomous expenditures", total income will be equal to the sum of autonomous total expenditures and stimulated expenditures. In this equation, the difference between disposable income and stimulated consumption will be equal to autonomous expenditures. Increases in income will stimulate stimulated investment, which is an increasing function of income. The multiplier mechanism is the expression of the principle that increases in stimulated investments create income and employment increases at a rate greater than the total amount of investment. Accordingly, the simple multiplier, which includes autonomous investments, is equal to 1/s, that is, 1/marginal propensity to save, under underemployment conditions. The super multiplier has been expanded to include the stimulated investments that will be created due to the increase in income resulting from autonomous investments, and investment increases increase investments as well as consumption. On the other hand, the Accelerator coefficient indicates that the increase in the demand for final consumption goods between periods leads to a much greater increase in the demand for investment goods.

It is possible to summarize the character of Keynes analysis, which does not include the dynamic analysis of accumulation and/or growth in addition to this mechanism, in three propositions; "(1) investment leads to savings, but saving does not lead to investment; (2) an increase in saving reduces income (paradox of savings); and (3) wage flexibility is not enough to move the economy to full employment" (Leijonhufvud, 2006, p.76). However, this structure shows inadequacies in explaining the relationships between different periods, that is, it does not allow a long-term dynamic analysis.

An attempt was made to determine the factors that characterized growth in the 1950s and 1960s. In this regard, Kaldor considers the relationships that appear to have emerged in the major industrialized countries - between the growth rate of production and capital and labor, and between factor prices and relative income shares - as a set of long-term relationships (Branson, 1995, p.560). has received. That is, growth has a dual character: on the one hand, there is the balance/relationship between total output growth and the volume of capital and labor force, and on the other hand, there is the balance/relationship between production factor prices and the relative income shares of these factors.

Although Keynes did not develop a specific long-term growth analysis, growth models were developed by economists in the Keynesian generation. Although the model is seen as developed independently of each other, it is the Harrod-Domar model that is considered together. The most basic feature of this model is that it is a "balanced economic growth model that requires the full use of both labor force and capital stock as the economy grows" (Branson, 1995, p.567).

Although the Harrod-Domar growth model develops independently of each other, it is a model that is considered together because they complement each other. The first assumption of the Harrod model, which is based on two basic assumptions, is that "the net saving of an economy in any period (t) is a certain and constant proportion (s) of that economy's income (Yt) in that period." What is meant by net saving is total saving minus total minus saving… [this] assumption in the model reveals a connection between actual saving and actual income" (Baumol, 1970, p.2) and states that planned saving and actual saving; The planned investment and the actual investment are equal.

The second assumption clarifies what the planned investment should be, assuming that actual savings and actual investment are equal. Accordingly, "entrepreneurs' desire to invest depends on the severity of the increase in income. To put it more clearly, the investment planned in period (t) is at a fixed and certain proportion (g) of the difference between the income in period (t) and the income in the previous, that is, period (t-1)… This second assumption is a part of the accelerating principle. It is called "form and its counterpart that accelerates to a constant ratio g" (Baumol, 1970, p.3-4). In short, it can create dynamic growth due to the accelerating principle of increases in investments depending on income, as the dynamics of growth.

Domar similarly examines the dynamic relationship between capital accumulation and employment. The basic assumptions of the Domar model are; "(a) there is a constant "general level of prices"; (b) there is no delay; (c) saving and investment belong to the income of the same period; (d) depreciation of both is deducted; (e) wear and tear is measured not by historical cost but by the cost of replacing an asset with another asset of the same production capacity; (f) the production capacity of an asset or the entire economy is a measurable concept" (Domar, 1946). The Harrod-Domar model, which can emerge when the ideas of both authors are considered together, can reveal the actual and natural growth rates required for the economy. Accordingly, the required growth rate is defined as the increase in income that makes the planned investment equal to the planned savings, which is the rate of increase in income in any (t) period compared to the previous (t-1) period. The actual growth rate is a deviation from the required growth rate and can be defined as the actual realization of an income greater or lower than the income increase that would equalize the planned investments to the planned savings. Finally, the natural growth rate is "the rate of production at a certain time and there is a maximum limit to the increase in production. This limit is determined according to the available workforce, natural resources, capital and equipment and technical knowledge level. This limit is called the natural growth rate by Harrod... If the economy continues to grow with the required growth rate, even if we accept the absolute income limit as above for a moment... the economy will sooner or later reach the natural limit and in this case, the actual growth or production increase rate will decrease" (Never, 1994, pp.85-92).

MARKET AS A NATURAL PROCESS OF ACCUMULATION

All accumulation models come from a single source; It arises from the creation of value and the accumulation of a surplus resulting from this value, and the continuity of this resource ensures its own continuity thanks to the driving and natural power of the "market" is a matter of deep debate among economists.

The main reason for opening this title regarding the concept of market and its functioning is to make sense of the functionality or non-functionality of the market mechanism, or under what conditions it works and under what conditions it does not work. Because, it is the market mechanism that gives its identity to the process and determines this triple phase of the process, starting from value formation, continuing with accumulation, and in the long period when accumulation is interrupted. In the economic cycle, it is necessary to focus on whether the market has achieved the task assigned to it or why it has not succeeded. The basic formal structure that moves the economic system is the market.

A simple definition of the concept of market such as "all physical or non-physical environments where buyers and sellers encounter" can be accepted by almost everyone. However, there are deep debates about the scope, functioning and socio-economic role of the market, that is, the confrontation between buyer and seller. While the market is a mechanism that can function perfectly for some, according to others it can never function perfectly and even carries the fundamental contradiction of one of the deepest contradictions of capitalism. On the one hand, there is a wide range of views between the extreme views that claim that the market mechanism cannot function perfectly (centralization and concentration) and that these flaws are the main problem of the system, while on the other hand, there are virtues of the perfect functioning of the market mechanism. Therefore, the market mechanism, its functionality, or hidden or obvious disruptions in its functionality, directly concern the accumulation process, and even the connection with the functionality of this mechanism is clearly present at the origin of the crisis explanations. Therefore, in order to make sense of different views on the functionality of the system, the meanings that different views attribute to the market will be quite revealing.

Mises (2010, p.257), one of the most prominent liberal thinkers, sees the concept of the market as a mechanism that "direct[s] the activities of individuals towards channels that will best serve the wishes of other people". However, Mises, one of the pioneers of neo-classical economics, was under the influence of Smith's "invisible hand" phenomenon. Because, it is essential that there is no "coercion and coercion" in the market system and that the state, as the most effective force of social coercion, does not intervene in market actors. And the sole function of the state is to act in a way that is abstract ("the market is not a place, an object, or a collective entity" in Mises's terms) and spontaneous ("activated by the interplay of actions of various individuals cooperating under the division of labor" in Mises's terms). It should not go beyond taking the necessary regulations and measures to ensure the functionality of the market. In fact, according to Mises, the market mechanism not only puts the economic system but also "the entire social system in order and gives it a meaning" (Mises, 2010, pp. 257-258). However, Mises also states that a purely implemented market economy has not been tried (Mises, 2010, p.264).

In general, the concept of market constitutes the basis of capitalism and the rotating mechanism of its production relations. In this regard, Mandel first asks "What brings movement to capitalist society?" He asks the question and gives the answer in one word: "competition". It treats competition as a concept with dual contradictory components and asks "what is the reason for competition?" He gives the following answer to the question: "The basis of competition consists of two concepts that are not necessarily compatible with each other. This is, firstly, the concept of the unlimited market, the market that is completely unrestricted without reservation. Secondly, there is the concept of diversity of decision centers, primarily in the field of investments and production." As a result, Mandel advises that capitalism cannot be talked about with the proposition that "if there is a single producer for all commodities and the market becomes completely stable and solidified and there is no possibility of expansion, competition will completely disappear" (Mandel, 1973, p.42-43).

Capital Accumulation Processes

Capital is a word with a very wide usage area. This range expands from the narrowest meaning, which includes the monetary and fixed means of production used by an entrepreneur in the production process, to the meaning in which it is used as a form of social structure. It would be appropriate for the purpose of this study to focus on two basic uses, especially within the science of economics, among many different purposes of use. First of all, “capital” is a production factor whose return is “profit”. However, although this definition keeps capital in a narrow framework as a factor of production, Capital also implies a social formation in a broad sense.

The main goal of mainstream economics is continuous growth, and all regulations should be implemented in a way that supports growth. Regular and continuous increase in GNP will result in people's living standards or social, cultural and social progress as a “result”. In the economy, the increase in the value of GNP (total monetary value of goods and services produced) from one period to another is an indicator of growth, and the proportional value of these increases gives the growth rate.

This pure meaning that mainstream economics attaches to the term “growth”, after a certain point, turned into “GNP fetishism”, in Weisskopf's term, and “growth and technical development targets turned into social goals under the influence of the ideology advocated by large companies” (Weisskopf, 1971, p.125). Again, according to Wisskopf, this view has replaced value-relativity in welfare economics.

Sen's views on the concept of “development”; Sen affirms the concept of development insofar as it helps liberation. According to him, increases in GNP are not an indicator of development on their own, and even the definition of “identifying it with the increase in individual income, industrialization, technological progress or social modernization” is a “narrow” meaning (Sen, 2004, p.17). Sen refers to the term “freedom” along with “other determinants such as the freedom to regulate social and economic regulations (education and health care) as well as civil and political rights (for example, the freedom to discuss matters of public concern and participate in supervision).” handles. Sen implicitly sees the term development as a holistic social progress with elements such as social, cultural and political, as well as economic growth. However, the most distinctive feature of this view is that it avoids establishing a linear cause-effect relationship between economic growth and the expansion of social, political and social freedoms, and defines development as a concept that provides integrity between growth and freedom and as a concept that includes a much deeper identity of simple linear causality. handles (Sen, 2004, p.20). Therefore, it distinguishes itself from views that link development solely to economic growth.

However, this attitude implicitly supports the arguments of mainstream economics. However, it is an indirect criticism and indirect support for the belief that the economy has “pure laws”, which are the most basic assumptions of mainstream economics.

State and Market: Analytical Determination

Based on the nature of the relationship Kant established between “concept” and “intuition”, it can be used as a determinant for the connections to be established between the market and the state, and between theory and practice. According to

Kant, "concepts without intuition are empty, intuitions without concepts are blind" (Kant, 2009, p.13). As a continuation of this idea, which is one of the basic propositions of Kant's philosophy, it is recommended that human thought and therefore the concept is more primary and superior than intuition, that is, experience. Accordingly, first of all, there is a level of a priori knowledge in human thought that becomes evident before observation. While agreeing with this proposition, it is also possible to argue that there is a cyclical causality relationship between intuition and concept and to talk about processes that feed each other. That is, a priori knowledge is expressed as a concept by a thinking subject in a certain time and place. For this process of expression, there are visions that force it to come out of the human understanding and be expressed. These visions remove the concept from the human mind and conceptualize it in a way that identifies with the vision. (This chain of propositions is also parallel to the problematic of differentiation of concepts in time, space and subject). When the concept matches the vision, the vision becomes richer. However, in this new state of the intuition, enriched with the concept, the subject attempts other and deeper observations, and then the intuition becomes richer each time compared to its previous state, and therefore the previous concept begins to become insufficient to coincide with the intuition. In addition, the mind of a second observer, directed towards the conceptualized vision, can reach other and broader concepts and meanings than the conceptualized vision presented to him, with his a priori knowledge. For the second observer, the unity of the first observer between the concept and vision given to him from outside; -And for the first observer, this unity is not simply absolute-it may contradict the a priori in itself. This contradiction also subjectively legitimizes the second observer's conceptualization of the unity predicted by the first observer as completely opposite. Therefore, the dialectical process requires a third observer. The concept-vision overlap of the first and second observers that comes to the third observer causes the third observer to attribute completely different meanings to the vision in his dialectical mind, but legitimizes his new conceptualization by only partially breaking away from the concepts of the previous observers. The main reason why the third observer cannot break away from the concepts of the previous observers, theoretically and practically, is due to the limited information that the human mind can obtain from vision. Because all observers are preoccupied with the same intuition, and intuitions basically contain abstract ideas from concepts. Dialectics continues until the essential unity of these ideas reaches the absolute and pure level, and the dialectic process that will produce pure and pure essential knowledge is endless. Because an observer at any point in time has the acquired concepts of previous observers, the concepts about vision acquired throughout history, and the experience of observing the dialectical processes in these concept-vision-temporary associations.

The second proposition that determines our interest in Kant in this study is the distinction between "analytic" and "synthetic" that he put forward in another work. According to this dilemma, which is far from the purpose of this study to subject it to a critical approach and judgment as above; Analytical judgments/propositions are "judgments in which the connection of the predicate with the subject is considered through identity; but the judgments in which this connection is considered without identity are called Synthetic judgments/propositions. In simpler terms, "the first [Analytic judgments] can be called explanatory, the second [Synthetic judgments] can be called extending-judgments, because the first [Analytical judgments] do not add anything to the subject's concept by predicate, but only by investigating the component already thought in it." solutions to concepts; On the other hand, the latter [Synthetic judgments] add to the subject's concept a predicate that has not been thought of in it in any way and cannot be deduced by any way of decomposing it" (Kant, 2000, pp.41-42).

In this study, in the first two chapters, an attempt is made to create analytical, synthetic and conceptual propositions and the theoretical infrastructure related to them, which will be subjected to empirical analysis in the third chapter. What is intended to be stated here is that an attempt has been made to determine an intellectual basis for the question to be examined. The question posed is to touch upon the relations between the market and the state in the process of economic development and to try to define these relations within a set of relations. For example, while in developed countries there are theories that emerge from natural situations, that is, the vision/phenomenon may emerge for the first time without a certain concept, in developing or underdeveloped countries, although the visions/phenomena emerge in their natural state, the conceptualization of them is based on preliminary visions/phenomenons. The cases are taken from developed countries. Moreover, the phenomena that occur in developing or underdeveloped countries do not arise independently of the policies of developed countries.

In short, while the phenomena occurring in developed economies have reached a certain conceptualization, it should be taken into consideration that, as a result of this conceptualization, developing countries cannot be handled with the same conceptualization purely because they also contain the effects of these phenomena.

State: The Best Theories

However, in mainstream economics, while the state is a self-functioning market mechanism that is most suitable for the optimal distribution of resources, public sector interventions and policies, as an external intervention, have disruptive effects on this natural situation. For example, according to Smith, state intervention disturbs a reasonable balance, which could cause this balance to be disturbed, "his attack on the aid of the poor [is not] because he does not feel sorry for the plight of these unfortunate people. On the contrary, the existing Poverty Laws, which require residence in a certain locality in order to benefit from the opportunities provided." He argued that "the practice reduces the rate of economic development by limiting the mobility of labor" (Barber, 2007, p.63). Therefore, on the basis of mainstream economics, such public expenditures are disruptive to a certain order not only in their economic dimensions but also in the social sphere. Today's writers say, "If private enterprise can supply goods and services of the desired quality and quantity by using fewer resources than state enterprises, private enterprise should be put in charge. "If the main state structure believes that consumer independence and private financiers operating private charities do not allow the poor to access goods and services of sufficient quality and quantity at affordable prices, the structure must determine the form and level of state aid to the poor" (Hanke, 1987, pp.1-3) advocate similar views.

The continuity of the economic system basically depends on the system's self-reproduction. A distinction is made between two stages in the expanded reproduction of capital [and the one that prevails from the Second World War until today is the "contemporary accumulation" stage. As can be seen, the general conditions in which accumulation takes place clearly move from one stage to another, both in terms of the situation of wage earners and the state's intervention in the economy" (Gouvernour, 2007, pp.238-239). That is, in this second stage, there is a parallel expansion in total supply and total demand.

In short, the main problem is the method to be followed in ensuring economic development. A market mechanism that operates spontaneously is accepted as the "best theory". However, at points where this theory does not work, it can be legitimized and theorized as the "second best theory", in which the public sector intervenes in the system in different dimensions, forms and levels. For example, it is thought that a union regulation that can be effective in eliminating the imbalance between total supply and total demand, socializing wages and bringing the wage earners to the level of minimum subsistence can only be established by the public authority.

Microfoundations: Firm Behaviors

Marxist economics has not explained firm behavior and inter-firm competition and mutual behavioral conditions in a formal structure. It focuses on a broader analysis of the conditions of inter-firm competition, including competition between capitalists and between capital fractions. Neo-Classical mainstream economics, on the other hand, focuses on intermediate market forms (incomplete competition markets) such as oligopoly and duopoly, based on two extreme theoretical and often uncommon models such as perfect competition and monopoly. However, both approaches analyze given market conditions and existing relationships between firms and capitals. For example, the assumptions of a perfect competition market are based on "n" number of firms and that entry and exit from the market are not limited. So much so that this "n" number of companies is so ineffective that they cannot have a determining power over prices. In monopoly, there is only one firm in the market from the very beginning, and it is uncertain how it came into existence. This monopolistic company produces a product that has no close substitutes and has surrounded the market for this non-substitutable good in such a way that there is no freedom of entry and exit, and prices are completely determined by the monopolistic company. The question is, how do the few firms that are subject to competition behave and what are the basic motivations that determine and influence their activities?

Like perfect competition and monopoly, its functioning is flawless - monopoly also works perfectly because competition is infinite in the perfect competition market, while competition is zero in monopoly - in the first of the formal markets, there is no need to follow the behavior of any of the "n" number of companies by the other because no company alone can do anything in the market., will not have any effect on a variable. Therefore, the main factor that affects the behavior of any market and the companies in that market is the power to influence prices. The power to set prices is also an inverse function of competition. As competition increases, the power to determine prices decreases, and as competition decreases, the power to determine prices increases.

Analysis of firm behavior will provide the basis for understanding and explaining the reasons why firms turn to public firms that are subject to privatization. In this analysis, profit maximization, technology, competition and search for profit are the key concepts. Because it is a result of the "search for profit opportunities" phase, which mostly occurs after passing these key concepts as a process, which leads companies to encourage the political power to privatize and purchase public companies.

Standard Firm Behavior: Mainstream Theory

Explanations of firm behavior, which is one of the fundamental views of mainstream economics, are handled in a way that closes firms and markets to all non-market influences and realizes the assumption that prices can only be formed in the market. In other words, firm behavior is analyzed under conditions where the market can regulate itself, driven by competition and in the absence of any non-market impact.

In summary, companies are envisaged as designed parts of the parts that will realize the general. Under these presuppositions, the focus here is on a firm's behavior.

The main axis of companies is profit maximization, and all behaviors are clearly and firmly committed to this basic goal. Profit is the inverse function of costs and the direct and simultaneous function of market prices. Therefore, for maximum profit, the company will simultaneously seek to reduce costs and increase market prices. Maximum profit is the production level at which the difference between the sales revenue at the market price and the costs is the highest positive difference as the production amount increases. Under all market conditions, firm equilibrium will occur at the production level where marginal cost equals marginal sales revenue.

A firm's sales revenue function is linear. So much so that multiplying the sales quantity by the market price always gives a linear function. However, the cost function is curvilinear. The main reason for this is that total costs consist of fixed and variable costs. While fixed costs provide an increase in production up to a certain production level and require new block fixed costs after this critical production level, variable costs have a linear relationship with the production amount. However, this linearity can also be changed under efficiency conditions. For example, for a worker who works eight hours, instead of hiring a new worker for more production, the existing worker can be employed under overtime conditions and the overtime costs of this worker will be less than the costs of employing a new worker.

Regarding the distribution of production costs, the amounts of capital and labor that will constitute production costs are expressed with the concept of "efficiency" and provide explanations on the determination of decisions regarding the labor-capital composition. Therefore, total cost, as the sum of fixed and variable costs, is formed by a choice between different combinations of labor and capital use. Here, how much labor and how much capital factor will be used for production can be produced in a labor-intensive or capital-intensive combination, depending on the nature of the goods produced, which is called "technical efficiency". When determining technical efficiency, the combination that will minimize the total cost will be selected among the same labor-intensive or capital-intensive combinations, taking into account factor prices depending on what the total cost will be, and this is called "economic efficiency". When making the most effective choice, companies take the market price and the attitudes of their competitors as data, in the determination of which there are no non-market factors. From the perspective of firm behavior, at first glance, competition appears as a driving mechanism to reduce costs and increase efficiency by using resources and production factors effectively. Companies are forced to compete in market conditions in order to hold on against their rivals. For this reason, it will always seek opportunities to increase the marginal productivity of capital or labor in order to increase its fixed and variable costs under competitive conditions.

Non-Standard Firm Behavior: Alternative Theory

The engine driving force of competition is shown as technology. However, companies may avoid technological innovations under some conditions. This is due to the fact that the production capacities of companies are focused on company profit maximization, not on social benefit.

In cases where competitive opportunities decrease, the market mechanism encounters a problem in controlling prices and keeping them at the socially "best" level. Companies that focus on profit maximization as their main goal conflict with the interests that are socially predicted to be "best" in situations where competitive opportunities are limited - monopoly, cartel, etc. According to Hahnel, there are three main reasons for this: non-competitive market structures, distorted price signals, and setting conflict theory. First of all, non-competitive markets will disrupt the efficient distribution and allocation of resources. "because monopolistic and cartelist market structures have incentives for profit-maximizing producers to keep output below socially productive levels." In this way, it focuses on its own profit maximization by restricting fixed capital investments in technological developments that will strengthen social benefit and resource allocation. Second, non-market factors other than resource and benefit allocation distortions "also lead to market prices that do not accurately reflect the true social cost of production." Thirdly, according to the "firm conflict theory", which is not discussed much in mainstream economics; "If more efficient technologies sufficiently reduce their bargaining power vis-à-vis workers, it explains why capitalists should choose less efficient technologies to maximize profits. The thesis is that there is a fundamental conflict of interest between employers and employees over how high or how low the wage rate should be and how much effort employees should put into their own wages. In short, if new technologies increase the bargaining power of employees against employers, employers may neglect new technology options. (Hahnel, 2003, p.106-107) and in these three basic points, non-market factors cause the society to move away from the "best" theory.

REFERENCES

Anikin, A. (1975). *A Science in its Youth: Pre-Marxian Political Economy*. Morkow: Progress Publishers.

Karaosmanoğlu, A. (1958). Keynes İktisadının Bugün Kabul Edilmiyen Tarafları. Ankara Üniversitesi SBF Dergisi, 13(04).

Baeshler, J. (1975). *The Origins of Capitalism*. Blackwell.

Baran, P. A. (1957). *The Political Economy of Growth*. Monthly Review Press.

Barber, W. J. (2007). *A History of Economic Thought*. Wesleyan University Press.

Baumol, W. J. (1970). *Economic Dynamics, an Introduction* (3rd ed.). MacMillan.

Branson, H. W. (1995). *Macroeconomics*. Harpercollins College.

Denis, H. (1978). Le rôle des "débouchés préalables" dans la croissance économique de l'Europe occidentale et des Etats-Unis d'Amérique. *Economia Aplicada*, 31(3-4), 643–690.

Dobb, M. (2012). Papers on Capitalism, Development and Planning, Routledge.

Domar, E. D. (1946). Capital expansion, rate of growth, and employment. *Econometrica*, 14(2), 137–147. 10.2307/1905364

Dornbush, R., Fisher, S., & Startz, R. (2010). *Macroeconomics* (11th ed.). McGraw-Hill.

Freeman, A. (2001). Has the empire struck back. In Albritton, R., Itoh, M., Westra, R., & Zuege, A. (Eds.), *Phases of Capitalist Development: Booms, Crises and Globalisations* (pp. 195–214). Palgrave. 10.1057/9781403900081_12

Gouverneur, J. (2005). The Foundations of Capitalist Economy. *Polity*.

Hahnel, R. (2003). *The ABC's of Political Economy: A Modern*. Pluto Press.

Hanke, S. (1987). Privatization versus nationalization. *Proceedings of the Academy of Political Science*, 36(3), 1–3. 10.2307/1174091

Harcourt, G. C. (2000). Contemparary capitalism and Keynes's General Theory. In Toporowski, J. (Ed.), *Political Economy and the New Capitalism: Essays in Honour of Sam Aaronovitch* (pp. 15–22). Routledge.

Hiç, M. (1994). *Büyüme ve Gelişme Ekonomisi*. Filiz Kitabevi.

Hunt, E. K. (2005). *History of Economic Thought*. Routledge.

Jones, G., & Sluyterman, K. (2007). British and Dutch business history. In Amatori, F., & Jones, G. (Eds.), *Business History around the World*. Cambridge University Press.

Kant, I. (1784). What is Enlightenment? https://www.nypl.org/sites/default/files/kant_whatisenlightenment.pdf

Kant, I. (2007). *Critique of Pure Reason* (2nd ed.). Palgrave Macmillan. 10.1007/978-1-137-10016-0

Kant, I. (2009). *Critique of Practical Reason*. Merchant Books.

Laidler, D. (2016). Keynes, John Maynard (New Perspectives), *in* R. Backhouse, B. W. Bateman (edt.). *The New Palgrave Dictionary of Economics*, (1-14), Palgrave.

Leijonhufvud, A. (2006). Keynes as a Marshallian. In *R.E. Backhouse, & B.W. Bateman (edt.). Keynes* (pp. 58–77). Cambidge University Press., 10.1017/CCOL0521840902.004

Levine, P. (2000). Unequal exchange re-visited. In Toporowski, J. (Ed.), *Political Economy and the New Capitalism: Essays in Honour of Sam Aaronovitch* (pp. 99–113). Routledge.

Mandel, E. (1973). *An Introduction to Marxist Economic Theory*. Pathfinder.

Mankiw, N. G. (2015). *Macroeconomics*. Worth Publishers.

Marx, K. (2016). *Capital, Vol.1, 2, 3.*, Fingerprint Publishing.

Marx, K., & Engels, F. (1998). The German Ideology. *Prometheus.*

Marx, K., & Engels, F. (2015). *The Communist Manifesto*. Penguin Classics. 10.2307/j.ctt184qq4k

Mises, L. (2010). *Human Action: A Treatise on Economics*. Ludwig von Mises Institute.

Saad-Filho, A. (2002). *The Value of Marx: Political Economy for Contemporary Capitalism*. Routledge.

Saad-Filho, A. (2006). *Marx's 'Capital*. Pluto Press.

Sen, A. (2004). *Development as Freedom*. Anchor.

Smith, A. (1994). *The Wealth of Nations*. Modern Library.

Smith, R. (2000). Military expenditure and globalization. In Toporowski, J. (Ed.), *Political Economy and the New Capitalism: Essays in Honour of Sam Aaronovitch* (pp. 76–86). Routledge.

Sweezy, P. (2018). *Theory of Capital Development*. Monthly Review Press.

Ülgener, S. (1991). *Milli Gelir, İstihdam ve İktisadi Büyüme* (7th ed.). Der Yayınları.

Ünsal, E. (2007). *İktisadi Büyüme*. İmaj Yayınevi.

Weisskopf, W. (1971). *Alienation and Economics*. Dutton.

Chapter 5
Capital Accumulation and State

ABSTRACT

The state is a central topic of debate in social sciences, defined by its institutional framework and legal authority as the embodiment of collective societal will. Its role and legitimacy are continually contested. The state wields a monopoly on legitimate violence and governs through laws and institutions, reflecting social consensus but often leading to divergent perspectives. Some view the state as a necessary evil, curbing individual freedoms for communal order and security, while others see it as a vehicle for social justice and welfare. Historically, the state's role has evolved, expanding during the rise of Keynesian economics to mitigate market failures and contracting under neoliberalism, which advocates for market efficiency, privatization, and deregulation. Ideological differences shape perceptions of the state: socialists see it as a tool for wealth redistribution and equality, while liberals favor a minimal state prioritizing individual liberty and market mechanisms.

CAPITAL ACCUMULATION PROCESSES AND THE STATE

All concepts, on which no consensus has been reached even at the theoretical level, come up again from time to time with an adjective before or after them, and can be the subject of research and debate. Even though consensus has not been reached on many concepts in almost all sciences in general and in social sciences in particular, and cannot be expected to be achieved, there are some concepts that can create an agenda of great debates in terms of their place at the core of human and social life. In fact, theoretical studies on some concepts seem to never end. Because these concepts surround human and social sciences as phenomena. Justice, state, freedom, human rights and civil society are among these concepts. The state, which we are interested in, is a concept on which practical and philosophical discussions

DOI: 10.4018/979-8-3693-5996-9.ch005

continue, under titles such as its place in economics, its duties, limits of authority and responsibility, justification for existence, qualities and continuity. "The state, as a whole of organization that can constantly change its structure in different forms from the emergence of the state to the present day, is abstract with laws, concrete with institutions and has the monopoly on the use of force" (Mann, 1984, pp.185-213: Wood, 2016, pp.30-33).) is an entity. This set of laws and institutions is a form of manifestation of social will. (The term "revelation of social will" that we mean here is not in full parallel with thinkers such as Kant, Locke, Rousseau and Hobbes, who argue that the source of existence of the state is the expression of will of the society. Because social will is not always free. This state of unfreedom is directed (or it can be revealed as the will of an engineered society) Will, on the other hand, is revealed as the desire to possess and use power that sometimes varies between God, sometimes morality, and sometimes race and ideas. Social will is transferred to someone else who will rule over it, on these and similar grounds. However, a mutual interest relationship also constitutes the source of consensus, at least at the intellectual level. However, this "relationship of interest" is beyond the meaning intended by Hume (2004, p.459-463). Because while Hume sees the "relationship of interest" as a part of human nature and natural, what we mean is a social interest relationship that is "convinced", "designed" or even "forced" that the "interest relationship" is "natural". In this state, society is not naturally built on relations of interest; It makes it necessary to keep a variation on the agenda that may be motivated in some way by a relationship of interest. For example, in a class social structure, slaves are not slaves because of the benefits they will gain as slaves; They were forced into slavery. For this reason, the adjectives assigned as prefixes to the state also differ at different levels of relationship. For example, the state, which is a set of laws and institutions with the prefix "dictator" for one segment, may acquire the prefix "sacred" for another segment, representing the social will and acting to realize social ideas. On the other hand, while some people think that supports that will mobilize market forces to expand freedoms make them talk about a "liberal" state, another group may evaluate the same practices with the "bourgeois" prefix.

The 1960s are quite interesting as the period in which theoretical studies on the state concentrated. Because these periods are witnessing several important developments and changes. First, World War II has ended and a new world system is being created both economically and politically. Second, Keynesian policies have effectively expanded their scope of application. Thirdly, development economics studies intensified and Keynesian policies, which began to be implemented in developed countries immediately after the Second War, began to develop suggestions in different forms for countries defined as "underdeveloped". Fourth, there is a marked increase in capital accumulation, described as the "golden age of capitalism". Fifth, it is a period when the global dominance of the United Kingdom ends and the expansion of the sovereignty of the United States accelerates. Sixth, confidence in the Bretton Woods monetary system is beginning to weaken rapidly. It is a period when the trust in the Dollar, in particular, began to fail to be resolved in the political arena due to the conflict areas maintained by the United States, and in the economic arena, the problems arising from the foreign payment system of developing countries could not be resolved. Seventhly, it is a period in which the "cold war" period, defined in the description of the "balance of terror", gradually intensifies, as Soviet Russia gradually increases its effectiveness in the economic and political fields. Eighth, Marxist analysis has concentrated its studies on the new form of state and capitalism, especially in Continental Europe. Many more political and economic events and features can be listed for the period of 1950-1970, when the core of today's features of the re-formed world system was formed.

In the relevant period, when neo-classical economics could not provide a solution to the 1929 crisis under the conditions of full employment balance and the resulting intense unemployment, Keynesian economics provided an explanation for maintaining the balance under public intervention and underemployment conditions. Keynes mostly gave a role to the public sector to eliminate the problems in ensuring the continuity of capitalist accumulation.

However, we are trying to focus not on "what" or "who" the state is, but on its "position in economic relations", which is the form that interests us. Therefore, here, the state taken as a given is limited by its economic activities. In a more specific area, it is considered as one of the parties of privatization activities, that is, an economic exchange, as the transfer of ownership within the economic development - accumulation - process.

While Kant defines the concept of "enlightenment", it means "man's liberation from a state of immaturity that he has fallen into through his own fault." He defines this immaturity as "the inability of a person to use his own mind without resorting to the guidance of someone else" (Kant, 1784). Therefore, enlightenment is nothing more than transferring the will directly to the mind itself, by removing it from the guidance of "other" things that limit or shape the human mind, such as God, Church, state, custom, and tradition. In fact, this justifies excluding the state as naturally and as much as possible in human thought, which the enlightenment thought tries to liberalize - individualize.

The individualization of the individual in almost every field, especially in the political field, directly refers to individualization and individual benefit in economic initiatives in the economic field. Individual initiative and, as a result, the maximization of individual interest precondition the indifferent success of the market and the exclusion of the factors limiting the market for this success. The most obvious regulation of market success comes from the state. For this reason, the state, as the only factor restraining market success in an individualized society, must be prevented from these limitations.

Examinations on the legitimacy of the state in the political field or the legitimacy of its legitimacy naturally necessitate the examination of the state's position in the economic field, without addressing its legitimacy or illegitimacy.

Public choice theory can be defined as "the economic analysis of non-market decision-making or simply the application of economics to political science. State theory, voting rules, voter behavior, party policies and bureaucracy, which are the subjects of political science, also constitute the subject of public choice (Mueller, 2008, p.1). Accordingly, the theory basically states that bureaucrats, politicians and voters pursue their interests as political and economic actors, and therefore focuses on achieving results by restricting the financial aspect of the state with legal obstacles in order to prevent politicians and bureaucrats from being market disruptors. With a highly designed economic constitution, it is planned to limit the borrowing and budget scope of the state and its administrators, politicians and bureaucrats.

In fact, under the dominant Keynesian policies, they are the efforts of liberal thought to provide an explanation through their own perception of the accepted policies of the state apparatus at the time. On the one hand, the inadequacy of traditional mainstream economics in explaining its period and the emergence of Keynesian policies and theories as highly effective and highly explanatory theories, and on the other hand, the unexpected growth and development trends shown by socialist economies are handled from a liberal perspective. Although socialist and Keynesian policies fundamentally have radically different perspectives on the state, they have inevitably brought to the agenda the evaluation of the effectiveness of the state and its policies, as the phenomenon they examine and attach importance to, from the liberal perspective. In short, it contains a liberal explanation of the state and the roles assigned to it in a perfectly functioning market world and a world of facts where the state cannot be truly neutralized.

These explanations about the state aim to be independent from the Keynesian and socialist policies that were very effective at the time, but at the same time, they aim to be a liberal approach that can explain the state. In this context, the term "social market economy" was brought to the agenda in 1949 and although it did not include harsh government policies, it was defined as "the basic principle on which it is based, market freedom provided with social justice". This unity of the public sector and market mechanism requires "the principle of coordination of a successful economic policy" (Armack, 1989). Therefore, instead of a Socialist absolutism or a Keynesian centrality, the state is assigned to the task of "coordination" in this concept. Following his definition above, Armack makes this determination by making a distinction between liberalism and neo-liberalism. According to him, he shares with neo-liberalism the view that "social and sociological problems are not given enough attention by classical mainstream economics, and although the functional importance of competition is recognized by "Old Liberalism", such problems are not given importance. "Unlike the old liberals, the new liberals do not intend to restructure the laisez-faire economy." In short, the power projected to the public sector "mixes central government control factors with those of the market economy to the point that they block each other and affect economic performance" (Armack, 1989). In summary, a public sector that strengthens the market mechanism is envisaged.

In the Institutional Economics approach, which is based on the works of W. Mitchell, J. R. Commons and T. Veblen, "the state is an important part of the economic system; [and] indeed the economic system cannot occur without the state. Both the basic economic institutions that determine the characteristics of the economic system and the structure of rights and powers that determine the power structure of the economy as well as the current economic importance of natural resources (De Gregori, 1987) are a function of the state" (Samuels, 1995). The state, as suggested by Marxist theory, in the service of the capitalist as the dominant class and as the provider of the continuity of its interests, also emerges in this form in institutional economics. However, this is not a situation that is negated as in Marxist economics, on the contrary, "it is an instrument for those who can control and use it [... and] the important thing is not the state in the face of statelessness; but they are benefits provided by the state in exchange for support. [...] The state is both a means of exercising superiority over private powers and a means of control over private power holders for control. The social system is formed through a kind of symbiosis of the beliefs and interests of public officials and private agents. In the view of institutional economists, both economics and politics have a common bond" (Samuels, 1995). Therefore, the state is not handled directly and only in parallel with capitalist interests, as in the Marxist approach, and it rises on the basis of a state form that contributes to the functionality of the market system.

While public choice theory excludes the failure of a functioning perfect market system, it places individual attitudes within the state system at the center of possible failures. The practices of bureaucrats and politicians within the system aimed at their individual interests are reflected in the economic system as market failures. However, the approach, which still focuses on the analysis of politician and bureaucrat behavior, focuses on legal and even constitutional limitations on the financial aspect of the state. In particular, the Constitutional Economics approach, pioneered by J. Buchanan and which can be placed within the public preferences approach, tries to determine the economic and financial position of the state through laws.

In short, the public sector and its interventions, which are excluded by neo-classical theory, are an explanation that the public sector, due to its own internal structure, deregulates the markets. The basis of these interventions and their deregulation refers to the self-interested behavior of individuals within the state apparatus.

Neo-Classical Theory and Market Failure

Neo-Classical Theory tries to bring a solution to the debates on state effectiveness in economic theory in the context of markets. As a continuation of the classical theory, neo-classical theory states that markets can be successful in their internal integrity and that under perfect competition conditions at a given price level, supply and demand in the economy will automatically come into balance, referring to the externality of situations where they do not. Walras's general equilibrium analysis expresses a static situation in which households and firms, as decision-making units, do not try to change their plans and their supply and demand are equal to each other. However, both Walras and other neo-classicals do not address the issue of "what is the origin of the resources in the economy and whether their distribution is more or less fair" in the general equilibrium state of the economy. For neo-classicals, the economist does not have to answer such a query, which concerns the domain of politics or morality. The economist must take the initial resources or this or that realizable situation as given, and compare it with other realizable situations, without being obliged to include any concept of social justice" (Guerrien, 1989, p.64). The changes between these "realizable alternative situations", under the assumption of interchangeability, are discussed in Pareto's analysis. Pareto optimum "occurs where it is impossible to improve someone's situation without worsening someone else's situation [and] it would be inefficient or wasteful not to implement a change in society that improves someone's situation and leaves no one worse off." Such a change is called a Pareto Increment, and a Pareto optimum or efficient outcome can be defined as an outcome that occurs where there are no other Pareto increment possibilities". (Hahnel, 2003, p.56). However, Pareto optimum does not represent a "fairness" situation. While one of the two individuals in the society obtains x unit of benefit and the other receives x/10 unit of benefit; Optimality is achieved if there is no way to increase the utility of the individual who obtains x units of utility without reducing the utility of the individual who benefits x/10 units. Pareto optimality receives criticism on two important points: "First, Pareto optimality is a weak case of "optimality": It says nothing about the total amount of welfare in a society or the distribution of that welfare. Second, [...] it is a probability theorem. He says that free markets can produce Pareto optimal results under some seemingly unlikely conditions. It does not show that genuine markets produce such results. It does not show that genuine markets produce such results" (O'Neil, 1998, p.96). As a matter of fact, Pareto's basic assumptions include "ideal" markets operating under full competition conditions. However, in the real world, ideal competitive markets may not be realized, and the reason for this is "public goods" and "external effects". In neo-classical theory, the state is involved in the economy with the task of regulating these market-distorting effects. However, this partial legitimacy attributed to the state is the most important gap in the theory for the periodic expansion of the state's fields of activity.

Welfare State and Welfare Economy

While there is generally no connection between the economic systems and political systems of countries in political sciences, and the economic system is perceived as a function of political systems; Within economics, the political system is respected as a function of the economic system. However, the definitions of "developed", "developing" or "underdeveloped" countries simultaneously imply both a political system and an economic system. Therefore, the political economy perspective considers the political and economic system simultaneously in their mutual connections. In short, the causalities between the terms "welfare state" and "welfare economy"; While the proposition "welfare economy as a sub-argument of the welfare state" can be put forward in terms of political sciences, the proposition "welfare state as a structure compatible with welfare economy" stands out in terms of economic sciences. However, from the perspective of political economy, there is a "simultaneous-counter-causal" relationship between both variables. In summary, these two terms; They are interconnected with simultaneous-counter-causality within a continuity mechanism that will ensure the continuity of a certain social formation. This continuity is the bond of "capital accumulation" continuity.

For example, Rosanvallan, who looks at the term welfare state mainly from the political field, argues that in an analysis to be made over the 19th and 20th centuries representing the emergence of the welfare state, the term is "a middle way between capitalism and socialism, a middle ground that will define the place of the social democracy initiative or the economic or social imbalances of capitalism." He makes the determination that "reading it as a compensatory move towards correction is not very enlightening as a result" and criticizes that this analysis "only sends the dynamics of the welfare state to the dynamics of capitalism" and finally draws the welfare state into the political field, understanding the concept and understanding the key to the power of the welfare state with its "contradictions and " It is not capitalism with its "logic" and the class conflict that accompanies it. He concludes: "The secret must be sought elsewhere, in the modern nation-state movement itself" (Rosanvallan, 2004, p.20-21). This approach shows a perspective on the term from the political field.

J. Hobson was the first author to explain the international expansion of states using purely economic variables. According to Hobson, the main reason for the international imperialist policies of states is the set of policies developed "neither for the [interests] of taxpayers, nor of merchants, nor of entrepreneurs, but only of finance capital [interests] in pursuit of profitable investment opportunities" and "according to Hobson Imperialism is a project of "restructuring within economically developed societies" (Münkler, 2007, p.42-43). Imperialism can be defined as "basically the systematic appropriation of one nation's values by another nation" (Carchedi, 2001, p.216). Therefore, welfare state initiatives in any country generally coincide with a period compatible with this financial mobility. As a matter of fact, the "poor states" in the proposition "poor countries are poor because they are poor" represent a welfare state proposal with a theoretical basis, a state model that seeks financial mobility and can be financed with a finance wave that can finance poverty. Thus, poor countries can finance welfare expenditures and even state economic enterprises; The way is opened for financial capital from developed countries, seeking new and profitable areas, and welfare states to enter into the same equation.

Three basic forms of the welfare state can be mentioned. Of these: Liberal model, Social-Democratic model and Conservative model. "The liberal model can be characterized by benefits as low as the mandate of limited social security schemes and income research assistance, equal amounts providing for the promotion of work income. In the social-democratic model, the social protection system is universal, based on subordination, increases social equality [...] and implies separation from the family; for example, individuals can achieve a high standard of living by living without market participation and independent of familial support. Finally, the Conservative model is oriented towards preserving status and ensuring unity within rather than between social groups" (Amable, 2003, p.19-20).

Liberal economics is shaped by adhering to the paradigm of individual freedom, which nourishes the basis of the political system and gives its philosophy. Thus, economics becomes an argument in support of a political goal such as individual freedom. Political liberalism, which is the basis/parallel of mainstream economics, poses the following philosophical questions to the welfare state: "What is the basis for the deprivation of freedom required [by the policies implemented by the Welfare State]? Or is this not a deprivation of freedom at all, but an increase in power (capacity) in the sense that it creates opportunities for individuals to do things they would not otherwise be able to do? On the other hand, even if these policies increase the use of coercion, wouldn't the reduction in inequality that welfare regulations are said to create justify the reduction in freedom? (Barry, 1974, p.285). As can be understood from these general questions, mainstream economics looks at the welfare state in a political sense and through the basic denominator of individual freedom. However, the point of discussion is that, in terms of adding new actors to the competing actors within the market mechanism, welfare state policies provide an infrastructure for these new actors to enter the competition mechanism and therefore ensure that the market system approaches full competition conditions; There are also opinions that freedom is restricted by emphasizing the negative effects it will have on the competitiveness of existing competitive elements due to tax policies, which are the most effective element in financing welfare expenditures.

"The failure to apply the general principles of liberalism to new problems manifested itself during the development of the modern Welfare State. Although it was possible to achieve many of the aims of the Welfare State within a liberal framework, this would require a slow experimental process; But the desire to achieve these aims directly by the most effective means led everywhere to the abandonment of liberal principles. In particular, while it is possible to provide most social insurance services by developing an institution for the purpose of truly competitive insurance, and even a guaranteed minimum income for all can be established within the liberal framework, it is not necessary to make the entire field of social insurance a government monopoly and for this purpose The decision to transform the entire constructed apparatus into a great machine for the redistribution of income led to a gradual expansion of that part of the economy under government control and a permanent contraction of that part of the economy in which liberal principles still prevailed" (Hayek, 2007, pp.197-224).

The term welfare state emerged in England in the 1940s [almost simultaneously with development economics] and was used to differentiate England from Nazi Germany. "A Welfare State is a state in which organized public power (through policy and administration) is used effectively to direct market forces in at least three areas. The first of these; to guarantee a minimum level of income to individuals and families, regardless of the market value of their assets, and secondly, to reduce the spread of insecurity, which would otherwise lead to personal and family problems (such as disease, old age and unemployment), by enabling individuals and families to overcome certain social risks. The third is to provide the best standards available to all citizens, regardless of status and class, within the framework of generally accepted social services" (Gough, 1979). This definition is important in two respects. The first one reveals a form of state that intervenes in the capitalist market economy. Secondly, it reveals that capitalism creates a class structure in society and that the lowest layers of these classes must be kept at a minimum standard of living by the state. In other words, it defines a state duty that requires it to try to provide solutions to poverty and inequalities, directly or indirectly. These duties include social security, security, education, preventing poverty and ensuring an average standard of living. The result obtained by looking at the welfare state from the economic field falls within the field of welfare economics, and basically the welfare expenditures made by the public sector are considered external to a general balance in the pure economic field and have a nature that disrupts this general balance.

These discussions also pave the way for the transition from the term welfare state to the term welfare economy. However, the connection is quite delicate. Namely; "There are three main forms of distribution of welfare: (1) collective organized social insurance, which is directed to financial rights in certain contingencies such as unemployment, illness, pregnancy, and retirement; (2) fiscal welfare assistance, not just transfer payments, and subsidized occupational welfare assistance, and property such as housing." redistribution through the fiscal-financial system, including its establishment by the private sector through state subsidies and other tax deductions; (3) collective consumption in the sense of public financing of public goods and services" (Jessop, 2003, p.232). While these functions of the welfare state are, on the one hand, a clear intervention in the market mechanism and an attempt to disrupt competition, on the other hand, they are perceived as a search for a solution to the process of destruction created by pure capitalism and a guarantee of continuity.

On the other hand, welfare economics is basically based on Pareto Judgment and Pareto Optimality. Accordingly, when the welfare of a single individual is increased, without changing the welfare of all other individuals in a society, the total welfare of the society increases. According to Pareto Optimum, based on the Pareto Judgment, it puts forward the proposition that optimality occurs if there is no possibility of increasing the welfare of a single individual in a society without reducing the welfare of others. This pure economic analysis identifies three basic elements that disrupt optimality, three basic externalities. The first of these is the property externality: it describes that the waste produced by an individual's production creates a social cost. The second is technology: it is the externality that arises under the assumption of increasing returns to scale in the production function, and it is claimed that increasing returns to scale paves the way for monopolization. The last externality element is "public goods": although full public goods are goods in which individuals do not prevent the use of one of these goods from the use of the other, there is a situation outside the rule of equality of marginal cost and marginal benefit. For this reason, there are opinions that public services will be transferred to the private sector over time, and their distorting externalities towards the welfare economy will be eliminated, due to the negative effects that welfare expenditures will create rather than the positive effects they provide (Lindbeck, 1995, p.9-15).

In short, public goods are theoretically a disruptive externality in the welfare economy, and the welfare state, due to its duties, envisages the proliferation of public goods. In summary, although the welfare state has provided the theoretical and political foundations for the emergence of public economic enterprises with welfare expenditures in a certain period of time in the accumulation process, the distorting effects of welfare expenditures in the welfare economy will emerge in another time period that will ensure the accumulation process, together with welfare expenditures. to eliminate public economic enterprises; provided the basis for privatization.

However, it is also a problematic area to consider the capital accumulation process, or in other words, capitalism, in a one-way causality process due to the above chain of propositions. As a matter of fact, in this context, the terms welfare state and welfare economy, as per the simultaneous-counter-causality term presented above, emerged as a phase in the historical process that will support the provision and continuity of capital accumulation required by capitalism as a social formation, based on political economy in the first chapter.

For this reason, the term welfare state, which helps the financial capital in developed countries to exceed the limits of the accumulated and more profitable areas, has also formed the basis and source for the financing of public economic enterprises along with other welfare state requirements, especially public goods. However, in the following period, when public goods and welfare state policies, especially public economic enterprises, were considered as an externality to the welfare economy within the general equilibrium analysis, privatization did not encounter any difficulty in gaining legitimacy.

Political liberalism, which is the basis/parallel of mainstream economics, poses the following philosophical questions to the welfare state: "What is the basis for the deprivation of freedom required [by the policies implemented by the Welfare State]? Or is this not a deprivation of freedom at all, but an increase in power (capacity) in the sense that it creates opportunities for individuals to do things they would not otherwise be able to do? On the other hand, even if these policies increase the use of coercion, wouldn't the reduction in inequality that welfare regulations are said to create justify the reduction in freedom? (Barry, 1974, p.285).

There are three main factors that disrupt the equilibrium situations in the welfare economics approach: incomplete competition conditions, externalities and public goods. Since these three elements directly affect the distribution of resources, they will also disrupt resource efficiency.

DEVIATION/BREAKS FROM THE ACCUMULATION CONTINUITY

This section has two main purposes. The first of these is to distinguish the terms "crisis" and "fluctuation" and the second is to reveal the mobility of capital fractions and their adaptation/change according to the crises and fluctuations experienced. As a matter of fact, based on the latter, it is tried to explain to what extent the change of hands of public ownership feeds and/or supports these circuits of capital fractions.

If the equation systems of economics were linear, accumulation processes would continue linearly with uninterrupted continuity. However, according to some, accumulation processes are interrupted due to periodic, according to some, random reasons, and according to others, due to structural reasons. Although the accumulation process shows an increasing trend in the long term, deviations and breaks are constantly experienced throughout this trend, and one of the most sophisticated subjects in economics is to produce propositions about the timing of these breaks and deviations. In fact, there is no consensus on the causes, effects and consequences of these deviations and breaks.

The main reason for keeping the terms Deviation and Breakage separate from each other is due to the difference in the terms "crisis" and "conjuncture". While crisis, with the meaning of "collapse", is a phenomenon that occurs in the economic system and changes almost all variables and even the equation, conjuncture movements do not always have an effect on the integrity of the system and can even be eliminated by the existing tools of the system. Although the term crisis in this study specifically refers to the crises of 1929 and 1974, as discussed in the first chapter, these crises had profound effects on the capitalist mode of production and organization. However, conjuncture movements do not affect production systems and processes with the same power. On the other hand, it is necessary to define the term crisis in its narrow and broad meanings. While the crisis in the broad sense has an impact on the capitalist mode of production and organization, as mentioned above, the crisis in the narrow sense is the countries that go through the adaptation process of any economy to the production and division of labor processes determined by the central capitalist countries - which in the future carry the term hegemony in its essence - in this articulation process. It covers the crises they experience. Because these economies in the process of articulation change and transform holistic forms of production and organization. In short, the term crisis in general refers to a change in the organization and production processes of capitalism; In a narrow sense, the term crisis implies changes and transformations in the production and organization of economies in the process of articulation.

Conjuncture, or in other words, cyclical movements, define deviations from the long-term trend function. These deviations are mainly due to the extended reproduction mechanism, or in other words, the mismatch between supply and demand. Just as the deep core of capitalism is "surplus value", the deep core of crises and business cycle fluctuations is the "expanded reproduction mechanism". In short, in this study, the terms "crisis" and "fluctuation" are considered as two different phenomena on the basis of cause, effect, form and effects.

Cyclical Fluctuations

While value should be considered as the starting point and source of capital accumulation, the change over time in the components that make up the value that creates accumulation can also take forms that may create breaks in the capital accumulation process. As one of the most controversial issues in the economic literature, these ruptures are subject to many names such as "crisis", "fluctuation", "cyclical movement", "conjuncture". The meanings attributed to almost each of these terms may differ from each other. Based on the above definitions, others give the same meaning, with the exception of the term "crisis".

"While British economists call short-term fluctuations cyclical fluctuations (trade business), nowadays they generally use the American term business cycle" (Fisher & Dornbusch, 2001, p.546). It has been experienced continuously in the economy since the 18th century, when economics started to gain its scientific identity, and it extends to all industrial and commercial fronts, first seen in 1825, and, according to Engels, recurs approximately every ten years (Engels, 1950, p. 315 cited by: Baby, 1967, p.180) and fluctuations that are tried to be explained in different ways are constantly experienced. These fluctuations constantly expose national and global economies, which continue to grow around a certain trend, to disruptions. In the most general sense, it is created by indicators such as "a rapid contraction in production, a fall in prices, a large number of bankruptcies, an increase in unemployment, a decline in wages, social tensions and the collapse of the stock market or banking system, often as an "explosive"" (Rosier, 1991, p.20). Economic shock is defined as a crisis. The crisis that emerges with these indicators is experienced in certain phases. Although the phases are generally similar to each other, there is no consensus in the literature on determining the timing, since the emergence, continuation and termination of the phases do not occur in the same time period. However, in general, they are theoretical studies that focus on accumulation, that is, growth, "the long-term growth path trend or potential growth path" (Branson, 1995, p.557). Breaks experienced in the short term are called "seasonal fluctuations", which in this context include purely external effects such as natural disasters and epidemics. However, although wars have a very effective and original effect on economic expansion, which is neglected but worth researching, they are not discussed in this study. In summary, "The concept of economic fluctuations is defined as non-periodic and consecutive positive-negative differences between the long-term growth rate and the annual growth rate" (Ünsal, 2000, p.14).

Although there is almost no consensus on the causes of business cycle movements, there are classical acceptances on their consequences and, more precisely, on their course of development. Within the framework of these assumptions, cyclical fluctuations are generally defined as four phases; It goes through the stages of Dip (Collapse), Revival (Expansion), Climax (Summit), Recession (Stagnation-Contraction), according to some it occurs periodically, and according to others it emerges as non-periodic random periods. A frequently used conjuncture definition that includes these terms; "It is a type of fluctuation that occurs in the total economic activities of societies in which cyclical activities are predominantly organized by firms. A business cycle consists of a period of expansion in many economic activities occurring simultaneously, followed by stagnation and contraction, and a period of revival combined with the expansion period of the next business cycle. Fluctuations are not periodic, but repeated changes, varying in time from one year to ten or twelve years (Kutlu, 2009, p.8, as cited in Burns and Mitchell). In the early periods when economic phenomena began to be analyzed, fluctuations in the economy were generally considered as external shocks created by seasonal changes, natural factors and extraordinary spending periods such as war.

Despite the different evaluation and analysis tools within themselves, classical economics and subsequent theoretical approaches inevitably reach the conclusion that the capitalist system is its own natural functioning, as they are heavily influenced by political liberalism. The most obvious exception to this was Keynes, who suggested that the economy could be restored to its own functioning by an artificial effect created by public intervention at the stagnation level of the economy until it reached the potential national income level of the classics. Because, especially as one of the most important classical economists, Say's proposition that "every supply creates its own demand" encountered major problems in the field of reality and was inadequate to explain the Great Depression of 1929. Thus, Keynes (2013) created a major break in the classical view with his proposition that "every demand creates its own supply", also known as "demand-side economics", and unlike the classics, he did not delve into the subject of "value" and became the founder of macroeconomics by working entirely on "total functions". has won. As a result, the most important break in classical economics is that it actually occurred during a crisis period. This is such a crisis that it has been tried to be explained with the concept of "effective demand" (Stewart, 1972, p.54-56). And the insufficiency in effective demand can only be covered by the fiscal policies of the public sector.

As will be discussed in the next topic, production and consumption possibilities have a chaotic structure in the market, where an infinite number of producers and consumers are as independent from each other as possible and decisions are made independently of each other due to benefit maximization, which is the root of "value" in neo-classical economics. Moreover, this unlimited number of producers and consumers, that is, economic agents, make decisions that will maximize their own benefits, instead of making decisions that are said to ensure the functionality of the system. All this information points to fluctuations that have continued historically but have not yet been agreed upon.

Explanations regarding the occurrence of trade crises, which were identified by Thomas Tooke in 1838 and Lord Overstone in 1839 and mentioned as recurring by Marx and Engels in 1848, were first defined by Clément Juglar in 1860 as crises, successive economic cycles. The term "economic cycles" was later named "Juglar cycles" by Schumpeter, and the classical cycles or fundamental cycles before Schumpeter were abandoned (Rosier, 1994, p.22).

However, it was suggested by Kondratieff that the cyclical movements carried out on the Jugs, lasting up to 10-12 years, were repeated in a much longer period. Kondratieff argued that economies go through long fluctuations over 50-year periods, similar to the 10-12 year periods put forward by Juglar. According to the statements of Kondratiyeff, who provides the broadest fluctuation explanation for capitalism, in the historical process of capitalism, there are long waves that repeat over longer periods of time, apart from the familiar boom-collapse processes/fluctuations. According to Kondratiev, the "rise" from 1790 to 1810-17; "decline" from 1810-17 to 1844-51, "rise" from 1844-51 to 1870-75; 1870-75 to 1890-96 "rise; It consists of "rise" periods from 1890 to 1914-20, with each wave going through periods of rise and fall approximately every 50 years. (Woods, 1997, p.8; Rosier, 1994, p.17-28)

Fisher and Dornbusch explain the reasons for the fluctuations; (in an analysis of the effects on aggregate demand) "an increase in the demand for exports, an increase in government spending, or decreases in interest rates lead to changes that increase aggregate demand in the short run": On the other hand, "an increase in tax rates, a decrease in export demand" or declines in firms' future profit expectations; It causes "a decrease in aggregate demand in the short run", which means that the occurrence of either of these two situations will shrink the aggregate demand in the short term and as a reaction to this, the total output will fluctuate. However, this causal relationship alone is not enough to explain cyclical fluctuations, nor does it explain why these effects on total demand occur in an orderly sequence (Fisher & Dornbusch, 2001, p.547).

As mentioned above, although there is almost a consensus on the formal process of fluctuations (at least it seems so), it is useful to briefly address the very deep debates on the causes of fluctuations. Although the main subject of the study is not crises or fluctuations, it is necessary to review these approaches in order to solve the characteristics of the public sector within the continuity of the accumulation process. Thus, if different and deep causes of fluctuations can be determined, propositions can be developed about the formal characteristics of the public sector's activities in these processes, and thus the position of changes in public ownership within these fluctuations can be determined.

As mentioned above, although a consensus has been reached on the process, many different theories have tried to explain the fluctuations in terms of their causes. Samuelson grouped these theories trying to explain the conjuncture under two very general headings and called them "external theories" and "internal theories". External theories are theories that try to explain the emergence of business cycles by attributing them to non-economic factors. Non-economic variables such as sunspots, climate changes, revolutions, political events, and population growth rate are some of these. Jevons and Moore are among those who put forward these views. However, even though major technological inventions, increased production of gold or other precious metals, or new discoveries are non-economic variables, these variables also have an impact on the economic trend as external factors. Internal theories, on the other hand, are theories that try to explain the circuits with internal variables within the economy. For example, machinery and equipment with an average economic life of 8-10 years will provide a very high level of output throughout this economic life. When the economy reaches the period when the machinery and equipment that have completed their life will be renewed, an inflationary expansion will occur, and with such a hypothetical model, the reasons for the fluctuations can be tried to be explained by the variables within the economy. The known ones of these models can be summarized as follows: "Cash theory; bases business cycle theories on the expansion and contraction of bank credit (Hawtrey); innovation theory links business cycles to the centralization of important inventions such as the railway (Schumpeter, Hansen); According to psychological theory, business cycles are caused by people influencing each other in a way that causes optimistic and pessimistic expectations to occur (Pigou, Bagehot); Underconsumption theories suggest that, relative to investment, a greater portion of income goes to the rich and is saved (Hobson, Foster, Catching); The theory of overinvestment suggests that high, rather than low, investment causes declines (Hayek, Mises)" (Samuelson, 1966, p.289-291).

However, in this general distinction between internal and external theories, which can be considered internal theories, the conjuncture analysis of almost every school has been different since the classical economists. For this reason, it is useful to outline the most basic business cycle theories. In this way, public sector activity can be periodized within the theories of business cycles and finally the place of privatization can be sought at the intersection of both phenomena.

Classical Business Cycle Theories

It should be noted right away that, in classical economic theory, it is not possible for a crisis/fluctuation to occur in the system. However, since the fluctuations in the system are not perceived as a crisis, there is no clear explanation. Because the economy operates under full employment conditions, only external shocks, namely wars, climatic conditions and, most importantly, unconscious and populist interventions of governments, cause fluctuations. Therefore, in classical theory, the main cause of business cycles is external shocks. Another important factor is that "industries producing capital goods are growing faster than those producing consumer goods". "The result of this was that, when full employment was achieved, the distribution of the country's resources between capital goods and consumer goods was disrupted" (Stewart, 1972, p.44-45).

Determining the components of the formation of full employment is necessary and sufficient to explain the non-emergence of business cycles (more generally, crisis). It is based on the French J.B. Say's proposition that "every supply creates its own demand" in the economic circulation, known as the Law of Exchanges/Say, which is essential in the formation of full employment. Accordingly, when there is a certain supply, this supply will definitely be met with demand. Because the prerequisite for being able to supply anything is to demand as much as that supply. Ricardo explains this situation as follows: "No one produces for any reason other than to consume or sell, and no one sells commodities except for the purpose of purchasing commodities that will not be useful to him or her or that will contribute to his future production. Thus, the person becomes either the consumer of the goods he produces himself or the person who buys and consumes the goods produced by another person" (Ricardo, 2004, p.273). In this way, there will be no overproduction and therefore no crisis situation will occur.

The general idea of the classical school envisions an exchange system based on a set of markets that are assumed to operate on the basis of "pure and perfect" competition. This means that many, many small independent producers and isolated consumers, with complete information, will come together, without affecting each other, to arrive at a price system that manually balances supply and demand. Hence the theory of general equilibrium, which shows mathematically that in a market economy it is normally impossible to experience any imbalances and, a fortiori, no crises. From here emerged the idea that the market should never be intervened" (Rosier, 1994, p.15). This general idea can only be disrupted by external shocks, giving rise to the term "surge". Early economic scientific studies observed some fall-rise processes in the economic system, but these fall-stay situations were not actively subject to theoretical studies and definitions. In 1802, Henry Thornton coined the term "crisis". The author, who specifically talked about the "great commercial crises", made suggestions regarding them and based this on the trade problems of 1793. Although Ricardo (1817) talked about severe contractions in trade, Lauderdale in 1804 and Malthus in his works dated 1820 did not use the term "crisis", although they talked about a deficiency in demand and a depressive state. However, Sismondi called what happened in England in 1819 the "trade crisis" (Hansen, 1951, p.213-215).

Classical economic theory uses the two concepts mentioned above at different times. However, it specifically uses the term crisis as fluctuations resulting from 1- Non-economic and 2- Intra-economic factors. Non-economic factors refer to uncontrollable changes in the economy caused by natural factors that arise outside the economy's own internal dynamics, such as disasters, epidemics, agricultural productivity, excessive rainfall or extreme climate differences, and changes in trade routes.

Marxist Surge [Crisis] Statements

One of the most important political consequences of Marxist theory is that capitalism will face a crisis that cannot be overcome, and as a result, capitalism will come to an end as a historical phase. This is such a crisis that it is the leading condition for socialism, the road to socialism will strengthen the class conflict (Burnham, 2002) and pioneer the historical necessity of the socialist revolution. On the contrary, ignoring the destructive effects of crises and assuming that capitalist accumulation progresses unlimitedly, "the most important ideological debate supporting socialist theory collapses; "The ideological basis of socialist action and proletarian class struggle ceases to reflect economic events and socialism ceases to be a historical necessity" (Luxemburg, 2003, p.249). In addition, "Luxemburg took imperialism as an externally determined phenomenon in her model, but applied neither financial capital nor monopoly power to explain the continuous reproduction of capitalism" (Desai, 2000, p.9). In short, the Marxist character of capitalism is that it contains internal contradictions that produce crises. This is one of the main objective reasons for the separation of the terms "crisis" and "fluctuation" in this study: if economic fluctuations are considered as crises, each crisis period will cause a search for signs of socialist historical necessity. However, when we consider the term crisis in its above form, this necessity disappears. In this way, the phenomena of fluctuation and crisis will be discussed as different subjects of analysis from a Marxist perspective.

The terminology used by almost every economic school is tried to be maintained with a certain consistency by those who continue the school. Under the same conditions, an effort to stay away from each other's concepts can be observed among alternative or competing movements. For example, Poulantzas argues that "concepts and ideas are never innocent, and by using his concepts in answering the opponent, one legitimizes them and allows them to continue. "Every idea or concept is meaningful only within the entire theoretical problematic that forms its basis: When it is removed from this problematic and imported "uncritically" into Marxism, it will have absolutely uncontrollable effects" (Poulantzas, 1975). indicates distinctions. This conceptual polarization and the avoidance of different schools from using each other's concepts is clearly evident in the concepts of "crisis" and "fluctuation". In simple words, while the Marxist school avoids the term "fluctuation", mainstream economics also avoids the concept of "crisis". Because the use of the concept of crisis implicitly affirms Marx, the term "fluctuation" is used explanatorily in order to give a concept to non-trend movements in the economy. However, the preference of this study is not to refrain from using any concepts in order to ensure the dialectical functioning of scientific knowledge.

While the term crisis is an economic depressive state that results in a change/ differentiation in the capitalist mode of production, we define the term fluctuation as movements around the long-term trend between actual output and actual demand/ consumption without causing a change in the mode of production. Therefore, while the term crisis includes the term fluctuation - a crisis is a fluctuation that changes the mode of production in addition to the scale size - the term fluctuation does not include crisis. That is, not every fluctuation is a crisis, but every crisis is a fluctuation. Before following the content of these terms, which are the basic propositions of this study, it deals with the generally used terms "crisis" and "fluctuation" and provides the necessary background for comparison. And this distinction is made "despite" Poulantzas' concerns and suggestions above.

In the Marxist view, the main cause and mechanism of economic fluctuations are hidden in the expanded reproduction mechanism. This simplest definition, which can be described as the self-feeding of the system, is also the source of capitalism's contradictions in creating natural fluctuations. "In Mark's own discussions, there is a contrast between his arithmetic examples of expanded reproduction and many of the treatments in his "literary" sections. Arithmetic examples – the "model" of expanding reproduction – are constructed to demonstrate the balanced and continuous growth of two sectors, under rather restrictive assumptions. When we look at the logic behind this balanced growth, many contradictions emerge" (Desai, 2000, p.89). [Deepening these discussions will distract us from our main goals. However, these discussions have been dealt with in depth and in a very impressive way in studies such as Desai (1974), Baran & Sweezy (1966), Mandel (1973), Luxemburg (2003), and Clarke (2001)]. The main reason for these criticisms is that Marx clearly presents a crisis. It is not surprising that he did not put forward a theory, since "the crisis tendency is the peak and, in a sense, the most superficial expression of the historical tendencies of the capitalist mode of production." Therefore, Marx's theory of crisis is presented as part of his broader description of the dynamics of the capitalist mode of production" (Clarke, 2001, p.22). However, second generation Marxists focused on this deficiency, and writers such as Kautsky, Hilferding, Bernstein, Tugan-Baranowsky, Luxemburg focused on crises and fluctuations. The main interest and focus of debate among these writers stems from Engels' explicit rejection of Lassalle's and Dühring's explanations of underconsumption in favor of overproduction in the Second International. For example, Kautsky argues that "the limits of the capitalist system lie in the tendency to overproduction, which is attributed to the fundamental contradiction between the tendency to develop the productive forces indefinitely, on the one hand, and, on the other hand, the tendency to restrict the consuming forces of the mass of the population by forcibly reducing the value of labor power and creating a relative surplus population." However, according to Kautsky, this tendency to chronic overproduction is not a cyclical tendency, as in Engels, but a concrete tendency. The tendency in question leads not to violent explosions but to final extinction" (Clarke, 2001, p.37). Another exemplary analysis comes from Luxemburg. In order for the smooth growth in Marx's two-section expanded reproduction model to continue, international exploitation will have to take place, that is, exploitation will become international (Luxemburg, 2003).

Since capitalism has internal dynamics that create crises, crisis will inevitably arise. However, in a broader sense, world capitalism will also experience crises [fluctuations] in certain periods, and this type of fluctuation is called "Long Waves". This approach was developed by N. Kondratieff. First of all, Kondratieff's analysis "stands on parallel grounds with Marx's analysis of the business cycle – the ordinary boom-bust cycle that is the main feature of capitalism... He takes Marx's view that the average cycle of capitalism is determined by the periodic reinvestment of fixed capital, but to this [he adds the assumption that] there is a change in the length of this cycle, in the period of production, and in the nature of fixed capital investments of different types" (Woods 2016, p.6). Stating that there are fluctuations in capitalism in periods of 7-10 years, but also "short waves" at intervals of 1.5-3 years, Kondratieff said that apart from these, "it is assumed that there are long waves with a length of 50 years" (Kondratieff, 2015, p.13) states that it is necessary.

The fluctuations in the new era capitalist formation defined as "modern capitalism" are now shaped on the effects of previous fluctuations. Moreover, the cores of a depression can be in the previous depression or in the eruption period/phase before it. For example, the crash of 1987 is stated by Clarke to be due to the sensitive base of the 1980 boom and was "based on the devaluation of capital. "The primary effects of the collapse were tried to be overcome by facilitating credit, bailing out banks, and international cooperation to regulate cash markets" (Clarke, 2001, p.87).

Keynes[ian] Business Cycle Theory

Keynes is a "crisis economist" who dealt with crises and fluctuations. In this study, "1. It is one of the most important actors of the 1929 Crisis, which we call "Crisis" and which deeply affected the capitalist system. Therefore, Keynes developed and put forward his theoretical work and views precisely in the practice of imbalances.

One connection between Keynes and Marx in general was "the inability of capitalists to find investment opportunities large enough to offset the increased level of savings generated by economic growth... Keynes's answer to the problem [...] Management can intervene when saving exceeds investment, borrowing the excess savings and then reducing the country's productive capacity." It could be spent on socially beneficial projects that would not increase or diminish future investment opportunities. It is thought that management spending will increase the injections in the spending tendency and create "full employment balance" (Hunt, 2005, p.515). In other words, "overproduction" in Marx is perceived as "underconsumption" in Keynes (Bleaney, 1979, p.179-180). However, while Marx talks about workers who cannot make demands, Keynes attributes the lack of demand to other reasons, the most fundamental reason for which is mostly based on expectations. In Keynes, the general cause of fluctuations is this "underconsumption": a clear imbalance between consumption and saving. Consumption lagged behind savings, and total savings far exceeded investment expenditures and consumption expenditures. Keynes' suggestion to absorb this excessive savings, which he saw as the cause of fluctuations, was public intervention. Therefore, since Keynes and his followers attribute fluctuations to a lack of demand, they approach and interpret fluctuations from the demand side. Accordingly, "in the upswing, aggregate demand begins to increase. It rises rapidly during the expansion phase. Then it starts to slow down and after peaking it may start to drop. In a recession, it falls or remains relatively stagnant. "Keynesians try to explain why aggregate demand fluctuates, and then try to design appropriate stabilization policies to soften these fluctuations" (Sloman, 1999), which shows that the cause of fluctuation in the classics emerges as a result of fluctuations in Keynes. The basic questions that Keynesians seek answers to regarding the fluctuation of aggregate demand are "why does aggregate demand continue to rise (or fall) once it starts to rise (or fall)?" Why does a boom or a recession end? In other words, why does aggregate demand continue to move in one direction but then stop and start moving in the other direction? What determines the length of the stages? Why do some recessions last several years while others last only a few weeks? What determines the size of the stages? Why are some recessions really severe, while others are just a "pause" before rapid growth? (Sloman, 1999).

Keynes, who adheres to the marginal productivity theory that wages are equal to the marginal productivity of the worker (Keynes, 2013), contradicts this assumption in his fluctuation analysis. The main reason for this is to provide the necessary support to governments that want to maintain capitalism. "Keynes rejected the view that if a capitalist economy started from a state of full employment, the interest rate would automatically equalize saving and investment, thus making aggregate demand equal to aggregate supply. His main deviation from the doctrines that constitute the neo-classical theory of spontaneity is twofold: First, although he accepted the neo-classical view that saving is affected by the rate of interest, he insisted that the level of total income has a much more important effect on the amount of savings than the rate of interest. Second, he argued that saving and investment do not determine the rate of interest. The interest rate was a price that equalized supply and demand; It was something completely different from investing and saving. Although Keynes did not realize this, these are very important observations, as they destroy not only the neo-classical theory of market spontaneity, but also two pillars of neo-classical ideology - the theory of marginal efficiency of allocation and the theory that a free, competitive market will result in Pareto optimal resource allocation" (Hunt, 2005, p.509).

Keynes, who gave the title of "classic" to classical economists, "claimed that in his economic model, the motivation of businessmen concentrated on C-C-C', as opposed to the C-C-C' problem in classical economists, and used Marx's realization problem as an analogy" (Moggridge, 1980, p.100) He started to create his General Theory. However, Keynes's greatest luck was that he lived the 1929 experience effectively. Skidelsky mentions two effects of the same experience on Keynes' success in explaining this experience. The first of these is that Keynes lost his faith in monetary policy, and the second is that the state intervenes in the economy to support and encourage new investments in underinvestment conditions (Skidelsky, 2003, p.108-109). One of the most important findings that Keynes observed from his deep experience in 1929 is on cyclical movements. Keynes explains this important observation about cyclical movement in his General Theory as follows: "The process that develops only in upward and downward directions is not a situation that, once started, continues in the same direction and eventually reverses. [by cyclical movement] What we mean is that, in addition to this last mentioned development, there is also a visible degree of regularity regarding the timing and duration of the upward and downward movements" (Keynes, 2013).

Moreover, Keynes states that the phenomenon of crisis is a qualitatively different form of business cycles. A crisis occurs in a cyclical movement where the downward trend replaces the upward trend, often occurring suddenly and harshly. However, as a rule, there is no drastic question at the turning point where the upward trend replaces the downward trend" (Keynes, 2013). In this case, the crisis is a phenomenon called "boom" that occurs at the maximum point of GDP and is a situation that occurs in the form of a sharp and sudden decrease in national income, that is, in investments and in the willingness to implement new investment projects. Although the beginning of the crisis shows that interest rates started to rise with the increase in demand for money for speculative and commercial purposes, the most important and determining factor is the "sudden collapse in the marginal efficiency of capital" and the fact that the liquidity preference does not increase, which makes this collapse uncontrollable. And finally, the beginning of the decline in interest rates will "become the condition for revival" (Keynes, 2013).

Keynes rejected Say's supply-side view, which gave its character to classical economics, and put forward an analysis of the demand side of the economy, arguing that demand would create supply. On this front, the main factor that will drive investments, which can be said as a simple equivalent to the term accumulation, is total demand. Therefore, making sense of accumulation, in Keynesian terms, will be about giving dynamism to investments. As a matter of fact, investment activity is also an expenditure and therefore an item of total demand. For this reason, investments are naturally one of the factors that stimulate total demand. Keynes explains the mechanism that keeps investments alive with the Multiplier-Accelerator model.

Increases in total demand - the investment expenditures of the public sector are also an element of this increase, and the companies created by the public sector are also expenditures in this manner. Therefore, the reversal of this mechanism of privatization, or at least the fact that public investments are no longer made, is an issue worth considering within the Multiplier-Accelerator model of the Keynesian model - its effect on total output and the equilibrium national income level is defined by the term "multiplier". The importance of public investments in this concept also stems from the pre-Keynesian form of the concept. Kahn (1931) defined the multiplier concept based on "the basic idea that if the consumption trend is taken as a given and monetary and other public authorities have decided to stimulate or delay investments, the change in the amount of employment will be a function of the net change in the amount of investment" (Keynes, 2013). In other words, "it is stated that the increase in employment created by public investments made in a stagnant economy that cannot fully utilize the workforce and consumption resources is much higher than the number of workers employed in these investments" (Karakayalı, 2002, p.167). However, Keynes also draws the line between his own multiplier analysis and Khan's acceptance. Accordingly, "[Khan's multiplier definition] gives the total employment increase ratio that occurs with the given increase in initial employment in investing industries, so we denote the multiplier put forward by Kahn with k' and call it the employment multiplier" (Keynes, 2013) and separates it from its own multiplier definition. On the other hand, Warming (1932) argued that "the leaks in the process are not the leaks emphasized by Keynes, but rather arise from the tendency of individuals to save a portion of the income they receive - a subject only touched upon by Kahn - and that the multiplier can be better understood if it is formulated on the basis of income rather than employment." [...] said that if households save 25% of the increase in their income and this is the only leak in the system, the multiplier process will result in an injection of new government spending that creates a fourfold increase in the economy's output" (Laidler, 2016). As a result, for Keynes, the multiplier is that the increase in autonomous public expenditures will increase the level of national income and therefore employment, and will enable us to get out of a period in which the private sector cannot invest because it is worried about profit opportunities and the economy is in stagnation. That is, $\Delta Y = k * \Delta I$ will be where k is the multiplier coefficient;

$$k = \frac{1}{1-c}$$

It is written as and c is equal to the marginal propensity to consume, that is, 1-s. s shows the marginal saving tendency and c+s=1. This set of relations, called the simple multiplier, is based on the effect of autonomous investments on national income. The super multiplier is expanded to show the effect on national income due to the income increase created by the combination of stimulated consumption and investment.

Real Business Cycle Theory

In this approach, which is called new classical economics and includes Chicago University economists with names like Lukas, the tools used to analyze the long term are adapted to analyze short-term fluctuations. As in classical economics, they treat fluctuations not in terms of aggregate demand but as fluctuations around the potential output level of output. The well-known classical assumption of perfect price elasticity forms the basis of these explanations, which is that prices are fully flexible in the short run and prices are determined within the market mechanism. The classical assumption is that the general level of money supply and prices (nominal variables) does not affect the levels of total output and employment (real variables). Fluctuations are explained by real variables, not nominal ones, such as production technologies. The first area of importance of the theory, which focuses on four basic variables, emphasizes that labor supply is the incentives that motivate workers to increase this supply. Accordingly, the financial rewards of workers are a very effective factor on the amount of labor supply, that is, on the willingness of workers to work. On the other hand, workers may also experience substitutable changes in their desire to work from period to period, which is called "inter-period substitution of labor force". The decision to work that can be substituted between periods will be determined by real wages. The worker who compares the real wage in a certain period t with the real wage in period t + 1; He will make a decision by comparing the real wage in period t+1 with the sum of the real wage in period t and the amount of interest he can earn until period t+1. In short; The relative wage between periods will be calculated as (1+r)Wt/Wt+1. For example, a household consumer's supply of labor and demand for goods are the result of an intertemporal choice, not an instantaneous one. So much so that lifetime income and lifetime consumption are considered together with initial wealth. Second, economic fluctuations move in tandem with technological fluctuations, and the level of output interacts directly with data technology. At the given level of technology, total output and real wages increase, and employment increases due to intertemporal labor substitution. Accordingly, when technological development declines, the process reverses and a recession occurs. The third is the assumption of neutrality of money, which is that money, as a nominal variable, is neutral, that is, ineffective, on the level of employment and output, which are real variables, and this assumption is the most radical assumption of the theory. Money only affects other nominal variables. The fourth and final assumption accepts that wages and prices are not sticky (rigid) and are adjusted regularly and very quickly by fluctuations, clearing the markets. Therefore, there is no disruption in the markets. The harshest criticisms of these statements are directed at the assumption that technology is in decline. Technological progress may stop, but it cannot regress. Additionally, the model deals with continuity, not direct fluctuations. Fluctuations can shake economies, but it is a significant setback that they think they do not have permanent effects. In addition, the fact that they made the above choice of working voluntarily (due to low wages) during the recession was generally not accepted and criticized. Criticisms continue that money is not always neutral and that there are data showing that periods of inflation and periods of high unemployment occur at the same time (Begg, Fischer & Dornbusch, 2005, p.550-552: Mankiw, 2015, p.593-603).

REFERENCES

Amable, B. (2003). *The Diversity of Modern Capitalism*. Oxford University Press. 10.1093/019926113X.001.0001

Armack, A. M. (1989). The meaning of social market economy. In Peacock, A., & Wilgerodt, H. (Eds.), *Germany's Social Market Economy: Origins and Evolution* (pp. 82–86). Macmillan. 10.1007/978-1-349-20145-7_6

Baby, J. (1967). *Principes Fondamentaux d'économie Politique*. Fronçois Maspero.

Baran, P. A., & Sweezy, P. (1966). *Monopoly Capital*. Monthly Review Press.

Barry, N. (1974). *Scientific Knowledge and Sociological Theory*. Routledge.

Begg, D., Fisher, S., & Dornbush, R. (2005). *Economics*. Mcgraw-Hill.

Bleaney, M. (1979). *Underconsumption Theories: A History and Critical Analysis*. International Publishers.

Branson, H. W. (1995). *Macroeconomics*. Harpercollins College.

Burnham, P. (2002). Class struggle, state and global circuits of capital. In *M. Rupert, & H. Smith (edt.), Historical Materialism and Globalization* (pp. 113–128). Routledge.

Carchedi, G. (2001). Imperialist contradictions at the threshold of the Third Millennium: A new phase? In Albritton, R., Itoh, M., Westra, R., & Zuege, A. (Eds.), *Phases of Capitalist Development: Booms, Crises and Globalisations* (pp. 215–229). Palgrave. 10.1057/9781403900081_13

Clarke, S. (2001). Class struggle and the global overaccumulation of capital. In Albritton, R., Itoh, M., Westra, R., & Zuege, A. (Eds.), *Phases of Capitalist Development: Booms, Crises and Globalisations* (pp. 76–92). Palgrave. 10.1057/9781403900081_5

Desai, M. (1974). *Marxian Economic Theory*. Gray-Mills Pub.

Fisher, S., & Dornbusch, R. (2001). *Macroeconomics*. Richard d Irwin.

Gough, I. (1979). *The Political Economy of the Welfare State*. Springer. 10.1007/978-1-349-16122-5

Guerrien, B. (1989). *L'economie Neo-Classique*. La Découverte.

Hahnel, R. (2003). *The ABC's of Political Economy: A Modern*. Pluto Press.

Hansen, A. H. (1951). *Business Cycles and National Income*. W. W. Norton & Company.

Hayek, F. A. (2007). *The Road to Serfdom*. University of Chicago Press. 10.7208/chicago/9780226320533.001.0001

Hume, D. (2004). *A Treatise of Human Nature*. Digireds.

Hunt, E. K. (2005). *History of Economic Thought*. Routledge.

Jessop, B. (2003). The Future of the Capitalist State. *Polity*.

Kahn, R. F. (1931). The relation of home investment to unemployment. *Economic Journal (London)*, 41(162), 173–198. 10.2307/2223697

Kant, I. (1784). What is Enlightenment? https://www.nypl.org/sites/default/files/kant_whatisenlightenment.pdf

Karakayalı, H. (2002). *Makro Ekonomi*. Umit Kitabevi.

Keynes, J. M. (2013). *The General Theory of Employment, Interest, and Money*. CreateSpace Independent Publishing Platform.

Kondratieff, N. D. (2015). *The Long Waves in Economic Life*. Ravenio Books.

Laidler, D. (2016). Keynes, John Maynard (New Perspectives), *in* R. Backhouse, B. W. Bateman (edt.). *The New Palgrave Dictionary of Economics*, (1-14), Palgrave.

Lindbeck, A. (1995). Hazardous Welfare State Dynamics. *The American Economic Review*, 85(2), 9–15.

Luxemburg, R. (2003). *The Accumulation of Capital*. Routledge.

Mandel, E. (1973). *An Introduction to Marxist Economic Theory*. Pathfinder.

Mann, M. (1984). The autonomous power of the state: Its origins, mechanisms, and results. *Archives Européennes de Sociologie*, 25(2), 185–213. 10.1017/S0003975600004239

Moggridge, D. E. (1980). *Keynes*. Macmillan.

Münkler, H. (2007). *Empires: The Logic of World Domination from Ancient Rome to the United States*. Polity Press.

O'Neill, J. (1998). *The Market: Ethics, Knowledge and Politics*. Routledge. 10.4324/9780203358467

Poulantzas, N. (1975). *Political Power and Social Classes*. Verso Books.

Ricardo, D. (2004). *The Principles of Political Economy and Taxation*. Dover Publications.

Rosanvallan, P. (2004). *The New Social Question: Rethinking the Welfare State*. Princeton University Press.

Rosier, B. (1991). *Les Theories des Crises Economiques*. Repères.

Samuels, W. J. (1995). The present state of institutional economics. *Cambridge Journal of Economics*, 19(4), 569–590. 10.1093/oxfordjournals.cje.a035331

Samuelson, P. (2010). *Economics*. McGraw-Hill.

Skidelsky, R. (2003). *Keynes*. Penguin Books.

Sloman, J. (1999). *Economics*. Prentice Hall.

Stewart, M. (1972). *Keynes and After*. Penguin.

Ünsal, E. (2007). *İktisadi Büyüme*. İmaj Yayınevi.

Wood, E. M. (1997). *Defence of History: Marxism and the Postmodern Agenda*. Verso.

Wood, E. M. (2016). *The Origin of Capitalism: A Longer View*. Verso.

Chapter 6
Capital Fractions and Public Sector

ABSTRACT

The relationship between individuals in society, driven by economic interests, defines societal character and poses challenges. Economicization views individuals as utilitarian agents within economic frameworks, a duality sparking debate. Proponents say it aligns with human nature and enhances freedom, while critics argue it erodes human essence. Political economy examines the dynamics among economic actors, focusing on the state's role. Historically, state involvement has shifted between central intervention and laissez-faire policies. Recent trends toward market efficiency and privatization highlight a reduced state role, fueling debate over its optimal function. Liberal economics, favoring minimal state interference, emphasizes market mechanisms for efficient resource allocation. Hayek's idea of organic societal structures opposes central planning, arguing that imposed orders disrupt economic balances. The principal-agent relationship reveals tensions in economic governance, especially in public enterprises.

DISCUSSION ON PUBLIC SECTOR ACTIVITIES

The fact that economic benefits and interests are the main determinants of relations between people gives society its character. This is where the whole problem stems from. The economicization of relations between people has led to the positioning of each of them as economic utilitarian agents. This is where the duality emerges; On the one hand, there are those who claim that this is in human nature, and on the other hand, there are those who claim that this destroys the human side of people and that this is a necessary phase that occurs historically. On the one hand, those who argue that man will achieve his "freedom" in this set of relationships; On the other hand, there are those who argue that this is a universal stage in man's attainment of

DOI: 10.4018/979-8-3693-5996-9.ch006

freedom. On the one hand, those who argue that the market is a unique and universal structure for people and that it will provide freedom, on the other hand, argue that the market is an artificial system, not human nature, since it is a mechanism that creates different power sources.

At this point, the concept of political economy/political economy emerges. In other words, it is a field of study that examines the determination of the relations between economic actors, but those who treat the market as a "neutral mechanism" among individual economic relations and those who start from the fact that the "market is imposed" see such an actor that they differ from each other in the behavior of this actor: the State. "After the period when the state was accepted as the central unit as the driving force of development (through planning and centralized distribution of resources, direct intervention in productive activities, regulation of the economy, realization of infrastructure and public services), the view that the state harms the economy only by encouraging the (incomplete) misallocation of resources outweighed. As a result of restrictive fiscal policies and privatization programs, the theoretical/ideological central shift led to a decrease in publicly allocated resources; and a phase was entered in which the role of the state decreased significantly" (Pio, 1983, p.117). However, despite these and similar views, the effectiveness, measure and style of the state in the economic field have a wide area of debate.

On the one hand, it is an actor that acts periodically to expand the functionality of the market and therefore human freedom, and must minimize its effectiveness when necessary. On the other hand, the state is an actor who sees that the market is artificial and tries to keep this artificial alive in favor of a certain class.

Then, the policies of the state are directly aimed at individual freedom. And in any case, it is an actor that restricts the freedom of the individual in a static situation. In this case, state activity should be considered within the framework of "market functioning".

The first use of the concept of Political Economy was to imply state activity in economic life. However, with Marx, the concept began to imply a larger-scale, holistic economic system. Moreover, the history of economic ideas is shaped on two basic axes. The first of these focuses on the individual, while the other focuses on the society.

According to Kuznets, public events consist of two parts. The first of these is the "positive elements that individuals, who are members of the society, purchase in their capacity as consumers" and the second is "a necessary prerequisite for the society to continue its economic activities, that is, it can be considered an intermediate good [...] it can be considered a pre-condition of the gross product rather than a gross product itself". infrastructure investments. At the same time, judicial, administrative, educational, etc. are included in the latter. It also includes public expenditures for specific purposes. The author's observations indicate that a significant portion of government expenditures are "expenses of institutions that actually contribute to the gross product rather than being a net contribution" (Kuznets, 1955).

Liberal Economics

The term liberal economics includes the reflections, perspectives and analyzes of political liberalism in the economic field. While neo-classical economics looks at a world that it designed by staying within the economic field, with a conceptualization and theorization centered on the economic field, liberal economics looks at the economic field with the concepts and theorization of political liberalism. Therefore, the central point of departure is political terms. The main focus of liberal economics is the assumption that state organization, which is considered as the most fundamental obstacle to individual political freedoms, is also the most fundamental obstacle to individual economic activities. While this body of views, conceptualized as the "economic theory of the state", essentially tries to analyze the state, it accepts that the restrictions on the individual, which are seen as a result of the existence of the state, are also valid for the economic activities of individuals. Accordingly, the state is considered as "an apparatus or institution for the production of public goods that should be resorted to only if market transactions do not meet the wishes of individuals" (Barry, 1974, p.74). This integrity does not implicitly or even explicitly accept market failure. However, state moves that appear only as external shocks and disrupt the general balance in the perfect market models in neo-classical economics have become partially internalized in liberal economics.

State activities emerge as a deviation from Pareto Optimality, which is an expression of general equilibrium in neo-classical economics. Simply put, if it is not possible to achieve any improvement in the situation of another individual without worsening the economic situation of another person, the resulting situation is defined as Pareto-Optimality.

Market, "economic theory holds that exchanges between individuals in a free market will provide an efficient or optimal allocation of resources. The decentralized market system allows individuals to maximize their own utility and is the way in which production reflects the desires of consumers. In a free market, individuals who maximize their utility will gain from trade; such that a market is sufficiently efficient to allow all exchange possibilities to be exhausted" (Barry, 1974, p.75).

Liberal economics is a general name that we try to give here to three liberal economic ideas based on liberal political thought. These three parallel views are categorized by the Grosseketts. According to him, all these approaches attempt three main areas of analysis and there are three basic questions they seek answers to: "What good reasons can liberals accept when the principle of subordination is applied to justify moving away from the idea of a society without oppression and therefore without government? To what extent does a liberal want premeditated institutions in addition to spontaneous ones? "Do a liberal believe in self-preserving or self-destructive competition in markets?" Three different liberal clusters emerge in terms of answering these questions. In continuation of the Austrian school, Hayek and his successors answer the questions about the reasonableness of a minimum state, obedience to the law, and the free market economy as the perfect option in the system. The second wing is the "social liberals", which are basically the opposite of Hayek on the basis of liberalism and seem to be used when a central government planning is necessary. In fact, it is seen as the "duty and responsibility" of the government to make regulations under the conditions of market unfavorable conditions. Thirdly, the Ordo-Liberals wing is located somewhere between these two extremes. "They have higher requirements for planning institutions than Hayek's supporters do. On the other hand, however, they want to limit the rights of the government much more strictly than the social liberals intend" (Grossekettler, 2009, pp.5-7: Böhm, Eucken & Dorth, 2009).

In short, the term "liberal economics", on the one hand, forms the intellectual basis of neo-classical economics, and on the other hand, it should sometimes be considered as an attempt to internalize the political field into the economic field and sometimes as an attempt to internalize the economic field into the political field. The term liberal economics injects many concepts, especially the concept of "freedom", which it takes from the political field, into economic theory. Although these initiatives date back to Smith, they have been carried over to the present day in the form of two basic movements, the first of which is Hayek and the second is Buchanan, which focuses more on financial fields.

Hayek, Buchanan and Public Choices

In the liberal economics approach, the public sector economy is considered external to the given market. But these two basic problems further give rise to two fundamental extreme perspectives: the economics-based view of sociality and the non-economic and especially political view of the economy. First of these, economism analyzes social change by taking economic changes as its origin. The second is to consider the changes in the economy through political variables.

More specifically, liberal economics, which is nourished by a liberal political infrastructure, assumes that the concepts in economic theory can be valid not only for actors in the economic field, but also for the behavior of actors in the political field. Therefore, the public choice approach universalizes the pragmatic understanding of the individual in neo-classical economics, especially in the political sphere. "If it is true that individuals behave as rational, self-interested actors in the marketplace, "it must be inferred that they will behave the same way in other, non-market behavioral settings" (Buchanan, 1999, p.22). The field of economic theory understood in this way is very general. In principle, it applies to any social setting, whether politics, family, community or any other organization" (O'Neill, 1998, pp.262-263). In fact, the body of thought that we conceptualize with the term liberal economics can be considered as the whole of attempts to internalize the political field externalized by neo-classical economics with the terms of the economic field. Within the term Liberal Economics, there are views that are fed by mainstream neo-classical economics but try to develop criticisms and regulations outside the framework of radical economics (in other words, political economy or political economy). In short, liberal economics can be considered as the whole of attempts to create a non-Marxist political economy. In other words, they are movements to develop an individual-based political economy instead of class and aim to internalize the public sector and make it internal to the market mechanism.

These initiatives arise from two basic roots, but it is noticeable that there is quite a lot of permeability between both. The first of these is "institutional economics", which is based on pioneers such as Veblen and Mitchell, and the other is the "public preferences" approach, which is based on Hayek and extends to Buchanan. While liberal economics, nourished by political liberalism, deepens the individual interest maximization approach, it is based on the fact that the bureaucrats who form the state organization and the politicians who govern also strive to maximize certain personal interests, and this is the main point where these views unite.

Hayek: On the basis of liberal economics, people have a tendency to think that "things that are consciously designed and planned to achieve some purposes will necessarily be better than those that develop naturally" (Butler, 2001, p.57). He argues that this tendency/tendency emerged to plan, design and direct people, political and economic areas. In fact, according to Butler, "in no field is this tendency more evident than in discussions about economic activity" (Butler, 2001, p.57). Although this perspective of thought goes back to the roots of political liberalism, its strongest advocate and foundation in recent times has been Hayek, and according to Hayek, these regulations are an intervention in the "natural" and have consequences that disrupt the order of the natural. Hayek, who discusses the term "Order", which generally implies "a state of relations", in two forms, introduces the terms "doing-order" and "grown-order". Emphasizing the necessity for every society to have an order, Hayek states that this order will "exist without being created by prior design." However, according to the distinction he makes, "made-order" is a created form of order created by an external effect on the natural structure, which, in terms of political liberalism, is a restriction of freedoms and an authoritarian form of order. On the other hand, the term "grown-order" refers to "self-generating or internal order". Hayek uses two terms from Ancient Greek for these two forms of order: the term "taxis" for artificial order, and the term cosmos, meaning "a correct order in a state or society" for enlarged order. Although Taxis serves or has served the interests of its designer now or in the past, the cosmos, that is, the self-grown order, does not have such a purpose. Finally, Hayek builds his main thesis on this distinction: "Very complex orders, encompassing a much larger amount of facts than any single mind can investigate or manipulate, can only be produced by forces that encourage the formation of spontaneous orders [the cosmos]" and "Since it is not created by a unit, such an order has no purpose, although its existence may be very useful to individuals acting within its framework", which is the spontaneous order "Market" (Hayek, 2022).

Actors in the market must demonstrate free mobility and adhere to the principle of free action. In this way, the economic sphere will organize itself and provide a spontaneous order. Hazlitt distinguishes these forms of organization in sharper terms as follows: "There are only two ways of organizing economic life. In the first, voluntary choice and voluntary cooperation of families and individuals organize economic life. This arrangement is called the free market. In the other, a dictator's orders do it. This is called command economy. The extreme form of the command economy, that is, the system in which an organized state retains ownership of the means of production, is called socialism or communism. Economic life is basically organized through one or the other of these systems" (Hazlitt, 2010, p.11).

Stating that Mises was inspired by how the economy becomes dysfunctional if it is planned, Hayek also emphasizes the moral foundations of this regulation that market actors will create spontaneously. This moral justification is the preservation of the functionality of the price mechanism. Hayek offers two options and defines his view with the following sentences: "Either you will set limits for yourself to create an institutional structure that will make this price system work as effectively as possible, or you will fight to disrupt its function. If it is true that prices are signals that will adapt our activities to unknown events and demands, there is no point in believing that we can control prices. You cannot develop a sign if you do not know what it indicates. It is not inconsistent to think that the price system does not take into account all the things we would want taken into account, even in a perfectly competitive market theory. However, if we cannot improve the system by directly intervening in prices, we must feed the market with information with new methods that have not been considered before" (Hayek, 2005, p.141-142).

The necessity of institutional structuring that will ensure and protect the price formations that will constitute data for the market is carried to the level of "financial constitution" by Buchanan in its advanced stage. However, the essence of Buchanan's approach also differs from Hayek. While Hayek focuses on social order, Buchanan focuses more on the financial sphere, and more specifically on the legal determinations of the financial and economic sphere.

Buchanan: The essence of Buchanan's thought is an economic view that he conceptualizes as Catallaxy, which implies a field of perfect exchange, but also includes political decision-making processes, that is, treats the political field as a field of exchange. In general, it tries to make an analysis that does not exclude the idealization of "pure" acquisition without intervention and therefore the political decision-making process. However, its analysis presents a unity that conceptualizes the economic field from the political field, rather than being a set of views looking at the political field from the economic field. The main reason for this is that, in his words, "under no circumstances in idealized perfect competition is there any definition or situation in which one force or one person is superior to another. In places and situations in the world where the encounter between the buyer of every good and service and its seller is costless, and where the encounter between the seller of every good and service and its buyer is costless, one has no power over the other. In such an environment, "economic power" becomes completely meaningless and contentless" (Buchanan, 2001). The solution to this "meaningless and contentless" situation will be possible by including "power" differences and therefore "power" relations into economic relations. However, Buchanan does not propose "to dwell on the many institutional differences in which both exchange and power elements coexist." Instead, he proposes that "the reason for making the largely categorical distinction is to suggest that, from an economic perspective, catallaxy is a natural extension of institutional formations within which individuals interact collectively, and that this is one aspect of looking at policy and governmental operations." Ultimately, "the public choice view is the view that makes model politics the last in the exchange paradigm" (Buchanan, 2001).

The term "catallaxy", which Hayek brought back from Ancient Greece, directly refers to exchange transactions, trade, agreements and contracts. In Buchanan's thought, this term goes beyond simple interplay and turns into an "analysis complex". "What is wanted to be defined by complex exchange is; He expands the term from Hayek by pointing out that "two, the magic number of economists, is a method of contractual agreement beyond the simple two persons and two goods to be exchanged" and directs his attention to the methods and transactions of these agreements. In this way, political science can be looked at through the principles, institutions and methods of complex exchange, and as a result, catallaxy can become a unifying method of analysis and perspective, without leaving a categorical difference between economics, political science and politics. From such a catallaxy perspective, privatization can be considered as a form of exchange between politicians and capital.

Public Choice: As mentioned above, the public preferences or public preferences approach of liberal economics combines the political and economic fields on the basis of "the individual who wants to maximize his interests" and universalizes this characteristic individual. In short, "public choice can be defined as the economic analysis of nonmarket decision-making or simply the application of economics to political science" (Mueller, 1979, p. 1). And so "the standard story in neo-classical economics is that state intervention is justified when it solves the problems of "market failures" that occur when genuine markets diverge from "ideal markets" (O'Neill, 1998, p.263). In other words, the public preferences approach to explain deviations from the Pareto optimum suggests that mainstream neo-classical economics sees bureaucrats and politicians as serving the "best" theory and are not "patriotic" characters, on the contrary, "the axioms that define the rational actor in neo-classical theory are bureaucrats and politicians". It also presupposes that politicians cease to be relevant behind closed office doors" (O'Neill, 1998, p.263). Accordingly, while politicians will build their actions in the economic field on winning new elections, bureaucrats will act with actions and thoughts in the economic field with the motivation of expanding their authority and budget areas. "According to Nisanken (1975), bureaucrats pursue their own interests and want to maximize their own benefits. The primary determinant of this situation is the size of the bureaucracy and the (discretionary) budgets under their control. This means that the more monopoly power the bureaucracy or government has, the more likely they are to spend more than necessary" (Bayliss, 2006). Of course, with such a bureaucratic and therefore management approach, it will be inevitable for public companies to become inefficient and ineffective management and market disruptors. In fact, this is exactly one of the mainstays of neo-classical and liberal economics, especially those in favor of privatization.

This perspective examines politician behavior in three main categories: "the behavior of representatives both at work and during their election campaigns to be elected; voters' behavior in electing representatives and the characteristics of representative democracy. Representatives, like voters, are assumed to be rational economic people who maximize their own utility" (Mueller, 1979, p.13). In fact, the constitutional economics perspective emerges from this very point, on the basis of being able to control the behavior of politicians.

However, it should be known that many economists who deal with the economic field on the basis of economic theory express the opinion that a theoretical relationship between politician behavior and election results does not yield consistent results. Because it is claimed that it emerged as a theory of political cyclical fluctuations and turned into a reductionism specific to elections and voter behavior aimed at explaining conjuncture movements. (e.g., Begg, Fischer, & Dornbusch, 2005, p.548). It is criticized that voters are not as narrow in their views as the model predicts, especially in perceiving the expansionary and contractionary policies put forward in the voter-politician and election trilogy.

Principal-Agent Relationship/Contradiction

In the theory of the firm, since the firm is motivated by an irresistible profit goal, the organizational structure of the firm is created and controlled in accordance with this purpose. First of all, for a simple company, there is the direct company/property/business owner on one side and a whole workforce on the other side, while as the company scale expands, the organizational structure also becomes more complex. There are many layers between the owner and employee duo in the basic company structure. Therefore, the simple boss-employee combination also starts to get complicated. As a matter of fact, in expanding company structures, although primarily senior management staff, many more layers emerge. Although these layers do not participate in the production of surplus value, that is, the product/service, like the employees directly involved in the production process, they carry out activities in many areas such as management and supervision of a large number of employees, and development of new plans and projects.

In the individual interest maximization model of liberal economics, it is claimed that employees can be motivated to serve the company's purpose by being subjected to strict control by the principal. However, when "proxies" as intermediate layers come into play, the situation becomes a little different. Principals are the company owners and agents are the management staff of the business. Principals must ensure that their agents act in accordance with their interests. The main condition for achieving this is the personal qualities of these senior executive deputies as well as the high wage levels offered to these deputies.

The basic assumption of liberal economics in the principal-agent relationship is that the managerial class, that is, the agents, in private companies is sufficiently concentrated for the purpose of business, and this concentration is necessary for the functioning of the market. That is, "business performance is monitored by shareholders and controlled through market incentives and competition. Stock options, which give managers a certain ownership chance in the companies they manage, also strengthen the motivation for high performance. Moreover, liquidity in capital markets allows shareholders to punish underperforming companies by selling their shares. "The threat of selling shares of unsuccessful companies serves to discipline company managers" (Chang & Grabel, 2005, p.114). However, in this table, there is an assumption that managers buy shares of the companies they manage. However, it cannot be known in advance that any manager will definitely buy the shares of the company he manages with his own savings. Criticizing this approach and an in-depth analysis of the behavior of the ruling class is beyond the scope of our study. However, while liberal economics treats the principal-agent relationship as a form of compatibility in the private sector, this relationship turns into a contradiction in the public sector, and this contradiction is treated as a theoretical basis for privatization.

When these relations are examined from a class perspective, it is observed that capitalism produces new forms in intra-company organization within the periodic stages of self-reproduction. "Fundamentally, empowering others in management has led to significant polarization, separating administrative work from other routine practices in the company. This distinction, whose precise boundaries are very difficult to draw, is based on the difference between the managerial staff and the workers [...] it is necessary to see the change not as a simple technical division of labor, but as the formation of class relations by the managerial staff that will determine the new ruling class in the future" (Dumenil & Levy, 2009, p.122-123). As a practical result of this separation, a new layer has emerged that is at least as concentrated on the profit motive as the owner of the company, defined as the capitalist. However, while the capitalist directly concentrates on the profit goal for his own accumulation, this new ruling class pursues this goal on behalf of the capitalist. The fact that the proxies undertake profit on behalf of the capitalist has brought about a formality from capitalist management to managerial capitalism.

However, in public economic enterprises, the situation emerges in a very different structure from the very beginning. Because the principal-agent-employee parties in companies are clearly evident due to private property ownership. However, in public companies, "the agents are typically the managers and executives of the business, and the principal is either the government or the shareholders" (Bayliss, 2006). However, the relationship should not be treated so superficially. As a matter of fact, since public economic enterprises are created with the taxes of the society, the property owners, that is, the nobles, are directly the public, that is, the people. The elected government is the representative of the nobles. On the other hand, managers, that is, bureaucrats, are the representatives of the representatives. In other words, while there is a "relationship" between a principal and an agent in the private sector, this situation becomes a "contradiction" in public companies, which is discussed in the third section.

Radical (Marxist) Economics

In general, liberal economics is based on basic assumptions such as the maximization of individual interests, the exclusion of public interventions, that is, non-economic intervention, and an economy that can operate mechanically with defined variables. However, Marxist economics is based on a historical social formation that it defines as "capitalism" and examining this social formation in the context of economic relations. Among all the economic ideas mentioned here, whose basic views on public activities are tried to be discussed, Marxist economics exhibits the most different and therefore "radical" approach, considering that other views can somehow be linked organically and inorganically to the public sector.

The term "radical" is/can be used to describe Marxist economics as the most important branch against Mainstream Economics. The source for this is the "liberal-radical economics" distinction that Hahnel frequently uses. In making this distinction, Hahnel acts on the basis of three different "rule" suggestions that emerge in ensuring economic justice. According to him, Conservatives "pay according to the value of a person's personal contribution and the contribution of the productive goods that person owns: The rationale behind the Conservative rule is that people should receive from the economy as much as they and their productive wealth contribute to it… [Liberals, on the other hand,] pay only according to the value of one's personal contribution." payment according to value: While supporters of the liberal rule find that most property income is unjustifiable, its defenders argue that everyone has the right to enjoy the "fruits of one's own labor"… [Radical economics, on the other hand,] payment according to effort or personal sacrifice: […] Differences in contribution, Even though it may be due to differences in talent, education, work done, luck and effort, the only factor that deserves the additional price is the additional effort. By "effort" is meant personal sacrifice for the sake of social enterprise" (Hahnel, 2003, p.46-55). In this state, a departure from both the orthodoxy and heterodoxy of Mainstream economics is mentioned, with a socially focused economic thinking characteristic rather than individual-centered.

A broad theory of the state is presented within the "bourgeois society" defined and explained by Marx, and subsequently within the "capitalist society" defined by Marxists, with a key role in the continuity of this social formation. However, "Marx postponed writing a theory of the state, as he did about social classes; This theory is present in a scattered form in his and Engels' writings" (Durand, 2018, pp.77-78). On the other hand, state discussions are almost the most controversial issue within the Marxist movement. However, in general, in Marxist economics, the state is at the most important point, which is often considered "relatively autonomous" from the economic field and yet is within the reproduction mechanism of the capitalist social system. First of all, while, on the one hand, there are theses that the influence and power of the "nation-state" view as the current form of the state is gradually disappearing and that globalization has created a "global capitalism", on the other hand, it is not possible to reduce the influence of "nation-states". There are theses that are far from each other, such as "the nation-state, in both its imperial and neo-colonial forms, has increased and expanded its activities" (Petras, 2002). Especially in the process of capitalistization, "whether growth and industrial transformation are state-led or natural results of market forces is one of the most prominent disputes" (Burkett & Hart-Landsberg, 2000).

In this state, in Marxist economics, the public sector, or more specifically the "state", is an arena of struggle for social classes. In this simplest definition, the state is in a mutual relationship with classes to ensure the continuity of the class structure that forms the character of the capitalist social order, and to protect the interests of the capitalist class. "They are nothing but the forms of organization that the bourgeoisie are forced to adopt for both internal and external purposes and for the mutual guarantee of their property and interests [...] therefore all common institutions are established with the help of the state and acquire a political form" (Marx, 2016, p.85-86). However, although Marx's view of the state is much more complex, the subject is not detailed in order not to go beyond the boundaries of this study.

The state has a dual function and the first of these is to ensure the continuity of the capitalist section in class society, while the second basic function is "national states because capitalism (as a global system) requires national organization to secure the internationalization of its production relations" (Corrigan, Ramsay & Sayer, 1980, p.208). Thus, the state is defined as a structure focused on the continuity of capitalism both domestically and globally. In fact, when states try to create obstacles in any way during this internationalization process, they are prevented from creating these problems themselves (Corm, 2013, p.23-24).

Radical economics carries out its analysis from this perspective about different state models brought to the agenda by mainstream economics or different approaches (for example, state interventionism, social state, welfare state, etc.) and makes such historical definitions oriented towards the continuity of capitalism, that is; He analyzes how capitalism, as a dynamic system, transforms the state in its own way.

The state is often defined as the "capitalist state" as a structure that moves together with capitalism and, moreover, adapts to the movement of capitalism. The capitalist state is based on the separation of politics and economics as different forms of social relations. This is what gives the capitalist state its distinctive feature. The separation in question is not the separation of the political from a pre-given economic field; It is about the establishment of the separation of the economic and the political through the disintegration of the capital relationship [...] through this disintegration, the integrated class relations specific to pre-capitalist societies are dispersed/disrupted." In other words, although capitalism divides society into classes, these classes are mutually interdependent and in relationship. (Holloway, 2003, p.424-425).

Radical economics sees the public sector/state as a part of a social order and considers the economic policies it implements within the framework of the degree of harmony with the integrity it is in. Therefore, economic policies are not considered as practices that can be considered individually, with certain results expected, but as different practices aimed at a single result, and that single result is the continuity of the capitalist social system.

For example, privatization, which can be defined as an economic policy, is more than an economic policy, it is about supporting a market-driven transition to the new economic and social regime of neo-liberalism. Privatization for the public sector requires liberalization and liberalization, a new legal and political environment and the imposition of commercial standards in the residual state sector, and passive support for market solutions in the private sector" (Jessop, 2013, p.385). Therefore, the main purpose of privatization or liberalization in general is an attempt to adapt to the constantly renewing economic and social system.

As a matter of fact, the state, that is, the public sector, is not considered as data and singularly. The state is the guarantee of a system in terms of its policies and is "a system of states, the form taken by the capitalist state is the nation-state form. Therefore, any argument regarding the capitalist state form must take into account the state both as an instrument of class domination and as an apparatus of competition between various segments of the bourgeoisie" (Barker, 2004, p. 249), and as such, it is also a tool for conflicts between capital fractions. The state again appears as a source of reconciliation. In this role, it is a mechanism that contributes to the continuity of accumulation.

In summary, economic policies, 1- to keep together the classes within the social system that are separated by the capitalist system and to guarantee the interests of the capitalist class while doing this; 2- In the process of internationalization of capitalism, it is seen as providing liberalization policies to guarantee the process.

Therefore, the capitalist state provides a "reproduction" mechanism. "The capitalist form of social reproduction has become generalized as the dominant form [...] capitalist social reproduction is social reproduction inverted: private production within a social context" (Bonefeld, 1992). Since the sociality of private production is not a matter of conscious decision by society, and the latter exists only in the inverted form of private fragmentation (the production of goods), the sociality of private production exists in the conditions of existence as private individuals within a social context.

In periods when capitalism enters into crisis and, as a result, restructuring, the position of the state is seen as one of the active elements and plays "a vital role in the continuity and reproduction of capital as a relationship of class domination" and "the historically determining form in society is the form drawn by the core relationship of class struggle" (Holloway & Picciotto, 2004, p.135-137).

However, the "relative autonomy" of the state is also emphasized and it is taken into account that the state is not a capitalist institution subject to capital, but "an institution that exists in all class societies, albeit in different forms." "Arguments that see the centrality of the state as a fundamental autonomy are based on the following three claims: a) the state represents the general interests of capital against the particular interests of particular capitals; b) the state is based on the abstraction of force from existing relations of production; c) the state is based on the abstract nature of the commodity form" (Clarke, 1991, p.225-228). Therefore, it is a structure suitable for the general capital form. And as a result, crises or fluctuations that may occur in the continuity of this general form affect the position of the state. For example, with the crisis that emerged in the 1970s, "the crisis experienced by Keynesianism, the disappearance of the welfare state, the emergence of strong tendencies towards re-privatization and the abandonment of demands for social equality" (Hirsch, 2004, p.188) can be seen as a form of this change in form.

In the context of this study, at the level of reproduction, that is, ensuring the continuity of the capitalist system, the state constantly keeps its position, position and policies dynamic in reshaping itself within certain historical stages. In line with the basic propositions, the state can base itself on "outward-closed" accumulation at a certain stage, and then turn to "outward-open" accumulation. Similarly, while an economic policy is carried out to create economic institutions based on public ownership in a period, the privatization of these institutions can later become the basic policy of the state. Again, a state that is effective on the markets aims to restrict this activity after a certain stage, but it still takes part in the markets with the "market regulatory institutions" it has created, and can only do this by transforming the active form of intervention.

Institutional Economics

Another important movement that opposes mainstream liberal economics but also brings a critical perspective to Marxist radical economics is the Institutional Economics approach. This approach, which is mostly filtered through mainstream theory and nourished by its terminology, strives to bring critical originality to many concepts and, frankly, aims to present a theoretical approach that includes the "real", that is, normative elements, while criticizing the micro theories and smoothness of mainstream economics. The main points that differentiate it from mainstream liberal economics can be listed as the perspective on the market, the position of public authority and methodological differences.

In general, "Institutional economics has at least three aspects: Institutional economics is a body of knowledge, an approach to problem solving, and a protest movement. Institutional economists criticize both orthodox neo-classical economics and radical Marxist economics and develop their own ideas in a positive way [...] Institutional economists argue that (a) economics encompasses more than the market and (b) the functional allocation mechanism has nothing to do with They argue that there is not a pure conceptual market but institutions or power structures that are shaped and operated through the real market... Although the institutional economics approach generally provides large-scale policy variables that are used in a less mechanical way, institutional economists can at least make their own analysis of policy issues in a way that is appropriate to them. "They are not very different from other economists who partly guide their work." (Samuels, 1995).

Although the reality that there is a situation of "uncertainty" is accepted in the method of institutional economics, it emphasizes "a radical determination on the limits of predicting the real future instead of predicting within the framework of a model" (Samuels, 1995) in order to eliminate this uncertainty and In this context, institutions are defined as "a guide to human interaction that reduces uncertainty by setting rules for daily life" (North, 1990, p.1).

Institutions are also structures that regulate economic relations and regulate the market mechanism, which mainstream institutional economics does not care about, and eliminate uncertainties. These institutions "determine to a large extent which people are able to achieve their personal goals and realize core values [...] they also influence the values on which people base themselves and the goals they pursue [...] so that the relationships between an individual and others within the community It reflects their subjective meaning and that their acceptance and enforcement are based precisely on the cultural ideas that society wants [...] Institutional economies, therefore, emphasize the need to analyze strictly human values" (Kasper & Streit, 1997, pp.27-28).

With this structure, it is possible to see institutional economics as an attempt to provide a meaningful definition/explanation of the public sector effect in eliminating market failures, without departing from liberal thought but from mainstream orthodox economics. Therefore, it can be said that it is an attempt to make public sector activity meaningful through institutional structures. In other words, it is an intellectual movement that accepts that market disruptions are "real" and aims to stabilize the continuity of the general economic order through regulations to be introduced through institutions, so as not to disrupt the functioning of the market mechanism, even if it disrupts the orthodoxy at the core of the market mechanism.

In general, it is envisaged that the effects of the public sector on the economy will be carried out by institutions limited and determined by law, in which political influences are reduced as much as possible. This is basically aimed at eliminating uncertainties and providing "trust" and "information" to market players. From this perspective, a parallelism can be observed with the idea of constitutional economics. As a matter of fact, Buchanan, who criticizes the use of mathematical models in explaining market failure, actually accepts it as one of the most fundamental factors affecting this failure and keeps it on his agenda that analyzes should be carried out "assuming that institutional limitations are completely unrelated to the people in the market" (Buchanan, 1999).

Institutional economics "emphasizes the inevitable presence of normative elements in economic theory—particularly those related to the state's practices in questioning its economic role and policy, and particularly those related to the social status quo." Accordingly, "the fundamental economic problem is the organization and control of the economy, that is, the reform of the power structure [...] the economy as a whole and the corporations in relation to legal rights, property, contract and power" (Samuels, 1995) is being examined.

As a result, institutional economics recommends the creation of a set of relations with certain rules between the public sector and markets. "At the appropriate time, the central government should establish the general rules of the game; players must choose their base class; should make arrangements to increase the source of information; For example, the details of institutional arrangements aimed at reducing the cost of collecting information from abroad by facilitating international cooperation should be revealed by trial and error among people involved in the relevant activity (Ostrom, 1990, narrated by Eggertsson, 1990, pp.665-671).

It should be noted that institutional economics, as a derivative of liberal economics, can easily be seen as an attempt to seek a suitable and harmonious position for the state in the functioning of the capitalist system, just as mentioned for Keynes. However, the most important point where it differs from mainstream liberal economics is the way institutions are perceived. Institutionalists would not have said anything new if, as in mainstream economic theory, they had considered constraints as elements that only produce ineffective results. Many [institutional economics] theorists actually say that institutions exist simply because they increase efficiency, even if they commit functional errors in doing so. But by using the discourse of "constraints," they perpetuate the myth that the free market is the natural order and argue that institutions are man-made substitute options that should be put in place only when the natural order is disrupted" (Chang & Evans, 2009, p.622). In other words, public sector activities that exclude institutional/public structures and are assumed to restrict the functionality of the market economy, which is constantly discussed in terms of being normative and/or theoretical, are included in the model; They are included in a new way as "institutions that can be operated properly and to the extent necessary"

Political Economics

In the context of this study, the term political economy carries a "critical" identity, apart from all the discussions on the term. While the forms of the term in different derivatives of mainstream economics are seen as "oversimplifying" and "detached from its historical roots", in Radical economics, it is not seen as suitable for a clear acceptance as it contains "necessary consequences". Therefore, this is the main reason for defining this study as a "political economy" study: Political economy deals with the dynamic economic analysis of a dynamic society with a wide range of interests.

Already in 1755, the term "political economy" was defined by Rousseau as follows. "[Economy] means the handling of household chores in accordance with reason and certain rules, for the common good of the whole family. The meaning of this term was later extended to include the management of the largest family, that is, the State. To distinguish between these two meanings, in the second case it is called general or political economy, in the other case it is called private economy or domestic economy" [emphasis added by the author] (Rousseau, 2006, p.7). This first period definition implies the management of certain material/financial conditions by the state within a certain community/society as a form of "togetherness" and/or "consensus" for this society. A primary meaning that needs to be drawn from here and a general meaning that can be extended; It is the effectiveness of the "consensus" that emerged as the "state" in ensuring this in the use and/or sharing of certain material conditions. However, this activity does not necessarily require focusing on state activity; the main point is that there are "material conditions that need to be agreed upon" and that there is no "balance of power" in sharing this. This means that there is an area of conflict, contention and polemic in the sharing of material conditions and there are power imbalances between the parties. In this state, as can be understood from the most primitive definition of the term, political economy involves the question of "who" and there is an imbalance of power between the parties that needs to be addressed.

Asking the "who" question also shapes the definitions of international political/political economy, and international political economy takes its principles from the term itself, that is, political economy. Accordingly, just as international political economy tries to find an answer to a classic question: Who wins, what, when and how? In researching the answer to this question, it constitutes the field of political economy as a social science that is fundamentally interdisciplinary and even supra-disciplinary, centers on economic development and aims to combine disciplines such as philosophy, sociology, history, anthropology and even psychology.

However, the term seems to be a term that has become obsolete and has become obsolete. Although the term is frequently used among radical economists, it is used with necessary consequences, as will be noted below. Liberal economics and its derivatives deal with the term rather superficially, mostly in the context of the politics-economy relationship.

For example, Lange's (2015) work "Political Economy" contains necessary consequences in terms of its content. As another example, Baby's work "Basic Principles of Political Economy" contains similar necessary conclusions, but in general, the social and historical meanings that these authors attribute to the term carry a content burden that cannot be ignored due to the meanings in which they use the term. The term Baby means "for scientific political economy, the basis of social connections, relations established between people for the purpose of production; in other words, it is the relations of production [...] it studies the economic activity of individuals, not as an activity in isolation, but always as subordinate to the relations of production. He defines it as "a person who is alone, apart from the community, is not a real person" (Baby, 1967, p.5-6). This definition expands the term political economy into a social scientific economy by bringing together many concepts such as "human", "society", "production" and "relationship".

The liberal perception of economics almost completely excludes sociology and therefore the dynamic and historical character of society from the term political economy. Definitions of the term within the mainstream can generally be summarized as follows: 1) by establishing mostly statistical relationships between voter behavior and its economic causes and consequences, or 2) It is treated as a finished and closed perspective.

Within the framework of this study, political economy covers a content that aims to analyze the economic dynamics of a society in the process of social development, together with the social qualities of the society, within the historical process. Thus, it creates a critical field that can ask the question "who" about economic events. Thus, the definition of political economy within the framework of this study; It makes it reasonable and necessary to base the historical, social and economic content of the perspective on economic phenomena in general and public sector activities in particular on certain philosophical and intellectual foundations.

CAPITAL FRACTIONS AND FRACTION CIRCUIT

The main issue that was tried to be shown in the previous sections was the essential characteristics of the accumulation process and the ways in which the breaks that may occur in this process are perceived and explained. The point that will be tried to be put forward here is to define the capital fractions and discuss the positions of these fractions within the general economy regarding the accumulation process. Then, by trying to determine the activity (Sovereignty and Hegemony) transformations of different fractions of the capital, especially in business cycles, it puts forward propositions on the role of the public sector in this activity. In this way, the effects of public sector capital fractions on efficiency transformation and business cycles will be tried to be associated with each other. The final proposition to be reached is whether the public sector is active in the transformation of capital fractions in business cycles, whether privatization is a form of this activity, and if so, how this activity progresses and to what extent it has the power to support capital fractions in establishing dominance or hegemony. . This study focuses on the assumption that there are three main sectors and therefore three main capital fractions in the economy; Industrial sector, Commercial sector and Financial sector: and analysis by creating a language through the conceptualization of these sectors as industrial (productive) capital, commercial (merchant) capital and financial (money) capital as indicators and capacities of their business volumes and effectiveness as economic-political actors. is being attempted. In addition to the fact that these fractions are highly dependent and dependent on each other, both organically and inorganically, financial capital has become remarkably specialized since the twentieth century, in terms of engaging in "maverick" movements, as Hilferding (1995, p.47) puts it. The type of fluctuation created by financial capital, which has become more evident in recent times and is called "financial crises", has emerged from the competitive conditions of capitalism and led to monopolization, that is, monopolization.

This means that, in general, a country's economy can characteristically rise if one of these three main sectors is stronger and more effective than the others. For example, the weight of the industrial capital of the German economy, the service/ merchant capital of the Dubai economy, and the financial capital of the British or Swiss economies can be seen at first glance.

Hegemony, Domination and Gramsci

The critical and key concepts at this stage of the study are the concepts of "Hegemony" and, accordingly, "Domination". The concept of hegemony began to be used extensively in the social science literature, with its framework determined by Gramsci. In fact, although the concept was not developed entirely by Gramsci, it is a concept that takes its current usage and intellectual load from Gramsci. Just as we define the term "politics" in this study as the ability of actors to take infinite positions in a movement/action space, in Hobsbawm's inference for Gramsci, politics for humans is "the central human activity; It is the means by which the unique consciousness is brought into contact with the social and natural world in all its aspects" (Hobsbawm, 1982, p.23 as cited in Carnoy, 2014, p.252). In other words, for humans, politics is a way of interacting with nature and society. Especially in the face of society and the individuals within it constantly developing positions, attitudes, ideas and policies, human beings are integrated into social vitality as a dynamic element by determining their own unique position and policy.

There is the concept of state that Gramsci used at the critical point of the intellectual process in which he developed the concept of hegemony. The first characteristic of the term "State thought" that he tries to develop "requires 'continuity' with both the past or tradition and the future, that is, every movement is a phase of a complex process that has already begun and will continue" (Gramsci, 2011, p.233).) requires.

A state that will ensure this continuity is "the complex totality of practical and theoretical activities through which the ruling class can not only justify and protect its rule, but also gain the effective consent of those it keeps under its rule" (Quoted in Gramsci, 1971, p.244; Carnoy, 2014, p.253). This consent, which is produced theoretically and practically and ensures the continuity of the state, is embodied in the concept of "hegemony". It deals with the terms "hegemony" and "historical bloc", which are among Gramsci's key concepts, and the "capitalist system" primarily in the national context. On the other hand, some Marxist writers state that capitalism is today evolving towards a transnational stage, differentiating from the national capitalist or imperialist capitalist system emphasized by classical Marxists. These authors [e.g. Robert Cox] analyze Gramsci's theses such as hegemony and historical bloc formation on a "world scale" (Gill & Law, 1988, p.64-65) and analyze them at a global level.

The concept of hegemony was used in many ways before Gramsci. Gramsci, who developed the concept of hegemony, which is often used with meanings such as "sovereignty", "superiority", "oppression", "domination", was influenced by many of these usages. After the Bolshevik "revolution" it became relatively unused in the Bolshevik party – for understandable reasons. Since its raison d'être was the issue of the role of the working class in the bourgeois revolution, it lost its functionality with the development of the socialist revolution." According to Anderson, the concept was clearly defined "for the first time" in 1922 and was addressed as "the dominance of the bourgeoisie over the proletariat, the bourgeoisie's ability to persuade the proletariat to distinguish between political and economic struggles, thus limiting it to a guild role" (Anderson, 2017, pp.31-35). The concept, which expanded to include the verbs "persuasion" and "interest", took its final form in Gramsci and; "The idea of hegemony requires taking into account the interests and tendencies of the segments to which hegemony will be exercised and establishing a certain balance of compromise; that is, the leading group must make sacrifices of the economic-corporate kind. However, there is no doubt that hegemony must be economic as well as moral and political. Because it must be based on the decisive work carried out by the leading group mainly in the decisive sectors of economic activity" (Gramsci, 1971, p.161 as cited in Anderson, 2017).

In Gramsci's phase, the concept implies "a unity in conflict". It is a type of sovereignty that, in order to maintain the existence of a dominant sovereign, will also take into account the interests of other elements that need to continue their existence, and is based on their consent and persuasion to "be governed and dominated".

Economic Hegemony/Domination and Fractions

However, at this point it is necessary to refer to Jessop's concepts. As a matter of fact, he argues that the validity of the growth model that defines the accumulation strategy depends on the relations between capital fractions. According to Jessop; An "accumulation strategy" defines a specific economic "growth model" complete with its various extra-economic prerequisites and draws a general strategy line suitable for its realization. "For such a model to be successful, it must unite different moments of capital circulation under the hegemony of a fraction" (Jessop, 1982, p.266). In the creation of this hegemony, within a certain conjuncture period, the state privatizes the institutions it has chosen to be suitable for the creation of this hegemony. At the stage when different fractions contribute to the continuity of the general process of accumulation by establishing hegemony in different periods, the state supports these fractions directly and indirectly, and this support appears in the form of privatization of institutions suitable for that fraction.

The heart of capital circulation is the production process itself. In popular parlance, wealth must be created before it is distributed. This means that the performance of productive capital is the ultimate economic determinant in the accumulation process, and the real rates of return on money capital and merchant capital as a whole depend on the continued price determination of long-term productive capital. (Jessop, 2003, p.267).

Jessop, who distinguishes the terms "economic hegemony" and "economic dominance" at a later stage, defines the concept of economic hegemony as "economic leadership gained through the general acceptance of an accumulation strategy". This strategy ensures that the long-term interests of the money capital are secured by controlling the allocation of money capital towards different investment areas that are advantageous for the dominant faction itself (in which areas both state and private banks have given loans), while at the same time integrating the capital circulation and other investment areas within this circulation. it expands the immediate interests of the factions" (Jessop, 2003, p.267). Economic domination, on the other hand, "can be established by any faction. And this faction can impose its own interests." The main difference between the two concepts is that, while Economic hegemony is incompatible with the continuous integration of social capital, Economic Hegemony is achieved by the integration of circulation and the continuous expansion of industrial capital even under the hegemony of a non-industrial fraction.

Capital Fractions

As mentioned above, three basic capital fractions are identified: financial capital, merchant capital and industrial capital. These fractions can take over the leadership at certain times within the framework of economic hegemony and act as the helm of the accumulation strategy. However, it should not be forgotten that the heart of capital cycle and accumulation is productive industrial capital. It should be noted that structural adjustment programs, as a form of the spread of capital on a world scale, also appear as a form of the mobility of fractions. However, it also shows "the main features of the accumulation regime, [...] as it emerged as a result of the implementation of the structural adjustment program, and the fact that social and sectoral segregations are much more intense in this new accumulation regime compared to the old regimes" (Teubal, 2001, p.29). .

Capital fractions are essentially interwoven. In Marx's terms, "the circuits of individual capitals intertwine, predict and necessitate each other, and create the movement of the total social capital within the mere network they weave" (Marx, 1992, p.316). However, changes in the dominance or hegemony of the fractions may occur during the business cycles that occur when this obligation is not complied with in the total capital cycle. "These functions of capital are wrongly treated as fractions of capital with different and mutually exclusive interests." "Productive capital and money capital (called financial capital), and sometimes productive capital and commercial capital, are defined as mutually exclusive concrete interest formations" (Ercan, 2009, p.33).

In general, it can be seen that international finance and money have been in a dominant position since the 1980s. Neo-liberal policies create a wave of short-term investment, currency speculation, financial instability and crisis all over the world (Brunhoff, 2009, p.173). As a matter of fact, the means of carrying value in international economic relations is financial capital, that is, the financial system, which has become more fluid and permeable with financial freedom. "The most defining feature of this financial hegemony is that shareholders' demands for high returns and high short-term corporate profits have become extremely strong. Bank loans and bonds are now much more dependent on international short-term profits. It provides loans to companies and countries that can pay high amounts. When these profits decline, major international banks cut off credit channels and money retreats to safer lands. As a result, weak currency loses its value, leading to financial crises and economic decline in "emerging" countries" (Brunhoff, 2009, p.174).

At this point, it becomes meaningful that the term "globalization" has come to the fore more effectively with neo-liberal policies. What characterizes globalization is the mobilization of factors of production, and it appears to be particularly prevalent in the financial and commercial fields. It should be particularly emphasized that one result of separating the concepts of growth and accumulation is seen here. Not every growth results in accumulation.

Natural Development/Sequence of Value, Accumulation and Fractions

Historically, the first capital fraction to emerge is trade/merchant capital. However, it should be noted immediately that the term "capital" at this stage refers to the accumulation of value, not a social formation. Merchants, who emerged especially at the end of the Middle Ages and were engaged in trade, began to accumulate valuable metals and gold by trading even internationally. Heilbroner states that "a small, irregular armed group on the roads of medieval Europe, consisting of a standard bearer at the head, a military leader, then footmen and horsemen carrying swords, and finally horses and mules loaded with sacks and sacks" came to India with trade trains. He states that this newly formed merchant class, which traded in an area extending to China, began to rise without even having a place within the fixed hierarchy of European feudalism. Moreover, business could not be done without these traveling merchants, who were humiliated in the hierarchy of the period and accused of "disturbing order". In other words, a natural dependency relationship was being established (Heilbroner, 1970, p.45-46). These developments in commerce paved the way for the formation of new cities, with the increase in the volume of trade and the introduction of ports as new transportation areas. In addition to being logistics centers, these cities are also "news, goods, capital, loans, people, orders [etc.] flow here and the same depart from here. Wholesale traders, sometimes extremely rich, make the law here" (Braudel, 1993, p.17). When this period approached the end of the eighteenth century, French physiocrats, led by Quesnay, claimed that capitalist agriculture was the basis of the growth of national income for economies based on trade in agricultural product production, which was the basis of trade. In the same period, Smith provides an explanation for England that, unlike agricultural capitalism, the growth of national income is based on the manufacturing industry, which is a result of the mechanization that came with the industrial revolution (Freeman & Soete, 2003, p.39). As the second stage, productive/industrial capital has begun to emerge. Although the general tendency of classical economists was to consider money only as a means of exchange, with the industrial capital reaching quite large scales and finally with the emergence of the credit mechanism and money transfers, banks providing these services and therefore financial institutions as a new capital fraction that earned returns from these transactions. It dates back to the emergence of money capital. In short, as of the historical development of capitalism, these three main fractions emerged in the order of trade, industrial and financial capitals.

When an individual entrepreneur/capitalist starts from simple commodity production and moves from the C-M-C circuit to the capitalist mode of production, he passes to the M-C-M' circuit. P' (output money) is greater than the amount of P (input money) put into the production process and constitutes the source of accumulation. However, such a situation must occur that the savings in the economy must somehow appear as a supply of funds and subsequently find a demand for funds.

Nowadays, the dominant layer of capital should be described as "oligopoly-finance capital". This is not because capitalists are in the financial sector of the system (banks and others); They have a privileged right to access the capital required for the development of their activities in different sectors of the economy (industrial production, commercialization, financial services, R&D). This privileged right of access provides them with a special and effective authority to intervene in the markets they shape according to their own interests" (Amin, 2010, p.2). Since this superiority can be used in line with one's own interests, it can be said that it falls under the definition of "economic hegemony".

Some Concepts of Jessop

Jessop's main interest is Marxist state theory and he has done a lot of work in this field. Although he works on state theory in general, it can be said that he deals with the state in the process of capital accumulation and more specifically the state within its mechanism and integrity that ensures the functioning of the capitalist system. Therefore, he analyzes capitalism through state theory, and in doing so, examines it in the context of the contribution of state activities to the transformative/changing and reproduction mechanism on production, distribution and consumption. For this reason, there is a holistic field of study originating from the state. In short, it makes comparative analyzes that can be summarized in terms of the state in capitalism and the capitalist state. The author himself describes his main focus as "theoretical and empirical criticism of political economy." It deals with the economic and political order and, more importantly, their strategic coordination and structural coupling" (Jessop, 2013, p.13).

As of this study, the concepts of "economic sovereignty" and "economic hegemony", which will be used from the Author, are important. In addition, the term "value form" is also discussed. Value Format; "In the field of production, the value-form is embodied in the organization of the labor process as a process of value determination (adding value) and its commitment to the need to reduce cost and/or increase output under competitive pressure. In relation to labor power, the value-form is associated with the commodification of labor power, its dependence on the control of capital in the labor process, its reproduction and compensation through the wage form" (Jessop, 1982, p.264). The importance of this term is because the core of the formation of the macroeconomic plane is in the concept of "value". In general, value shapes the entire accumulation process and is the source of fluctuations as deviations from the process. On the other hand, as of this study, the term "crisis" is a macroeconomic imbalance that can lead to a change in the production function/form of production, or more clearly in the "value-producing-mechanism": a crisis is a shocking event that can cause a change in the value-producing mechanism. contains effects.

he value form is a cost reduction initiative and is an initiative that changes/affects the mode/function of production. This initiative varies as market prices fluctuate around. The reason for this fluctuation is the uncoordinated movement of capital chasing profit opportunities. On the other hand, "the distribution of labor time between different production activities is the mechanism that drives the fluctuation in market prices around production prices that reflect the socially necessary labor time embedded in different commodities" (Jessop, 2003, pp.264-265). These interconnected elements of the value form define the parameters within which accumulation will occur and can therefore determine the process of fluctuation and crisis. "The real essence of value depends on the ability of capital to control wage labor in the very process of production, and this in turn depends on the consequences of the economic class struggle in which the balance of forces is shaped by many factors beyond the value-form [...] the circulation of capital has neither an essential unity nor a predetermined It means there is no pattern of accumulation. The rhythm and direction of capitalist development vary greatly within the matrix formed by the value-form. In this sense, the value-form forms the basis for various efforts in the reproduction of capital relations; The nature of accumulation depends on the success or failure of these efforts" (Jessop, 1982, p.265-266).

One of the basic propositions of this study is that the state has a specific place in the processes of value production and accumulation. So much so that, although we agree with Jessop's proposition that "there is no specified accumulation pattern", the economic policies of the public sector also play a role within this matrix of value production accumulation. In this context, while privatization, that is, the acquisition of property (production property) by the public, is a historical phase of capitalism and a role it plays in the value accumulation process, privatization is a role undertaken by the public sector in another phase, and both roles are included in the matrix mentioned by Jessop. gets. In line with this thesis, when we look at the employment and wage levels in privatized organizations, I think it will be seen that although there will be no wage increase, working conditions will worsen, that is, there will be an increase in the productivity of labor. Accordingly, of course, employment opportunities will also shrink.

The public sector, which is trying to withdraw from the production area of the economy through privatization, causes the public sector to occupy a larger place in the general economy in the field of expenditures with the revenues obtained from the same privatization. In other words, the state does not shrink within the economy where it withdraws from the production side, on the contrary, it grows even more. This transformation is yet another form change within the same matrix, and its main purpose is to support the accumulation process.

Therefore, when the accumulation strategy is mentioned, openness to the outside world or closedness to the outside world should not be understood. Again, even if openness to the outside world is considered only as an argument that ensures the continuity of accumulation, a broader matrix should be mentioned and another important argument of this matrix in this study is that the public sector is withdrawn from the productive area and transferred to the consumer area. is to pass. More generally, although the effectiveness of the state in the economy is an argument in the accumulation process, the state can play different roles in the process. Only one of these roles is customization.

On the other hand, the terms "economic sovereignty" and "economic hegemony", as two important concepts, are defined as follows. Economic domination can be "established by various fractions of capital and is a form of superiority and dominance that occurs when these fractions are able to impose their particular interests on others without regard to and/or to the detriment of the interests of other fractions" (Jessop, 1982, pp.266-267). is a form of guidance.

The term economic hegemony is defined as "economic leadership achieved by the general adoption of a certain accumulation strategy". The main difference between both terms is that they "secure the long-term interests of the hegemonic segment." Thus, although economic hegemony may be incompatible with the process of seamless integration of total social capital, they differ from each other in that economic hegemony can move towards the integration of the cycle and the maintenance of the expansion of industrial capital even if non-industrial fractions are hegemonic (Jessop, 1982, p.267).

In these processes, the state is one of the most important supply points of the accumulation process and is considered as the "capitalist state". The basic features of the capitalist state are, in brief, as follows: 1) ensuring the formal legal regulations and property rights assurance necessary for capital accumulation, 2) ensuring the fictional commodification of land, money, labor power and knowledge, 3) labor market regulations that will ensure that capital controls labor power. 4) Defining the boundaries of the economic and the extra-economic, 5) Supporting capital-intensive infrastructure, 6) "Managing the fundamental contradiction between the increasingly social nature of the productive forces and the distribution of surplus labor and the constantly private and competitive nature of the social relations of production", 7) being concerned with the broader political and social implications of the changing ways in which the contradictions of capitalism are mediated in and through specific forms of political organization and social mobilization" (Jessop, 2013, p.89). As of this study, the most important point here is that the state mechanism is a mechanism that directly supports the state in the accumulation process and can make the necessary legal and institutional arrangements to continue this process. As a matter of fact, privatization can also be facilitated through laws and can be effective and decisive on the dominance and/or hegemonic positions of capital in general and capital fractions in particular within the economy.

REFERENCES

Amin, S. (2010). *Global History: A View from the South*. Pambazuka Press.

Anderson, P. (2017). *The Antinomies of Antonio Gramsci*. Verso.

Baby, J. (2000). Ekonomi Politiğin Temel Prensipleri. C. Karakaya (çev.). İstanbul: Sosyal Yayınları.

Barry, N. (1974). *Scientific Knowledge and Sociological Theory*. Routledge.

Bayliss, K. (2006). Privatization theory and practice. In Jomo, K. S., & Fine, B. (Eds.), *The New Development Economics: Post Washington Consensus Neoliberal Thinking* (pp. 144–161). Zed Books.

Begg, D., Fisher, S., & Dornbush, R. (2005). *Economics*. Mcgraw-Hill.

Böhm, Eucken & Dorth, 2009

Böhm-Bawerk, E. (2011). *Karl Marx and the Close of His System*. Ludwig von Mises Institute.

Bonefeld, W. (1992). Social constitution and the from the capitalist sate, *in* W. Bonefeld, R. Gunn, & K. Psychopedis (edt.), *Open Marxizm Vol.1*. (93-132), Pluto.

Braudel, F. (1993). *A History of Civilizations*. Penguin Books.

Brunhoff, S. (2009). *Marx on Money*. Verso Book.

Buchanan, J. M. (1999). *Public Principles of Public Debt: A Defense and Restatement*. Liberty Fund.

Buchanan, J. M. (2001). *Externalities and Public Expenditure Theory*. Liberty Fund.

Burkett, P., & Hart-Landsberg, M. (2000). *Development, Crisis, and Class Struggle*. MacMillan Press.

Carnoy, M. (2014). *The State and Political Theory*. Princeton University Press.

Chang, H.J. (2007). *Kalkınma Reçetelerinin Gerçek Yüzü*. T. Onmuş (çev.), İletişim Yayınları.

Chang, H.-J., & Evans, P. (2007). *Institutional Change and Economic Development*. United Nations.

Chang, H.-J., & Grabel, I. (2014). *Reclaiming Development: An Alternative Economic Policy Manual*. Zed Books. 10.5040/9781350222137

Clarke, S. (1991). *The State Debate*. Palgrave Macmillan. 10.1007/978-1-349-21464-8

Corm, G. (2013). *Le Nouveau Gouvernement du Monde*. La Découverte.

Corrigan, P., Ramsay, H., & Sayer, D. (1980). The state as a relation of production. In Corrigan, P. (Ed.), *Capitalism, State Formation and Marxist Theory: Historical Investigations* (pp. 1–25). Quartet Books.

Duménil, G., & Lévy, D. (2009). *La grande bifurcation En finir avec le néolibéralisme*. Ouvrières.

Durand, J. P. (2018). *La sociologie de Marx*. La Découverte. 10.3917/dec.duran.2018.01

Eggertsson, T. (1990). *Economic Behavior and Institutions: Principles of Neoinstitutional Economics*. Cambridge University Press. 10.1017/CBO9780511609404

Ercan, F. (2006). *Modernizm, Kapitalizm ve Azgelişmişlik*. Bağlam Yayıncılık.

Freeman, C., & Soete, L. (2003). *The Economics of Industrial Innovation*. Psychology Press.

Gill, S., & Law, D. (1988). *The Global Political Economy: Perspective, Problems, and Policies*. John Hopkins University Press. 10.56021/9780801837630

Gramsci, A. (2011). *Prison Notebooks*. Columbia University Press.

Grossekettler, H. G. (1994). On designing an institutional infrastructure for economies: The Freiburg Legacy After 50 Years. *Journal of Economic Studies (Glasgow, Scotland)*, 21(4), 9–24. 10.1108/01443589410070761

Hahnel, R. (2003). *The ABC's of Political Economy: A Modern*. Pluto Press.

Hayek, F. A. (2007). *The Road to Serfdom*. University of Chicago Press. 10.7208/chicago/9780226320533.001.0001

Hayek, F. A. (2022). *Law, Legislation, and Liberty*. University of Chicago Press.

Hazlitt, H. (2010). *The ABC of a Market Economy*. Crown Currency.

Heilbroner, R. L. (1970). On the limits of economic prediction. *Diogenes*, 18(70), 27–40. 10.1177/039219217001807002

Hilferding, R. (1995). *Finance Capital*. Routledge.

Hirsch, B. (2004). What do unions do for economic performance? *Journal of Labor Research*, 25(3), 415–456. 10.1007/s12122-004-1023-8

Hobsbawm, E. (1996). *The Age of Revolution: 1789-1848*. Vintage.

Hobsbawm, E. (1996a). *The Age of Capital: 1848-1875*. Vintage.

Hobsbawm, E. (1998). *On History*. The New Press.

Holloway, J. (2003). Devlet ve gündelik mücadele, A. Güney (çev.). *Praksis Dergisi*, 9, 411–442.

Holloway, J., & Picciotto, S. (1978). *State and Capital: A Marxist Debate*. Edward Arnold.

Jessop, B. (1982). *The Capitalist State*. New York University Press.

Jessop, B. (2003). The Future of the Capitalist State. *Polity*.

Jessop, B. (2013). State Theory: Putting the Capitalist State in Its Place. *Polity*.

Kasper, W., & Streit, M. E. (1998). *Institutional Economics, Social Order and Public Policy*. Edward Elgar.

Kuznets, S. (1955). Economic growth and income inequality. *The American Economic Review*, 45(1), 1–28.

Lange, O. (2015). *Political Economy*. Pergamon.

Marx, K. (1988). The Economic and Philosophic Manuscripts of 1844 and the Communist Manifesto. *Prometheus*.

Marx, K. (2016). *Capital, Vol.1, 2, 3.*, Fingerprint Publishing.

Marx, K., & Engels, F. (1998). The German Ideology. *Prometheus*.

Mueller, D. C. (1979). *Public Choice*. Cambridge University Press.

Nisanken, W. A. (1975). Bureaucrats and politicians. *The Journal of Law & Economics*, 18(3), 617–643. 10.1086/466829

North, D. (1990). *Institutions, Institutional Change and Economic Performance*. Cambridge University Press. 10.1017/CBO9780511808678

O'Neill, J. (1998). *The Market: Ethics, Knowledge and Politics*. Routledge. 10.4324/9780203358467

Petras, J. (2002). The centrality of the state in the contemporary World, *CSCAweb*. sa.1-12.

Pio, A. (1994). New growth theory and old development problems: How recent developments in endogenous growth theory apply to developing countries. *Development Policy Review*, 12(3), 277–300. 10.1111/j.1467-7679.1994.tb00068.x

Rousseau, J. J. (2006). *A Discourse on Political Economy*. Waking Lion Press.

Samuels, W. J. (1995). The present state of institutional economics. *Cambridge Journal of Economics*, 19(4), 569–590. 10.1093/oxfordjournals.cje.a035331

Teubal, M. (2001). Structural adjustment and social disarticulation: The case of Argentina. *Science and Society*, 64(4), 460–480.

Chapter 7
Conjuncture, Capital Fractions, and Public Property

ABSTRACT

This chapter explores economic theories within the context of capitalism, public sector activities, and privatization. The first part establishes a philosophical and historical foundation, identifying key concepts and their definitions within different levels of capitalism. The second part examines terms like strategy, development, policy, accumulation, and growth, differentiating their roles in economic theories and practices. It distinguishes between economic growth (total output increase) and accumulation (capacity to produce output increase), highlighting their implications for development and policy. The chapter critically analyzes capitalism's tendencies to generate crises and cyclical fluctuations, exploring their impact on social structures and public sector activities. It also examines capitalism's historical continuity, recognizing its renewal and adaptation. A significant portion contrasts economic theories regarding public ownership and privatization, highlighting ideological and practical differences in addressing economic challenges within capitalist frameworks.

GRASP THE CONJUNCTURE

In the first of the first two parts of the study, it includes determining the elements that make up the main and side propositions on which the study is built, discussing these elements, and what kind of usage method is adopted according to the level and form of use in reaching the main proposition, and more precisely, the philosophical, intellectual and historical background that is adopted to be used. . The reason for this is to emphasize historical continuity. Thus, it is to consider the static

DOI: 10.4018/979-8-3693-5996-9.ch007

situation as a unified process with its historical roots and to determine a paradigm basis on the direction, form and principles of change. However, when adopting an intellectual-philosophical paradigm, privileged importance can be attributed to certain concepts. For this reason, these concepts have been tried to be determined and, based on the importance attributed to them, these concepts have been defined and developed in a way to form a semantic and epistemological integrity, and this has been tried to be done in the context of different definitions and levels of capitalism.

In summary, the first chapter is devoted to determining the space of concepts surrounding the basic proposition and shaping the concepts. Therefore, it aims to create conceptual integrity. That is, it tries to explain the observer's perspective and position.

In the second part, the elements that constitute the main and subsidiary propositions of the study were tried to be determined more specifically. Moreover, in this section, the determinations made on the terms that make up the whole and the discussion of their conceptual loads are made in order to create a pre-determination and pre-supposition regarding the whole and the part. These premises are intended to provide conceptual clarity in the way of perceiving the whole. Based on the data of the first chapter, where the relationship of concepts with facts is revealed, there is an attempt to update the concepts in understanding and explaining "today". The meanings given to the terms strategy, development, policy, accumulation and growth have been tried to be made in accordance with their development and change processes, and attempts have been made to give meaning and explain the concepts within this line of development-change, without separating the "today" from its historical roots. A second importance of the chapter is discussed by comparing the ways of handling and understanding these concepts in the theoretical sense and in the pure economic sense. Thus, an attempt was made to integrate the semantics, epistemology and paradigm of the first chapter into the synthetic components of different approaches, and this was done through basic theoretical explanations explaining growth and accumulation.

In summary, the second part tries to establish the connection between the basic proposition and the space of different approaches of economic theory as the premises surrounding the basic proposition and aims to determine the position of the basic proposition in this space. In other words, it tries to reveal the specific phenomenon towards which the observer is directed and the general integrity within which the specific phenomenon exists. This very simple and basic summary of both sections forms the basis for revealing the propositions, which are grouped into two categories below, again in a very simple language.

Conceptual Propositions (Semantic and Analytical Propositions)

1. Strategy does not always have a positive meaning. Strategy is based on making choices, and not every choice is always optimal. Planning to achieve a certain goal, that is, the variables in the equation established for that purpose, requires some elements to be excluded from the equation. Therefore, it is inevitable that there will be contradictions between the variables outside the equation and the expected result of the equation.
2. A policy implementation does not always have linear consequences. When policy is defined in the broad sense of "position taking," policy implementation by any political actor stimulates all other actors and directly affects the linear expectations of the policy. Because the political actors who are warned immediately determine new positions, that is, they revitalize their own policies. Therefore, the political position space is anarchic.
3. The terms economic accumulation and growth are distinguished from each other. While growth is the increase in total output, accumulation is defined as the increase in the capacity to produce output. There are two significances in this. First, to understand the continuity of growth and to distinguish between "bubble" and second, because the public sector in general and privatization in particular have different effects on growth and accumulation, these differences are included in the basic proposition.
4. Capitalism includes mechanisms that create both crises and fluctuations. It aims to distinguish between the two concepts and to make sense of economic development and the economic basis of the social transformation it creates. While the crisis causes "system" change and even transformation at a level that can cause change in the capitalist production system (shaking the micro theory), fluctuations are growth and accumulation that occur in the form of systematic cycles (rise, contraction, etc.) that are at a scale that does not change the production system but can be attributed to different reasons. defined as deviations from the process.
5. Capitalism, as a form of historical and social organization, contains neither pure rupture nor pure continuity as a historical social entity, but rupture and continuity inherent in historicity. However, there is a scale problem. (for example, while the exploited were in one country at first, they later started to be in other countries).

Synthetic Propositions

Capitalism is a social structure that can renew itself from time to time and cannot be adhered to. While the structure tries to organize its own internal qualities, it also tends to organize and design social life.

Capitalism characteristically creates crises. In addition, it also characteristically creates cyclical fluctuations. Both forms of discontinuity have an impact on the behavior of key actors. In particular, and what concerns us, the perception of the economic structure (which forms of discontinuity also affect social structures) and the public sector seem to be activated or activated from time to time and/or change their form in accordance with the conjuncture and crisis periods.

Modeling within economic theory is nothing more than explaining the positions of actors. Therefore, a universal economic model cannot be developed, but the economic universe is designed for the continuity of capitalism. In other words, although a generally valid economic model cannot be developed, what can be done is to make sense of the static position within the dynamic process. Therefore, while theories that explain the effectiveness of the public sector are adopted in some periods, theories that ignore or limit this activity are adopted in other times. Essentially, this situation comes down to the before-after timing contradiction between fact and theory in social sciences, but this study does not address this contradiction.

Although capital is a set of social relations in a broad sense, capital in a narrow sense consists of three basic fractions, and these fractions have "sovereignty" over the economy in general, according to the periodic characteristics of capitalism (especially in periods of crisis and/or conjuncture, and also in periods such as expansion and contraction). " or establishes "hegemony".

Privatization is also shaped as a movement in public ownership in accordance with the dominance or hegemony of capital fractions that are active in the periodic identity of the economy, and this formation is in accordance with the dominance/hegemony of capital fractions. This may also make sense of a nationalization attempt that may occur in the future, other than socialism.

The final proposition is that while the dominance and/or hegemony of capital fractions occurs in harmony with the capital accumulation process, public sector activities are also compatible with this and privatization is one of the strong links of this harmony. In order to establish this harmony, privatizations are made in areas that will support accumulation and fractionation. Because for a dominant and/or hegemonic capital fraction, privatization is an answer to the demand for "seeking profit opportunities". This is a concrete indicator of the internal continuity of capitalism.

PUBLIC OWNERSHIP AND EFFICIENCY APPROACHES

From the perspective of political economy, it is possible to look at public sector activity from three main fronts: Liberal Economics, Keynesian Economics, Marxist Economics and Political Economics. However, of course, there are also derivative approaches under these three main approaches. It is also possible to reduce these three basic approaches to two main fronts. Liberal economics, that is, mainstream orthodox economics and the second, heterodox economics. Although there are many characteristics that distinguish these two main movements, they fundamentally differ on two points. Firstly, there is a difference in terms of value theory and secondly, there is a difference in terms of perspective on the future of the capitalist system. From the perspective of value theory, liberal orthodox economics argues that capitalism is an ultimate human system through the subjective marginal value theory. Heteredox radical economics, on the other hand, is based on the labor theory of value and argues that capitalism is a historical phase and will come to an end. Keynesian economics, which is located between these two approaches and the three main currents listed above, envisages effective public sector interventions in the markets from the points that liberal economics sees as market failure, and the continuity of capitalism with such interventions. For this reason, although it seems at first glance to be a derivative of liberal economics, it is based on the inadequacy of the "optimism" of liberal economics for the continuity of capitalism.

Liberal economics treats public sector interventions as completely external. Therefore, one of the main reasons for market failures is public sector activities. Its extensions, such as Hayek, Friedman, Buchanan, and Solow, which are derivatives of liberal economics, still consider public sector activities as external and adopt models and approaches that include mechanisms to control the activities of the public sector.

Keynesian economics and its derivatives, on the other hand, accept market failures that may occur during the continuity of the system, but adopt public sector activities to replace these failures and therefore continue the system.

In Marxist economics, public ownership, like other public sector activities, is subjected to a class analysis and is treated as attempts to maintain the functioning of capitalism with temporary arrangements, although it will eventually disappear with its own contradictions.

All real and monetary activities of the public sector, including derivative approaches, are not discussed with a detailed comparison of public sector activities, which is not within the scope of this study. Here it is necessary to focus only on the functioning of state economic enterprises, which is implied by the general term public ownership, and the place of privatization of these enterprises in the basic proposition. However, first of all, it is necessary to reveal the formation of economic organizations as public property and the expectations from these organizations. The basic theme that this section tries to focus on is that while a phenomenon within economic theory is affirmed at a certain stage within capitalist development, in line with practical developments, the same phenomenon may be negated at advanced stages of the system. As a matter of fact, while public property that is specifically subject to privatization can be considered as the main element of economic development for a certain period, the same public property can later be privatized and become an element of economic development.

PUBLIC OWNERSHIP AND ACTIVITY

In general, the most basic expectation from economic development is empirically to increase the gross national product and, of course, to increase the total personal consumption of people. In this context, although there is no consensus on what methods and structures will be used to increase these two basic elements of the economy - production and consumption - increasing the quality of human life is the main starting point. The most general and fundamental point of differentiation is where the public sector stands in directing the economic variables in achieving this basic starting point, and moreover, whether the main actor that will determine the performance of the economy in achieving economic goals will be the market or the public sector or a rhythmic component of both.

The answer to this problem and the ways and methods to be determined to achieve economic goals can be limited to the term "economic policy". However, the scope of this limitation, "that is, the research subject of economic policy theory, is determined by the "fundamental question" asked when investigating the truth, that is, by the posing of the problem [...] "Economic policy can be defined as follows: Economic policy is a sub-branch of (general) policy. The concept of "policy" can be considered broadly to include not only the behavior of the state, but also the behavior of individuals and groups (Pütz, 1994, pp.20-21). The author who made this definition considers the term "policy" as a general and superior concept, and defines the term "economic policy" as a sub-branch within it. So, while a social continuity is "policy", economic regulations within that general social continuity are "economic policy". However, as mentioned before in this study, although the same terminology is used by the author, different contents are attributed. Because the author defines the term "politics", which he considers as a superordinate concept, with the state, that is, legislative and executive activities and behaviors. However, in this working terminology, although an "economic policy" may be directed by governments, the activities of the state are not independent of individuals and groups as subunits. Therefore, in the parent term "policy", just like in the term "economic policy", there is bias of the individual, the market and other pressure groups, and this should not be neglected. If we accept that the individual, the market and other economic actors are ineffective on the economic policies of the state and that the state acts independently, then we have to accept that there is no influence other than government decisions for privatization, and that almost all economic policies, including privatization practices, are There are non-governmental influences and guidance in its practices. In this context, although politics is a superordinate term, it is not limited to state activities and interacts with all other individuals and groups. Accordingly, it is more appropriate for the consistency of the study to define economic policy as economic activities that include these connections more deeply and shape the economic relations and connections of the state with other individuals and groups.

Although economic policies are defined differently in different aspects, with the content of the state directing individuals and groups by directing the economy or the content of the state positioning itself in line with the demands of individuals and groups, ultimately, for the state as a non-market economic actor within the economy, creating public economic enterprises in a certain period of time is an important part of the economy. We have been going through a period of economic policy based on the privatization of these organizations since the 1980s. In particular, privatization, which has recently gained momentum in Eastern European countries, is on the agenda with "reform" programs, mostly influenced by the experiences of other central Western European countries (Bolton, 1992, p.276).

When it comes to this period, there are some elements that can form the basis for privatization in the periodization that capitalism has gone through. Therefore, determining the general periodic picture of the post-1980 period, when privatization was an active item of economic policies, is effective in making sense of these policies.

First, "By the early 1970s "Chicago economists [von Hayek and Friedman in particular] had hardly entered the consciousness of most Americans" [(McGraw, 1984, p.9)]; According to one study investigating its influence on policy in the 1980s, "But over the next twelve years, the Chicago School exerted a profound influence on America's public sector and especially its regulatory policies" [(McGraw, 1984, p.9)]" (Martin, 1993, p.73). These ideas, generally collected under the title of "neo-liberal policy proposals", represent the intellectual foundations of restricting public sector activities.

Secondly, it created a new field of acceptance in terms of liberal economics and policies, after the failure of Keynesian economics, which remained effective until the mid-1970s and was based on the trade-off between unemployment and inflation, to explain stagflation. Theoretical approaches that linked economic development to a "strong state" with Keynes gave way to "strong market, minimal state" theories for economic development in the 1970s.

While liberal economics, which could not remain indifferent to the success of planning in socialist countries, accepted Keynes and public sector efficiency in liberal theory and legitimized a type of planning even if it was not socialist, in the 1980s, following the failures in socialist countries, it had to remove public sector efficiency from the agenda again. In fact, although this is not clearly a socialist orientation, it can be considered as an emulation originating from policy success. However, ironically, within the Marxist movement, a "new socialism" was created on the basis of Keynes. "This theory argues that social ownership of the means of production is no longer the essence of socialism; The Fabian version revives the view of gradual progress that had been shattered by the depression and unemployment of the interwar period; It has been suggested that "in order to move towards socialism, it is necessary to start by repairing capitalism" (Eaton, 1951, p.66). D. Jay, one of the pioneers of this view, put forward this approach, which he called Keynesian socialism, as a three-stage transition to socialism project. Accordingly, "the first step is to tax income and inheritance to cover social service expenses; second, "taxes, subsidies, price control, utilities, etc. and thirdly, the nationalization of some industrial, financial and commercial sectors" (Eaton, 1951, p.71). In short, while Keynes, on the one hand, highlights public activity for the advancement of capitalism for some, on the other hand, Keynesianism for socialism suggests applicability for the first two of these three stages. This irony of the 1930s manifests itself with a parallel line of thought, although not with similar thoughts, in the 1980s.

Thirdly, although "strong market, minimal state" approaches are not actually valid for central capitalist countries, they are a suggestion for transition economies and third world economies and, frankly, a set of policies that will force integration into these economies. However, these suggestions of the central countries are heavily criticized on the grounds that they do not actually implement them but "effectively recommend" them to non-central countries. Early capitalist countries show that they did not implement these "effective suggestions" policy proposals they made in the post-1980 period at all, in the initial stages of their capitalist development, that is, their economic development. For example, protectionist strategies against "infant industries" were first seen in the USA. Likewise, stating that the claim that England's development was based on free trade is not true, Chang said that England started to impose bans on imports from the colonies when it threatened its own industries, to protecting the agricultural sectors with the practices introduced by the Corn Laws. It deals with practices regarding the effectiveness of protectionist policies as opposed to free trade (Chang, 2007, pp.48-52). However, after the central capitalist countries completed their development phases and experienced marginal levels of public sector contributions to effective demand, especially in the post-War II period, policy proposals were made to eliminate protectionist walls, regardless of their level of development, under the general name of globalization, in order to ensure the opportunities of the companies of these countries to open up to new markets. have become active.

Fourthly, the narrowing of the gap between investment profitability rates and interest rates in developed countries has created the need to search for new investment areas for this capital. The need for high-yield areas, whether fixed investment or interest income, has manifested itself as financial liberalization. Therefore, as mentioned above, a political presupposition has emerged for trade liberalization, parallel to and even leading to trade liberalization, and subsequently for the integration of the financial and finally production areas. The reason for this is the belief that global resource allocation will be achieved in the most effective way if an integrated world economy directs world resources by market actors. "A global and integrated perspective [is emerging] on the 'process of adjustment', defined as a decline in the role of the state in economic management and a greater reliance on market forces, and that structural adjustment is a worldwide process that is in a relationship of interdependence and mutual reinforcement with the process of globalization" (Ghai, 1995)., p.39-40) is considered as a case. The general name of this approach is gathered under "structural adjustment" policies. One of the basic propositions of this structural adjustment policies process is the decrease in state effectiveness, and one of the basic elements of it is privatization initiatives. Of course, there are also serious views opposing this structural harmony-based integration. The most prominent of these are writers of South American origin.

The basic proposition of the group of thought called "Dependency School", especially led by A. G. Frank; It points to a transformation that forces the integration of the world division of labor system and, as a result, the integration of the third world economies, due to the depression that the industrialized capitalist and socialist economies, defined as the first and second world countries, entered, especially due to the economic and political crises in the 1970s. In this process, nation states "become oppressive" in a way that encourages this articulation, and "various "sections" of the world gradually integrate into a single economic system" (Frank, 2014, p.131). In connection with our thesis, within the new organization of the system, the state will give up the previous -apparent- protectionisms and somehow necessitate the transfer of public sector property to the private sector, especially in the wave of globalization that will increase the permeability and mobility of capital.

The fifth element can be considered as the fact that the political relations between international political actors have become based on economic relations, in line with the general character of capitalism. Political actors shape their economic-based political relations on two basic levels. While the first of these is based on political and ideological cooperation and organizations that will ensure political integration, the second is realized as cooperation based on the impulses of market forces to provide the expansion areas required by market actors.

Despite all these general and special periodic characteristics, it is claimed that the main reason for privatization on water is to create a minimal public sector and that the market can use resources more effectively, but causes public waste of resources. This claim is originally based on M. Friedman's (1962) claim that since the state is typically inefficient and bureaucratic, its intervention is cumbersome and inflexible. The problem of market disruptions is counterposed to the problem of state disruptions" (Caslin, 1993, p.302). In other words, while at first the obstacle to economic development was seen as market failures and public sector activity to compensate for this, later the obstacle to economic development was seen as public sector failure and it was observed that neo-liberal policies including effective privatization and deregulation were adopted.

In addition, the historical periodicity of capitalism, the necessity of capitalism to expand capital and seek new profit opportunities, the desire and activity of the current pole to design the world system in the unipolar world shaped by the disappearance of the Eastern Bloc, the development of new production opportunities that will support the expansion of consumption opportunities in developed capitalist countries. In harmony with the need for production factors, especially labor, and the application areas of recent endogenous growth theories, the withdrawal of the public sector from the production areas in a very different and wide range, such as the public sectors of the central capitalist countries turning to sub-share investments and the withdrawal of the economy from the production areas, can be explained. Therefore, privatization, as the transfer of public ownership in production areas to the private sector, can be addressed at many different levels in theoretical and practical areas.

Bailey also emphasizes the ambiguity of the concept and defines it in his study on this ambiguity as follows: "It is a general effort to alleviate the factors that prevent public institutions from operating effectively by placing them under the influence of the incentives of private markets" (Bailey, 1987, p. 138). With this situation, Bailey's definition is considered as a policy to contribute to the functionality of the market, within the definition categories given below. As a matter of fact, Bailey's proposition that "words lose their intelligibility when they start to become a political weapon" (Bailey, 1987, p.139) also shows that the concept of privatization can be handled in different meanings by different segments of society. People or institutions that take a "political" stance can turn even a simple definition into a complex area of debate.

As another definition, Dodgson emphasizes the content of the concept and defines it as "the sale of public assets[,] Liberalization, in other words, the abolition of public monopolies and deregulation, that is, the removal of institutional regulations [and...] the provision of government-financed activities by private companies, and in general, this It is based on competition between private companies to undertake activities" (Dodgson, 1987, pp. 261-262). This definition, or rather a differential definition, distinguishes between the privatization of property in the hands of the public sector, the abolition of legal regulations as mechanisms for the public authority to influence the markets, and thirdly, the outsourcing of public services to the private sector through the tender method.

However, Dodgson advises that the concept of deregulation, that is, deregulation or liberalization, which implies the removal of restrictions that market actors may face, should be used with caution and says, "Although some regulations are aimed at increasing competition, in many past practices this has served the interests of the regulated industry and protected this industry against competitive pressures." has been observed. He states that this situation is seen especially in the United States, where regulations are more common than public ownership (Dodgson, 1987, p.261).

Savas, on the other hand, builds privatization on the term "public", which expresses three different situations: "state ownership, widespread ownership and widespread access". "It implies that state ownership – and by extension state intervention – is not necessary for popular (i.e. public) interests. Privatization is the disposal of an airline, a factory, a coal mine owned by the state [...] in a way that serves the interests of society in order to meet the desires and needs of a wide range of ownership and activity relations based on this fact, the importance of which is not sufficiently appreciated; "The state stops insuring mortgage loans or operating urban buses and transfers the provision of these services to the market" (Savas, 1994, p.4) is also defined as privatization. However, as will be seen later, the transfer of almost every service to the private sector produces results contrary to the principle of public interest, and this is where the most fundamental criticism of privatization comes from.

First of all, privatization, which is the transfer of public enterprises to the private sector, ostensibly in line with the main purpose of strengthening and activating market functioning, brings two different concepts of capitalism to the agenda. The first of these is market capitalism, which is based on the determination of prices, values and growth entirely by market actors. However, state capitalism is defined as "trying to achieve the growth goal by operating nationalized industries and seriously intervening in the functioning of private firms and markets" (Hanke, 1987, p.1), based on seeing the state as the engine of development. State capitalism has played as active a role as possible in economies that are generally defined as mixed economic systems and in which the public sector plays a leading role in the capital accumulation that has not yet been realized through large companies in order to ensure economic growth. Mostly, privatization can be considered as a means of gradually ending the practice of state capitalism as capital accumulation in the country reaches a level that can ensure the functionality of market conditions and resource efficiency.

Especially with the Great Depression of 1929, there were intense increases in the economic efficiency of the public sector. Immediately after this period, state activity in the planning of economies became widespread, while public investments also increased their effectiveness. However, since the 1980s, economic theory has focused on the possibility that transferring public property to the private sector could be a solution to market failures. This theoretical tendency has also found its counterpart in the practical field, and a privatization policy process has been initiated throughout the world, starting from England. Privatization, which started in England with Thatcher, spread all over the world by the mid-1980s (Meggison, 2000, p.14-15).

REFERENCES

Bailey, R. (1987). Uses and misuses of privatization. *Proceedings of the Academy of Political Science*, 36(3), 138–152. 10.2307/1174104

Bolton, P., Roland, G., Vickers, J., & Burda, M. (1992). Privatization in Central and Eastern Europe. *Economic Policy*, 7(15), 275–309. 10.2307/1344544

Caslin, T. (1993). *Devlet ve ekonomi, M. Akgün (çev.). Liberalizm, Refah Devleti, Eleştiriler. K. Saybaşılı (drl.).* Bağlam Yayıncılık.

Chang, H. J. (2007). *Kalkınma Reçetelerinin Gerçek Yüzü. T. Onmuş (çev.).* İletişim Yayınları.

Dodgson, J. (1987). *Current Controversies in Economics*. Blackwell.

Eaton, J. (1951). *Marx against Keynes*. Lawrence and Wishart Ltd.

Frank, A. G. (2014). *The World System: Five Hundred Years or Five Thousand?* Routledge.

Friedman, M. (1962). *Capitalism and Freedom*. University of Chicago Press.

Ghai, D. (1995). Yapısal uyum, küresel bütünleşme ve sosyal demokrasi, İ. Eser (çev). In Prendergast, R., & Stewart, F. (Eds.), *Piyasa Güçleri ve Küresel Kalkınma*. Yapı Kredi Yayınları.

Hanke, S. (1987). Privatization versus nationalization. *Proceedings of the Academy of Political Science*, 36(3), 1–3. 10.2307/1174091

Martin, S. (1993). Private and social incentives to form R&D joint ventures. *Review of Industrial Organization*, 9(2), 157–171. 10.1007/BF01035655

Meggison, W. L. (2000). From state to market: A survey of empirical studies on privatization. *Journal of Economic Literature*, 39(2), 321–389. 10.1257/jel.39.2.321

Pütz, T. (1994). *Grundlagen der Theoretischen Wirtschaftspolitik*. Gustav Fischer Verlag.

Savas, E.S. (1994). *Özelleştirme*. MPM Yayınları, No.517.

Chapter 8
Results and General Evaluation

ABSTRACT

This chapter distinguishes between analytical and synthetic propositions in social sciences, focusing on their roles in knowledge production and empirical validation. Analytical propositions, such as "Privatization is an economic policy," are true by definition and need no empirical verification. In contrast, synthetic propositions, like "Privatization fosters capital accumulation," require empirical evidence to validate. The chapter also discusses the holistic integration of phenomena within broader frameworks, emphasizing their interconnected, context-dependent nature. Concepts evolve over time and across different contexts due to subjective interpretations, challenging uniform application. Theoretical foundations in surplus-value formation and economic crises are explored, showing how capital accumulation fluctuations influence public sector strategies. Shifts from public ownership to privatization reflect changing alignments with dominant capital factions, illustrating cyclical transformations in public policy under varying economic conditions.

RESULTS AND GENERAL EVALUATION

Scientific studies are created on analytical and/or synthetic premises. In an analytical proposition, while the predicate of the proposition does not give any information/new information about its subject, the definition of the terms that make up the predicate completes the proposition. A completed analytic proposition is true by the rules of logic. Therefore, its accuracy is outside of reality and it does not require any proof, that is, experiment or observation, for its accuracy. In fact, analytic propositions are tautological, that is, they repeat any information. The proposition "Privatization is an economic policy" is an analytical proposition, and the definition of concepts completes the proposition, but at the same time, this proposition does

DOI: 10.4018/979-8-3693-5996-9.ch008

not give new information about privatization. While there are pre-defined concepts such as "privatization" and "policy", this proposition is a proposition that does not produce information and is true in terms of being analytical and does not require proof of its accuracy.

As for a synthetic proposition, the information that the predicate gives about the subject cannot be completed only by the rules of logic and the definition of terms. This is why synthetic propositions are the basic mechanism that produces knowledge, and the knowledge they put forward cannot be completed within the proposition, and must be investigated based on scientific principles. For this reason, propositions should be put into empirical analysis, observed and tested. In the proposition "Privatization is compatible with the capital accumulation process", he does not complete the proposition by merely defining capital accumulation. Testing this at the same time can be subject to scientific examination.

On the other hand, the second condition for analyzing any phenomenon is the holistic relationship of the phenomenon with other phenomena in the space of phenomena and finally with the whole space. In short, no analyzed phenomenon is a whole or a part independent of the whole. Therefore, each fact is a whole with other facts and finally with the space of facts and is a part of the whole. Then, the specific phenomenon to be analyzed must be considered within the entirety of the space of facts. The first and indispensable stage of this discussion is possible with abstraction, that is, by determining a starting point. The first stage of this abstraction is history, the analytical and/or synthetic structure and epistemological-semantic processes that produce propositions. History includes the acceptance that any phenomenon is in the past as it is finished and completed, but that the results it creates in the direction of the ongoing arrow of time cause other phenomena. The analytical-synthetic structure that produces propositions implies separating any phenomenon into its components and/or clarifying the system of intellectual equations that produces propositions by synthesizing different facts into a certain whole. The epistemological-semantic process consists of handling the acceptances and objections regarding the information load of the concepts, taking into account the information usage mechanism used in analyzing the phenomenon and the development of the concepts throughout history.

In social sciences, propositions and equation systems created with linear formal logic rules do not have a deterministic character. For this reason, contrary to what linear formal logic predicts, "fuzzy logic" paves the way for creating more creative propositions for social sciences. In the "Fact"-"Observation"-"Theory" system (which is preliminary and after each theory, new facts emerge, new observations are made and re-theorized to include the effects of the theory), the initial conditions on which the emergence of the phenomenon depends, the effects on the process. and due to the effects of dynamic actors in the process, observation may lead to different results in observations of the same phenomena made by different observers.

However, a phenomenon is conceptualized and theorized where it is first observed. In addition to the power to explain a certain phenomenon, the concept also carries a certain meaning. However, historical transformations in the phenomenon show that the content of the concept also has a dynamic character. For this reason, the concept formed by observations of a phenomenon that occurred in any "place" and "time" may be incompatible with the form of the same phenomenon that occurred "elsewhere" and "at another time". The main reason for this is that the effects of "active people" in the content of a concept produced in social scientific facts, which includes observational and cause-effect relationships, create perception differences for "other active people" when the concept appears in another place. In other words, the active person who produces a concept also includes that person's subjective judgments. For this reason, in another place where a similar phenomenon occurs, the same concept does not have the same explanatory and content power (since the phenomenon is dynamic and the phenomenon constantly emerges in different modes), it can also be influenced and interpreted by the active person who perceives the concept and puts it into practice as a policy.

The dynamic character of a phenomenon, in terms of the consequences of the explanatory concept that is put forward in one place, spreads where it spreads, due to the tendency of these consequences to spread; Under the assumption that the concept first emerged and gave the expected results to some extent, this is because the actors who want to achieve these positive results in the area of expansion are a directly effective element on the initial conditions in the new place. On the positive side, this can be observed in the flying formation of a flock of geese. The goose in the front row flies by consuming a great deal of energy, but the air gap created by the goose in front makes it easier for the geese flying behind to fly, and therefore the amount of energy consumed by the geese in the back row is constantly decreasing. Negatively speaking, for a fleet of jet aircraft flying in formation, the air gap created by the aircraft in front makes it difficult for the aircraft behind them to fly. In short, the act of "flying" can have different results depending on who performs it under the "same form". For this reason, social scientific concepts may not be used elsewhere with the same content load by different observers and for different observations, as they carry different content loads depending on the phenomenon and observation that gave rise to the concept and the observer. For this reason, the terms strategy, policy, growth/accumulation, capital fractions and public ownership, which are the basic concepts that form the language of the study, were defined in the study to create a synthetic proposition. In particular, the main hypothesis; Although the concepts were put forward as analytical propositions, they were also used as synthetic propositions linked to each other in order to explain the transformation of a harmonious public activity area with the development stages of capital fractions compatible with the capital accumulation process in general and the capital accumulation process in particular.

In the first part, although the general characteristics of the concepts and their definitions from different perspectives are discussed, a certain perception of economic development and, based on this, theoretical explanations regarding the stages of development are tried to be determined. Within the framework of this perception of history and development, the concept of strategy does not always have a positive meaning and has been given a meaning considering that among alternative strategies, some of the elements that make up the strategy are/may be neglected. The term politics is based on the assumption that people are political beings; It is defined not only as practices carried out by the public sector, but also based on the acceptance that almost every person or segment of the population involved in the practice acts politically and takes their own unique positions. Thus, in the face of any public policy, it has been accepted that the results expected from the policy will not always give the linear results expected when the policy is put forward. Therefore, the assumption has been made that economic policies in one place cannot produce the same results in other places. The main reason for this is that, in addition to the unpredictability in the positioning space between political actors, countries that have previously implemented economic development strategies and achieved results are also actors for the policies implemented "here" and "now", and therefore they are also actors for the policies that are intended to be implemented "here" and "now". It has been tried to place them in a logical system in which they are effective actors on economic development strategy or economic policy.

In the second part, the theoretical foundations of surplus-value formation and the accumulation of this surplus-value, which constitutes the source of the capital accumulation process, are discussed. Accordingly, an attempt has been made to ground the fluctuations and crisis situations that occur in the accumulation process. Additionally, the terms crisis and fluctuation are distinguished from each other; Deviations from economic accumulation that have permanent effects on the mode of production, crisis; Movements that occur periodically and cause shocks in macro economies, although they do not change the mode of production, are defined as fluctuations, that is, conjuncture movements. However, the dominance or hegemony of capital fractions in an economy created by these fluctuations or crises that may occur in the capital accumulation process has been tried to be explained cyclically. Thus, while trying to show that public sector activity affects public sector activities in periods of crisis and/or fluctuation, it has also been tried to show that there is a transformation of public activity in the capital accumulation process that is compatible with the development of capital fractions.

Therefore, as the accumulation process continues, a general reorganization mechanism of the system continues to operate. These mechanisms shape the activities of the public sector in line with the capital accumulation process. For example, while the creation of public ownership was compatible with accumulation in a certain period, today privatization is a public sector intervention that ensures the continuity of accumulation. This book tried to show that privatization policies, which emerged in harmony with the capital accumulation process, are a type of intervention in the public sector, and in line with this, it also tried to show the relationship between the development course of capital fractions. Accordingly, it seems that privatization practices were carried out in accordance with the development period of capital fractions.

Compilation of References

Albertini, J. M. (1983). *Mécanisme du sous développement et développement*. Ouvrières.

AlHussaini, W., & Molz, R. (2009). A Post-Keynesian regulatory model of privatization. *Journal of Socio-Economics*, 38(2), 391–398. 10.1016/j.socec.2008.10.011

Althusser, L. (1967). *Philosophie et philosophie spontanée des savants*. Fronçois Maspero.

Althusser, L. (2011). *Sur la reproduction: Préface d'Étienne Balibar* (2nd ed.). Fronçois Maspero. 10.3917/puf.althu.2011.01

Amable, B. (2003). *The Diversity of Modern Capitalism*. Oxford University Press. 10.1093/019926113X.001.0001

Amin, S. (2010). *Global History: A View from the South*. Pambazuka Press.

Amsden, A. (1990). The world industrialization: 'Global Fordism' or a new model. *New Left Review*, 182, 5–31.

Anderson, P. (2017). *The Antinomies of Antonio Gramsci*. Verso.

Anikin, A. (1975). *A Science in its Youth: Pre-Marxian Political Economy*. Morkow: Progress Publishers.

Aren, S., & Gorvine, A. (1956). İktisadi Kalkınma ve Totaliter Liberaller. *Journal of SBF*, 11(3), 387–394. 10.1501/SBFder0000000254

Armack, A. M. (1989). The meaning of social market economy. In Peacock, A., & Wilgerodt, H. (Eds.), *Germany's Social Market Economy: Origins and Evolution* (pp. 82–86). Macmillan. 10.1007/978-1-349-20145-7_6

Assidon, E. (1996). Les conceptions Nord-Sud: un oubli et le marché, *in* S. Cordellier (Edt.). *La fin du Tiers Monde?* La Decouverte.

Baby, J. (2000). Ekonomi Politiğin Temel Prensipleri. C. Karakaya (çev.). İstanbul: Sosyal Yayınları.

Baby, J. (1967). *Principes Fondamentaux d'économie Politique*. Fronçois Maspero.

Baeshler, J. (1975). *The Origins of Capitalism*. Blackwell.

Bailey, R. (1987). Uses and misuses of privatization. *Proceedings of the Academy of Political Science*, 36(3), 138–152. 10.2307/1174104

Balaam, D. N., & Veseth, M. (2001). *Introduction to International Political Economy*. Prentice-Hall Inc.

Ballance, R. H., Ansari, J. A., & Singer, H. W. (1985). *The International Economy and Industrial Development*. Impetus.

Bapat, B. G. (1981). İthalat kısıtlamaları ya da karşılaştırmalı üstünlüklerin değişmesi, O. Esen (çev.). *Ekonomik Yaklaşım*, 2(5), 89–106. 10.5455/ey.10101

Baran, P. A. (1957). *The Political Economy of Growth*. Monthly Review Press.

Baran, P. A., & Sweezy, P. (1966). *Monopoly Capital*. Monthly Review Press.

Barber, W. J. (2007). *A History of Economic Thought*. Wesleyan University Press.

Barro, R. (1999). Human capital and growth in cross country regressions. *Swedish Economic Policy Review*, 6, 237–277.

Barry, N. (1974). *Scientific Knowledge and Sociological Theory*. Routledge.

Başkaya, F. (2000). *Kalkınma İktisadının Yükselişi ve Düşüşü* (3rd ed.). İmge Kitabevi.

Baumol, W. J. (1970). *Economic Dynamics, an Introduction* (3rd ed.). MacMillan.

Beesley, M., & Littlechild, S. (1989). The regulation of privatized monopolies in the United Kingdom. *The RAND Journal of Economics*, 20(3), 454–472. 10.2307/2555582

Begg, D., Fisher, S., & Dornbush, R. (2005). *Economics*. Mcgraw-Hill.

Bernstein, E. M., & Patel, I. G. (1952). *Inflation in Relation to Economic Development*. IMF. 10.2307/3866200

Bessis, S. (1998). The current state of the third world, *in* S. Cordellier (Edt.). *La fin du Tiers Monde?* La Decouverte.

Bina, C., & Yaghmanian, B. (1988). Import substitution and export promotion within the context of the internationalization of capital. *The Review of Radical Political Economics*, 20(2-3), 234–240. 10.1177/048661348802000235

Bleaney, M. (1979). *Underconsumption Theories: A History and Critical Analysis*. International Publishers.

Bock, K. (2004). Theories of progress, development, evolution. In Bottomore, T., & Bisbet, R. (Eds.), *A History of Sociological Analysis*. Heinemann.

Böhm, Eucken & Dorth, 2009

Böhm-Bawerk, E. (2011). *Karl Marx and the Close of His System*. Ludwig von Mises Institute.

Bolton, P., Roland, G., Vickers, J., & Burda, M. (1992). Privatization in Central and Eastern Europe. *Economic Policy*, 7(15), 275–309. 10.2307/1344544

Bonefeld, W. (1992). Social constitution and the from the capitalist sate, *in* W. Bonefeld, R. Gunn, & K. Psychopedis (edt.), *Open Marxizm Vol.1*. (93-132), Pluto.

Braudel, F. (1993). *A History of Civilizations*. Penguin Books.

Brunhoff, S. (2009). *Marx on Money*. Verso Book.

Bruton, H. J. (1966). Growth models and underdeveloped economies. *Journal of Political Economy*, 63(4), 322–336. 10.1086/257679

Bryson, J. M., & Einsweiler, R. C. (1988). *Strategic Planning: Threat and Opportunities for Planners*. Planner Press.

Buchanan, J. M. (1999). *Public Principles of Public Debt: A Defense and Restatement*. Liberty Fund.

Buchanan, J. M. (2001). *Externalities and Public Expenditure Theory*. Liberty Fund.

Burkett, P., & Hart-Landsberg, M. (2000). *Development, Crisis, and Class Struggle*. MacMillan Press.

Callinicos, A. (2001). Periodising capitalism and analysing imperialism: Classical Marxism and capitalist evolution. In Albritton, R., Itoh, M., Westra, R., & Zuege, A. (Eds.), *Phases of Capitalist Development: Booms, Crises and Globalisations* (pp. 230–245). Palgrave. 10.1057/9781403900081_14

Callinicos, A. (2007). *Social Theory: A Historical Introduction* (2nd ed.). Polity.

Carnoy, M. (2014). *The State and Political Theory*. Princeton University Press.

Carr, E. (1991). *What Is History*. Penguin.

Caslin, T. (1993). *Devlet ve ekonomi, M. Akgün (çev.). Liberalizm, Refah Devleti, Eleştiriler. K. Saybaşılı (drl.)*. Bağlam Yayıncılık.

Chang, H.J. (2007). *Kalkınma Reçetelerinin Gerçek Yüzü*. T. Onmuş (çev.), İletişim Yayınları.

Chang, H. J. (2007). *Kalkınma Reçetelerinin Gerçek Yüzü. T. Onmuş (çev.)*. İletişim Yayınları.

Chang, H.-C. (2007). *Kicking Away the Ladder: Development Strategy in Historical Perspective*. Anthem Press.

Chang, H.-J., & Evans, P. (2007). *Institutional Change and Economic Development*. United Nations.

Chang, H.-J., & Grabel, I. (2014). *Reclaiming Development: An Alternative Economic Policy Manual*. Zed Books. 10.5040/9781350222137

Chenery, H. B., & Kretschmer, K. S. (1969). Resource allocation for economic development. *Econometrica*, 24(4), 365–399. 10.2307/1905490

Claessen, H., & Skalnik, P. (1978). *The Early State*. DeGruyter Books., 10.1515/9783110813326

Clarke, S. (1991). *The State Debate*. Palgrave Macmillan. 10.1007/978-1-349-21464-8

Clausewitz, C. (1989). *On War*. Princeton University Press.

Cohn, E. J. (1966). *Yenilikçiler'in Rolü, Azgelişmiş Ülkeler*. Milliyet Kültür.

Colas, A. (2002). The class of globalisation, historical materialism and globalization. In *M. Rupert, & H. Smith (edt.), Historical Materialism and Globalization* (pp. 191–209). Routledge.

Colm, G., & Geiger, T. (1962). İktisadi ve toplumsal kalkınmada kamu planlaması ve ferdi karar alma, N. Serin (çev.). *SBF Dergisi*, 19(2), 11–29.

Corm, G. (2013). *Le Nouveau Gouvernement du Monde*. La Découverte.

Corrigan, P., Ramsay, H., & Sayer, D. (1980). The state as a relation of production. In Corrigan, P. (Ed.), *Capitalism, State Formation and Marxist Theory: Historical Investigations* (pp. 1–25). Quartet Books.

Denis, H. (1978). Le rôle des "débouchés préalables" dans la croissance économique de l'Europe occidentale et des Etats-Unis d'Amérique. *Economia Aplicada*, 31(3-4), 643–690.

Desai, M. (1974). *Marxian Economic Theory*. Gray-Mills Pub.

Dobb, M. (2012). Papers on Capitalism, Development and Planning, Routledge.

Dodgson, J. (1987). *Current Controversies in Economics*. Blackwell.

Domar, E. D. (1946). Capital expansion, rate of growth, and employment. *Econometrica*, 14(2), 137–147. 10.2307/1905364

Dornbush, R., Fisher, S., & Startz, R. (2010). *Macroeconomics* (11th ed.). McGraw-Hill.

Dowd, D. (2006). *Capitalism and Its Economics: A Critical History*. Pluto Press.

Duménil, G., & Lévy, D. (2009). *La grande bifurcation En finir avec le néolibéralisme*. Ouvrières.

Dunn, R. M., & Mutti, J. (2004). *International Economics* (6th ed.). Routledge. 10.4324/9780203462041

Durand, J. P. (2018). *La sociologie de Marx*. La Découverte. 10.3917/dec.duran.2018.01

Easterlin, R. A. (1981). Why isn't the whole World developed? *The Journal of Economic History*, 41(1), 1–17. 10.1017/S0022050700042674

Eaton, J. (1951). *Marx against Keynes*. Lawrence and Wishart Ltd.

Egeli, H. A. (2001). Dış ticaret açısından sanayileşme stratejileri ve Türkiye açısından değerlendirilmesi. *Sosyal Bilimler Dergisi*, 2, 149–161.

Eggertsson, T. (1990). *Economic Behavior and Institutions: Principles of Neoinstitutional Economics*. Cambridge University Press. 10.1017/CBO9780511609404

Einstein, A. (2002). *Relativity: The Special And The General Theory*. Fingerprint Publishing.

Ercan, F. (2006). *Modernizm, Kapitalizm ve Azgelişmişlik*. Bağlam Yayıncılık.

Feynman, R. (2017). *The Character of Physical Law*. Piper Books. 10.7551/mit-press/11068.001.0001

Frank, A. G. (2014). *The World System: Five Hundred Years or Five Thousand?* Routledge.

Freeman, C., & Soete, L. (2003). *The Economics of Industrial Innovation*. Psychology Press.

Freyssinet, J. (1980). *Le Concept de Sous-Développement*. Walter de Gruyter.

Friedman, M. (1962). *Capitalism and Freedom*. University of Chicago Press.

Ghai, D. (1995). Yapısal uyum, küresel bütünleşme ve sosyal demokrasi, İ. Eser (çev). In Prendergast, R., & Stewart, F. (Eds.), *Piyasa Güçleri ve Küresel Kalkınma*. Yapı Kredi Yayınları.

Gibson, H. D., & Tsakalatos, E. (1992). The international debt crisis: Causes, consequences and solutions. In Hewitt, T., Johnson, H., & Wield, D. (Eds.), *Industrialization and Development*. Oxford University Press.

Giddens, A. (1995). *A Contemporary Critique of Historical Materialism*. Palgrave. 10.1007/978-1-349-24187-3

Giddens, A. (1999). The Constitution of Society: Outline of the Theory of Structuration. *Polity*.

Giddens, A. (2013). The Nation-State and Violence. *Polity*.

Gill, S., & Law, D. (1988). *The Global Political Economy: Perspective, Problems, and Policies*. John Hopkins University Press. 10.56021/9780801837630

Goethe, J. W. (2008). *Faust*. Oxford University Press.

Gough, I. (1979). *The Political Economy of the Welfare State*. Springer. 10.1007/978-1-349-16122-5

Gouverneur, J. (2005). The Foundations of Capitalist Economy. *Polity*.

Gramsci, A. (2011). *Prison Notebooks*. Columbia University Press.

Gréau, J. L. (2005). *L'Avenir du Capitalisme*. Gallimard.

Grossekettler, H. G. (1994). On designing an institutional infrastructure for economies: The Freiburg Legacy After 50 Years. *Journal of Economic Studies (Glasgow, Scotland)*, 21(4), 9–24. 10.1108/01443589410070761

Guerrien, B. (1989). *L'economie Neo-Classique*. La Découverte.

Guichaoua, A. (1981). *Sciences Sociales et Développement*. CNRS Éditions.

Gülalp, H. (1987). *Gelişme Stratejileri ve Gelişme İdeolojileri*. Yurt Yayınları.

Güran, N., & Aktürk, İ. (1999). *Uluslararası İktisadi Kuruluşlar*. Tuğra Ofset.

Haar, C., Higgins, B., & Rodwin, L. (1961). Metropolitan policy for developing areas. *Daedalus*, 90(1), 132–146.

Hahnel, R. (2003). *The ABC's of Political Economy: A Modern*. Pluto Press.

Hanke, S. (1987). Privatization versus nationalization. *Proceedings of the Academy of Political Science*, 36(3), 1–3. 10.2307/1174091

Hansen, A. H. (1951). *Business Cycles and National Income*. W. W. Norton & Company.

Harrison, B. (1996). Küçük firmalar miti, K. Tanyılmaz (çev.). *Ekonomik Yaklaşım*, 7(20), 77–94.

Hart, B. H. L. (1991). *Strategy*. Plume.

Harvey, D. (1991). *The Condition of Postmodernity: An Enquiry into the Origins of Cultural Change*. Wiley-Blackwell.

Hawking, S. (1998). *A Brief History of Time: From the Big Bang to Black Holes*. Bantam Press.

Hayek, F. A. (2007). *The Road to Serfdom*. University of Chicago Press. 10.7208/chicago/9780226320533.001.0001

Hayek, F. A. (2022). *Law, Legislation, and Liberty*. University of Chicago Press.

Hazlitt, H. (2010). *The ABC of a Market Economy*. Crown Currency.

Heaton, H. (1948). *Economic History of Europe*, Harper & Brothers.

Hegel, G. W. F. (2004). *The Philosophy of History*. Dover Publications.

Heilbroner, R. L. (1970). On the limits of economic prediction. *Diogenes*, 18(70), 27–40. 10.1177/039219217001807002

Hiç, M. (1994). *Büyüme ve Gelişme Ekonomisi*. Filiz Kitabevi.

Hilferding, R. (1995). *Finance Capital*. Routledge.

Hirsch, B. (2004). What do unions do for economic performance? *Journal of Labor Research*, 25(3), 415–456. 10.1007/s12122-004-1023-8

Hirschman, A. (1958). *The Strategy of Economic Development*. Yale University Press.

Hirst, P., & Thompson, G. (2018). *Globalization in Question*. Rawat.

Hobsbawm, E. (1996). *The Age of Revolution: 1789-1848*. Vintage.

Hobsbawm, E. (1996a). *The Age of Capital: 1848-1875*. Vintage.

Hobsbawm, E. (1998). *On History*. The New Press.

Hodgson, G. (2006). Demokratik ekonomi: Planlama, piyasa ve iktidara yeni bir bakış, S. Çaklı (çev.). *Ekonomik Yaklaşım*, 17(59), 99–113. 10.5455/ey.10612

Hollinger, R. (1994). *Postmodernism and the Social Sciences: A Thematic Approach*. Sage Publications.

Holloway, J. (2003). Devlet ve gündelik mücadele, A. Güney (çev.). *Praksis Dergisi*, 9, 411–442.

Holloway, J., & Picciotto, S. (1978). *State and Capital: A Marxist Debate*. Edward Arnold.

Hume, D. (2004). *A Treatise of Human Nature*. Digireds.

Hunt, E. K. (2005). *History of Economic Thought*. Routledge.

Husserl, E. (1975). *Introduction to the Logical Investigations: A Draft of a Preface to the Logical Investigations*. Springer. 10.1007/978-94-010-1655-1

Husson, M. (2010). *Marxist İktisat Teorisi, Çağdaş Kapitalizm ve Kriz*. S. Binaltı (çev.). İstanbul: Yazın Yayıncılık.

Jenkins, R. (2003). *Corporate Responsibility and Labour Rights: Codes of Conduct in the Global Economy*. Routledge.

Jessop, B. (1982). *The Capitalist State*. New York University Press.

Jessop, B. (2003). The Future of the Capitalist State. *Polity*.

Jessop, B. (2013). State Theory: Putting the Capitalist State in Its Place. *Polity*.

Jones, G. (2011). Multinationals. In Amatori, F., & Jones, G. (Eds.), *Business History around the World*. Cambridge University Press.

Kahn, R. F. (1931). The relation of home investment to unemployment. *Economic Journal (London)*, 41(162), 173–198. 10.2307/2223697

Kant, I. (1784). What is Enlightenment? https://www.nypl.org/sites/default/files/kant_whatisenlightenment.pdf

Kant, I. (2007). *Critique of Pure Reason* (2nd ed.). Palgrave Macmillan. 10.1007/978-1-137-10016-0

Kant, I. (2009). *Critique of Practical Reason*. Merchant Books.

Karakayalı, H. (2002). *Makro Ekonomi*. Umit Kitabevi.

Karaosmanoğlu, A. (1958). Keynes İktisadının Bugün Kabul Edilmiyen Tarafları. Ankara Üniversitesi SBF Dergisi, 13(04).

Kasper, W., & Streit, M. E. (1998). *Institutional Economics, Social Order and Public Policy*. Edward Elgar.

Keyder, Ç. (1987). İthal ikameci sanayileşme stratejisi ve çelişkileri, *in* Boratav, Ç. Keyder ve Ş. Pamuk (der.), *Kriz, Gelir Dağılımı ve Türkiye'nin Alternatif Sorunu*, (pp. 13-36), Kaynak Yayınları.

Keynes, J. M. (2013). *The General Theory of Employment, Interest, and Money*. CreateSpace Independent Publishing Platform.

Kimura, F., & Kiyota, K. (2004). Foreing-owned versus domestically-owned firms: Economic performance in Japan. *Review of Development Economics*, 11(1), 31–48. 10.1111/j.1467-9361.2006.00347.x

Kojéve, A. (1980). *Introduction to the Reading of Hegel: Lectures on the "Phenomenology of Spirit"*. Cornell University Press.

Kondratieff, N. D. (2015). *The Long Waves in Economic Life*. Ravenio Books.

Koselleck, R. (2004). *Futures Past: On the Semantics of Historical Time*. Columbia University Press.

Koutsoyiannis, A. (1979). *Modern Microeconomics*, 2Rev Ed Edition, Palgrave. 10.1007/9781349160778

Kumar, K. (2004). *Sanayi Sonrası Toplumdan Postmodern Topluma Çağdaş Dünyanın Yeni Kuramları*. Dost Kitabevi.

Kuznets, S. (1955). Economic growth and income inequality. *The American Economic Review*, 45(1), 1–28.

Laidler, D. (2016). Keynes, John Maynard (New Perspectives), *in* R. Backhouse, B. W. Bateman (edt.). *The New Palgrave Dictionary of Economics*, (1-14), Palgrave.

Lall, S. (2005). Reinventing industrial strategy: The role of government policy in building industrial competitiveness, *in* K.P. Gallanger (edt.), *Putting Development First: The Importance of Policy Space in the WTO and International Financial Institutions*, (pp.144-161), Zed Books.

Landes, D. S. (1990). Why are we so rich and they so poor? *The American Economic Review*, 80(2), 1–13.

Lange, O. (2015). *Political Economy*. Pergamon.

Lazonick, W. (2007). The US stock market and the governance of innovative enterprise. *Industrial and Corporate Change*, 16(6), 983–1035. 10.1093/icc/dtm030

Lefebvre, H. (1966). Sociologie de Marx. *Revue Philosophique de Louvain*, 86, 173–241.

Leijonhufvud, A. (2006). Keynes as a Marshallian. In *R.E. Backhouse, & B.W. Bateman (edt.). Keynes* (pp. 58–77). Cambidge University Press., 10.1017/CCOL0521840902.004

Levi-Faur, D. (2005). The global diffusion of regulatory capitalism. *The Annals of the American Academy of Political and Social Science*, 598(1), 12–32. 10.1177/0002716204272371

Lewis, W. A. (1954). Economic Development with Unlimited Supplies of Labour. *Manchester School*, 22(2), 139–191. 10.1111/j.1467-9957.1954.tb00021.x

Lindbeck, A. (1995). Hazardous Welfare State Dynamics. *The American Economic Review*, 85(2), 9–15.

Luxemburg, R. (2003). *The Accumulation of Capital*. Routledge.

MacIntyre, A. (2002). *A Short History of Ethics*. Routledge.

Maillet, J. (1953). *Histoire des faits économiques*. Payot.

Mandel, E. (1973). *An Introduction to Marxist Economic Theory*. Pathfinder.

Mann, M. (1984). The autonomous power of the state: Its origins, mechanisms, and results. *Archives Européennes de Sociologie*, 25(2), 185–213. 10.1017/S0003975600004239

Martin, S. (1993). Private and social incentives to form R&D joint ventures. *Review of Industrial Organization*, 9(2), 157–171. 10.1007/BF01035655

Marx, K. (2016). *Capital, Vol.1, 2, 3.*, Fingerprint Publishing.

Marx, K. (1988). The Economic and Philosophic Manuscripts of 1844 and the Communist Manifesto. *Prometheus.*

Marx, K., & Engels, F. (2003). The German Ideology. *Prometheus.*

Marx, K., & Engels, F. (2003b). *The Communist Manifesto*. Penguin Classics. 10.1522/cla.mak.man

Mason, E. S. (1964). Kalkınma planlamasında metodoloji: Kalkınma planlamasında izlenen stratejinin yönleri", N. Serin (çev.). *SBF Dergisi*, 19(1), 39–57.

Meggison, W. L. (2000). From state to market: A survey of empirical studies on privatization. *Journal of Economic Literature*, 39(2), 321–389. 10.1257/jel.39.2.321

Millikan, M. F. (1965). İktisadi planlamada karar alma kriteri gelişen ülkelerde planlama hareketi ve planlama amaçları, N. Serin (çev.). *SBF Dergisi*, 20(1), 63–76.

Mises, L. (2010). *Human Action: A Treatise on Economics*. Ludwig von Mises Institute.

Moggridge, D. E. (1980). *Keynes*. Macmillan.

Mueller, D. C. (1979). *Public Choice*. Cambridge University Press.

Münkler, H. (2007). *Empires: The Logic of World Domination from Ancient Rome to the United States*. Polity Press.

Murphy, J. (1989). *Postmodern Social Analysis and Criticism*. Praeger.

Myint, H. (1973). Ekonomi teorisi ve kalkınma politikası", A.Y. Gökdere (çev.). *SBF Dergisi*, 29(3-4), 313–328.

Nair, S. (2000). İktisadi Liberalizmin Dünya Ölçeğinde Yayılması, S. Köm (çev.). Bir Uygarlık Siyaseti. İstanbul: Om Yayınevi.

Nisanken, W. A. (1975). Bureaucrats and politicians. *The Journal of Law & Economics*, 18(3), 617–643. 10.1086/466829

North, D. (1990). *Institutions, Institutional Change and Economic Performance*. Cambridge University Press. 10.1017/CBO9780511808678

Noy, I. (2004). Financial liberalization, prudential supervision, and the onset of banking crises. *Emerging Markets Review*, 5(3), 341–359. 10.1016/j.ememar.2004.05.001

Nunnenkamp, P. (1991). What are the future prospects for the Third World? Current problems and conclusions for development co-operation. *Economics*, 43, 7–27.

Nurkse, R. (1953). *Problems of Capital Formation in Underdeveloped Countries*. Oxford University Press.

O'Neill, J. (1998). *The Market: Ethics, Knowledge and Politics*. Routledge. 10.4324/9780203358467

Petras, J. (2002). The centrality of the state in the contemporary World, *CSCAweb*. sa.1-12.

Pieterse, J. N. (2013). Trends in development theory, *in* R. Palan (Edt.), *Global Political Economy: Contemporary Theories*. (pp.197-214), Routledge.

Pio, A. (1994). New growth theory and old development problems: How recent developments in endogenous growth theory apply to developing countries. *Development Policy Review*, 12(3), 277–300. 10.1111/j.1467-7679.1994.tb00068.x

Poulantzas, N. (1975). *Political Power and Social Classes*. Verso Books.

Poulantzas, N. (2008). *Marxism, Law and the State*. Verso.

Power, M. (1994). *The Audit Explosion*. Demos.

Pütz, T. (1994). *Grundlagen der Theoretischen Wirtschaftspolitik*. Gustav Fischer Verlag.

Ricardo, D. (2004). *The Principles of Political Economy and Taxation*. Dover Publications.

Ringer, F. (2000). *Max Weber's Methodology*. Harvard University Press.

Robinson, W. (2002). Capitalist Globalization and the Transnationalization of the State, *in* M. Rupert, & H. Smith (edt.), *Historical Materialism and Globalization*. (pp.210-229), Routledge.

Robinson, W. I. (2004). *A Theory of Blobal Capitalism: Production, Class, And State in A Transnational World*. Johns Hopkins University Press. 10.56021/9780801878848

Rosanvallan, P. (2004). *The New Social Question: Rethinking the Welfare State*. Princeton University Press.

Rosier, B. (1991). *Les Theories des Crises Economiques*. Repères.

Rostow, W. W. (1966). *The Stages of Economic Growth: A Non-Communist Manifesto*. Barakaldo Books.

Rousseau, J. J. (2006). *A Discourse on Political Economy*. Waking Lion Press.

Saad-Filho, A. (2002). *The Value of Marx: Political Economy for Contemporary Capitalism*. Routledge.

Saad-Filho, A. (2006). *Marx's 'Capital*. Pluto Press.

Samuels, W. J. (1995). The present state of institutional economics. *Cambridge Journal of Economics*, 19(4), 569–590. 10.1093/oxfordjournals.cje.a035331

Savas, E.S. (1994). *Özelleştirme*. MPM Yayınları, No.517.

Schmitt, C. (2006). *The Concept of the Political*. The University of Chicago Press.

Schmitz, H., & Musyck, B. (1994). Industrial districts in Europe: Policy lessons for developing countries? *World Development*, 22(6), 889–910. 10.1016/0305-750X(94)90060-4

Schumpeter, J. A. (2007). *Capitalism, Socialism and Democracy*. Lebooks Editora.

Sen, A. (2004). *Development as Freedom*. Anchor.

Seyidoğlu, H. (1998). *Uluslararası İktisat*. Güzem Yayınları.

Shafaeddin, S. M. (2005). Towards an alternative perspective on trade and industrial policies. *Development and Change*, 36(6), 1143–1162. 10.1111/j.0012-155X.2005.00453.x

Simmel, G. (2019). *Superiority and Subordination as Subject-Matter of Sociology*. LM Publishers.

Smith, A. (1994). *The Wealth of Nations*. Modern Library.

Smith, R. (2000). Military expenditure and globalization. In Toporowski, J. (Ed.), *Political Economy and the New Capitalism: Essays in Honour of Sam Aaronovitch* (pp. 76–86). Routledge.

Sombart, W. (1967). *Luxury and Capitalism*. University of Michigan Press.

Stewart, M. (1972). *Keynes and After*. Penguin.

Sutcliffe, B. (2002). How many capitalism? Historical materyalism in the debates about imperialism and globalization, *in* M. Rupert, & H. Smith (edt.), *Historical Materialism and Globalization*. (pp.40-58), Routledge

Sweezy, P. (2018). *Theory of Capital Development*. Monthly Review Press.

Teubal, M. (2001). Structural adjustment and social disarticulation: The case of Argentina. *Science and Society*, 64(4), 460–480.

Thorbecke, E. (2009). The evolution of the development doctrine, *in* G. Mavrotas, & A. Shorrocks, *Advancing Development: Core Themes in Global Economics*, (pp.3-36), Springer. https://doi.org/10.1057/9780230801462_1

Tinbergen, J. (1965). *A planning model for the educational requirements of economic development, Econometric Models of Education*. OECD.

Tokol, A. (2001). Çokuluslu şirketler ve endüstri ilişkilerine etkileri, *İş- Güç Dergisi*, 3(2), 35-52.

Touraine, A. (2007). *New Paradigm for Understanding Today s World*. Polity Press.

Toye, J. (2005). The significance of Keynes for development economies. In Jomo, K. S., & Fine, B. (Eds.), *The New Development Economics: Post Washington Consensus Neoliberal Thinking* (pp. 123–124). Zed Books.

Tubiana, L. (1998). The end of economic models, *in* S. Cordellier (Edt.). *La fin du Tiers Monde?* La Decouverte.

Türkay, M. (1994). *Gelişme iktisadı: Ekonomik büyüme merkezli yaklaşımın yükseliş ve gerilemesi, Yayınlanmamış Doktora Tezi.* Marmara Üniversitesi SBE.

Ülgener, S. (1991). *Milli Gelir, İstihdam ve İktisadi Büyüme* (7th ed.). Der Yayınları.

Ünsal, E. (2007). *İktisadi Büyüme.* İmaj Yayınevi.

Uzun, A. (2002). Yeni iktisat tarihi akımı ve iktisat tarihi yazımına katkıları. *CÜ İİBF Dergisi*, 2(1), 80–93.

Wade, R. H. (2003). What strategies are viable for developing countries today? The World Trade Organization and the shrinking of 'development space'. *Review of International Political Economy*, 10(4), 621–644. 10.1080/09692290310001601902

Weisskopf, W. (1971). *Alienation and Economics.* Dutton.

Wood, E. M. (2002). Global capital, national state, *in* M. Rupert, & H. Smith (edt.), *Historical Materialism and Globalization.* (pp.17-39), Routledge.

Wood, E. M. (1997). *Defence of History: Marxism and the Postmodern Agenda.* Verso.

Wood, E. M. (2016). *The Origin of Capitalism: A Longer View.* Verso.

Related References

To continue our tradition of advancing information science and technology research, we have compiled a list of recommended IGI Global readings. These references will provide additional information and guidance to further enrich your knowledge and assist you with your own research and future publications.

Arteta, A. (2019). *Democracy and Government: Making Decisions*. IGI Global. 10.4018/978-1-5225-7558-0.ch001

Camillo, A. (2021). *Legal Matters, Risk Management, and Risk Prevention: From Forming a Business to Legal Representation*. IGI Global. 10.4018/978-1-7998-4342-9.ch004

Abdel-Hameid, S. O., & Wilson, E. (2018). Gender, Organization, and Change in Sudan. In Mahtab, N., Haque, T., Khan, I., Islam, M., & Wahid, I. (Eds.), *Handbook of Research on Women's Issues and Rights in the Developing World* (pp. 107–120). Hershey, PA: IGI Global. 10.4018/978-1-5225-3018-3.ch007

Abdullahi, R. B. (2018). Volunteerism in Urban Development the Case of Non-Cash, Non-Digital Crowdfunding Growth in Nigeria. In Benna, U., & Benna, A. (Eds.), *Crowdfunding and Sustainable Urban Development in Emerging Economies* (pp. 188–210). Hershey, PA: IGI Global. 10.4018/978-1-5225-3952-0.ch010

Abioye, T. O., Oyesomi, K., Ajiboye, E., Omidiora, S., & Oyero, O. (2017). Education, Gender, and Child-Rights: Salient Issues in SDGS Years in ADO-ODO/OTA Local Government Area of Ogun State, Nigeria. In Nelson, O., Ojebuyi, B., & Salawu, A. (Eds.), *Impacts of the Media on African Socio-Economic Development* (pp. 141–154). Hershey, PA: IGI Global. 10.4018/978-1-5225-1859-4.ch009

Abir, T., & Khan, M. Y. (2022). Importance of ICT Advancement and Culture of Adaptation in the Tourism and Hospitality Industry for Developing Countries. In Ramos, C., Quinteiro, S., & Gonçalves, A. (Eds.), *ICT as Innovator Between Tourism and Culture* (pp. 30–41). IGI Global. https://doi.org/10.4018/978-1-7998-8165-0.ch003

Abir, T., & Khan, M. Y. (2022). Importance of ICT Advancement and Culture of Adaptation in the Tourism and Hospitality Industry for Developing Countries. In Ramos, C., Quinteiro, S., & Gonçalves, A. (Eds.), *ICT as Innovator Between Tourism and Culture* (pp. 30–41). IGI Global. https://doi.org/10.4018/978-1-7998-8165-0.ch003

Adalı, G. K. (2022). Measuring the Attitudes of Governmental Policies and the Public Towards the COVID-19 Pandemic. In Omeraki Çekirdekci, Ş., İngün Karkış, Ö., & Gönültaş, S. (Eds.), *Handbook of Research on Interdisciplinary Perspectives on the Threats and Impacts of Pandemics* (pp. 163–187). IGI Global. https://doi.org/10.4018/978-1-7998-8674-7.ch009

Adisa, W. B. (2018). Land Use Policy and Urban Sprawl in Nigeria: Land Use and the Emergence of Urban Sprawl. In Eneanya, A. (Ed.), *Handbook of Research on Environmental Policies for Emergency Management and Public Safety* (pp. 256–274). Hershey, PA: IGI Global. 10.4018/978-1-5225-3194-4.ch014

Afenyo-Agbe, E., & Mensah, I. (2022). Principles, Benefits, and Barriers to Community-Based Tourism: Implications for Management. In Mensah, I., & Afenyo-Agbe, E. (Eds.), *Prospects and Challenges of Community-Based Tourism and Changing Demographics* (pp. 1–29). IGI Global. 10.4018/978-1-7998-7335-8.ch001

Afolabi, O. S., Amao-Kolawole, T. G., Shittu, A. K., & Oguntokun, O. O. (2018). Rule of Law, Governance, and Sustainable Development: The Nigerian Perspective. In Teshager Alemu, K., & Abebe Alebachew, M. (Eds.), *Handbook of Research on Sustainable Development and Governance Strategies for Economic Growth in Africa* (pp. 273–290). Hershey, PA: IGI Global. 10.4018/978-1-5225-3247-7.ch015

Agbo, V. M. (2022). Distributive Justice Issues in Community-Based Tourism. In Mensah, I., & Afenyo-Agbe, E. (Eds.), *Prospects and Challenges of Community-Based Tourism and Changing Demographics* (pp. 107–129). IGI Global. https://doi.org/10.4018/978-1-7998-7335-8.ch005

Agrawal, S. (2017). The Impact of Emerging Technologies and Social Media on Different Business(es): Marketing and Management. In Rishi, O., & Sharma, A. (Eds.), *Maximizing Business Performance and Efficiency Through Intelligent Systems* (pp. 37–49). Hershey, PA: IGI Global. 10.4018/978-1-5225-2234-8.ch002

Agyemang, O. S. (2018). Institutional Structures and the Prevalence of Foreign Ownership of Firms: Empirical Evidence From Africa. In Teshager Alemu, K., & Abebe Alebachew, M. (Eds.), *Handbook of Research on Sustainable Development and Governance Strategies for Economic Growth in Africa* (pp. 455–479). Hershey, PA: IGI Global. 10.4018/978-1-5225-3247-7.ch024

Ahmad, A., & Johari, S. (2022). Georgetown as a Gastronomy Tourism Destination: Visitor Awareness Towards Revisit Intention of Nasi Kandar Restaurant. In Valeri, M. (Ed.), *New Governance and Management in Touristic Destinations* (pp. 71–83). IGI Global. https://doi.org/10.4018/978-1-6684-3889-3.ch005

Alsaç, U. (2017). EKAP: Turkey's Centralized E-Procurement System. In Shakya, R. (Ed.), *Digital Governance and E-Government Principles Applied to Public Procurement* (pp. 126–150). Hershey, PA: IGI Global. 10.4018/978-1-5225-2203-4.ch006

Amadi, L. A., & Igwe, P. (2018). Open Government and Bureaucratic Secrecy in the Developing Democracies: Africa in Perspective. In Kok, A. (Ed.), *Proliferation of Open Government Initiatives and Systems* (pp. 1–28). Hershey, PA: IGI Global. 10.4018/978-1-5225-4987-1.ch001

Antosova, G., Sabogal-Salamanca, M., & Krizova, E. (2021). Human Capital in Tourism: A Practical Model of Endogenous and Exogenous Territorial Tourism Planning in Bahía Solano, Colombia. In Costa, V., Moura, A., & Mira, M. (Eds.), *Handbook of Research on Human Capital and People Management in the Tourism Industry* (pp. 282–302). IGI Global. https://doi.org/10.4018/978-1-7998-4318-4.ch014

Arble, E., & Arnetz, B. B. (2021). Four Fundamental Principles to Enhance Police Performance and Community Safety. In Arble, E., & Arnetz, B. (Eds.), *Interventions, Training, and Technologies for Improved Police Well-Being and Performance* (pp. 231–245). IGI Global. https://doi.org/10.4018/978-1-7998-6820-0.ch015

Arora, G. C. (2020). The Problem of Climate-Induced Displacement: Analyzing the International Framework on Protection of Rights of Climate Migrants. In Das, R., & Mandal, N. (Eds.), *Interdisciplinary Approaches to Public Policy and Sustainability* (pp. 67–82). IGI Global. https://doi.org/10.4018/978-1-7998-0315-7.ch004

Arora, T., & Mehra, N. (2021). Administration of Civil Justice in India: Ancient and Modern Perspectives. In Yin, E., & Kofie, N. (Eds.), *Advancing Civil Justice Reform and Conflict Resolution in Africa and Asia: Comparative Analyses and Case Studies* (pp. 17–45). IGI Global. https://doi.org/10.4018/978-1-7998-7898-8.ch002

Arsenijević, O. M., Orčić, D., & Kastratović, E. (2017). Development of an Optimization Tool for Intangibles in SMEs: A Case Study from Serbia with a Pilot Research in the Prestige by Milka Company. In Vemić, M. (Ed.), *Optimal Management Strategies in Small and Medium Enterprises* (pp. 320–347). Hershey, PA: IGI Global. 10.4018/978-1-5225-1949-2.ch015

Asante, M., & Botchway, T. P. (2021). Shielding Members of Parliament Against Court Summons: Interrogating the Question of Parliamentary Immunity. In Yin, E., & Kofie, N. (Eds.), *Advancing Civil Justice Reform and Conflict Resolution in Africa and Asia: Comparative Analyses and Case Studies* (pp. 210–229). IGI Global. https://doi.org/10.4018/978-1-7998-7898-8.ch012

Asero, V., & Billi, S. (2022). New Perspective of Networking in the DMO Model. In Valeri, M. (Ed.), *New Governance and Management in Touristic Destinations* (pp. 105–118). IGI Global. https://doi.org/10.4018/978-1-6684-3889-3.ch007

Ateş, V. (2021). Critical Antecedents of Trust in E-Government Services in Turkey. In Babaoğlu, C., Akman, E., & Kulaç, O. (Eds.), *Handbook of Research on Global Challenges for Improving Public Services and Government Operations* (pp. 94–116). IGI Global. https://doi.org/10.4018/978-1-7998-4978-0.ch006

Atiku, S. O., & Fields, Z. (2017). Multicultural Orientations for 21st Century Global Leadership. In Baporikar, N. (Ed.), *Management Education for Global Leadership* (pp. 28–51). Hershey, PA: IGI Global. 10.4018/978-1-5225-1013-0.ch002

Atiku, S. O., & Fields, Z. (2018). Organisational Learning Dimensions and Talent Retention Strategies for the Service Industries. In Baporikar, N. (Ed.), *Global Practices in Knowledge Management for Societal and Organizational Development* (pp. 358–381). Hershey, PA: IGI Global. 10.4018/978-1-5225-3009-1.ch017

Ávila, L., & Teixeira, L. (2018). The Main Concepts Behind the Dematerialization of Business Processes. In M. Khosrow-Pour, D.B.A. (Ed.), *Encyclopedia of Information Science and Technology, Fourth Edition* (pp. 888-898). Hershey, PA: IGI Global. https://doi.org/10.4018/978-1-5225-2255-3.ch076

Ayeni, A. O. (2018). Environmental Policies for Emergency Management and Public Safety: Implementing Green Policy and Community Participation. In Eneanya, A. (Ed.), *Handbook of Research on Environmental Policies for Emergency Management and Public Safety* (pp. 40–59). Hershey, PA: IGI Global. 10.4018/978-1-5225-3194-4.ch003

Ayodele, J. O. (2017). The Influence of Migration and Crime on Development in Lagos, Nigeria. In Afolayan, G., & Akinwale, A. (Eds.), *Global Perspectives on Development Administration and Cultural Change* (pp. 192–230). Hershey, PA: IGI Global. 10.4018/978-1-5225-0629-4.ch009

Ayorekire, J., Mugizi, F., Obua, J., & Ampaire, G. (2022). Community-Based Tourism and Local People's Perceptions Towards Conservation: The Case of Queen Elizabeth Conservation Area, Uganda. In Mensah, I., & Afenyo-Agbe, E. (Eds.), *Prospects and Challenges of Community-Based Tourism and Changing Demographics* (pp. 56–82). IGI Global. https://doi.org/10.4018/978-1-7998-7335-8.ch003

Baarda, R. (2017). Digital Democracy in Authoritarian Russia: Opportunity for Participation, or Site of Kremlin Control? In Luppicini, R., & Baarda, R. (Eds.), *Digital Media Integration for Participatory Democracy* (pp. 87–100). Hershey, PA: IGI Global. 10.4018/978-1-5225-2463-2.ch005

Balakrishnan, K. (2017). The Rationale for Offsets in Defence Acquisition from a Theoretical Perspective. In Burgess, K., & Antill, P. (Eds.), *Emerging Strategies in Defense Acquisitions and Military Procurement* (pp. 263–276). Hershey, PA: IGI Global. 10.4018/978-1-5225-0599-0.ch015

Banerjee, S. (2017). Globalization and Human Rights: How Globalization Can Be a Tool to Protect the Human Rights. In Akrivopoulou, C. (Ed.), *Defending Human Rights and Democracy in the Era of Globalization* (pp. 1–16). Hershey, PA: IGI Global. 10.4018/978-1-5225-0723-9.ch001

Bartens, Y., Chunpir, H. I., Schulte, F., & Voß, S. (2017). Business/IT Alignment in Two-Sided Markets: A COBIT 5 Analysis for Media Streaming Business Models. In De Haes, S., & Van Grembergen, W. (Eds.), *Strategic IT Governance and Alignment in Business Settings* (pp. 82–111). Hershey, PA: IGI Global. 10.4018/978-1-5225-0861-8.ch004

Bashayreh, A. M. (2018). Organizational Culture and Organizational Performance. In Lee, W., & Sabetzadeh, F. (Eds.), *Contemporary Knowledge and Systems Science* (pp. 50–69). Hershey, PA: IGI Global. 10.4018/978-1-5225-5655-8.ch003

Bechthold, L., Lude, M., & Prügl, R. (2021). Crisis Favors the Prepared Firm: How Organizational Ambidexterity Relates to Perceptions of Organizational Resilience. In Zehrer, A., Glowka, G., Schwaiger, K., & Ranacher-Lackner, V. (Eds.), *Resiliency Models and Addressing Future Risks for Family Firms in the Tourism Industry* (pp. 178–205). IGI Global. https://doi.org/10.4018/978-1-7998-7352-5.ch008

Bedford, D. A. (2018). Sustainable Knowledge Management Strategies: Aligning Business Capabilities and Knowledge Management Goals. In Baporikar, N. (Ed.), *Global Practices in Knowledge Management for Societal and Organizational Development* (pp. 46–73). Hershey, PA: IGI Global. 10.4018/978-1-5225-3009-1.ch003

Bekjanov, D., & Matyusupov, B. (2021). Influence of Innovative Processes in the Competitiveness of Tourist Destination. In Soares, J. (Ed.), *Innovation and Entrepreneurial Opportunities in Community Tourism* (pp. 243–263). IGI Global. https://doi.org/10.4018/978-1-7998-4855-4.ch014

Bessant, J. (2017). Digital Humour, Gag Laws, and the Liberal Security State. In Luppicini, R., & Baarda, R. (Eds.), *Digital Media Integration for Participatory Democracy* (pp. 204–221). Hershey, PA: IGI Global. 10.4018/978-1-5225-2463-2.ch010

Bharwani, S., & Musunuri, D. (2018). Reflection as a Process From Theory to Practice. In M. Khosrow-Pour, D.B.A. (Ed.), *Encyclopedia of Information Science and Technology, Fourth Edition* (pp. 1529-1539). Hershey, PA: IGI Global. 10.4018/978-1-5225-2255-3.ch132

Bhat, M. Y. (2020). Environmental Problems of Delhi and Governmental Concern. In Merviö, M. (Ed.), *Global Issues and Innovative Solutions in Healthcare, Culture, and the Environment* (pp. 133–167). IGI Global. https://doi.org/10.4018/978-1-7998-3576-9.ch008

Bhat, R. A. (2021). Identification of Various Dimensions and Indicators of Immigrant Integration Into Global Scenarios. In Mafukata, M. (Ed.), *Impact of Immigration and Xenophobia on Development in Africa* (pp. 247–260). IGI Global. https://doi.org/10.4018/978-1-7998-7099-9.ch014

Bhushan, M., & Yadav, A. (2017). Concept of Cloud Computing in ESB. In Bhadoria, R., Chaudhari, N., Tomar, G., & Singh, S. (Eds.), *Exploring Enterprise Service Bus in the Service-Oriented Architecture Paradigm* (pp. 116–127). Hershey, PA: IGI Global. 10.4018/978-1-5225-2157-0.ch008

Binder, D., & Miller, J. W. (2021). A Generations' Perspective on Employer Branding in Tourism. In Costa, V., Moura, A., & Mira, M. (Eds.), *Handbook of Research on Human Capital and People Management in the Tourism Industry* (pp. 152–174). IGI Global. https://doi.org/10.4018/978-1-7998-4318-4.ch008

Birch Freeman, A. A., Mensah, I., & Antwi, K. B. (2022). Smiling vs. Frowning Faces: Community Participation for Sustainable Tourism in Ghanaian Communities. In Mensah, I., & Afenyo-Agbe, E. (Eds.), *Prospects and Challenges of Community-Based Tourism and Changing Demographics* (pp. 83–106). IGI Global. https://doi.org/10.4018/978-1-7998-7335-8.ch004

Biswas, A., & De, A. K. (2017). On Development of a Fuzzy Stochastic Programming Model with Its Application to Business Management. In Trivedi, S., Dey, S., Kumar, A., & Panda, T. (Eds.), *Handbook of Research on Advanced Data Mining Techniques and Applications for Business Intelligence* (pp. 353–378). Hershey, PA: IGI Global. 10.4018/978-1-5225-2031-3.ch021

Boachie, C. (2017). Public Financial Management and Systems of Accountability in Sub-National Governance in Developing Economies. In Schoburgh, E., & Ryan, R. (Eds.), *Handbook of Research on Sub-National Governance and Development* (pp. 193–217). Hershey, PA: IGI Global. 10.4018/978-1-5225-1645-3.ch009

Boachie, C., & Adu-Darko, E. (2018). Socio-Economic Impact of Foreign Direct Investment in Developing Countries. In Malepati, V., & Gowri, C. (Eds.), *Foreign Direct Investments (FDIs) and Opportunities for Developing Economies in the World Market* (pp. 66–81). Hershey, PA: IGI Global. 10.4018/978-1-5225-3026-8.ch004

Boragnio, A., & Faracce Macia, C. (2021). "Taking Care of Yourself at Home": Use of E-Commerce About Food and Care During the COVID-19 Pandemic in the City of Buenos Aires. In Korstanje, M. (Ed.), *Socio-Economic Effects and Recovery Efforts for the Rental Industry: Post-COVID-19 Strategies* (pp. 45–71). IGI Global. https://doi.org/10.4018/978-1-7998-7287-0.ch003

Borges, V. D. (2021). Happiness: The Basis for Public Policy in Tourism. In Perinotto, A., Mayer, V., & Soares, J. (Eds.), *Rebuilding and Restructuring the Tourism Industry: Infusion of Happiness and Quality of Life* (pp. 1–25). IGI Global. https://doi.org/10.4018/978-1-7998-7239-9.ch001

Borràs, S. (2017). Rights of Nature to Protect Human Rights in Times of Environmental Crisis. In Akrivopoulou, C. (Ed.), *Defending Human Rights and Democracy in the Era of Globalization* (pp. 225–261). Hershey, PA: IGI Global. 10.4018/978-1-5225-0723-9.ch010

Bouaziz, F. (2021). E-Government and Digital Transformation: A Conceptual Framework for Risk Factors Identification. In Sandhu, K. (Ed.), *Disruptive Technology and Digital Transformation for Business and Government* (pp. 67–90). IGI Global. https://doi.org/10.4018/978-1-7998-8583-2.ch004

Brusca, I., Olmo, J., & Labrador, M. (2018). Characterizing the Risk Factors for Financial Sustainability in Spanish Local Governments. In Rodríguez Bolívar, M., & López Subires, M. (Eds.), *Financial Sustainability and Intergenerational Equity in Local Governments* (pp. 206–223). Hershey, PA: IGI Global. 10.4018/978-1-5225-3713-7.ch009

Bücker, J., & Ernste, K. (2018). Use of Brand Heroes in Strategic Reputation Management: The Case of Bacardi, Adidas, and Daimler. In Erdemir, A. (Ed.), *Reputation Management Techniques in Public Relations* (pp. 126–150). Hershey, PA: IGI Global. 10.4018/978-1-5225-3619-2.ch007

Budd, J. R., & Littrell, M. W. (2021). Law Enforcement Challenges to Gathering Intelligence in the Street: The Fourth Amendment. In de Silva, E., & Abeyagoonesekera, A. (Eds.), *Intelligence and Law Enforcement in the 21st Century* (pp. 18–40). IGI Global. https://doi.org/10.4018/978-1-7998-7904-6.ch002

Buluk Eşitti, B. (2021). COVID-19 and Alternative Tourism: New Destinations and New Tourism Products. In Demir, M., Dalgıç, A., & Ergen, F. (Eds.), *Handbook of Research on the Impacts and Implications of COVID-19 on the Tourism Industry* (pp. 786–805). IGI Global. https://doi.org/10.4018/978-1-7998-8231-2.ch038

Bureš, V. (2018). Industry 4.0 From the Systems Engineering Perspective: Alternative Holistic Framework Development. In Brunet-Thornton, R., & Martinez, F. (Eds.), *Analyzing the Impacts of Industry 4.0 in Modern Business Environments* (pp. 199–223). Hershey, PA: IGI Global. 10.4018/978-1-5225-3468-6.ch011

Bush, C. L. (2021). Policing Strategies and Approaches to Improving Community Relations: Black Citizens' Perceptions of Law Enforcement Efforts to Intentionally Strengthen Relationships. In Pittaro, M. (Ed.), *Global Perspectives on Reforming the Criminal Justice System* (pp. 56–75). IGI Global. https://doi.org/10.4018/978-1-7998-6884-2.ch004

Buzady, Z. (2017). Resolving the Magic Cube of Effective Case Teaching: Benchmarking Case Teaching Practices in Emerging Markets – Insights from the Central European University Business School, Hungary. In Latusek, D. (Ed.), *Case Studies as a Teaching Tool in Management Education* (pp. 79–103). Hershey, PA: IGI Global. 10.4018/978-1-5225-0770-3.ch005

Canto Moniz, G. (2020). Is There Anything Left of the Portuguese Law Implementing the GDPR?: The Decision of the Portuguese Supervisory Authority. In Tzanou, M. (Ed.), *Personal Data Protection and Legal Developments in the European Union* (pp. 125–139). IGI Global. https://doi.org/10.4018/978-1-5225-9489-5.ch007

Căpusneanu, S., & Topor, D. I. (2018). Business Ethics and Cost Management in SMEs: Theories of Business Ethics and Cost Management Ethos. In Oncioiu, I. (Ed.), *Ethics and Decision-Making for Sustainable Business Practices* (pp. 109–127). Hershey, PA: IGI Global. 10.4018/978-1-5225-3773-1.ch007

Casoria, M., & AlSarraf, E. M. (2020). The Impact of the GDPR on Extra-EU Legal Systems: The Case of the Kingdom of Bahrain. In Tzanou, M. (Ed.), *Personal Data Protection and Legal Developments in the European Union* (pp. 224–237). IGI Global. https://doi.org/10.4018/978-1-5225-9489-5.ch011

Chan, R. L., Mo, P. L., & Moon, K. K. (2018). Strategic and Tactical Measures in Managing Enterprise Risks: A Study of the Textile and Apparel Industry. In Strang, K., Korstanje, M., & Vajjhala, N. (Eds.), *Research, Practices, and Innovations in Global Risk and Contingency Management* (pp. 1–19). Hershey, PA: IGI Global. 10.4018/978-1-5225-4754-9.ch001

Charlier, S. D., Burke-Smalley, L. A., & Fisher, S. L. (2018). Undergraduate Programs in the U.S: A Contextual and Content-Based Analysis. In Mendy, J. (Ed.), *Teaching Human Resources and Organizational Behavior at the College Level* (pp. 26–57). Hershey, PA: IGI Global. 10.4018/978-1-5225-2820-3.ch002

Chaves, A. (2022). Government Response Capacity to the COVID-19 Pandemic: Estimating the Impact of Lockdown Measures in Colombia. In Antošová, G. (Ed.), *Innovative Strategic Planning and International Collaboration for the Mitigation of Global Crises* (pp. 114–137). IGI Global. https://doi.org/10.4018/978-1-7998-8339-5.ch008

Chen, M., & Su, F. (2017). Global Civic Engagement as an Empowering Device for Cross-Ethnic and Cross-Cultural Understanding in Taiwan. In Shin, R. (Ed.), *Convergence of Contemporary Art, Visual Culture, and Global Civic Engagement* (pp. 24–45). Hershey, PA: IGI Global. 10.4018/978-1-5225-1665-1.ch002

Chigwata, T. C. (2017). Fiscal Decentralization: Constraints to Revenue-Raising by Local Government in Zimbabwe. In Schoburgh, E., & Ryan, R. (Eds.), *Handbook of Research on Sub-National Governance and Development* (pp. 218–240). Hershey, PA: IGI Global. 10.4018/978-1-5225-1645-3.ch010

Chowdhury, M. A. (2017). The Nexus Between Institutional Quality and Foreign Direct Investments (FDI) in South Asia: Dynamic Heterogeneous Panel Approach. In Dorożyński, T., & Kuna-Marszałek, A. (Eds.), *Outward Foreign Direct Investment (FDI) in Emerging Market Economies* (pp. 293–310). Hershey, PA: IGI Global. 10.4018/978-1-5225-2345-1.ch015

Christopher, M. E., & Tsushima, V. G. (2017). Police Interactions with Persons-in-Crisis: Emergency Psychological Services and Jail Diversion. In Mitchell, C., & Dorian, E. (Eds.), *Police Psychology and Its Growing Impact on Modern Law Enforcement* (pp. 274–294). Hershey, PA: IGI Global. 10.4018/978-1-5225-0813-7.ch014

Chumillas, J., Güell, M., & Quer, P. (2022). The Use of ICT in Tourist and Educational Literary Routes: The Role of the Guide. In Ramos, C., Quinteiro, S., & Gonçalves, A. (Eds.), *ICT as Innovator Between Tourism and Culture* (pp. 15–29). IGI Global. https://doi.org/10.4018/978-1-7998-8165-0.ch002

Ciftci, D. (2022). Digital Citizenship and E-Government Integration: The Case of North Cyprus. In Öngün, E., Pembecioğlu, N., & Gündüz, U. (Eds.), *Handbook of Research on Digital Citizenship and Management During Crises* (pp. 34–55). IGI Global. https://doi.org/10.4018/978-1-7998-8421-7.ch003

Citro, F., Lucianelli, G., & Santis, S. (2018). Financial Conditions, Financial Sustainability, and Intergenerational Equity in Local Governments: A Literature Review. In Rodríguez Bolívar, M., & López Subires, M. (Eds.), *Financial Sustainability and Intergenerational Equity in Local Governments* (pp. 101–124). Hershey, PA: IGI Global. 10.4018/978-1-5225-3713-7.ch005

Correa de Mello, M. B. (2019). The Information Access Law as a Full Constitutional Citizenship Instrument. In Melro, A., & Oliveira, L. (Eds.), *Constitutional Knowledge and Its Impact on Citizenship Exercise in a Networked Society* (pp. 55–72). IGI Global. https://doi.org/10.4018/978-1-5225-8350-9.ch003

Covell, C. E. (2018). Theoretical Application of Public Sector Planning and Budgeting. In Rodríguez Bolívar, M., & López Subires, M. (Eds.), *Financial Sustainability and Intergenerational Equity in Local Governments* (pp. 248–279). Hershey, PA: IGI Global. 10.4018/978-1-5225-3713-7.ch011

Cunha, A. M., Ferreira, A. D., & Fernandes, M. J. (2018). The Impact of Accounting Information and Socioeconomic Factors in the Re-Election of Portuguese Mayors. In Azevedo, G., da Silva Oliveira, J., Marques, R., & Ferreira, A. (Eds.), *Handbook of Research on Modernization and Accountability in Public Sector Management* (pp. 406–432). Hershey, PA: IGI Global. 10.4018/978-1-5225-3731-1.ch019

da Rosa, I., & de Almeida, J. (2017). Digital Transformation in the Public Sector: Electronic Procurement in Portugal. In Shakya, R. (Ed.), *Digital Governance and E-Government Principles Applied to Public Procurement* (pp. 99–125). Hershey, PA: IGI Global. 10.4018/978-1-5225-2203-4.ch005

Dahlberg, T., Kivijärvi, H., & Saarinen, T. (2017). IT Investment Consistency and Other Factors Influencing the Success of IT Performance. In De Haes, S., & Van Grembergen, W. (Eds.), *Strategic IT Governance and Alignment in Business Settings* (pp. 176–208). Hershey, PA: IGI Global. 10.4018/978-1-5225-0861-8.ch007

Damnjanović, A. M. (2017). Knowledge Management Optimization through IT and E-Business Utilization: A Qualitative Study on Serbian SMEs. In Vemić, M. (Ed.), *Optimal Management Strategies in Small and Medium Enterprises* (pp. 249–267). Hershey, PA: IGI Global. 10.4018/978-1-5225-1949-2.ch012

Daneshpour, H. (2017). Integrating Sustainable Development into Project Portfolio Management through Application of Open Innovation. In Vemić, M. (Ed.), *Optimal Management Strategies in Small and Medium Enterprises* (pp. 370–387). Hershey, PA: IGI Global. 10.4018/978-1-5225-1949-2.ch017

Daniel, A. D., & Reis de Castro, V. (2018). Entrepreneurship Education: How to Measure the Impact on Nascent Entrepreneurs. In Carrizo Moreira, A., Guilherme Leitão Dantas, J., & Manuel Valente, F. (Eds.), *Nascent Entrepreneurship and Successful New Venture Creation* (pp. 85–110). Hershey, PA: IGI Global. 10.4018/978-1-5225-2936-1.ch004

Daramola, O. (2018). Revisiting the Legal Framework of Urban Planning in the Global South: An Explanatory Example of Nigeria. In Teshager Alemu, K., & Abebe Alebachew, M. (Eds.), *Handbook of Research on Sustainable Development and Governance Strategies for Economic Growth in Africa* (pp. 258–271). Hershey, PA: IGI Global. 10.4018/978-1-5225-3247-7.ch014

Dau, L. A., Moore, E. M., Soto, M. A., & LeBlanc, C. R. (2017). How Globalization Sparked Entrepreneurship in the Developing World: The Impact of Formal Economic and Political Linkages. In Christiansen, B., & Kasarcı, F. (Eds.), *Corporate Espionage, Geopolitics, and Diplomacy Issues in International Business* (pp. 72–91). Hershey, PA: IGI Global. 10.4018/978-1-5225-1031-4.ch005

David, R., Swami, B. N., & Tangirala, S. (2018). Ethics Impact on Knowledge Management in Organizational Development: A Case Study. In Baporikar, N. (Ed.), *Global Practices in Knowledge Management for Societal and Organizational Development* (pp. 19–45). Hershey, PA: IGI Global. 10.4018/978-1-5225-3009-1.ch002

De Man, P. (2019). In-Situ Resource Utilization: Legal Aspects. In Nakarada Pecujlic, A., & Tugnoli, M. (Eds.), *Promoting Productive Cooperation Between Space Lawyers and Engineers* (pp. 211–224). IGI Global. https://doi.org/10.4018/978-1-5225-7256-5.ch013

Denholm, J., & Lee-Davies, L. (2018). Success Factors for Games in Business and Project Management. In *Enhancing Education and Training Initiatives Through Serious Games* (pp. 34–68). Hershey, PA: IGI Global. 10.4018/978-1-5225-3689-5.ch002

Deshpande, M. (2017). Best Practices in Management Institutions for Global Leadership: Policy Aspects. In Baporikar, N. (Ed.), *Management Education for Global Leadership* (pp. 1–27). Hershey, PA: IGI Global. 10.4018/978-1-5225-1013-0.ch001

Deshpande, M. (2018). Policy Perspectives for SMEs Knowledge Management. In Baporikar, N. (Ed.), *Knowledge Integration Strategies for Entrepreneurship and Sustainability* (pp. 23–46). Hershey, PA: IGI Global. 10.4018/978-1-5225-5115-7.ch002

Domingos, D., Respício, A., & Martinho, R. (2017). Reliability of IoT-Aware BPMN Healthcare Processes. In Reis, C., & Maximiano, M. (Eds.), *Internet of Things and Advanced Application in Healthcare* (pp. 214–248). Hershey, PA: IGI Global. 10.4018/978-1-5225-1820-4.ch008

Drenner, K. (2017). Introduction to Faith in State Legislatures: Land of the Brave and the Home of the Free – The Star-Spangled Banner. In *Impacts of Faith-Based Decision Making on the Individual-Level Legislative Process: Emerging Research and Opportunities* (pp. 1–25). Hershey, PA: IGI Global. 10.4018/978-1-5225-2388-8.ch001

Drenner, K. (2017). The Holy Wars of Marriage. In *Impacts of Faith-Based Decision Making on the Individual-Level Legislative Process: Emerging Research and Opportunities* (pp. 92–116). Hershey, PA: IGI Global. 10.4018/978-1-5225-2388-8.ch004

Drenner, K. (2017). The Implications of Religious Liberty. In *Impacts of Faith-Based Decision Making on the Individual-Level Legislative Process: Emerging Research and Opportunities* (pp. 143–162). Hershey, PA: IGI Global. 10.4018/978-1-5225-2388-8.ch006

Duncan, S. T., & Geczi, H. (2021). Body-Worn Cameras: Panacea or Distraction for Increased Police Use of Force Accountability? In Pittaro, M. (Ed.), *Global Perspectives on Reforming the Criminal Justice System* (pp. 1–25). IGI Global. https://doi.org/10.4018/978-1-7998-6884-2.ch001

Duran, D. Ş. (2019). Reflections of the Multi-Level Governance Approach on the Turkish Metropolitan Municipality System: Evaluations on the Metropolitan Law No 6360. In Uysal, T., & Aldemir, C. (Eds.), *Multi-Level Governance in Developing Economies* (pp. 52–91). IGI Global. https://doi.org/10.4018/978-1-5225-5547-6.ch003

Edwards, J. S. (2018). Integrating Knowledge Management and Business Processes. In M. Khosrow-Pour, D.B.A. (Ed.), *Encyclopedia of Information Science and Technology, Fourth Edition* (pp. 5046-5055). Hershey, PA: IGI Global. 10.4018/978-1-5225-2255-3.ch437

Ehalaiye, D., Redmayne, N. B., & Laswad, F. (2020). The Case of Accounting Information for Infrastructural Assets Reporting: Local Government Borrowings and Investment Choices in the Context of Moral Hazard and Local Government Politics. In Cunha, A., Ferreira, A., Fernandes, M., & Gomes, P. (Eds.), *Financial Determinants in Local Re-Election Rates: Emerging Research and Opportunities* (pp. 176–201). IGI Global. https://doi.org/10.4018/978-1-5225-7820-8.ch007

Eichelberger, S., & Peters, M. (2021). Family Firm Management in Turbulent Times: Opportunities for Responsible Tourism. In Zehrer, A., Glowka, G., Schwaiger, K., & Ranacher-Lackner, V. (Eds.), *Resiliency Models and Addressing Future Risks for Family Firms in the Tourism Industry* (pp. 103–124). IGI Global. https://doi.org/10.4018/978-1-7998-7352-5.ch005

Ejiogu, A. O. (2018). Economics of Farm Management. In *Agricultural Finance and Opportunities for Investment and Expansion* (pp. 56–72). Hershey, PA: IGI Global. 10.4018/978-1-5225-3059-6.ch003

Ekanem, I., & Alrossais, L. A. (2017). Succession Challenges Facing Family Businesses in Saudi Arabia. In Zgheib, P. (Ed.), *Entrepreneurship and Business Innovation in the Middle East* (pp. 122–146). Hershey, PA: IGI Global. 10.4018/978-1-5225-2066-5.ch007

Elena, S., & van Schalkwyk, F. (2017). Open Data for Open Justice in Seven Latin American Countries. In Jiménez-Gómez, C., & Gascó-Hernández, M. (Eds.), *Achieving Open Justice through Citizen Participation and Transparency* (pp. 210–231). Hershey, PA: IGI Global. 10.4018/978-1-5225-0717-8.ch011

Eneanya, A. N. (2018). Integrating Ecosystem Management and Environmental Media for Public Policy on Public Health and Safety. In Eneanya, A. (Ed.), *Handbook of Research on Environmental Policies for Emergency Management and Public Safety* (pp. 321–338). Hershey, PA: IGI Global. 10.4018/978-1-5225-3194-4.ch017

Erickson, G. S. (2019). Sharing Knowledge With the Government: Implications of FOIA Requests. In Albastaki, Y., Al-Alawi, A., & Abdulrahman Al-Bassam, S. (Eds.), *Handbook of Research on Implementing Knowledge Management Strategy in the Public Sector* (pp. 143–158). IGI Global. https://doi.org/10.4018/978-1-5225-9639-4.ch007

Essien, E. D. (2018). Strengthening Performance of Civil Society Through Dialogue and Critical Thinking in Nigeria: Its Ethical Implications. In Chhabra, S. (Ed.), *Handbook of Research on Civic Engagement and Social Change in Contemporary Society* (pp. 82–102). Hershey, PA: IGI Global. 10.4018/978-1-5225-4197-4.ch005

Eweida, A. M. (2021). Urban Laws in Harmony or at Odds With Knowledge-Based Urban Policies: A Case Study on Egypt. In Galaby, A., & Abdrabo, A. (Eds.), *Handbook of Research on Creative Cities and Advanced Models for Knowledge-Based Urban Development* (pp. 23–40). IGI Global. https://doi.org/10.4018/978-1-7998-4948-3.ch002

Fanaian, T. (2017). The Theocratic Deception Trap: Khomeini's Persuasion Techniques and Communication Patterns in His Books, Guardianship of the Jurist 1979 and Testament 1989. In Lewin, E., Bick, E., & Naor, D. (Eds.), *Comparative Perspectives on Civil Religion, Nationalism, and Political Influence* (pp. 62–105). Hershey, PA: IGI Global. 10.4018/978-1-5225-0516-7.ch003

Fawsitt, J. (2020). Government Policy and the Disintegration of Village Community Life and Individual Identity in Urbanising Japan. In Merviö, M. (Ed.), *Recent Social, Environmental, and Cultural Issues in East Asian Societies* (pp. 76–94). IGI Global. https://doi.org/10.4018/978-1-7998-1807-6.ch005

Fidanoski, F., Sergi, B. S., Simeonovski, K., Naumovski, V., & Sazdovski, I. (2018). Effects of Foreign Capital Entry on the Macedonian Banking Industry: Two-Edged Sword. In Sergi, B., Fidanoski, F., Ziolo, M., & Naumovski, V. (Eds.), *Regaining Global Stability After the Financial Crisis* (pp. 308–338). Hershey, PA: IGI Global. 10.4018/978-1-5225-4026-7.ch015

Figueira, L. M., Honrado, G. R., & Dionísio, M. S. (2021). Human Capital Management in the Tourism Industry in Portugal. In Costa, V., Moura, A., & Mira, M. (Eds.), *Handbook of Research on Human Capital and People Management in the Tourism Industry* (pp. 1–19). IGI Global. 10.4018/978-1-7998-4318-4.ch001

Franconi, A. I. (2018). Economic Variations and Their Impact on Labor Legislation Throughout History in Argentina. In Amine, S. (Ed.), *Employment Protection Legislation in Emerging Economies* (pp. 77–98). Hershey, PA: IGI Global. 10.4018/978-1-5225-4134-9.ch004

Friedrich, P., & Chebotareva, M. (2017). Options for Applying Functional Overlapping Competing Jurisdictions (FOCJs) for Municipal Cooperation in Russia. In Lewandowski, M., & Kożuch, B. (Eds.), *Public Sector Entrepreneurship and the Integration of Innovative Business Models* (pp. 73–107). Hershey, PA: IGI Global. 10.4018/978-1-5225-2215-7.ch004

Gao, S. S., Oreal, S., & Zhang, J. (2018). Contemporary Financial Risk Management Perceptions and Practices of Small-Sized Chinese Businesses. In I. Management Association (Ed.), *Global Business Expansion: Concepts, Methodologies, Tools, and Applications* (pp. 917-931). Hershey, PA: IGI Global. 10.4018/978-1-5225-5481-3.ch041

Garg, R., & Berning, S. C. (2017). Indigenous Chinese Management Philosophies: Key Concepts and Relevance for Modern Chinese Firms. In Christiansen, B., & Koc, G. (Eds.), *Transcontinental Strategies for Industrial Development and Economic Growth* (pp. 43–57). Hershey, PA: IGI Global. 10.4018/978-1-5225-2160-0.ch003

Garita, M. (2018). The Negotiation and Effects of Fiscal Privileges in Guatemala. In Garita, M., & Bregni, C. (Eds.), *Economic Growth in Latin America and the Impact of the Global Financial Crisis* (pp. 119–137). Hershey, PA: IGI Global. 10.4018/978-1-5225-4981-9.ch008

Gascó-Hernández, M. (2017). Digitalizing Police Requirements: Opening up Justice through Collaborative Initiatives. In Jiménez-Gómez, C., & Gascó-Hernández, M. (Eds.), *Achieving Open Justice through Citizen Participation and Transparency* (pp. 157–172). Hershey, PA: IGI Global. 10.4018/978-1-5225-0717-8.ch008

Gáspár-Szilágyi, S. (2017). Human Rights Conditionality in the EU's Newly Concluded Association Agreements with the Eastern Partners. In Akrivopoulou, C. (Ed.), *Defending Human Rights and Democracy in the Era of Globalization* (pp. 50–79). Hershey, PA: IGI Global. 10.4018/978-1-5225-0723-9.ch003

Gavrielides, T. (2017). Reconciling Restorative Justice with the Law for Violence Against Women in Europe: A Scheme of Structured and Unstructured Models. In Halder, D., & Jaishankar, K. (Eds.), *Therapeutic Jurisprudence and Overcoming Violence Against Women* (pp. 106–120). Hershey, PA: IGI Global. 10.4018/978-1-5225-2472-4.ch007

Gechlik, M., Dai, D., & Beck, J. C. (2017). Open Judiciary in a Closed Society: A Paradox in China? In Jiménez-Gómez, C., & Gascó-Hernández, M. (Eds.), *Achieving Open Justice through Citizen Participation and Transparency* (pp. 56–92). Hershey, PA: IGI Global. 10.4018/978-1-5225-0717-8.ch004

Gencer, Y. G. (2017). Supply Chain Management in Retailing Business. In Akkucuk, U. (Ed.), *Ethics and Sustainability in Global Supply Chain Management* (pp. 197–210). Hershey, PA: IGI Global. 10.4018/978-1-5225-2036-8.ch011

Gera, R., Arora, S., & Malik, S. (2021). Emotional Labor in the Tourism Industry: Strategies, Antecedents, and Outcomes. In Costa, V., Moura, A., & Mira, M. (Eds.), *Handbook of Research on Human Capital and People Management in the Tourism Industry* (pp. 73–91). IGI Global. https://doi.org/10.4018/978-1-7998-4318-4.ch004

Gerger, A. (2021). Technologies for Connected Government Implementation: Success Factors and Best Practices. In Mahmood, Z. (Ed.), *Web 2.0 and Cloud Technologies for Implementing Connected Government* (pp. 36–66). IGI Global. https://doi.org/10.4018/978-1-7998-4570-6.ch003

Germann, S. K. (2019). The International Space Station: Legal Aspects. In Nakarada Pecujlic, A., & Tugnoli, M. (Eds.), *Promoting Productive Cooperation Between Space Lawyers and Engineers* (pp. 96–113). IGI Global. 10.4018/978-1-5225-7256-5.ch007

Giacosa, E. (2018). The Increasing of the Regional Development Thanks to the Luxury Business Innovation. In Carvalho, L. (Ed.), *Handbook of Research on Entrepreneurial Ecosystems and Social Dynamics in a Globalized World* (pp. 260–273). Hershey, PA: IGI Global. 10.4018/978-1-5225-3525-6.ch011

Gillath, N. (2017). Avoiding Conscription in Israel: Were Women Pawns in the Political Game? In Lewin, E., Bick, E., & Naor, D. (Eds.), *Comparative Perspectives on Civil Religion, Nationalism, and Political Influence* (pp. 226–256). Hershey, PA: IGI Global. 10.4018/978-1-5225-0516-7.ch009

Glowka, G., Tusch, M., & Zehrer, A. (2021). The Risk Perception of Family Business Owner-Manager in the Tourism Industry: A Qualitative Comparison of the Intra-Firm Senior and Junior Generation. In Zehrer, A., Glowka, G., Schwaiger, K., & Ranacher-Lackner, V. (Eds.), *Resiliency Models and Addressing Future Risks for Family Firms in the Tourism Industry* (pp. 126–153). IGI Global. https://doi.org/10.4018/978-1-7998-7352-5.ch006

Gomes, J., & Romão, M. (2017). Aligning Information Systems and Technology with Benefit Management and Balanced Scorecard. In De Haes, S., & Van Grembergen, W. (Eds.), *Strategic IT Governance and Alignment in Business Settings* (pp. 112–131). Hershey, PA: IGI Global. 10.4018/978-1-5225-0861-8.ch005

Górski, J. (2019). Northern Sea Route: International Law Perspectives. In Erokhin, V., Gao, T., & Zhang, X. (Eds.), *Handbook of Research on International Collaboration, Economic Development, and Sustainability in the Arctic* (pp. 292–313). IGI Global. https://doi.org/10.4018/978-1-5225-6954-1.ch014

Grant, B., Woods, R., & Tan, S. F. (2017). Subnational Finance in Australia and China: The Case for Municipal Bond Banks. In Schoburgh, E., & Ryan, R. (Eds.), *Handbook of Research on Sub-National Governance and Development* (pp. 150–166). Hershey, PA: IGI Global. 10.4018/978-1-5225-1645-3.ch007

Gurpinar, B. (2018). Supporter, Activist, Rebel, Terrorist: Children in Syria. In Akrivopoulou, C. (Ed.), *Global Perspectives on Human Migration, Asylum, and Security* (pp. 97–114). Hershey, PA: IGI Global. 10.4018/978-1-5225-2817-3.ch005

Gussen, B. F. (2018). The United States. In *Ranking Economic Performance and Efficiency in the Global Market: Emerging Research and Opportunities* (pp. 109–136). Hershey, PA: IGI Global. 10.4018/978-1-5225-2756-5.ch005

Haider, A., & Saetang, S. (2017). Strategic IT Alignment in Service Sector. In Rozenes, S., & Cohen, Y. (Eds.), *Handbook of Research on Strategic Alliances and Value Co-Creation in the Service Industry* (pp. 231–258). Hershey, PA: IGI Global. 10.4018/978-1-5225-2084-9.ch012

Halder, D., & Bhati, D. (2021). Culture, Ethnicity, and Hate Crimes: A Comparative Analysis of Preventive Laws Between India and the USA. In Pittaro, M. (Ed.), *Global Perspectives on Reforming the Criminal Justice System* (pp. 236–245). IGI Global. https://doi.org/10.4018/978-1-7998-6884-2.ch013

Haldorai, A., Ramu, A., & Murugan, S. (2018). Social Aware Cognitive Radio Networks: Effectiveness of Social Networks as a Strategic Tool for Organizational Business Management. In Bansal, H., Shrivastava, G., Nguyen, G., & Stanciu, L. (Eds.), *Social Network Analytics for Contemporary Business Organizations* (pp. 188–202). Hershey, PA: IGI Global. 10.4018/978-1-5225-5097-6.ch010

Hanifah, H., Halim, H. A., Ahmad, N. H., & Vafaei-Zadeh, A. (2017). Innovation Culture as a Mediator Between Specific Human Capital and Innovation Performance Among Bumiputera SMEs in Malaysia. In Ahmad, N., Ramayah, T., Halim, H., & Rahman, S. (Eds.), *Handbook of Research on Small and Medium Enterprises in Developing Countries* (pp. 261–279). Hershey, PA: IGI Global. 10.4018/978-1-5225-2165-5.ch012

Haque, T. (2018). Women-Friendly Working Environment in Bangladesh: Critical Analysis. In Mahtab, N., Haque, T., Khan, I., Islam, M., & Wahid, I. (Eds.), *Handbook of Research on Women's Issues and Rights in the Developing World* (pp. 52–68). Hershey, PA: IGI Global. 10.4018/978-1-5225-3018-3.ch004

Hartlieb, S., & Silvius, G. (2017). Handling Uncertainty in Project Management and Business Development: Similarities and Differences. In Raydugin, Y. (Ed.), *Handbook of Research on Leveraging Risk and Uncertainties for Effective Project Management* (pp. 337–362). Hershey, PA: IGI Global. 10.4018/978-1-5225-1790-0.ch016

Hass, K. B. (2017). Living on the Edge: Managing Project Complexity. In Raydugin, Y. (Ed.), *Handbook of Research on Leveraging Risk and Uncertainties for Effective Project Management* (pp. 177–201). Hershey, PA: IGI Global. 10.4018/978-1-5225-1790-0.ch009

Hawking, P., & Carmine Sellitto, C. (2017). Developing an Effective Strategy for Organizational Business Intelligence. In Tavana, M. (Ed.), *Enterprise Information Systems and the Digitalization of Business Functions* (pp. 222–237). Hershey, PA: IGI Global. 10.4018/978-1-5225-2382-6.ch010

Heuva, W. E. (2017). Deferring Citizens' "Right to Know" in an Information Age: The Information Deficit in Namibia. In Mhiripiri, N., & Chari, T. (Eds.), *Media Law, Ethics, and Policy in the Digital Age* (pp. 245–267). Hershey, PA: IGI Global. 10.4018/978-1-5225-2095-5.ch014

Hwangbo, Y. (2022). Government Challenges Over Global Electronic Commerce Using FinTech: Design of Consumer Payment Tax (CPT) System. In Anshari, M., Almunawar, M., & Masri, M. (Eds.), *FinTech Development for Financial Inclusiveness* (pp. 197–213). IGI Global. https://doi.org/10.4018/978-1-7998-8447-7.ch011

Igbinakhase, I. (2017). Responsible and Sustainable Management Practices in Developing and Developed Business Environments. In Fields, Z. (Ed.), *Collective Creativity for Responsible and Sustainable Business Practice* (pp. 180–207). Hershey, PA: IGI Global. 10.4018/978-1-5225-1823-5.ch010

Islam, M. R. (2018). Abuse Among Child Domestic Workers in Bangladesh. In Tshabangu, I. (Ed.), *Global Ideologies Surrounding Children's Rights and Social Justice* (pp. 1–21). Hershey, PA: IGI Global. 10.4018/978-1-5225-2578-3.ch001

Iwata, J. J., & Hoskins, R. G. (2017). Managing Indigenous Knowledge in Tanzania: A Business Perspective. In Jain, P., & Mnjama, N. (Eds.), *Managing Knowledge Resources and Records in Modern Organizations* (pp. 198–214). Hershey, PA: IGI Global. 10.4018/978-1-5225-1965-2.ch012

Jain, P. (2017). Ethical and Legal Issues in Knowledge Management Life-Cycle in Business. In Jain, P., & Mnjama, N. (Eds.), *Managing Knowledge Resources and Records in Modern Organizations* (pp. 82–101). Hershey, PA: IGI Global. 10.4018/978-1-5225-1965-2.ch006

James, S., & Hauli, E. (2017). Holistic Management Education at Tanzanian Rural Development Planning Institute. In Baporikar, N. (Ed.), *Management Education for Global Leadership* (pp. 112–136). Hershey, PA: IGI Global. 10.4018/978-1-5225-1013-0.ch006

Jankovic-Milic, V., & Džunić, M. (2017). Measuring Governance: The Application of Grey Relational Analysis on World Governance Indicators. In Stanković, J., Delias, P., Marinković, S., & Rochhia, S. (Eds.), *Tools and Techniques for Economic Decision Analysis* (pp. 104–128). Hershey, PA: IGI Global. 10.4018/978-1-5225-0959-2.ch005

Janošková, M., Csikósová, A., & Čulková, K. (2018). Measurement of Company Performance as Part of Its Strategic Management. In Leon, R. (Ed.), *Managerial Strategies for Business Sustainability During Turbulent Times* (pp. 309–335). Hershey, PA: IGI Global. 10.4018/978-1-5225-2716-9.ch017

Jean-Vasile, A., & Alecu, A. (2017). Theoretical and Practical Approaches in Understanding the Influences of Cost-Productivity-Profit Trinomial in Contemporary Enterprises. In Jean Vasile, A., & Nicolò, D. (Eds.), *Sustainable Entrepreneurship and Investments in the Green Economy* (pp. 28–62). Hershey, PA: IGI Global. 10.4018/978-1-5225-2075-7.ch002

Jenkins, B., Semple, T., Quail, J., & Bennell, C. (2021). Optimizing Scenario-Based Training for Law Enforcement. In Arble, E., & Arnetz, B. (Eds.), *Interventions, Training, and Technologies for Improved Police Well-Being and Performance* (pp. 18–37). IGI Global. https://doi.org/10.4018/978-1-7998-6820-0.ch002

Jiménez-Gómez, C. E. (2017). Open Judiciary Worldwide: Best Practices and Lessons Learnt. In Jiménez-Gómez, C., & Gascó-Hernández, M. (Eds.), *Achieving Open Justice through Citizen Participation and Transparency* (pp. 1–15). Hershey, PA: IGI Global. 10.4018/978-1-5225-0717-8.ch001

Juma, A., & Mzera, N. (2017). Knowledge Management and Records Management and Competitive Advantage in Business. In Jain, P., & Mnjama, N. (Eds.), *Managing Knowledge Resources and Records in Modern Organizations* (pp. 15–28). Hershey, PA: IGI Global. 10.4018/978-1-5225-1965-2.ch002

Kabra, G., Ghosh, V., & Ramesh, A. (2018). Enterprise Integrated Business Process Management and Business Intelligence Framework for Business Process Sustainability. In Paul, A., Bhattacharyya, D., & Anand, S. (Eds.), *Green Initiatives for Business Sustainability and Value Creation* (pp. 228–238). Hershey, PA: IGI Global. 10.4018/978-1-5225-2662-9.ch010

Karatzimas, S., & Miquela, C. G. (2018). Two Approaches on Local Governments' Financial Sustainability: Law vs. Practice in Catalan Municipalities. In Rodríguez Bolívar, M., & López Subires, M. (Eds.), *Financial Sustainability and Intergenerational Equity in Local Governments* (pp. 58–81). Hershey, PA: IGI Global. 10.4018/978-1-5225-3713-7.ch003

Katuu, S. (2018). A Comparative Assessment of Enterprise Content Management Maturity Models. In Gwangwava, N., & Mutingi, M. (Eds.), *E-Manufacturing and E-Service Strategies in Contemporary Organizations* (pp. 93–118). Hershey, PA: IGI Global. 10.4018/978-1-5225-3628-4.ch005

Khan, M. Y., & Abir, T. (2022). The Role of Social Media Marketing in the Tourism and Hospitality Industry: A Conceptual Study on Bangladesh. In Ramos, C., Quinteiro, S., & Gonçalves, A. (Eds.), *ICT as Innovator Between Tourism and Culture* (pp. 213–229). IGI Global. https://doi.org/10.4018/978-1-7998-8165-0.ch013

Khan, S. A., & Alag, A. (2020). Arbitration in Patent Disputes: To What Extent Is It Possible? In Dewani, N., & Gurtu, A. (Eds.), *Intellectual Property Rights and the Protection of Traditional Knowledge* (pp. 76–102). IGI Global. https://doi.org/10.4018/978-1-7998-1835-9.ch004

Kirsanov, S., Safonov, E., Tuzcuoglu, F., & Mammadov, Z. (2022). Modern Problems of Staff Training for State and Municipal Services in Russia. In Kulaç, O., Babaoğlu, C., & Akman, E. (Eds.), *Public Affairs Education and Training in the 21st Century* (pp. 325–337). IGI Global. https://doi.org/10.4018/978-1-7998-8243-5.ch021

Kita, Y. (2017). An Analysis of a Lay Adjudication System and Open Judiciary: The New Japanese Lay Adjudication System. In Jiménez-Gómez, C., & Gascó-Hernández, M. (Eds.), *Achieving Open Justice through Citizen Participation and Transparency* (pp. 93–109). Hershey, PA: IGI Global. 10.4018/978-1-5225-0717-8.ch005

Klein, A. Z., Sabino de Freitas, A., Machado, L., Freitas, J. C.Jr, Graziola, P. G.Jr, & Schlemmer, E. (2017). Virtual Worlds Applications for Management Education. In Tomei, L. (Ed.), *Exploring the New Era of Technology-Infused Education* (pp. 279–299). Hershey, PA: IGI Global. 10.4018/978-1-5225-1709-2.ch017

Kővári, E., Saleh, M., & Steinbachné Hajmásy, G. (2022). The Impact of Corporate Digital Responsibility (CDR) on Internal Stakeholders' Satisfaction in Hungarian Upscale Hotels. In Valeri, M. (Ed.), *New Governance and Management in Touristic Destinations* (pp. 35–51). IGI Global. https://doi.org/10.4018/978-1-6684-3889-3.ch003

Kożuch, B., & Jabłoński, A. (2017). Adopting the Concept of Business Models in Public Management. In Lewandowski, M., & Kożuch, B. (Eds.), *Public Sector Entrepreneurship and the Integration of Innovative Business Models* (pp. 10–46). Hershey, PA: IGI Global. 10.4018/978-1-5225-2215-7.ch002

Kuatova, A., Bekbasarova, T., & Abdrashev, R. (2020). Introducing E-Government in Kazakhstan: The Concept of E-Democracy for the State-Public Interaction. In Tazhina, G., & Parker, J. (Eds.), *Toward Sustainability Through Digital Technologies and Practices in the Eurasian Region* (pp. 1–16). IGI Global. https://doi.org/10.4018/978-1-7998-2551-7.ch001

Kumari, S., Patil, Y., & Rao, P. (2017). An Approach to Sustainable Watershed Management: Case Studies on Enhancing Sustainability with Challenges of Water in Western Maharashtra. In Rao, P., & Patil, Y. (Eds.), *Reconsidering the Impact of Climate Change on Global Water Supply, Use, and Management* (pp. 252–271). Hershey, PA: IGI Global. 10.4018/978-1-5225-1046-8.ch014

Kumburu, N. P., & Pande, V. S. (2018). Decentralization and Local Governance in Tanzania: Theories and Practice on Sustainable Development. In Teshager Alemu, K., & Abebe Alebachew, M. (Eds.), *Handbook of Research on Sustainable Development and Governance Strategies for Economic Growth in Africa* (pp. 131–148). Hershey, PA: IGI Global. 10.4018/978-1-5225-3247-7.ch007

Kunock, A. I. (2017). Boko Haram Insurgency in Cameroon: Role of Mass Media in Conflict Management. In Mhiripiri, N., & Chari, T. (Eds.), *Media Law, Ethics, and Policy in the Digital Age* (pp. 226–244). Hershey, PA: IGI Global. 10.4018/978-1-5225-2095-5.ch013

Kurebwa, J. (2019). Young People-Sensitive and Participatory Governance Approaches: Lessons for the Zimbabwean Government. In Kurebwa, J., & Dodo, O. (Eds.), *Participation of Young People in Governance Processes in Africa* (pp. 80–99). IGI Global. https://doi.org/10.4018/978-1-5225-9388-1.ch005

Latusi, S., & Fissore, M. (2021). Pilgrimage Routes to Happiness: Comparing the Camino de Santiago and Via Francigena. In Perinotto, A., Mayer, V., & Soares, J. (Eds.), *Rebuilding and Restructuring the Tourism Industry: Infusion of Happiness and Quality of Life* (pp. 157–182). IGI Global. https://doi.org/10.4018/978-1-7998-7239-9.ch008

Lawrie, A. (2017). The Subnational Region: A Utopia? The Challenge of Governing Through Soft Power. In Schoburgh, E., & Ryan, R. (Eds.), *Handbook of Research on Sub-National Governance and Development* (pp. 96–115). Hershey, PA: IGI Global. 10.4018/978-1-5225-1645-3.ch005

Lazzareschi, V. H., & Brito, M. S. (2017). Strategic Information Management: Proposal of Business Project Model. In Jamil, G., Soares, A., & Pessoa, C. (Eds.), *Handbook of Research on Information Management for Effective Logistics and Supply Chains* (pp. 59–88). Hershey, PA: IGI Global. 10.4018/978-1-5225-0973-8.ch004

Lechuga Sancho, M. P., & Martín Navarro, A. (2022). Evolution of the Literature on Social Responsibility in the Tourism Sector: A Systematic Literature Review. In Fernandes, G. (Ed.), *Challenges and New Opportunities for Tourism in Inland Territories: Ecocultural Resources and Sustainable Initiatives* (pp. 169–186). IGI Global. https://doi.org/10.4018/978-1-7998-7339-6.ch010

Lee, I. (2017). A Social Enterprise Business Model and a Case Study of Pacific Community Ventures (PCV). In Potocan, V., Ünğan, M., & Nedelko, Z. (Eds.), *Handbook of Research on Managerial Solutions in Non-Profit Organizations* (pp. 182–204). Hershey, PA: IGI Global. 10.4018/978-1-5225-0731-4.ch009

Lentzis, D. (2020). Revisiting the Basics of EU Data Protection Law: On the Material and Territorial Scope of the GDPR. In Tzanou, M. (Ed.), *Personal Data Protection and Legal Developments in the European Union* (pp. 19–33). IGI Global. https://doi.org/10.4018/978-1-5225-9489-5.ch002

Levy, C. L., & Elias, N. I. (2017). SOHO Users' Perceptions of Reliability and Continuity of Cloud-Based Services. In Moore, M. (Ed.), *Cybersecurity Breaches and Issues Surrounding Online Threat Protection* (pp. 248–287). Hershey, PA: IGI Global. 10.4018/978-1-5225-1941-6.ch011

Levy, M. (2018). Change Management Serving Knowledge Management and Organizational Development: Reflections and Review. In Baporikar, N. (Ed.), *Global Practices in Knowledge Management for Societal and Organizational Development* (pp. 256–270). Hershey, PA: IGI Global. 10.4018/978-1-5225-3009-1.ch012

Lewandowski, M. (2017). Public Organizations and Business Model Innovation: The Role of Public Service Design. In Lewandowski, M., & Kożuch, B. (Eds.), *Public Sector Entrepreneurship and the Integration of Innovative Business Models* (pp. 47–72). Hershey, PA: IGI Global. 10.4018/978-1-5225-2215-7.ch003

Lewin, E., & Bick, E. (2017). Introduction: Civil Religion and Nationalism on a Godly-Civil Continuum. In Lewin, E., Bick, E., & Naor, D. (Eds.), *Comparative Perspectives on Civil Religion, Nationalism, and Political Influence* (pp. 1–31). Hershey, PA: IGI Global. 10.4018/978-1-5225-0516-7.ch001

Lopez-Fernandez, M., Perez-Perez, M., Serrano-Bedia, A., & Cobo-Gonzalez, A. (2021). Small and Medium Tourism Enterprise Survival in Times of Crisis: "El Capricho de Gaudí. In Toubes, D., & Araújo-Vila, N. (Eds.), *Risk, Crisis, and Disaster Management in Small and Medium-Sized Tourism Enterprises* (pp. 103–129). IGI Global. 10.4018/978-1-7998-6996-2.ch005

Luyombya, D. (2018). Management of Records and Archives in Uganda's Public Sector. In Ngulube, P. (Ed.), *Handbook of Research on Heritage Management and Preservation* (pp. 275–297). Hershey, PA: IGI Global. 10.4018/978-1-5225-3137-1.ch014

Mabe, M., & Ashley, E. A. (2017). The Local Command Structure and How the Library Fits. In *In The Developing Role of Public Libraries in Emergency Management: Emerging Research and Opportunities* (pp. 44–60). Hershey, PA: IGI Global. 10.4018/978-1-5225-2196-9.ch004

Macilotti, G. (2020). Online Child Pornography: Conceptual Issues and Law Enforcement Challenges. In Balloni, A., & Sette, R. (Eds.), *Handbook of Research on Trends and Issues in Crime Prevention, Rehabilitation, and Victim Support* (pp. 226–247). IGI Global. https://doi.org/10.4018/978-1-7998-1286-9.ch013

Maher, C. (2018). Legal Framework, Funding, and Procurement Polices to Accelerate the Growth of the Social Enterprise Ecosystem. In *Influence of Public Policy on Small Social Enterprises: Emerging Research and Opportunities* (pp. 52–83). Hershey, PA: IGI Global. 10.4018/978-1-5225-2770-1.ch003

Mahmood, M. (2019). Transformation of Government and Citizen Trust in Government: A Conceptual Model. In Molnar, A. (Ed.), *Strategic Management and Innovative Applications of E-Government* (pp. 107–122). IGI Global. https://doi.org/10.4018/978-1-5225-6204-7.ch005

Mahmood, Z. (2021). Cloud Computing Technologies for Connected Digital Government. In Mahmood, Z. (Ed.), *Web 2.0 and Cloud Technologies for Implementing Connected Government* (pp. 19–35). IGI Global. https://doi.org/10.4018/978-1-7998-4570-6.ch002

Malega, P. (2017). Small and Medium Enterprises in the Slovak Republic: Status and Competitiveness of SMEs in the Global Markets and Possibilities of Optimization. In Vemić, M. (Ed.), *Optimal Management Strategies in Small and Medium Enterprises* (pp. 102–124). Hershey, PA: IGI Global. 10.4018/978-1-5225-1949-2.ch006

Malewska, K. M. (2017). Intuition in Decision-Making on the Example of a Non-Profit Organization. In Potocan, V., Ünğan, M., & Nedelko, Z. (Eds.), *Handbook of Research on Managerial Solutions in Non-Profit Organizations* (pp. 378–399). Hershey, PA: IGI Global. 10.4018/978-1-5225-0731-4.ch018

Malik, I., Putera, V. S., & Putra, I. E. (2018). Traditional Leaders in the Reconciliation of Muslim-Christian Conflicts in Moluccas. In Campbell, A. (Ed.), *Global Leadership Initiatives for Conflict Resolution and Peacebuilding* (pp. 235–248). Hershey, PA: IGI Global. 10.4018/978-1-5225-4993-2.ch011

Maroofi, F. (2017). Entrepreneurial Orientation and Organizational Learning Ability Analysis for Innovation and Firm Performance. In Baporikar, N. (Ed.), *Innovation and Shifting Perspectives in Management Education* (pp. 144–165). Hershey, PA: IGI Global. 10.4018/978-1-5225-1019-2.ch007

Marques, M., Moleiro, D., Brito, T. M., & Marques, T. (2021). Customer Relationship Management as an Important Relationship Marketing Tool: The Case of the Hospitality Industry in Estoril Coast. In M. Dinis, L. Bonixe, S. Lamy, & Z. Breda (Eds.), *Impact of New Media in Tourism* (pp. 39-56). IGI Global. https://doi.org/10.4018/978-1-7998-7095-1.ch003

Martin, S. M. (2017). Transnational Crime and the American Policing System. In M. Dawson, D. Kisku, P. Gupta, J. Sing, & W. Li (Eds.), *Developing Next-Generation Countermeasures for Homeland Security Threat Prevention* (pp. 72-92). Hershey, PA: IGI Global. https://doi.org/10.4018/978-1-5225-0703-1.ch004

Mayer, V. F., Fraga, C. C., & Silva, L. C. (2021). Contributions of Neurosciences to Studies of Well-Being in Tourism. In Perinotto, A., Mayer, V., & Soares, J. (Eds.), *Rebuilding and Restructuring the Tourism Industry: Infusion of Happiness and Quality of Life* (pp. 108–128). IGI Global. https://doi.org/10.4018/978-1-7998-7239-9.ch006

McKee, J. (2018). Architecture as a Tool to Solve Business Planning Problems. In M. Khosrow-Pour, D.B.A. (Ed.), *Encyclopedia of Information Science and Technology, Fourth Edition* (pp. 573-586). Hershey, PA: IGI Global. 10.4018/978-1-5225-2255-3.ch050

McMurray, A. J., Cross, J., & Caponecchia, C. (2018). The Risk Management Profession in Australia: Business Continuity Plan Practices. In Bajgoric, N. (Ed.), *Always-On Enterprise Information Systems for Modern Organizations* (pp. 112–129). Hershey, PA: IGI Global. 10.4018/978-1-5225-3704-5.ch006

Meddah, I. H., & Belkadi, K. (2018). Mining Patterns Using Business Process Management. In Hamou, R. (Ed.), *Handbook of Research on Biomimicry in Information Retrieval and Knowledge Management* (pp. 78–89). Hershey, PA: IGI Global. 10.4018/978-1-5225-3004-6.ch005

Mekonnen, G. A., & Kassie, W. A. (2020). Fiscal Decentralization at Local Government of Ethiopia: Theory vs Practices. In Chhabra, S., & Kumar, M. (Eds.), *Civic Engagement Frameworks and Strategic Leadership Practices for Organization Development* (pp. 171–197). IGI Global. https://doi.org/10.4018/978-1-7998-2372-8.ch008

Melian, A. G., & Camprubí, R. (2021). The Accessibility of Museum Websites: The Case of Barcelona. In Eusébio, C., Teixeira, L., & Carneiro, M. (Eds.), *ICT Tools and Applications for Accessible Tourism* (pp. 234–255). IGI Global. https://doi.org/10.4018/978-1-7998-6428-8.ch011

Mendes, L. (2017). TQM and Knowledge Management: An Integrated Approach Towards Tacit Knowledge Management. In Jaziri-Bouagina, D., & Jamil, G. (Eds.), *Handbook of Research on Tacit Knowledge Management for Organizational Success* (pp. 236–263). Hershey, PA: IGI Global. 10.4018/978-1-5225-2394-9.ch009

Mhiripiri, N. A., & Chikakano, J. (2017). Criminal Defamation, the Criminalisation of Expression, Media and Information Dissemination in the Digital Age: A Legal and Ethical Perspective. In Mhiripiri, N., & Chari, T. (Eds.), *Media Law, Ethics, and Policy in the Digital Age* (pp. 1–24). Hershey, PA: IGI Global. 10.4018/978-1-5225-2095-5.ch001

Mnjama, N. M. (2017). Preservation of Recorded Information in Public and Private Sector Organizations. In Jain, P., & Mnjama, N. (Eds.), *Managing Knowledge Resources and Records in Modern Organizations* (pp. 149–167). Hershey, PA: IGI Global. 10.4018/978-1-5225-1965-2.ch009

Mokoqama, M., & Fields, Z. (2017). Principles of Responsible Management Education (PRME): Call for Responsible Management Education. In Fields, Z. (Ed.), *Collective Creativity for Responsible and Sustainable Business Practice* (pp. 229–241). Hershey, PA: IGI Global. 10.4018/978-1-5225-1823-5.ch012

Morim, A. C., Inácio, H., & Vieira, E. (2018). Internal Control in a Public Hospital: The Case of Financial Services Expenditure Department. In Azevedo, G., da Silva Oliveira, J., Marques, R., & Ferreira, A. (Eds.), *Handbook of Research on Modernization and Accountability in Public Sector Management* (pp. 77–102). Hershey, PA: IGI Global. 10.4018/978-1-5225-3731-1.ch005

Muniapan, B. (2017). Philosophy and Management: The Relevance of Vedanta in Management. In Ordóñez de Pablos, P. (Ed.), *Managerial Strategies and Solutions for Business Success in Asia* (pp. 124–139). Hershey, PA: IGI Global. 10.4018/978-1-5225-1886-0.ch007

Mupepi, M. G. (2017). Developing Democratic Paradigms to Effectively Manage Business, Government, and Civil Society: The African Spring. In Schoburgh, E., & Ryan, R. (Eds.), *Handbook of Research on Sub-National Governance and Development* (pp. 432–462). Hershey, PA: IGI Global. 10.4018/978-1-5225-1645-3.ch020

Murad, S. E., & Dowaji, S. (2017). Using Value-Based Approach for Managing Cloud-Based Services. In Turuk, A., Sahoo, B., & Addya, S. (Eds.), *Resource Management and Efficiency in Cloud Computing Environments* (pp. 33–60). Hershey, PA: IGI Global. 10.4018/978-1-5225-1721-4.ch002

Mwakisisya, H. J., Rugeiyamu, R., & Cyprian, S. (2021). Blending Local Government Authorities and Grassroots for Industrial Economy Through Participatory Development Communication in Tanzania. In Nafukho, F., & Boniface Makulilo, A. (Eds.), *Handbook of Research on Nurturing Industrial Economy for Africa's Development* (pp. 74–98). IGI Global. https://doi.org/10.4018/978-1-7998-6471-4.ch005

Naidoo, V. (2017). E-Learning and Management Education at African Universities. In Baporikar, N. (Ed.), *Management Education for Global Leadership* (pp. 181–201). Hershey, PA: IGI Global. 10.4018/978-1-5225-1013-0.ch009

Naidoo, V., & Igbinakhase, I. (2018). Opportunities and Challenges of Knowledge Retention in SMEs. In Baporikar, N. (Ed.), *Knowledge Integration Strategies for Entrepreneurship and Sustainability* (pp. 70–94). Hershey, PA: IGI Global. 10.4018/978-1-5225-5115-7.ch004

Naidoo, V., & Nzimakwe, T. I. (2019). M-Government and Its Application on Public Service Delivery. In Abassi, R., & Ben Chehida Douss, A. (Eds.), *Security Frameworks in Contemporary Electronic Government* (pp. 1–14). IGI Global. https://doi.org/10.4018/978-1-5225-5984-9.ch001

Naumov, N., & Costandachi, G. (2021). Creativity and Entrepreneurship: Gastronomic Tourism in Mexico. In Soares, J. (Ed.), *Innovation and Entrepreneurial Opportunities in Community Tourism* (pp. 90–108). IGI Global. https://doi.org/10.4018/978-1-7998-4855-4.ch006

Navaratnam, R., & Lee, I. Y. (2017). Globalization as a New Framework for Human Rights Protection. In Akrivopoulou, C. (Ed.), *Defending Human Rights and Democracy in the Era of Globalization* (pp. 17–49). Hershey, PA: IGI Global. 10.4018/978-1-5225-0723-9.ch002

Nayak, S., & Prabhu, N. (2017). Paradigm Shift in Management Education: Need for a Cross Functional Perspective. In Baporikar, N. (Ed.), *Management Education for Global Leadership* (pp. 241–255). Hershey, PA: IGI Global. 10.4018/978-1-5225-1013-0.ch012

Nedelko, Z., & Potocan, V. (2017). Management Solutions in Non-Profit Organizations: Case of Slovenia. In Potocan, V., Ünğan, M., & Nedelko, Z. (Eds.), *Handbook of Research on Managerial Solutions in Non-Profit Organizations* (pp. 1–22). Hershey, PA: IGI Global. 10.4018/978-1-5225-0731-4.ch001

Nedelko, Z., & Potocan, V. (2017). Priority of Management Tools Utilization among Managers: International Comparison. In Wang, V. (Ed.), *Encyclopedia of Strategic Leadership and Management* (pp. 1083–1094). Hershey, PA: IGI Global. 10.4018/978-1-5225-1049-9.ch075

Nedelko, Z., Raudeliūnienė, J., & Črešnar, R. (2018). Knowledge Dynamics in Supply Chain Management. In Baporikar, N. (Ed.), *Knowledge Integration Strategies for Entrepreneurship and Sustainability* (pp. 150–166). Hershey, PA: IGI Global. 10.4018/978-1-5225-5115-7.ch008

Nemec, J., Meričková, B. M., Svidroňová, M. M., & Klimovský, D. (2017). Co-Creation as a Social Innovation in Delivery of Public Services at Local Government Level: The Slovak Experience. In Schoburgh, E., & Ryan, R. (Eds.), *Handbook of Research on Sub-National Governance and Development* (pp. 281–303). Hershey, PA: IGI Global. 10.4018/978-1-5225-1645-3.ch013

Neupane, A., Soar, J., Vaidya, K., & Aryal, S. (2017). Application of E-Government Principles in Anti-Corruption Framework. In Shakya, R. (Ed.), *Digital Governance and E-Government Principles Applied to Public Procurement* (pp. 56–74). Hershey, PA: IGI Global. 10.4018/978-1-5225-2203-4.ch003

Nguyen, H. T., & Hipsher, S. A. (2018). Innovation and Creativity Used by Private Sector Firms in a Resources-Constrained Environment. In Hipsher, S. (Ed.), *Examining the Private Sector's Role in Wealth Creation and Poverty Reduction* (pp. 219–238). Hershey, PA: IGI Global. 10.4018/978-1-5225-3117-3.ch010

Njie, S. N., Wogu, I. A., Ogbuehi, U. K., Misra, S., & Udoh, O. D. (2021). Rising Global Challenges in Energy Demand and the Politics of Climate Change in Government Operations: Policy and Economic Development Implications. In Babaoğlu, C., Akman, E., & Kulaç, O. (Eds.), *Handbook of Research on Global Challenges for Improving Public Services and Government Operations* (pp. 242–263). IGI Global. https://doi.org/10.4018/978-1-7998-4978-0.ch013

Obicci, P. A. (2017). Risk Sharing in a Partnership. In *Risk Management Strategies in Public-Private Partnerships* (pp. 115–152). Hershey, PA: IGI Global. 10.4018/978-1-5225-2503-5.ch004

Ogunde, O. (2017). Democracy and Child Rights Protection: The Problem of the Nigerian Constitution. In Akrivopoulou, C. (Ed.), *Defending Human Rights and Democracy in the Era of Globalization* (pp. 123–144). Hershey, PA: IGI Global. 10.4018/978-1-5225-0723-9.ch006

Ojedokun, U. A. (2017). Crime Witnesses' Non-Cooperation in Police Investigations: Causes and Consequences in Nigeria. In Egharevba, S. (Ed.), *Police Brutality, Racial Profiling, and Discrimination in the Criminal Justice System* (pp. 89–99). Hershey, PA: IGI Global. 10.4018/978-1-5225-1088-8.ch005

Okeke, G. S. (2018). The Politics of Environmental Pollution in Nigeria: Emerging Trends, Issues, and Challenges. In Eneanya, A. (Ed.), *Handbook of Research on Environmental Policies for Emergency Management and Public Safety* (pp. 300–320). Hershey, PA: IGI Global. 10.4018/978-1-5225-3194-4.ch016

Ökten, S., Akman, E., & Akman, Ç. (2018). Modernization and Accountability in Public-Sector Administration: Turkey Example. In Azevedo, G., da Silva Oliveira, J., Marques, R., & Ferreira, A. (Eds.), *Handbook of Research on Modernization and Accountability in Public Sector Management* (pp. 18–39). Hershey, PA: IGI Global. 10.4018/978-1-5225-3731-1.ch002

Oladapo, O. A., & Ojebuyi, B. R. (2017). Nature and Outcome of Nigeria's #NoToSocialMediaBill Twitter Protest against the Frivolous Petitions Bill 2015. In Nelson, O., Ojebuyi, B., & Salawu, A. (Eds.), *Impacts of the Media on African Socio-Economic Development* (pp. 106–124). Hershey, PA: IGI Global. 10.4018/978-1-5225-1859-4.ch007

Olivera, V. A., & Carrillo, I. M. (2021). Organizational Culture: A Key Element for the Development of Mexican Micro and Small Tourist Companies. In Soares, J. (Ed.), *Innovation and Entrepreneurial Opportunities in Community Tourism* (pp. 227–242). IGI Global. 10.4018/978-1-7998-4855-4.ch013

Olmos, S., & Nares, J. J. (2020). Applying Fault Trees to the Analysis at the Minimum Age for Sexual Consent in the Criminal Law of México. In Balloni, A., & Sette, R. (Eds.), *Handbook of Research on Trends and Issues in Crime Prevention, Rehabilitation, and Victim Support* (pp. 60–78). IGI Global. https://doi.org/10.4018/978-1-7998-1286-9.ch005

Olukolu, Y. R. (2017). Harmful Traditional Practices, Laws, and Reproductive Rights of Women in Nigeria: A Therapeutic Jurisprudence Approach. In Halder, D., & Jaishankar, K. (Eds.), *Therapeutic Jurisprudence and Overcoming Violence Against Women* (pp. 1–14). Hershey, PA: IGI Global. 10.4018/978-1-5225-2472-4.ch001

Onyebadi, U., & Mbunyuza-Memani, L. (2017). Women and South Africa's Anti-Apartheid Struggle: Evaluating the Political Messages in the Music of Miriam Makeba. In Onyebadi, U. (Ed.), *Music as a Platform for Political Communication* (pp. 31–51). Hershey, PA: IGI Global. 10.4018/978-1-5225-1986-7.ch002

Osmani, A. R. (2017). Tipaimukh Multipurpose Hydroelectric Project: A Policy Perspective – Indo-Bangla Priorities, Indigenous Peoples' Rights, and Environmental Concerns. In Rao, P., & Patil, Y. (Eds.), *Reconsidering the Impact of Climate Change on Global Water Supply, Use, and Management* (pp. 227–251). Hershey, PA: IGI Global. 10.4018/978-1-5225-1046-8.ch013

Ossorio, M. (2022). Corporate Museum Experiences in Enogastronomic Tourism. In R. Augusto Costa, F. Brandão, Z. Breda, & C. Costa (Eds.), *Planning and Managing the Experience Economy in Tourism* (pp. 107-121). IGI Global. https://doi.org/10.4018/978-1-7998-8775-1.ch006

Ossorio, M. (2022). Enogastronomic Tourism in Times of Pandemic. In Fernandes, G. (Ed.), *Challenges and New Opportunities for Tourism in Inland Territories: Eco-cultural Resources and Sustainable Initiatives* (pp. 241–255). IGI Global. https://doi.org/10.4018/978-1-7998-7339-6.ch014

Owolabi, T. O. (2018). Free Media and Bank Reforms in West Africa: Implications for Sustainable Development. In Salawu, A., & Owolabi, T. (Eds.), *Exploring Journalism Practice and Perception in Developing Countries* (pp. 18–39). Hershey, PA: IGI Global. 10.4018/978-1-5225-3376-4.ch002

Özekici, Y. K. (2022). ICT as an Acculturative Agent and Its Role in the Tourism Context: Introduction, Acculturation Theory, Progress of the Acculturation Theory in Extant Literature. In Ramos, C., Quinteiro, S., & Gonçalves, A. (Eds.), *ICT as Innovator Between Tourism and Culture* (pp. 42–66). IGI Global. https://doi.org/10.4018/978-1-7998-8165-0.ch004

Öztürk, N. K. (2021). Government Systems and Control of Bureaucracy. In Babaoğlu, C., Akman, E., & Kulaç, O. (Eds.), *Handbook of Research on Global Challenges for Improving Public Services and Government Operations* (pp. 133–150). IGI Global. https://doi.org/10.4018/978-1-7998-4978-0.ch008

Pacheco, F. M., & Alves, D. R. (2019). The New Paths of Fundamental Rights in the 21st Century: Globalization and Knowledge in a Digital Age as a Proposal. In Melro, A., & Oliveira, L. (Eds.), *Constitutional Knowledge and Its Impact on Citizenship Exercise in a Networked Society* (pp. 1–26). IGI Global. https://doi.org/10.4018/978-1-5225-8350-9.ch001

Pal, K. (2018). Building High Quality Big Data-Based Applications in Supply Chains. In Kumar, A., & Saurav, S. (Eds.), *Supply Chain Management Strategies and Risk Assessment in Retail Environments* (pp. 1–24). Hershey, PA: IGI Global. 10.4018/978-1-5225-3056-5.ch001

Palos-Sanchez, P. R., & Correia, M. B. (2018). Perspectives of the Adoption of Cloud Computing in the Tourism Sector. In Rodrigues, J., Ramos, C., Cardoso, P., & Henriques, C. (Eds.), *Handbook of Research on Technological Developments for Cultural Heritage and eTourism Applications* (pp. 377–400). Hershey, PA: IGI Global. 10.4018/978-1-5225-2927-9.ch018

Panda, P., & Sahu, G. P. (2017). Public Procurement Framework in India: An Overview. In Shakya, R. (Ed.), *Digital Governance and E-Government Principles Applied to Public Procurement* (pp. 229–248). Hershey, PA: IGI Global. 10.4018/978-1-5225-2203-4.ch010

Pande, V. S., & Kumburu, N. P. (2018). An Overview of Population Growth and Sustainable Development in Sub-Saharan Africa. In Teshager Alemu, K., & Abebe Alebachew, M. (Eds.), *Handbook of Research on Sustainable Development and Governance Strategies for Economic Growth in Africa* (pp. 480–499). Hershey, PA: IGI Global. 10.4018/978-1-5225-3247-7.ch025

Papadopoulou, G. (2021). Promoting Gender Equality and Women Empowerment in the Tourism Sector. In F. Brandão, Z. Breda, R. Costa, & C. Costa (Eds.), *Handbook of Research on the Role of Tourism in Achieving Sustainable Development Goals* (pp. 152-174). IGI Global. https://doi.org/10.4018/978-1-7998-5691-7.ch009

Patiño, B. E. (2017). New Generation Management by Convergence and Individual Identity: A Systemic and Human-Oriented Approach. In Baporikar, N. (Ed.), *Innovation and Shifting Perspectives in Management Education* (pp. 119–143). Hershey, PA: IGI Global. 10.4018/978-1-5225-1019-2.ch006

Pattnaik, P. N., & Shukla, M. K. (2020). Understanding Indian Political Parties Through the Lens of Marketing Management: Towards a Conceptual Political Marketing Model. In Kavoğlu, S., & Salar, M. (Eds.), *Political Propaganda, Advertising, and Public Relations: Emerging Research and Opportunities* (pp. 170–190). IGI Global. https://doi.org/10.4018/978-1-7998-1734-5.ch008

Pawliczek, A., & Rössler, M. (2017). Knowledge of Management Tools and Systems in SMEs: Knowledge Transfer in Management. In Bencsik, A. (Ed.), *Knowledge Management Initiatives and Strategies in Small and Medium Enterprises* (pp. 180–203). Hershey, PA: IGI Global. 10.4018/978-1-5225-1642-2.ch009

Pejic-Bach, M., Omazic, M. A., Aleksic, A., & Zoroja, J. (2018). Knowledge-Based Decision Making: A Multi-Case Analysis. In Leon, R. (Ed.), *Managerial Strategies for Business Sustainability During Turbulent Times* (pp. 160–184). Hershey, PA: IGI Global. 10.4018/978-1-5225-2716-9.ch009

Perano, M., Hysa, X., & Calabrese, M. (2018). Strategic Planning, Cultural Context, and Business Continuity Management: Business Cases in the City of Shkoder. In Presenza, A., & Sheehan, L. (Eds.), *Geopolitics and Strategic Management in the Global Economy* (pp. 57–77). Hershey, PA: IGI Global. 10.4018/978-1-5225-2673-5.ch004

Pereira, R., Mira da Silva, M., & Lapão, L. V. (2017). IT Governance Maturity Patterns in Portuguese Healthcare. In De Haes, S., & Van Grembergen, W. (Eds.), *Strategic IT Governance and Alignment in Business Settings* (pp. 24–52). Hershey, PA: IGI Global. 10.4018/978-1-5225-0861-8.ch002

Perelló-Sobrepere, M. (2017). Building a New State from Outrage: The Case of Catalonia. In Adria, M., & Mao, Y. (Eds.), *Handbook of Research on Citizen Engagement and Public Participation in the Era of New Media* (pp. 344–359). Hershey, PA: IGI Global. 10.4018/978-1-5225-1081-9.ch019

Pérez-Uribe, R. I., Torres, D. A., Jurado, S. P., & Prada, D. M. (2018). Cloud Tools for the Development of Project Management in SMEs. In Perez-Uribe, R., Salcedo-Perez, C., & Ocampo-Guzman, D. (Eds.), *Handbook of Research on Intrapreneurship and Organizational Sustainability in SMEs* (pp. 95–120). Hershey, PA: IGI Global. 10.4018/978-1-5225-3543-0.ch005

Petrisor, I., & Cozmiuc, D. (2017). Global Supply Chain Management Organization at Siemens in the Advent of Industry 4.0. In Saglietto, L., & Cezanne, C. (Eds.), *Global Intermediation and Logistics Service Providers* (pp. 123–142). Hershey, PA: IGI Global. 10.4018/978-1-5225-2133-4.ch007

Pierce, J. M., Velliaris, D. M., & Edwards, J. (2017). A Living Case Study: A Journey Not a Destination. In Silton, N. (Ed.), *Exploring the Benefits of Creativity in Education, Media, and the Arts* (pp. 158–178). Hershey, PA: IGI Global. 10.4018/978-1-5225-0504-4.ch008

Pohl, G. M. (2017). The Role of Social Media in Enforcing Environmental Justice around the World. In Demirhan, K., & Çakır-Demirhan, D. (Eds.), *Political Scandal, Corruption, and Legitimacy in the Age of Social Media* (pp. 123–156). Hershey, PA: IGI Global. 10.4018/978-1-5225-2019-1.ch006

Popescu, C. R. (2022). Environmental, Social, and Corporate Governance by Avoiding Management Bias and Tax Minimization: Reaching a General Consensus Regarding a Minimum Global Tax Rate. In Popescu, C. (Ed.), *COVID-19 Pandemic Impact on New Economy Development and Societal Change* (pp. 94–132). IGI Global. https://doi.org/10.4018/978-1-6684-3374-4.ch006

Popoola, T. (2017). Ethical and Legal Challenges of Election Reporting in Nigeria: A Study of Four General Elections, 1999-2011. In Mhiripiri, N., & Chari, T. (Eds.), *Media Law, Ethics, and Policy in the Digital Age* (pp. 78–100). Hershey, PA: IGI Global. 10.4018/978-1-5225-2095-5.ch005

Poulaki, P., Kritikos, A., Vasilakis, N., & Valeri, M. (2022). The Contribution of Female Creativity to the Development of Gastronomic Tourism in Greece: The Case of the Island of Naxos in the South Aegean Region. In Valeri, M. (Ed.), *New Governance and Management in Touristic Destinations* (pp. 246–258). IGI Global. https://doi.org/10.4018/978-1-6684-3889-3.ch015

Prakash, O. (2020). History, Policy Making, and Sustainability. In Das, R., & Mandal, N. (Eds.), *Interdisciplinary Approaches to Public Policy and Sustainability* (pp. 1–17). IGI Global. https://doi.org/10.4018/978-1-7998-0315-7.ch001

Provazníková, R., Sobotková, L., & Sobotka, M. (2021). Local Government Development in the Czech Republic: Dilemmas and Challenges. In Babaoğlu, C., Akman, E., & Kulaç, O. (Eds.), *Handbook of Research on Global Challenges for Improving Public Services and Government Operations* (pp. 151–171). IGI Global. https://doi.org/10.4018/978-1-7998-4978-0.ch009

Qawasmeh, F. A. (2022). Understanding the Field of Public Policy in the Context of Public Administration Evolution. In Kulaç, O., Babaoğlu, C., & Akman, E. (Eds.), *Public Affairs Education and Training in the 21st Century* (pp. 22–44). IGI Global. https://doi.org/10.4018/978-1-7998-8243-5.ch002

Radosavljevic, M., & Andjelkovic, A. (2017). Multi-Criteria Decision Making Approach for Choosing Business Process for the Improvement: Upgrading of the Six Sigma Methodology. In Stanković, J., Delias, P., Marinković, S., & Rochhia, S. (Eds.), *Tools and Techniques for Economic Decision Analysis* (pp. 225–247). Hershey, PA: IGI Global. 10.4018/978-1-5225-0959-2.ch011

Radovic, V. M. (2017). Corporate Sustainability and Responsibility and Disaster Risk Reduction: A Serbian Overview. In Camilleri, M. (Ed.), *CSR 2.0 and the New Era of Corporate Citizenship* (pp. 147–164). Hershey, PA: IGI Global. 10.4018/978-1-5225-1842-6.ch008

Raghunath, K. M., Devi, S. L., & Patro, C. S. (2018). Impact of Risk Assessment Models on Risk Factors: A Holistic Outlook. In Strang, K., Korstanje, M., & Vajjhala, N. (Eds.), *Research, Practices, and Innovations in Global Risk and Contingency Management* (pp. 134–153). Hershey, PA: IGI Global. 10.4018/978-1-5225-4754-9.ch008

Rahman, M. S. (2017). Politics-Administration Relations and the Effect on Local Governance and Development: The Case of Bangladesh. In Schoburgh, E., & Ryan, R. (Eds.), *Handbook of Research on Sub-National Governance and Development* (pp. 256–279). Hershey, PA: IGI Global. 10.4018/978-1-5225-1645-3.ch012

Ramachandran, M., Chelliah, P. R., & Soundarabai, P. B. (2021). Towards Connected Government Services: A Cloud Software Engineering Framework. In Mahmood, Z. (Ed.), *Web 2.0 and Cloud Technologies for Implementing Connected Government* (pp. 113–135). IGI Global. https://doi.org/10.4018/978-1-7998-4570-6.ch006

Raman, A., & Goyal, D. P. (2017). Extending IMPLEMENT Framework for Enterprise Information Systems Implementation to Information System Innovation. In Tavana, M. (Ed.), *Enterprise Information Systems and the Digitalization of Business Functions* (pp. 137–177). Hershey, PA: IGI Global. 10.4018/978-1-5225-2382-6.ch007

Rao, Y., & Zhang, Y. (2017). The Construction and Development of Academic Library Digital Special Subject Databases. In Ruan, L., Zhu, Q., & Ye, Y. (Eds.), *Academic Library Development and Administration in China* (pp. 163–183). Hershey, PA: IGI Global. 10.4018/978-1-5225-0550-1.ch010

Ravasan, A. Z., Mohammadi, M. M., & Hamidi, H. (2018). An Investigation Into the Critical Success Factors of Implementing Information Technology Service Management Frameworks. In Jakobs, K. (Ed.), *Corporate and Global Standardization Initiatives in Contemporary Society* (pp. 200–218). Hershey, PA: IGI Global. 10.4018/978-1-5225-5320-5.ch009

Razzante, R. (2020). The Fight Against Corruption. In Balloni, A., & Sette, R. (Eds.), *Handbook of Research on Trends and Issues in Crime Prevention, Rehabilitation, and Victim Support* (pp. 167–186). IGI Global. 10.4018/978-1-7998-1286-9.ch010

Reddy, P. S. (2017). Political-Administrative Interface at the Local Sphere of Government with Particular Reference to South Africa. In Schoburgh, E., & Ryan, R. (Eds.), *Handbook of Research on Sub-National Governance and Development* (pp. 242–255). Hershey, PA: IGI Global. 10.4018/978-1-5225-1645-3.ch011

Richards, V., Matthews, N., Williams, O. J., & Khan, Z. (2021). The Challenges of Accessible Tourism Information Systems for Tourists With Vision Impairment: Sensory Communications Beyond the Screen. In Eusébio, C., Teixeira, L., & Carneiro, M. (Eds.), *ICT Tools and Applications for Accessible Tourism* (pp. 26–54). IGI Global. https://doi.org/10.4018/978-1-7998-6428-8.ch002

Rodrigues de Souza Neto, V., & Marques, O. (2021). Rural Tourism Fostering Welfare Through Sustainable Development: A Conceptual Approach. In Perinotto, A., Mayer, V., & Soares, J. (Eds.), *Rebuilding and Restructuring the Tourism Industry: Infusion of Happiness and Quality of Life* (pp. 38–57). IGI Global. https://doi.org/10.4018/978-1-7998-7239-9.ch003

Romano, L., Grimaldi, R., & Colasuonno, F. S. (2017). Demand Management as a Success Factor in Project Portfolio Management. In Romano, L. (Ed.), *Project Portfolio Management Strategies for Effective Organizational Operations* (pp. 202–219). Hershey, PA: IGI Global. 10.4018/978-1-5225-2151-8.ch008

Rombo, D. O., & Lutomia, A. N. (2018). Tracing the Rights of Domestic and International Kenyan House Helps: Profiles, Policy, and Consequences. In Mahtab, N., Haque, T., Khan, I., Islam, M., & Wahid, I. (Eds.), *Handbook of Research on Women's Issues and Rights in the Developing World* (pp. 1–18). Hershey, PA: IGI Global. 10.4018/978-1-5225-3018-3.ch001

Rouzbehani, K. (2017). Health Policy Implementation: Moving Beyond Its Barriers in United States. In Wickramasinghe, N. (Ed.), *Handbook of Research on Healthcare Administration and Management* (pp. 541–552). Hershey, PA: IGI Global. 10.4018/978-1-5225-0920-2.ch032

Rubio-Escuderos, L., & García-Andreu, H. (2021). Competitiveness Factors of Accessible Tourism E-Travel Agencies. In Eusébio, C., Teixeira, L., & Carneiro, M. (Eds.), *ICT Tools and Applications for Accessible Tourism* (pp. 196–217). IGI Global. https://doi.org/10.4018/978-1-7998-6428-8.ch009

Rucci, A. C., Porto, N., Darcy, S., & Becka, L. (2021). Smart and Accessible Cities?: Not Always – The Case for Accessible Tourism Initiatives in Buenos Aries and Sydney. In Eusébio, C., Teixeira, L., & Carneiro, M. (Eds.), *ICT Tools and Applications for Accessible Tourism* (pp. 115–145). IGI Global. https://doi.org/10.4018/978-1-7998-6428-8.ch006

Ruhi, U. (2018). Towards an Interdisciplinary Socio-Technical Definition of Virtual Communities. In M. Khosrow-Pour, D.B.A. (Ed.), *Encyclopedia of Information Science and Technology, Fourth Edition* (pp. 4278-4295). Hershey, PA: IGI Global. 10.4018/978-1-5225-2255-3.ch371

Ryan, L., Catena, M., Ros, P., & Stephens, S. (2021). Designing Entrepreneurial Ecosystems to Support Resource Management in the Tourism Industry. In Costa, V., Moura, A., & Mira, M. (Eds.), *Handbook of Research on Human Capital and People Management in the Tourism Industry* (pp. 265–281). IGI Global. https://doi.org/10.4018/978-1-7998-4318-4.ch013

Ryan, R., & Woods, R. (2017). Decentralization and Subnational Governance: Theory and Praxis. In Schoburgh, E., & Ryan, R. (Eds.), *Handbook of Research on Sub-National Governance and Development* (pp. 1–33). Hershey, PA: IGI Global. 10.4018/978-1-5225-1645-3.ch001

Sabao, C., & Chingwaramusee, V. R. (2017). Citizen Journalism on Facebook and the Challenges of Media Regulation in Zimbabwe: Baba Jukwa. In Mhiripiri, N., & Chari, T. (Eds.), *Media Law, Ethics, and Policy in the Digital Age* (pp. 193–206). Hershey, PA: IGI Global. 10.4018/978-1-5225-2095-5.ch011

Sabuncu, I. (2021). Understanding Tourist Perceptions and Expectations During Pandemic Through Social Media Big Data. In Demir, M., Dalgıç, A., & Ergen, F. (Eds.), *Handbook of Research on the Impacts and Implications of COVID-19 on the Tourism Industry* (pp. 330–350). IGI Global. https://doi.org/10.4018/978-1-7998-8231-2.ch016

Sahoo, J., Pati, B., & Mohanty, B. (2017). Knowledge Management as an Academic Discipline: An Assessment. In Gunjal, B. (Ed.), *Managing Knowledge and Scholarly Assets in Academic Libraries* (pp. 99–126). Hershey, PA: IGI Global. 10.4018/978-1-5225-1741-2.ch005

Saidane, A., & Al-Sharieh, S. (2019). A Compliance-Driven Framework for Privacy and Security in Highly Regulated Socio-Technical Environments: An E-Government Case Study. In Abassi, R., & Ben Chehida Douss, A. (Eds.), *Security Frameworks in Contemporary Electronic Government* (pp. 15–50). IGI Global. https://doi.org/10.4018/978-1-5225-5984-9.ch002

Saini, D. (2017). Relevance of Teaching Values and Ethics in Management Education. In Baporikar, N. (Ed.), *Management Education for Global Leadership* (pp. 90–111). Hershey, PA: IGI Global. 10.4018/978-1-5225-1013-0.ch005

Sánchez-Fernández, M. D., & Manríquez, M. R. (2018). The Entrepreneurial Spirit Based on Social Values: The Digital Generation. In Isaias, P., & Carvalho, L. (Eds.), *User Innovation and the Entrepreneurship Phenomenon in the Digital Economy* (pp. 173–193). Hershey, PA: IGI Global. 10.4018/978-1-5225-2826-5.ch009

Sanchez-Ruiz, L., & Blanco, B. (2017). Process Management for SMEs: Barriers, Enablers, and Benefits. In Vemić, M. (Ed.), *Optimal Management Strategies in Small and Medium Enterprises* (pp. 293–319). Hershey, PA: IGI Global. 10.4018/978-1-5225-1949-2.ch014

Sandill, S. (2020). Law, Equality, and Entrepreneurship Through a Gendered Lens: Bridging the Gap Between Academia, Legislature, and Politics. In Moeke-Pickering, T., Cote-Meek, S., & Pegoraro, A. (Eds.), *Critical Reflections and Politics on Advancing Women in the Academy* (pp. 124–149). IGI Global. https://doi.org/10.4018/978-1-7998-3618-6.ch008

Santos, H. R., & Tonelli, D. F. (2019). Smart Government and the Maturity Levels of Sociopolitical Digital Interactions: Analysing Temporal Changes in Brazilian E-Government Portals. In Molnar, A. (Ed.), *Strategic Management and Innovative Applications of E-Government* (pp. 176–199). IGI Global. https://doi.org/10.4018/978-1-5225-6204-7.ch008

Sanz, L. F., Gómez-Pérez, J., & Castillo-Martinez, A. (2018). Analysis of the European ICT Competence Frameworks. In Ahuja, V., & Rathore, S. (Eds.), *Multidisciplinary Perspectives on Human Capital and Information Technology Professionals* (pp. 225–245). Hershey, PA: IGI Global. 10.4018/978-1-5225-5297-0.ch012

Saponaro, A. (2021). "Visible" and "Invisible" Victims in the Criminal Justice System: Victim-Oriented Paradigms and Models. In Blasdell, R., Krieger-Sample, L., & Kilburn, M. (Eds.), *Invisible Victims and the Pursuit of Justice: Analyzing Frequently Victimized Yet Rarely Discussed Populations* (pp. 1–23). IGI Global. 10.4018/978-1-7998-7348-8.ch001

Saxena, G. G., & Saxena, A. (2021). Host Community Role in Medical Tourism Development. In Singh, M., & Kumaran, S. (Eds.), *Growth of the Medical Tourism Industry and Its Impact on Society: Emerging Research and Opportunities* (pp. 105–127). IGI Global. https://doi.org/10.4018/978-1-7998-3427-4.ch006

Saygili, E. E., & Saygili, A. T. (2017). Contemporary Issues in Enterprise Information Systems: A Critical Review of CSFs in ERP Implementations. In Tavana, M. (Ed.), *Enterprise Information Systems and the Digitalization of Business Functions* (pp. 120–136). Hershey, PA: IGI Global. 10.4018/978-1-5225-2382-6.ch006

Schwaiger, K. M., & Zehrer, A. (2021). The COVID-19 Pandemic and Organizational Resilience in Hospitality Family Firms: A Qualitative Approach. In Zehrer, A., Glowka, G., Schwaiger, K., & Ranacher-Lackner, V. (Eds.), *Resiliency Models and Addressing Future Risks for Family Firms in the Tourism Industry* (pp. 32–49). IGI Global. https://doi.org/10.4018/978-1-7998-7352-5.ch002

Scott, N., & Campos, A. C. (2022). Cognitive Science of Tourism Experiences. In R. Augusto Costa, F. Brandão, Z. Breda, & C. Costa (Eds.), *Planning and Managing the Experience Economy in Tourism* (pp. 1-21). IGI Global. https://doi.org/10.4018/978-1-7998-8775-1.ch001

Seidenstricker, S., & Antonino, A. (2018). Business Model Innovation-Oriented Technology Management for Emergent Technologies. In M. Khosrow-Pour, D.B.A. (Ed.), *Encyclopedia of Information Science and Technology, Fourth Edition* (pp. 4560-4569). Hershey, PA: IGI Global. 10.4018/978-1-5225-2255-3.ch396

Selvi, M. S. (2021). Changes in Tourism Sales and Marketing Post COVID-19. In Demir, M., Dalgıç, A., & Ergen, F. (Eds.), *Handbook of Research on the Impacts and Implications of COVID-19 on the Tourism Industry* (pp. 437–460). IGI Global. 10.4018/978-1-7998-8231-2.ch021

Senaratne, S., & Gunarathne, A. D. (2017). Excellence Perspective for Management Education from a Global Accountants' Hub in Asia. In Baporikar, N. (Ed.), *Management Education for Global Leadership* (pp. 158–180). Hershey, PA: IGI Global. 10.4018/978-1-5225-1013-0.ch008

Seyal, A. H., & Rahman, M. N. (2017). Investigating Impact of Inter-Organizational Factors in Measuring ERP Systems Success: Bruneian Perspectives. In Tavana, M. (Ed.), *Enterprise Information Systems and the Digitalization of Business Functions* (pp. 178–204). Hershey, PA: IGI Global. 10.4018/978-1-5225-2382-6.ch008

Shakya, R. K., & Schapper, P. R. (2017). Digital Governance and E-Government Principles: E-Procurement as Transformative. In Shakya, R. (Ed.), *Digital Governance and E-Government Principles Applied to Public Procurement* (pp. 1–28). Hershey, PA: IGI Global. 10.4018/978-1-5225-2203-4.ch001

Shambare, R. (2019). Facilitating Consumers' Adoption of E-Government in South Africa: Supply Side-Driven Virtuous Cycles. In Gbadamosi, A. (Ed.), *Exploring the Dynamics of Consumerism in Developing Nations* (pp. 243–265). IGI Global. https://doi.org/10.4018/978-1-5225-7906-9.ch011

Sharma, A. J. (2017). Enhancing Sustainability through Experiential Learning in Management Education. In Baporikar, N. (Ed.), *Management Education for Global Leadership* (pp. 256–274). Hershey, PA: IGI Global. 10.4018/978-1-5225-1013-0.ch013

Shetty, K. P. (2017). Responsible Global Leadership: Ethical Challenges in Management Education. In Baporikar, N. (Ed.), *Innovation and Shifting Perspectives in Management Education* (pp. 194–223). Hershey, PA: IGI Global. 10.4018/978-1-5225-1019-2.ch009

Siphambe, H., Kolobe, M., & Oageng, I. P. (2018). Employment Protection Legislation and Unemployment in Botswana. In Amine, S. (Ed.), *Employment Protection Legislation in Emerging Economies* (pp. 157–191). Hershey, PA: IGI Global. 10.4018/978-1-5225-4134-9.ch008

Skokic, V. (2021). How Small Hotel Owners Practice Resilience: Longitudinal Study Among Small Family Hotels in Croatia. In Zehrer, A., Glowka, G., Schwaiger, K., & Ranacher-Lackner, V. (Eds.), *Resiliency Models and Addressing Future Risks for Family Firms in the Tourism Industry* (pp. 50–73). IGI Global. 10.4018/978-1-7998-7352-5.ch003

Song, M. Y., & Abelson, J. (2017). Public Engagement and Policy Entrepreneurship on Social Media in the Time of Anti-Vaccination Movements. In Adria, M., & Mao, Y. (Eds.), *Handbook of Research on Citizen Engagement and Public Participation in the Era of New Media* (pp. 38–56). Hershey, PA: IGI Global. 10.4018/978-1-5225-1081-9.ch003

Sood, P., Malhotra, M., & Nijjer, S. (2021). Government Policies During Lockdown: Indian vs. International Perspective. In Kumar, V., & Malhotra, G. (Eds.), *Stakeholder Strategies for Reducing the Impact of Global Health Crises* (pp. 18–39). IGI Global. https://doi.org/10.4018/978-1-7998-7495-9.ch002

Sousa, M. J., Cruz, R., Dias, I., & Caracol, C. (2017). Information Management Systems in the Supply Chain. In Jamil, G., Soares, A., & Pessoa, C. (Eds.), *Handbook of Research on Information Management for Effective Logistics and Supply Chains* (pp. 469–485). Hershey, PA: IGI Global. 10.4018/978-1-5225-0973-8.ch025

Spremic, M., Turulja, L., & Bajgoric, N. (2018). Two Approaches in Assessing Business Continuity Management Attitudes in the Organizational Context. In Bajgoric, N. (Ed.), *Always-On Enterprise Information Systems for Modern Organizations* (pp. 159–183). Hershey, PA: IGI Global. 10.4018/978-1-5225-3704-5.ch008

Stacey, E. (2018). Networked Protests: A Review of Social Movement Literature and the Hong Kong Umbrella Movement (2017). In Chhabra, S. (Ed.), *Handbook of Research on Civic Engagement and Social Change in Contemporary Society* (pp. 347–363). Hershey, PA: IGI Global. 10.4018/978-1-5225-4197-4.ch020

Stamatakis, N. (2017). Authority and Legitimacy: A Quantitative Study of Youth's Perceptions on the Brazilian Police. In Egharevba, S. (Ed.), *Police Brutality, Racial Profiling, and Discrimination in the Criminal Justice System* (pp. 151–213). Hershey, PA: IGI Global. 10.4018/978-1-5225-1088-8.ch009

Steenkamp, A. L. (2018). Some Insights in Computer Science and Information Technology. In *Examining the Changing Role of Supervision in Doctoral Research Projects: Emerging Research and Opportunities* (pp. 113–133). Hershey, PA: IGI Global. 10.4018/978-1-5225-2610-0.ch005

Steinert, S. W. (2021). An Interview With Chief Sargent of the Worcester, MA Police Department. In Arble, E., & Arnetz, B. (Eds.), *Interventions, Training, and Technologies for Improved Police Well-Being and Performance* (pp. 185–197). IGI Global. https://doi.org/10.4018/978-1-7998-6820-0.ch011

Stipanović, C., Rudan, E., & Zubović, V. (2022). Reaching the New Tourist Through Creativity: Sustainable Development Challenges in Croatian Coastal Towns. In Valeri, M. (Ed.), *New Governance and Management in Touristic Destinations* (pp. 231–245). IGI Global. https://doi.org/10.4018/978-1-6684-3889-3.ch014

Sugars, J. M. (2017). Refoulement and Refugees. In Akrivopoulou, C. (Ed.), *Defending Human Rights and Democracy in the Era of Globalization* (pp. 181–197). Hershey, PA: IGI Global. 10.4018/978-1-5225-0723-9.ch008

Takaya-Umehara, Y. (2019). Suborbital Spaceflight: Legal Aspects. In Nakarada Pecujlic, A., & Tugnoli, M. (Eds.), *Promoting Productive Cooperation Between Space Lawyers and Engineers* (pp. 64–78). IGI Global. https://doi.org/10.4018/978-1-5225-7256-5.ch005

Tam, G. C. (2017). Project Manager Sustainability Competence. In *Managerial Strategies and Green Solutions for Project Sustainability* (pp. 178–207). Hershey, PA: IGI Global. 10.4018/978-1-5225-2371-0.ch008

Tambo, T. (2018). Fashion Retail Innovation: About Context, Antecedents, and Outcome in Technological Change Projects. In I. Management Association (Ed.), *Fashion and Textiles: Breakthroughs in Research and Practice* (pp. 233-260). Hershey, PA: IGI Global. https://doi.org/10.4018/978-1-5225-3432-7.ch010

Tan, S. F. (2017). Local Representation in Australia: Preliminary Findings of a National Survey. In Schoburgh, E., & Ryan, R. (Eds.), *Handbook of Research on Sub-National Governance and Development* (pp. 368–384). Hershey, PA: IGI Global. 10.4018/978-1-5225-1645-3.ch017

Tantau, A. D., & Frăţilă, L. C. (2018). Information and Management System for Renewable Energy Business. In *Entrepreneurship and Business Development in the Renewable Energy Sector* (pp. 200–244). Hershey, PA: IGI Global. 10.4018/978-1-5225-3625-3.ch006

Tavares, M. D., & Rodrigues, L. L. (2018). Strategic Responses of Public Sector Entities to GRI Sustainability Reports. In Azevedo, G., da Silva Oliveira, J., Marques, R., & Ferreira, A. (Eds.), *Handbook of Research on Modernization and Accountability in Public Sector Management* (pp. 159–188). Hershey, PA: IGI Global. 10.4018/978-1-5225-3731-1.ch008

Teixeira, N., Pardal, P. N., & Rafael, B. G. (2018). Internationalization, Financial Performance, and Organizational Challenges: A Success Case in Portugal. In Carvalho, L. (Ed.), *Handbook of Research on Entrepreneurial Ecosystems and Social Dynamics in a Globalized World* (pp. 379–423). Hershey, PA: IGI Global. 10.4018/978-1-5225-3525-6.ch017

Teixeira, P., Teixeira, L., Eusébio, C., Silva, S., & Teixeira, A. (2021). The Impact of ICTs on Accessible Tourism: Evidence Based on a Systematic Literature Review. In Eusébio, C., Teixeira, L., & Carneiro, M. (Eds.), *ICT Tools and Applications for Accessible Tourism* (pp. 1–25). IGI Global. 10.4018/978-1-7998-6428-8.ch001

Thakre, A. G. (2017). Sexual Harassment of Women in Workplace in India: An Assessment of Implementation of Preventive Laws and Practicing of Therapeutic Jurisprudence in New Delhi. In Halder, D., & Jaishankar, K. (Eds.), *Therapeutic Jurisprudence and Overcoming Violence Against Women* (pp. 135–146). Hershey, PA: IGI Global. 10.4018/978-1-5225-2472-4.ch009

Tiwary, A. (2017). Key Elements of CEAF. In *Driving Efficiency in Local Government Using a Collaborative Enterprise Architecture Framework: Emerging Research and Opportunities* (pp. 25–61). Hershey, PA: IGI Global. 10.4018/978-1-5225-2407-6.ch002

Toscano, J. P. (2017). Social Media and Public Participation: Opportunities, Barriers, and a New Framework. In Adria, M., & Mao, Y. (Eds.), *Handbook of Research on Citizen Engagement and Public Participation in the Era of New Media* (pp. 73–89). Hershey, PA: IGI Global. 10.4018/978-1-5225-1081-9.ch005

Trad, A., & Kalpić, D. (2018). The Business Transformation and Enterprise Architecture Framework: The Financial Engineering E-Risk Management and E-Law Integration. In Sergi, B., Fidanoski, F., Ziolo, M., & Naumovski, V. (Eds.), *Regaining Global Stability After the Financial Crisis* (pp. 46–65). Hershey, PA: IGI Global. 10.4018/978-1-5225-4026-7.ch003

Trad, A., & Kalpić, D. (2018). The Business Transformation Framework, Agile Project and Change Management. In M. Khosrow-Pour, D.B.A. (Ed.), *Encyclopedia of Information Science and Technology, Fourth Edition* (pp. 620-635). Hershey, PA: IGI Global. https://doi.org/10.4018/978-1-5225-2255-3.ch054

Tsabedze, V. W. (2020). Strategies for Managing E-Records for Good Governance: Reflection on E-Government in the Kingdom of Eswatini. In Rodríguez Bolívar, M., & Cortés Cediel, M. (Eds.), *Digital Government and Achieving E-Public Participation: Emerging Research and Opportunities* (pp. 63–86). IGI Global. https://doi.org/10.4018/978-1-7998-1526-6.ch004

Tshishonga, N. (2017). Operation Sukuma-Sakhe: A New Social Contract for Decentralized Service Delivery and Responsive Governance in KwaZulu-Natal. In Schoburgh, E., & Ryan, R. (Eds.), *Handbook of Research on Sub-National Governance and Development* (pp. 304–323). Hershey, PA: IGI Global. 10.4018/978-1-5225-1645-3.ch014

Tsygankov, S., & Gasanova, E. (2017). Electronification of the Public Procurement System: A Comparative Analysis of the Experience of the Russian Federation and Ukraine. In Shakya, R. (Ed.), *Digital Governance and E-Government Principles Applied to Public Procurement* (pp. 267–277). Hershey, PA: IGI Global. 10.4018/978-1-5225-2203-4.ch013

Turulja, L., & Bajgoric, N. (2018). Business Continuity and Information Systems: A Systematic Literature Review. In Bajgoric, N. (Ed.), *Always-On Enterprise Information Systems for Modern Organizations* (pp. 60–87). Hershey, PA: IGI Global. 10.4018/978-1-5225-3704-5.ch004

Tüzünkan, D. (2018). The International Migration Movements and Immigrant Policies From the Ottoman Empire 1299 to Republican Turkey 2016. In Erçetin, Ş. (Ed.), *Social Considerations of Migration Movements and Immigration Policies* (pp. 13–45). Hershey, PA: IGI Global. 10.4018/978-1-5225-3322-1.ch002

Ullah, Z. (2022). Violent Extremism and the Politics of Education in Pakistan: An Analysis of the Links Between Anti-Terror Laws, the Curriculum, and the Islamised Public Sphere. In Kulaç, O., Babaoğlu, C., & Akman, E. (Eds.), *Public Affairs Education and Training in the 21st Century* (pp. 256–275). IGI Global. https://doi.org/10.4018/978-1-7998-8243-5.ch017

Valenzuela, R., & Ochoa, A. (2018). Open Mexico Network in the Implementation of National Open Data Policy. In Kok, A. (Ed.), *Proliferation of Open Government Initiatives and Systems* (pp. 50–67). Hershey, PA: IGI Global. 10.4018/978-1-5225-4987-1.ch003

Valera-Ordaz, L., & Humanes, M. L. (2022). What Drives Selective Exposure to Political Information in Spain? Comparing Political Interest and Ideology. In Palau-Sampio, D., López García, G., & Iannelli, L. (Eds.), *Contemporary Politics, Communication, and the Impact on Democracy* (pp. 93–112). IGI Global. https://doi.org/10.4018/978-1-7998-8057-8.ch006

Vargas-Hernández, J. G. (2017). Professional Integrity in Business Management Education. In Baporikar, N. (Ed.), *Management Education for Global Leadership* (pp. 70–89). Hershey, PA: IGI Global. 10.4018/978-1-5225-1013-0.ch004

Varnacı Uzun, F. (2021). The Destination Preferences of Foreign Tourists During the COVID-19 Pandemic and Attitudes Towards: Marmaris, Turkey. In Demir, M., Dalgıç, A., & Ergen, F. (Eds.), *Handbook of Research on the Impacts and Implications of COVID-19 on the Tourism Industry* (pp. 285–306). IGI Global. https://doi.org/10.4018/978-1-7998-8231-2.ch014

Vijayan, G., & Kamarulzaman, N. H. (2017). An Introduction to Sustainable Supply Chain Management and Business Implications. In Khan, M., Hussain, M., & Ajmal, M. (Eds.), *Green Supply Chain Management for Sustainable Business Practice* (pp. 27–50). Hershey, PA: IGI Global. 10.4018/978-1-5225-0635-5.ch002

Vlachvei, A., & Notta, O. (2017). Firm Competitiveness: Theories, Evidence, and Measurement. In Vlachvei, A., Notta, O., Karantininis, K., & Tsounis, N. (Eds.), *Factors Affecting Firm Competitiveness and Performance in the Modern Business World* (pp. 1–42). Hershey, PA: IGI Global. 10.4018/978-1-5225-0843-4.ch001

Wang, C., Schofield, M., Li, X., & Ou, X. (2017). Do Chinese Students in Public and Private Higher Education Institutes Perform at Different Level in One of the Leadership Skills: Critical Thinking?: An Exploratory Comparison. In Wang, V. (Ed.), *Encyclopedia of Strategic Leadership and Management* (pp. 160–181). Hershey, PA: IGI Global. 10.4018/978-1-5225-1049-9.ch013

Wodecka-Hyjek, A. (2017). Co-Operation between the Public Administration and Non-Profit Organisations as a Condition of the Development of Public Entrepreneurship: On the Example of the Selected World Solutions. In Potocan, V., Üngan, M., & Nedelko, Z. (Eds.), *Handbook of Research on Managerial Solutions in Non-Profit Organizations* (pp. 253–275). Hershey, PA: IGI Global. 10.4018/978-1-5225-0731-4.ch012

Wolf, R., & Thiel, M. (2018). Advancing Global Business Ethics in China: Reducing Poverty Through Human and Social Welfare. In Hipsher, S. (Ed.), *Examining the Private Sector's Role in Wealth Creation and Poverty Reduction* (pp. 67–84). Hershey, PA: IGI Global. 10.4018/978-1-5225-3117-3.ch004

Yablonsky, S. (2018). Innovation Platforms: Data and Analytics Platforms. In *Multi-Sided Platforms (MSPs) and Sharing Strategies in the Digital Economy: Emerging Research and Opportunities* (pp. 72–95). Hershey, PA: IGI Global. 10.4018/978-1-5225-5457-8.ch003

Yang, K. C., & Kang, Y. (2017). Social Media, Political Mobilization, and Citizen Engagement: A Case Study of the March 18, 2014, Sunflower Student Movement in Taiwan. In Adria, M., & Mao, Y. (Eds.), *Handbook of Research on Citizen Engagement and Public Participation in the Era of New Media* (pp. 360–388). Hershey, PA: IGI Global. 10.4018/978-1-5225-1081-9.ch020

Yang, K. C., & Kang, Y. (2020). Will Microblogs Shape China's Civil Society Under President's Xi's Surveillance State?: The Case of Anti-Extradition Law Protests in Hong Kong. In Kumar, V., & Malhotra, G. (Eds.), *Examining the Roles of IT and Social Media in Democratic Development and Social Change* (pp. 156–184). IGI Global. https://doi.org/10.4018/978-1-7998-1791-8.ch007

Yaşar, B. (2021). The Impact of COVID-19 on Volatility of Tourism Stocks: Evidence From BIST Tourism Index. In Demir, M., Dalgıç, A., & Ergen, F. (Eds.), *Handbook of Research on the Impacts and Implications of COVID-19 on the Tourism Industry* (pp. 23–44). IGI Global. https://doi.org/10.4018/978-1-7998-8231-2.ch002

Yavuz, N., Karkın, N., & Sevinç Çubuk, E. B. (2020). Explaining Government Crowdsourcing Decisions: A Theoretical Model. In Rodríguez Bolívar, M., & Cortés Cediel, M. (Eds.), *Digital Government and Achieving E-Public Participation: Emerging Research and Opportunities* (pp. 159–183). IGI Global. https://doi.org/10.4018/978-1-7998-1526-6.ch008

Yusoff, A., Ahmad, N. H., & Halim, H. A. (2017). Agropreneurship among Gen Y in Malaysia: The Role of Academic Institutions. In Ahmad, N., Ramayah, T., Halim, H., & Rahman, S. (Eds.), *Handbook of Research on Small and Medium Enterprises in Developing Countries* (pp. 23–47). Hershey, PA: IGI Global. 10.4018/978-1-5225-2165-5.ch002

Zacher, D., & Pechlaner, H. (2021). Resilience as an Opportunity Approach: Challenges and Perspectives for Private Sector Participation on a Community Level. In Zehrer, A., Glowka, G., Schwaiger, K., & Ranacher-Lackner, V. (Eds.), *Resiliency Models and Addressing Future Risks for Family Firms in the Tourism Industry* (pp. 75–102). IGI Global. https://doi.org/10.4018/978-1-7998-7352-5.ch004

Zanin, F., Comuzzi, E., & Costantini, A. (2018). The Effect of Business Strategy and Stock Market Listing on the Use of Risk Assessment Tools. In *Management Control Systems in Complex Settings: Emerging Research and Opportunities* (pp. 145–168). Hershey, PA: IGI Global. 10.4018/978-1-5225-3987-2.ch007

Zgheib, P. W. (2017). Corporate Innovation and Intrapreneurship in the Middle East. In Zgheib, P. (Ed.), *Entrepreneurship and Business Innovation in the Middle East* (pp. 37–56). Hershey, PA: IGI Global. 10.4018/978-1-5225-2066-5.ch003

Zhaleleva, S., Zhaleleva, R., & Pasternak, A. (2020). Evolution of Business-Government Interaction Models: Their Use and Management. In Tazhina, G., & Parker, J. (Eds.), *Toward Sustainability Through Digital Technologies and Practices in the Eurasian Region* (pp. 17–35). IGI Global. https://doi.org/10.4018/978-1-7998-2551-7.ch002

Zhao, B. (2018). A Privacy Perspective of Open Government: Sex, Wealth, and Transparency in China. In Kok, A. (Ed.), *Proliferation of Open Government Initiatives and Systems* (pp. 29–48). Hershey, PA: IGI Global. 10.4018/978-1-5225-4987-1.ch002

Abdul Razak, R., & Mansor, N. A. (2021). Instagram Influencers in Social Media-Induced Tourism: Rethinking Tourist Trust Towards Tourism Destination. In M. Dinis, L. Bonixe, S. Lamy, & Z. Breda (Eds.), *Impact of New Media in Tourism* (pp. 135-144). IGI Global. https://doi.org/10.4018/978-1-7998-7095-1.ch009

Altinay Ozdemir, M. (2021). Virtual Reality (VR) and Augmented Reality (AR) Technologies for Accessibility and Marketing in the Tourism Industry. In C. Eusébio, L. Teixeira, & M. Carneiro (Eds.), *ICT Tools and Applications for Accessible Tourism* (pp. 277-301). IGI Global. https://doi.org/10.4018/978-1-7998-6428-8.ch013

Baleiro, R. (2022). Tourist Literature and the Architecture of Travel in Olga Tokarczuk and Patti Smith. In R. Baleiro & R. Pereira (Eds.), *Global Perspectives on Literary Tourism and Film-Induced Tourism* (pp. 202-216). IGI Global. https://doi.org/10.4018/978-1-7998-8262-6.ch011

Barbosa, C. A., Magalhães, M., & Nunes, M. R. (2021). Travel Instagramability: A Way of Choosing a Destination? In M. Dinis, L. Bonixe, S. Lamy, & Z. Breda (Eds.), *Impact of New Media in Tourism* (pp. 173-190). IGI Global. https://doi.org/10.4018/978-1-7998-7095-1.ch011

Bari, M. W., & Khan, Q. (2021). Pakistan as a Destination of Religious Tourism. In E. Alaverdov & M. Bari (Eds.), *Global Development of Religious Tourism* (pp. 1-10). IGI Global. https://doi.org/10.4018/978-1-7998-5792-1.ch001

Bogdanoski, M., Stoilkovski, M., & Risteski, A. (2020). Novel First Responder Digital Forensics Tool as a Support to Law Enforcement. In I. Management Association (Ed.), *Improving the Safety and Efficiency of Emergency Services: Emerging Tools and Technologies for First Responders* (pp. 239-270). IGI Global. https://doi.org/10.4018/978-1-7998-2535-7.ch011

Bradford, A. C., McElroy, H. K., & Rosenblatt, R. (2019). Social Climate Change and the Modern Police Department: Millennials, Marijuana, and Mass Media. In I. Management Association (Ed.), *Police Science: Breakthroughs in Research and Practice* (pp. 34-51). IGI Global. https://doi.org/10.4018/978-1-5225-7672-3.ch003

De Uña-Álvarez, E., & Villarino-Pérez, M. (2022). Fostering Ecocultural Resources, Identity, and Tourism in Inland Territories (Galicia, NW Spain). In G. Fernandes (Ed.), *Challenges and New Opportunities for Tourism in Inland Territories: Ecocultural Resources and Sustainable Initiatives* (pp. 1-16). IGI Global. https://doi.org/10.4018/978-1-7998-7339-6.ch001

Durnalı, M., & Eriçok, B. (2019). Legal Challenges on Developing Education Policy for Immigrants in Turkey. In I. Management Association (Ed.), *Immigration and Refugee Policy: Breakthroughs in Research and Practice* (pp. 223-237). IGI Global. https://doi.org/10.4018/978-1-5225-8909-9.ch013

Eide, D., Hjalager, A., & Hansen, M. (2022). Innovative Certifications in Adventure Tourism: Attributes and Diffusion. In R. Augusto Costa, F. Brandão, Z. Breda, & C. Costa (Eds.), *Planning and Managing the Experience Economy in Tourism* (pp. 161-175). IGI Global. https://doi.org/10.4018/978-1-7998-8775-1.ch009

Goyal, A. (2021). Communicating and Building Destination Brands With New Media. In M. Dinis, L. Bonixe, S. Lamy, & Z. Breda (Eds.), *Impact of New Media in Tourism* (pp. 1-20). IGI Global. https://doi.org/10.4018/978-1-7998-7095-1.ch001

Guasca, M., Van Broeck, A. M., & Vanneste, D. (2021). Tourism and the Social Reintegration of Colombian Ex-Combatants. In J. da Silva, Z. Breda, & F. Carbone (Eds.), *Role and Impact of Tourism in Peacebuilding and Conflict Transformation* (pp. 66-86). IGI Global. https://doi.org/10.4018/978-1-7998-5053-3.ch005

Ibrahim, F., Suhip, H., Kura, K. M., & Noor, H. M. L. (2022). Exploratory Study on User Satisfaction of E-HRM: Evidence From Brunei Government Employee Management System (GEMS). In P. Ordóñez de Pablos (Eds.), *Handbook of Research on Developing Circular, Digital, and Green Economies in Asia* (pp. 243-271). IGI Global. https://doi.org/10.4018/978-1-7998-8678-5.ch014

Leote, F. J., Teixeira, N. M., & Galvão, R. (2021). Entrepreneurship and Unemployment: Government Grants and Challenges in a Pandemic Context. In N. Teixeira, & I. Lisboa (Eds.), *Handbook of Research on Financial Management During Economic Downturn and Recovery* (pp. 20-40). IGI Global. https://doi.org/10.4018/978-1-7998-6643-5.ch002

Mahajan, A., Maidullah, S., & Hossain, M. R. (2022). Experience Toward Smart Tour Guide Apps in Travelling: An Analysis of Users' Reviews on Audio Odigos and Trip My Way. In R. Augusto Costa, F. Brandão, Z. Breda, & C. Costa (Eds.), *Planning and Managing the Experience Economy in Tourism* (pp. 255-273). IGI Global. https://doi.org/10.4018/978-1-7998-8775-1.ch014

Menezes, V. D., & Cavagnaro, E. (2021). Communicating Sustainable Initiatives in the Hotel Industry: The Case of the Hotel Jakarta Amsterdam. In F. Brandão, Z. Breda, R. Costa, & C. Costa (Eds.), *Handbook of Research on the Role of Tourism in Achieving Sustainable Development Goals* (pp. 224-234). IGI Global. https://doi.org/10.4018/978-1-7998-5691-7.ch013

Menezes, V. D., & Cavagnaro, E. (2021). Communicating Sustainable Initiatives in the Hotel Industry: The Case of the Hotel Jakarta Amsterdam. In F. Brandão, Z. Breda, R. Costa, & C. Costa (Eds.), *Handbook of Research on the Role of Tourism in Achieving Sustainable Development Goals* (pp. 224-234). IGI Global. https://doi.org/10.4018/978-1-7998-5691-7.ch013

Mitas, O., Bastiaansen, M., & Boode, W. (2022). If You're Happy, I'm Happy: Emotion Contagion at a Tourist Information Center. In R. Augusto Costa, F. Brandão, Z. Breda, & C. Costa (Eds.), *Planning and Managing the Experience Economy in Tourism* (pp. 122-140). IGI Global. https://doi.org/10.4018/978-1-7998-8775-1.ch007

Monteiro, A., Lopes, S., & Carbone, F. (2021). Academic Mobility: Bridging Tourism and Peace Education. In J. da Silva, Z. Breda, & F. Carbone (Eds.), *Role and Impact of Tourism in Peacebuilding and Conflict Transformation* (pp. 275-301). IGI Global. https://doi.org/10.4018/978-1-7998-5053-3.ch016

Papp-Váry, Á. F., & Tóth, T. Z. (2022). Analysis of Budapest as a Film Tourism Destination. In R. Baleiro & R. Pereira (Eds.), *Global Perspectives on Literary Tourism and Film-Induced Tourism* (pp. 257-279). IGI Global. https://doi.org/10.4018/978-1-7998-8262-6.ch014

Parikh, M., & Krishna, V. S. (2021). Recent Trends and Repercussions in Civil and Criminal Justice Systems: A Comparative Analysis of England, Singapore, and India. In E. Yin, & N. Kofie (Ed.), *Advancing Civil Justice Reform and Conflict Resolution in Africa and Asia: Comparative Analyses and Case Studies* (pp. 230-242). IGI Global. https://doi.org/10.4018/978-1-7998-7898-8.ch013

Patro, C. S. (2021). Digital Tourism: Influence of E-Marketing Technology. In M. Dinis, L. Bonixe, S. Lamy, & Z. Breda (Eds.), *Impact of New Media in Tourism* (pp. 234-254). IGI Global. https://doi.org/10.4018/978-1-7998-7095-1.ch014

Pipia, S., & Pipia, S. (2021). Challenges of Religious Tourism in the Conflict Region: An Example of Jerusalem. In E. Alaverdov & M. Bari (Eds.), *Global Development of Religious Tourism* (pp. 135-148). IGI Global. https://doi.org/10.4018/978-1-7998-5792-1.ch009

Ravotti, N. (2020). In the [Source] C\ode of the Conquerors: On the Need for Culturally-Minded Tribal Law Research Databases. In S. Edwards III, & D. Santos (Eds.), *Digital Transformation and Its Role in Progressing the Relationship Between States and Their Citizens* (pp. 124-137). IGI Global. https://doi.org/10.4018/978-1-7998-3152-5.ch006

Trengereid, V. (2022). Conditions of Network Engagement: The Quest for a Common Good. In R. Augusto Costa, F. Brandão, Z. Breda, & C. Costa (Eds.), *Planning and Managing the Experience Economy in Tourism* (pp. 69-84). IGI Global. https://doi.org/10.4018/978-1-7998-8775-1.ch004

Trompetter, P. S. (2019). A History of Police Psychology. In I. Management Association (Eds.), *Police Science: Breakthroughs in Research and Practice* (pp. 377-402). IGI Global. https://doi.org/10.4018/978-1-5225-7672-3.ch019

Tryma, K., & Salnikova, N. (2021). The Influence of Religion on Political Parties of the European Union. In E. Alaverdov & M. Bari (Eds.), *Global Development of Religious Tourism* (pp. 98-112). IGI Global. https://doi.org/10.4018/978-1-7998-5792-1.ch007

van der Vliet-Bakker, J. M. (2019). Environmentally Forced Migration and Human Rights. In I. Management Association (Eds.), *Immigration and Refugee Policy: Breakthroughs in Research and Practice* (pp. 336-362). IGI Global. https://doi.org/10.4018/978-1-5225-8909-9.ch019

Yasmeen, H., Wang, Y., Zameer, H., & Ismail, H. (2020). Modeling the Role of Government, Firm, and Civil Society for Environmental Sustainability. In I. Management Association (Ed.), *Developing Eco-Cities Through Policy, Planning, and Innovation: Can It Really Work?* (pp. 62-83). IGI Global. https://doi.org/10.4018/978-1-7998-0441-3.ch003

Abtahi, M. S., Behboudi, L., & Hasanabad, H. M. (2017). Factors Affecting Internet Advertising Adoption in Ad Agencies. *International Journal of Innovation in the Digital Economy*, 8(4), 18–29. 10.4018/IJIDE.2017100102

Aham-Anyanwu, N. M., & Li, H. (2017). E-State: Realistic or Utopian? *International Journal of Public Administration in the Digital Age*, 4(2), 56–76. 10.4018/IJPADA.2017040105

Al Balushi, T., & Ali, S. (2020). Theoretical Approach for Instrument Development in Measuring User-Perceived E-Government Service Quality: A Case of Oman E-Government Services. *International Journal of Electronic Government Research*, 16(1), 40–58. 10.4018/IJEGR.2020010103

Al-Jamal, M., & Abu-Shanab, E. (2018). Open Government: The Line between Privacy and Transparency. *International Journal of Public Administration in the Digital Age*, 5(2), 64–75. 10.4018/IJPADA.2018040106

Alkhatib, G., & Bayouq, S. T. (2021). A TAM-Based Model of Technological Factors Affecting Use of E-Tourism. *International Journal of Tourism and Hospitality Management in the Digital Age*, 5(2), 50–67. https://doi.org/10.4018/IJTHMDA.20210701.oa1

Anantharaman, R. N., Rajeswari, K. S., Angusamy, A., & Kuppusamy, J. (2017). Role of Self-Efficacy and Collective Efficacy as Moderators of Occupational Stress Among Software Development Professionals. *International Journal of Human Capital and Information Technology Professionals*, 8(2), 45–58. 10.4018/IJHCITP.2017040103

Aninze, F., El-Gohary, H., & Hussain, J. (2018). The Role of Microfinance to Empower Women: The Case of Developing Countries. *International Journal of Customer Relationship Marketing and Management*, 9(1), 54–78. 10.4018/IJCRMM.2018010104

Aryanto, V. D., Wismantoro, Y., & Widyatmoko, K. (2018). Implementing Eco-Innovation by Utilizing the Internet to Enhance Firm's Marketing Performance: Study of Green Batik Small and Medium Enterprises in Indonesia. *International Journal of E-Business Research*, 14(1), 21–36. 10.4018/IJEBR.2018010102

Atsa'am, D. D., & Kuset Bodur, E. (2021). Pattern Mining on How Organizational Tenure Affects the Psychological Capital of Employees Within the Hospitality and Tourism Industry: Linking Employees' Organizational Tenure With PsyCap. *International Journal of Tourism and Hospitality Management in the Digital Age*, 5(2), 17–28. https://doi.org/10.4018/IJTHMDA.2021070102

Barat, S. (2021). Looking at the Future of Medical Tourism in Asia. *International Journal of Tourism and Hospitality Management in the Digital Age*, 5(1), 19–33. https://doi.org/10.4018/IJTHMDA.2021010102

Bhatt, G. D., Wang, Z., & Rodger, J. A. (2017). Information Systems Capabilities and Their Effects on Competitive Advantages: A Study of Chinese Companies. *Information Resources Management Journal*, 30(3), 41–57. 10.4018/IRMJ.2017070103

Bhushan, S. (2017). System Dynamics Base-Model of Humanitarian Supply Chain (HSCM) in Disaster Prone Eco-Communities of India: A Discussion on Simulation and Scenario Results. *International Journal of System Dynamics Applications*, 6(3), 20–37. 10.4018/IJSDA.2017070102

Delias, P., & Lakiotaki, K. (2018). Discovering Process Horizontal Boundaries to Facilitate Process Comprehension. *International Journal of Operations Research and Information Systems*, 9(2), 1–31. 10.4018/IJORIS.2018040101

Dezdar, S. (2017). ERP Implementation Projects in Asian Countries: A Comparative Study on Iran and China. *International Journal of Information Technology Project Management*, 8(3), 52–68. 10.4018/IJITPM.2017070104

Dosumu, O., Hussain, J., & El-Gohary, H. (2017). An Exploratory Study of the Impact of Government Policies on the Development of Small and Medium Enterprises in Developing Countries: The Case of Nigeria. *International Journal of Customer Relationship Marketing and Management*, 8(4), 51–62. 10.4018/IJCRMM.2017100104

Durst, S., Bruns, G., & Edvardsson, I. R. (2017). Retaining Knowledge in Smaller Building and Construction Firms. *International Journal of Knowledge and Systems Science*, 8(3), 1–12. 10.4018/IJKSS.2017070101

Edvardsson, I. R., & Durst, S. (2017). Outsourcing, Knowledge, and Learning: A Critical Review. *International Journal of Knowledge-Based Organizations*, 7(2), 13–26. 10.4018/IJKBO.2017040102

Ekanem, I., & Abiade, G. E. (2018). Factors Influencing the Use of E-Commerce by Small Enterprises in Nigeria. *International Journal of ICT Research in Africa and the Middle East*, 7(1), 37–53. 10.4018/IJICTRAME.2018010103

El Faquih, L., & Fredj, M. (2017). Ontology-Based Framework for Quality in Configurable Process Models. *Journal of Electronic Commerce in Organizations*, 15(2), 48–60. 10.4018/JECO.2017040104

Faisal, M. N., & Talib, F. (2017). Building Ambidextrous Supply Chains in SMEs: How to Tackle the Barriers? *International Journal of Information Systems and Supply Chain Management*, 10(4), 80–100. 10.4018/IJISSCM.2017100105

Faura-Martínez, U., & Cifuentes-Faura, J. (2020). Does E-Government Promote Transparency and the Fight Against Corruption in the European Union? *International Journal of Electronic Government Research*, 16(4), 42–57. https://doi.org/10.4018/IJEGR.2020100103

Fernandes, T. M., Gomes, J., & Romão, M. (2017). Investments in E-Government: A Benefit Management Case Study. *International Journal of Electronic Government Research*, 13(3), 1–17. 10.4018/IJEGR.2017070101

Garad, A., & Qamari, I. N. (2021). Determining Factors Influencing Establishing E-Service Quality in Developing Countries: A Case Study of Yemen E-Government. *International Journal of Electronic Government Research*, 17(1), 15–30. https://doi.org/10.4018/IJEGR.2021010102

Glykas, M., & George, J. (2017). Quality and Process Management Systems in the UAE Maritime Industry. *International Journal of Productivity Management and Assessment Technologies*, 5(1), 20–39. 10.4018/IJPMAT.2017010102

Glykas, M., Valiris, G., Kokkinaki, A., & Koutsoukou, Z. (2018). Banking Business Process Management Implementation. *International Journal of Productivity Management and Assessment Technologies*, 6(1), 50–69. 10.4018/IJPMAT.2018010104

Gomes, J., & Romão, M. (2017). The Balanced Scorecard: Keeping Updated and Aligned with Today's Business Trends. *International Journal of Productivity Management and Assessment Technologies*, 5(2), 1–15. 10.4018/IJPMAT.2017070101

Grefen, P., & Turetken, O. (2017). Advanced Business Process Management in Networked E-Business Scenarios. *International Journal of E-Business Research*, 13(4), 70–104. 10.4018/IJEBR.2017100105

Hajilari, A. B., Ghadaksaz, M., & Fasghandis, G. S. (2017). Assessing Organizational Readiness for Implementing ERP System Using Fuzzy Expert System Approach. *International Journal of Enterprise Information Systems*, 13(1), 67–85. 10.4018/IJEIS.2017010105

Hall, O. P.Jr. (2017). Social Media Driven Management Education. *International Journal of Knowledge-Based Organizations*, 7(2), 43–59. 10.4018/IJKBO.2017040104

Hawking, P., & Sellitto, C. (2017). A Fast-Moving Consumer Goods Company and Business Intelligence Strategy Development. *International Journal of Enterprise Information Systems*, 13(2), 22–33. 10.4018/IJEIS.2017040102

Hawking, P., & Sellitto, C. (2017). Business Intelligence Strategy: Two Case Studies. *International Journal of Business Intelligence Research*, 8(2), 17–30. 10.4018/IJBIR.2017070102

Hee, W. J., Jalleh, G., Lai, H., & Lin, C. (2017). E-Commerce and IT Projects: Evaluation and Management Issues in Australian and Taiwanese Hospitals. *International Journal of Public Health Management and Ethics*, 2(1), 69–90. 10.4018/IJPHME.2017010104

Hernandez, A. A. (2018). Exploring the Factors to Green IT Adoption of SMEs in the Philippines. *Journal of Cases on Information Technology*, 20(2), 49–66. 10.4018/JCIT.2018040104

Hollman, A., Bickford, S., & Hollman, T. (2017). Cyber InSecurity: A Post-Mortem Attempt to Assess Cyber Problems from IT and Business Management Perspectives. *Journal of Cases on Information Technology*, 19(3), 42–70. 10.4018/JCIT.2017070104

Ibrahim, F., & Zainin, N. M. (2021). Exploring the Technological Impacts: The Case of Museums in Brunei Darussalam. *International Journal of Tourism and Hospitality Management in the Digital Age*, 5(1), 1–18. https://doi.org/10.4018/IJTHMDA.2021010101

Joia, L. A., & Correia, J. C. (2018). CIO Competencies From the IT Professional Perspective: Insights From Brazil. *Journal of Global Information Management*, 26(2), 74–103. 10.4018/JGIM.2018040104

Kaoud, M. (2017). Investigation of Customer Knowledge Management: A Case Study Research. *International Journal of Service Science, Management, Engineering, and Technology*, 8(2), 12–22. 10.4018/IJSSMET.2017040102

Khachaturyan, M., & Klicheva, E. (2021). Risks of Introducing E-Governance Into Strategic Management Systems of Russian Companies in the Context of the Pandemic. *International Journal of Electronic Government Research*, 17(4), 84–102. https://doi.org/10.4018/IJEGR.2021100105

Kinnunen, S., Ylä-Kujala, A., Marttonen-Arola, S., Kärri, T., & Baglee, D. (2018). Internet of Things in Asset Management: Insights from Industrial Professionals and Academia. *International Journal of Service Science, Management, Engineering, and Technology*, 9(2), 104–119. 10.4018/IJSSMET.2018040105

Kumar, J., Adhikary, A., & Jha, A. (2017). Small Active Investors' Perceptions and Preferences Towards Tax Saving Mutual Fund Schemes in Eastern India: An Empirical Note. *International Journal of Asian Business and Information Management*, 8(2), 35–45. 10.4018/IJABIM.2017040103

Lavassani, K. M., & Movahedi, B. (2017). Applications Driven Information Systems: Beyond Networks toward Business Ecosystems. *International Journal of Innovation in the Digital Economy*, 8(1), 61–75. 10.4018/IJIDE.2017010104

Lederer, M., Kurz, M., & Lazarov, P. (2017). Usage and Suitability of Methods for Strategic Business Process Initiatives: A Multi Case Study Research. *International Journal of Productivity Management and Assessment Technologies*, 5(1), 40–51. 10.4018/IJPMAT.2017010103

Leon, L. A., Seal, K. C., Przasnyski, Z. H., & Wiedenman, I. (2017). Skills and Competencies Required for Jobs in Business Analytics: A Content Analysis of Job Advertisements Using Text Mining. *International Journal of Business Intelligence Research*, 8(1), 1–25. 10.4018/IJBIR.2017010101

Lhannaoui, H., Kabbaj, M. I., & Bakkoury, Z. (2017). A Survey of Risk-Aware Business Process Modelling. *International Journal of Risk and Contingency Management*, 6(3), 14–26. 10.4018/IJRCM.2017070102

Li, J., Sun, W., Jiang, W., Yang, H., & Zhang, L. (2017). How the Nature of Exogenous Shocks and Crises Impact Company Performance?: The Effects of Industry Characteristics. *International Journal of Risk and Contingency Management*, 6(4), 40–55. 10.4018/IJRCM.2017100103

Martins, P. V., & Zacarias, M. (2017). A Web-based Tool for Business Process Improvement. *International Journal of Web Portals*, 9(2), 68–84. 10.4018/IJWP.2017070104

Matthies, B., & Coners, A. (2017). Exploring the Conceptual Nature of e-Business Projects. *Journal of Electronic Commerce in Organizations*, 15(3), 33–63. 10.4018/JECO.2017070103

Mensah, I. K., Luo, C., & Abu-Shanab, E. (2021). Citizen Use of E-Government Services Websites: A Proposed E-Government Adoption Recommendation Model (EGARM). *International Journal of Electronic Government Research*, 17(2), 19–42. https://doi.org/10.4018/IJEGR.2021040102

Mishaal, D. A., & Abu-Shanab, E. A. (2017). Utilizing Facebook by the Arab World Governments: The Communication Success Factor. *International Journal of Public Administration in the Digital Age*, 4(3), 53–78. 10.4018/IJPADA.2017070105

Mutahar, A. M., Daud, N. M., Thurasamy, R., Isaac, O., & Abdulsalam, R. (2018). The Mediating of Perceived Usefulness and Perceived Ease of Use: The Case of Mobile Banking in Yemen. *International Journal of Technology Diffusion*, 9(2), 21–40. 10.4018/IJTD.2018040102

Obidallah, W. J., & Raahemi, B. (2017). Managing Changes in Service Oriented Virtual Organizations: A Structural and Procedural Framework to Facilitate the Process of Change. *Journal of Electronic Commerce in Organizations*, 15(1), 59–83. 10.4018/JECO.2017010104

Ojo, O. (2017). Impact of Innovation on the Entrepreneurial Success in Selected Business Enterprises in South-West Nigeria. *International Journal of Innovation in the Digital Economy*, 8(2), 29–38. 10.4018/IJIDE.2017040103

Okdinawati, L., Simatupang, T. M., & Sunitiyoso, Y. (2017). Multi-Agent Reinforcement Learning for Value Co-Creation of Collaborative Transportation Management (CTM). *International Journal of Information Systems and Supply Chain Management*, 10(3), 84–95. 10.4018/IJISSCM.2017070105

Paulin, A. A. (2017). Informating Public Governance: Towards a Basis for a Digital Ecosystem. *International Journal of Public Administration in the Digital Age*, 4(2), 14–32. 10.4018/IJPADA.2017040102

Rezaie, S., Mirabedini, S. J., & Abtahi, A. (2018). Designing a Model for Implementation of Business Intelligence in the Banking Industry. *International Journal of Enterprise Information Systems*, 14(1), 77–103. 10.4018/IJEIS.2018010105

Safari, M. R., & Jiang, Q. (2018). The Theory and Practice of IT Governance Maturity and Strategies Alignment: Evidence From Banking Industry. *Journal of Global Information Management*, 26(2), 127–146. 10.4018/JGIM.2018040106

Sambhanthan, A. (2017). Assessing and Benchmarking Sustainability in Organisations: An Integrated Conceptual Model. *International Journal of Systems and Service-Oriented Engineering*, 7(4), 22–43. 10.4018/IJSSOE.2017100102

Sambhanthan, A., & Potdar, V. (2017). A Study of the Parameters Impacting Sustainability in Information Technology Organizations. *International Journal of Knowledge-Based Organizations*, 7(3), 27–39. 10.4018/IJKBO.2017070103

Sarvepalli, A., & Godin, J. (2017). Business Process Management in the Classroom. *Journal of Cases on Information Technology*, 19(2), 17–28. 10.4018/JCIT.2017040102

Saygili, E. E., Ozturkoglu, Y., & Kocakulah, M. C. (2017). End Users' Perceptions of Critical Success Factors in ERP Applications. *International Journal of Enterprise Information Systems*, 13(4), 58–75. 10.4018/IJEIS.2017100104

Sensuse, D. I., & Cahyaningsih, E. (2018). Knowledge Management Models: A Summative Review. *International Journal of Information Systems in the Service Sector*, 10(1), 71–100. 10.4018/IJISSS.2018010105

Seth, M., Goyal, D., & Kiran, R. (2017). Diminution of Impediments in Implementation of Supply Chain Management Information System for Enhancing its Effectiveness in Indian Automobile Industry. *Journal of Global Information Management*, 25(3), 1–20. 10.4018/JGIM.2017070101

Shaikh, A. K., Ahmad, N., Khan, I., & Ali, S. (2021). E-Participation Within E-Government: A Bibliometric-Based Systematic Literature Review. *International Journal of Electronic Government Research*, 17(4), 15–39. https://doi.org/10.4018/IJEGR.2021100102

Shaqrah, A. A. (2018). Analyzing Business Intelligence Systems Based on 7s Model of McKinsey. *International Journal of Business Intelligence Research*, 9(1), 53–63. 10.4018/IJBIR.2018010104

Sinthupundaja, J., & Kohda, Y. (2017). Effects of Corporate Social Responsibility and Creating Shared Value on Sustainability. *International Journal of Sustainable Entrepreneurship and Corporate Social Responsibility*, 2(1), 27–38. 10.4018/IJSECSR.2017010103

Škarica, I., & Hrgović, A. V. (2018). Implementation of Total Quality Management Principles in Public Health Institutes in the Republic of Croatia. *International Journal of Productivity Management and Assessment Technologies*, 6(1), 1–16. 10.4018/IJPMAT.2018010101

Smuts, H., Kotzé, P., Van der Merwe, A., & Loock, M. (2017). Framework for Managing Shared Knowledge in an Information Systems Outsourcing Context. *International Journal of Knowledge Management*, 13(4), 1–30. 10.4018/IJKM.2017100101

Tabach, A., & Croteau, A. (2017). Configurations of Information Technology Governance Practices and Business Unit Performance. *International Journal of IT/Business Alignment and Governance*, 8(2), 1–27. 10.4018/IJITBAG.2017070101

Talaue, G. M., & Iqbal, T. (2017). Assessment of e-Business Mode of Selected Private Universities in the Philippines and Pakistan. *International Journal of Online Marketing*, 7(4), 63–77. 10.4018/IJOM.2017100105

Vasista, T. G., & AlAbdullatif, A. M. (2017). Role of Electronic Customer Relationship Management in Demand Chain Management: A Predictive Analytic Approach. *International Journal of Information Systems and Supply Chain Management*, 10(1), 53–67. 10.4018/IJISSCM.2017010104

Vieru, D., & Bourdeau, S. (2017). Survival in the Digital Era: A Digital Competence-Based Multi-Case Study in the Canadian SME Clothing Industry. *International Journal of Social and Organizational Dynamics in IT*, 6(1), 17–34. 10.4018/IJSODIT.2017010102

Waller, P. (2017). Co-Production and Co-Creation in Public Services: Resolving Confusion and Contradictions. *International Journal of Electronic Government Research*, 13(2), 1–17. 10.4018/IJEGR.2017040101

Wang, J. (2017). Multi-Agent based Production Management Decision System Modelling for the Textile Enterprise. *Journal of Global Information Management*, 25(4), 1–15. 10.4018/JGIM.2017100101

Wiedemann, A., & Gewald, H. (2017). Examining Cross-Domain Alignment: The Correlation of Business Strategy, IT Management, and IT Business Value. *International Journal of IT/Business Alignment and Governance*, 8(1), 17–31. 10.4018/IJITBAG.2017010102

About the Author

Bilal Kargı After his undergraduate and graduate studies, he received his Doctorate degree from Marmara University. All his education is in economics. After Ph.D., 2012 Assistant professor; He received the title of Associate Professor in 2017. He is especially an expert on economic growth and development. In addition, he also has studies on economic philosophy, history of economic ideas and economic sociology. He currently works as an Associate Professor at Ankara Yıldırım Beyazıt University. He has collaborated with world-renowned economists such as Steve Hanke, Mario Coccia and Hrabrin Bachev.

Index

K

L

M

N

O

P

R

S

T

V

W

www.ingramcontent.com/pod-product-compliance
Lightning Source LLC
LaVergne TN
LVHW081331021026
849161LV00008BA/1931